Banding Together

Banding Together

The Rise of National Associations

in American Higher Education, 1887–1950

Hugh Hawkins

The Johns Hopkins University Press

BALTIMORE AND LONDON

This book has been brought to publication with
the generous assistance of the Amherst College Faculty Fund.

The Johns Hopkins University Press
701 West 40th Street
Baltimore, Maryland 21211-2190
The Johns Hopkins Press Ltd., London

LIBRARY OF CONGRESS
CATALOGING-IN-PUBLICATION DATA

Hawkins, Hugh.
    Banding together : the rise of national
associations in American higher education, 1887–
1950 / Hugh Hawkins.
        p.   cm.
    Includes bibliographical references (p.   ) and
index.
    ISBN 0-8018-4370-7
    1. Education, Higher—United States—
History.   2. Universities and colleges—United
States—Societies, etc.—History.   3. Associations,
institutions, etc.—United States—History.   I.
Title.
LA226.H355   1992
378.73—dc20   92-2929

Contents

Tables

Introduction

AMERICANS like to think that in their country higher education is neither centralized nor highly systematized. Academics have in recent years found themselves irritated, even dismayed, by the increase in controls from state coordination programs, federal regulations, and court actions. They complain about loss of institutional autonomy, about "delocalization." It is too little recognized that American colleges and universities, near the turn of the century, themselves launched a program of coordination through various institutional associations which led to what, in the American idiom, may be called a voluntary system. Educators chose to sacrifice a measure of institutional autonomy to gain the benefits of cooperation. This book approaches the history of American higher education through five of these associations.

Elsewhere in American society at about the same time analogues of these associations were appearing—the American Federation of Labor (1886), the Federal Council of Churches (1905), the Chamber of Commerce of the United States (1912), the Motion Picture Producers and Distributors Association (1922). Their emergence revealed a shift away from local autonomy and isolated institutional decision making toward national coordination and the common pursuit of shared interests. The old Tocquevillian term *voluntary association* fit these national bodies only loosely. They were groupings not of individuals, but of more or less complex institutions. Although membership was not legally mandated, to remain apart was to risk being considered a disorderly element and perhaps to lose credibility with clients or constituents.

The principal associations treated in this book grew out of the notion that the national government ought not to control educational affairs, but that more control was necessary. The association builders saw disarray threatening academic institutions—overproliferation, fraud, and corruption by special interests. They saw institutional isolation as breeding poverty and powerlessness, arbitrariness and poor education. Associations made existence risky for mavericks, casting doubt on the acceptability of their degrees and endangering enrollment and financial support.

To refer to associations' "ideology" may exaggerate the theoretical self-consciousness of their early leaders, but they and their successors gave at least piecemeal expression to an underlying social philosophy. This view, which can conveniently be called *associationalism*, recognized and justified the multiplicity of power centers in society. From such an affirmation, it followed that education, as one of a variety of interests (though superior to most, since its social benefits seemed unquestionable), needed leadership and organization. These educators favored a pluralistic approach not just in society at large, but also within the educational realm. That is to say, different levels and patterns of educational institutions called for separate organizations, and state and regional bodies had a legitimate place. Since academic leaders embraced both sorts of pluralism (social and educational), they were sometimes perplexed in distinguishing between occasions when higher education should organize to speak with one voice and occasions when a virtue could be made of variety. A group of institutions might legitimately form a specialized organization, but there would be pressure on that organization to make common cause with others in seeking national standards, coordination, and visibility for higher education. In this process of centralization, however, educators remained associationalists, largely skeptical of activism by the central government.

The institutional associations did things that the national government, in their view, could not, would not, or should not do. But they did not want the federal government to eschew all educational activity. From their beginnings the associations had congenial relations with the U.S. Bureau of Education and other federal agencies such as the Department of Agriculture. Government was seen as a source of financial support, and support implied at least a modicum of supervision. It was understandably difficult for an association to object to government provision of funds for its deserving and needy member institutions. There often seemed good reason to have government collect information that aided coordination and assumed certain standards in its mode of classification, but government, associationalists maintained, should not regulate in educational matters. Washington was entreated to give but not to govern. Although the exigencies of World Wars I and II made federal officials more willing to assert themselves educationally, these crises also tended to strengthen the associations' case for an independent role. They could spare the government the distraction of coordinating, advising, or directing educational institutions. At the same time, associations offered their members some protection against efforts to control educational affairs in the name of national security.

Their longevity suggests the usefulness of these associations in the American educational setting, although inertia and bureaucratic self-preservation doubtless have played some part. An association of institutions of higher education, once it got as far as a ratified constitution, tended strongly to persist. It might spin off new associations, it might merge with others, and it was virtually certain to enter a federation. It might change its name and revise its basis for membership. But it would not disband. The account that follows says less of the associations' formal undertakings than of their origins, self-presentations, strategies for survival, and, above all, visions of the place of higher education in American society.

In a historical work, there is danger of overdefinition of the subject matter. A typology has a fixity that, while useful for clarity, contradicts the changes occurring in the historical process. It is the growing edge or the burst seam that most interests historians. Let it suffice here to say that the subject of this book is a process, the process by which colleges and universities have banded together at the national level. What motivated them, what organizations they created, how these new entities developed and took on complex identities, what purposes they sought to serve—that is the stuff of the history that follows.

I began this study as a middle course between histories of single institutions and the general history of higher education, assuming that the associations were comprehensive enough to reveal much of the history of American academic affairs during the last century. I also expected that this approach would make it easier to set educational history in a broader context of social change. Readers of this book will, I hope, include not only fellow historians, but participants in higher education who are curious about its past. There should be some grist here, also, for the mills of organizational theorists. To policy-oriented scholars who have written about the recent past, I owe a great deal, both for useful conceptualization and for interviewing persons no longer alive. Although essentially this account ends in 1950, selected as a date long enough after World War II for major new patterns to have emerged, certain later interorganizational developments find mention in chapter 9 and the postlude.

Of course, some readers will turn to this book to find out about a particular association. Chapter subheadings and the index make this easy to do. Like most authors, however, I hold that the whole of the book is more than the sum of its parts. I encourage users with special interests at least to examine chapter introductions and conclusions.

Individuals matter, even in organizations made up of other organizations. As the index readily reveals, scores of persons appear by name. Inevitably, most such appearances are brief. I have tried, however, to give the reader some sense of the lively and at times contentious personalities involved in the quest for cooperation. Some educational leaders, like James B. Conant, are already familiar to most academics. Others, like Samuel P. Capen, have been unjustly forgotten.

In an effort to vivify the associations themselves, I have included at least one "interlude" on each, tracing an annual meeting in considerable detail. Much of the activity of these groups occurred in other settings, but here at its "convention" an association reached an annual pinnacle of self-awareness. Here the followers as well as the leaders were gathered together. At ten-year intervals, from 1895 to 1945, I have reported on an annual meeting, taking the five associations in order of founding, with a bonus in one case. My simultaneous variation of time and association admittedly deprives these interludes of elaborate comparative possibilities, but the accounts are principally intended to convey more of the flavor of each group than is allowed by the thematic chapters. Drawn from standard printed accounts of proceedings, the interludes also give reader and author a respite from endnotes.

Some readers will prefer the history of a single institution, perhaps one to which they feel personal loyalty. Some excellent works in that genre are available, many cited in my notes. Other readers may be waiting for a broad synthetic history of twentieth-century American higher education. Scholars working in the field suspect that it will be slow in coming. I hope in this book to have provided some of the specificity of institutional histories while delineating broader patterns that include all American colleges and universities.

An Apology for Acronyms

HISTORIANS generally avoid direct address, perhaps hoping that impersonality suggests omniscience. With a sensitive matter like the one I discuss here, however, a more intimate tone is appropriate. I want to make these pages seem more inviting than does a preliminary glance at their splotches of grouped capital letters. Beyond aesthetic objections, I note that this capitalizing gives terms more typographical weight than is merited by their significance in the text. Still, I have relied heavily on acronyms (in which initial letters are grouped into a pronounced word—*AIDS*) and initialisms (in which initial letters are grouped but pronounced separately—*CPA*). This preliminary comment aims to counteract their hazards to fluent reading.*

To help ourselves cope with the modern world's verbal fecundity, we shorten word clusters by using initials, and we do it more and more often. At first we used decorous periods after each. Remember the A. F. of L.? But this form slowly gave way to that of WPA, CIA, and OPEC. Company names, diseases, drugs, sports terms, sexual identifications in personal ads—all have undergone initialization. Maybe it began for Americans when the first of them jotted down "O.K." Sometimes the eye is spared by lowercasing. The shift from RADAR to radar came quickly, and Unesco has been gaining on UNESCO. Readily pronounced short forms, it seems, become acronyms and are eventually made lowercase, while others remain initialisms. Today, the full names of new organizations are often circumlocutions that provide easily remembered and pronounced initials.

---

* For a brief, sympathetic treatment, see Ellen T. Crowley (ed.), "Preface to the Seventh Edition," *Acronyms, Initialisms, and Abbreviations Dictionary*, 7th ed. (Detroit, 1980), vii–xi. This guide had some 12,000 entries in 1960 and over 211,000 by 1980.

Early participants in the associations central to this book avoided initializing their names, lengthy though they sometimes were. I have taken authorial license to commit this anachronism, adding yet another trick to those the present plays on the past. When repetitions would have made an initialism tedious or the context would have caused confusion, I sometimes used the full title and sometimes sought other strategies for identification.

The organizational protagonists of this volume cause other troubles besides aesthetic ones. Their names are in some cases annoyingly similar to each other. One of them kept changing its name, attaining five variants in seventy-eight years. I offer some suggestions to make reading easier.

Let's begin with two of the groups: the Association of American *Universities* (AAU) and the Association of American *Colleges* (AAC). With the eye habituated to pick up the last letter, the distinction is readily recognized. The American Council on Education (ACE) offers a likely candidate for an initialism to become an acronym, and "Ace" would be a suitable name for this peak association (one that includes others). Staff at ACE headquarters, however, resist the process.

The association with the many name changes was long known as "the land-grant association," a happy basis for consistency of nomenclature, to say nothing of minimizing initialism. Its names were longer than those of most other associations. In reading this book you can assume that AAACES, ALGC, and ALGCU stand for the land-grant group under one of its successive designations. Spotting the internal "LG" also helps.

I have saved for last the National Association of State Universities (NASU), a group that existed independently from 1895 to 1963, when it merged with the land-grant association. During its existence, the NASU preserved the same name; although no longer familiar in academic circles, it survives in the opening letters of the merged association, which also has the longest name of all—National Association of State Universities and Land-Grant Colleges (NASULGC). (The usual pronunciation by its participants these days is "naSULjick." Perhaps its very length forced it over the line from initialism to acronym.)

One last forewarning: the United States Bureau of Education (USBE) changed its name to the United States Office of Education (USOE) in 1929. New feathers for the same bird.

For those who like such matters schematized, I insert here a list of the five associations central to this study, with founding dates, name changes, and identification of persons who headed central offices. (A full list of acronyms, initialisms, and other abbreviations precedes the notes.)

AAACES Association of American Agricultural Colleges and
        Experiment Stations (land-grant association name from
        founding, 1887, to 1919)
AAC   Association of American Colleges (founded 1915)
            Robert L. Kelly, executive secretary, 1918–37
            Guy E. Snavely, executive director, 1937–54
AAU   Association of American Universities (founded 1900)
ACE   American Council on Education (founded 1918)
            Samuel P. Capen, director, 1919–22
            Charles Riborg Mann, director, 1922–34
            George F. Zook, director, 1934–35, president, 1935–50
ALGC   Association of Land-Grant Colleges (1920–25)
ALGCU   Association of Land-Grant Colleges and Universities
        (1926–55)
            Russell I. Thackrey appointed executive secretary-
            treasurer, 1947
NASU   National Association of State Universities (founded 1895)

Banding Together

CHAPTER 1

Going National

EVERYONE seemed to be banding together. At any rate, educators were far from alone in moving to formalize group relations. The period between the creation of the first association of institutions of higher education, in 1887, and the creation of the most inclusive, in 1918, roughly approximates "the organizational revolution," as Kenneth Boulding and other scholars have come to call it. In these years the country shifted from a rapidly growing economy that stressed expansion over space, exploitation of natural resources, and individual self-enrichment to a "mature" economy, putting greater emphasis on intensive development and technological advance. Increasingly, corporate structures brought individuals into complex relationships that encouraged both specialization and interdependence. With heightened differentiation came a need for closer articulation. Charles W. Eliot's scorn for the jack of all trades presaged new attitudes.[1]

In a nation where nearly everything was getting bigger and more highly organized, the dominant mood was optimistic. But a series of social observers noted the paradox that gratifying progress often occurred amid deplorable poverty. Farmers, losing their land and sinking into debt peonage, and immigrant laborers in cities, crowded into slums and trapped in sweatshops, had firsthand experience of the underside of American progress.

Higher education was chiefly the province of the middle class. For these people, too, the times proved unsettling, breeding fears of radicalism, distress at the impersonality of cities or their all-too-personal corruption, and dismay at the economic unsteadiness of the 1880s and the tenacious depression of the midnineties. Giant corporations challenged old ideals of individual enterprise, and monopolism, a persistent threat to liberal values, had become a recognizable trend.

In political life, men began to lose their strong party loyalties, and electoral participation declined sharply after the bitter Bryan-

McKinley contest of 1896. Voter turnout reached its low point in 1920.
As party discipline weakened and gave less direction to government,
new groups organized to advance particular interests. Much of the
ferment loosely categorized as "Progressivism" was in fact the effort
of these groups to reshape government policy. No ivory towers, American academic institutions had to pursue their goals in this confusing,
rapidly changing ambience, and some leaders concluded that the creation of national organizations could help.[2]

Baseball teams organized nationally for somewhat different reasons
than churches, and the National Association of Manufacturers did
not have quite the same plan as the American Federation of Labor.
Still, there was a commonality in the rise of national organizations
that indicated deep-running transformations in American life. The
American Social Science Association sought to be general, to combine
learning and social improvement in many areas, but was itself un-
dermined by the rise of disciplinary and professional specialism that
spun off other associations. It had collapsed by 1910, having demonstrated that those aspiring to authority could no longer count on
gaining it from gentility, benevolence, or ascribed status. Ironically,
the very organizations that had abandoned the American Social Science Association soon found themselves forming national coordinating bodies, such as the American Council of Learned Societies.[3]

Americans had long been thought of as joiners, and there was no
reason for that reputation to fade. New technologies of travel favored
convention delegates, and as communication grew swifter and text
duplication cheaper, it was easier for members to stay in touch. In
this, they were aided by national officers or even (portentous term)
"the national office." In an increasingly centralized society, to remain
local, or even regional, appeared to court impotence, insignificance,
and perhaps oblivion.

The years 1880–1920, which saw colleges and universities enter
new relationships within institutional associations, brought so many
changes to American higher education as to invite the label "academic
revolution." Although dwarfed by later expansion, measurable increases were striking. The relatively modest rise in the number of
institutions of higher education from about eight hundred in 1880 to
about one thousand in 1920 was overshadowed by the quintupling of
students enrolled (from 116,000 to 598,000). As a proportion of the
United States population aged eighteen to twenty-one, enrollment in
higher education climbed from 3 to 8 percent. The average enrollment
in an institution of higher education was 574 in 1920 (up from 143
in 1880), but the range that year went from small colleges like Gooding
in Idaho, with 122 students, to the "giant" universities: Harvard with

4,650, Columbia with 8,510, and Chicago with 11,300. In Muncie, Indiana, in the mid-1920s the Lynds found high school attendance soaring. Although education was often "taken for granted by the business class," it evoked in many members of the working class "the fervor of a religion, a means of salvation." Of 124 working class families studied, nearly a quarter planned for the younger generation to attend college. Determined somehow get his children through college, one father declared, "A boy without an education today just ain't *anywhere!*"[4]

University was not a term reserved for large entities. Full of ambiguities in 1880, the name was still legally available in 1920 to a wide range of institutions. Among academics, however, there was general agreement that it meant a complex institution including liberal studies for the bachelor's degree, a faculty committed to research, and training of advanced students in research and preparation for the professions.

The colleges, which had applied highly various admission standards in 1880, with many offering preparatory training, were clearly located on an educational ladder by 1920. Their program followed four years of secondary education and led to the bachelor's degree representing four more years of study. An institution that did not exist in 1880, the two-year junior college, though not yet widespread, was clearly established by 1920.

No less impressive than the rise in numbers or the new definitional clarity was the increasing public approval of higher education. Institutions associated in 1880 with exclusiveness, esoteric learning, and narrow preparation for traditional professions had by 1920 gained a reputation for accessibility and curricular reach. Higher education's middle-class rhetoric of openness and upward mobility, combined with institutional proliferation and rising enrollments, created a strong democratic aura.

If coverage in newspapers and magazines can serve as a guide, higher education stirred wide public interest. Intercollegiate sports, like the annual University of Texas–Texas A&M football game, were often front-page news. Human interest stories from academia abounded. People cared that Wellesley's Alice Freeman married Harvard's George Herbert Palmer. Through their connection with science and technology, the universities became levers of change in an industrializing society. Institutions that in 1880 had been bastions of classical culture produced scientists for crash programs in World War I. If many people knew that Thomas Edison had not gone to college, many also knew that the laboratories at the Massachusetts Institute of Technology (MIT) had produced crucial antisubmarine weaponry. Industrial laboratories, pioneered by the General Electric company before the war, were taking their models from research counterparts at universities. Journalists and politicians (and academics) celebrated "the Wisconsin Idea"—state university extension courses and expert counseling by faculty members for legislative and regulatory agencies. Private institutions similarly expanded into public service activities.[5]

Within universities, the ethos was not as service oriented as sympathetic commentators suggested. Other attitudes were prominent among professors, such as insistence on pursuing new knowledge for its own sake or on the preservation of the humanist heritage. Within student subcultures, athletics and social life often dominated. Although idealism and dedication to learning could be found on the campuses, frivolity seemed on the increase. Already noticeable before World War I, student hedonism during the Jazz Age drew mounting attention from journalists, novelists, and social critics. Everybody had an opinion about the flappers and their boyfriends from the frats.[6]

University presidents had become national figures. Andrew D. White at Cornell had shown that it was possible to combine public and private funding, useful and esoteric learning, and education of men and women, besides continuing his career in politics and diplomacy. Charles W. Eliot had spread the gospel of the elective system and made himself a household image with his editorship of the Harvard Classics for home education. William Rainey Harper had taken by storm the Baptists, John D. Rockefeller, the Chicago business community, and restless faculty members at older institutions. In the 1890s Harper's new University of Chicago, which summed up the innovations recently made at other universities, awed the academic world and drew almost as much public admiration as its temporary neighbor, the World's Columbian Exposition. For Woodrow Wilson, academic leadership at Princeton had preceded a brilliant foray into politics that shortly put him in the White House.

Labeling change as progress did not keep it from being unsettling. Among academic administrators, self-confidence often alternated with anxiety. Both emotions contributed to the creation of institutional associations. Like others, educators shared in what Robert Wiebe has fruitfully called "the search for order."[7]

GOVERNMENT SUBSIDY AND ORGANIZATIONAL INNOVATION: ORIGINS OF THE LAND-GRANT ASSOCIATION

The first successful effort to organize colleges nationally responded to the federal government's recently increased involvement in higher education. Similar to an earlier bill resisted by Southern state's-righters and vetoed by President Buchanan, the Morrill Act became law in

1862 with little fanfare, an assertion of free-labor ideology, belief in governmental efficacy, and eagerness to put public lands on the market. Even though institutions that owed their existence or part of their funds to the act followed widely varied paths, they found that they had important common interests.

The act provided that scrip redeemable in public lands be distributed to each state to support "at least one college where the leading object shall be, without excluding other scientific and classical studies, and including military tactics, to teach such branches of learning as are related to agriculture and the mechanic arts, in such manner as the legislatures of the States may respectively prescribe." Offspring of the act ranged from the University of Arkansas, established to receive the grant but given little additional aid by the state, to Cornell University, where donor munificence and administrative imagination created a model for educational reformers of the day. The act directed the colleges to circulate reports but did not provide for central supervision. The commissioners of agriculture and of education made gestures toward information gathering and guidance, the latter sending Yale's Daniel Coit Gilman traveling among the institutions, urging that they not allow themselves to become mere trade schools and putting in a good word for Latin. But the college leaders were largely on their own.[8]

One beneficiary of the act, the Illinois Industrial University, reacted to attacks from disillusioned farmers by seeking cooperation with other Morrill colleges. As a result, a group of "friends of agricultural education" met in Chicago in 1871. The call had stressed possibilities for advancing agricultural experimentation, but besides scientific matters, the meeting discussed administrative problems of the colleges. Suggestions for a permanent organization of these institutions, however, came to nothing.[9]

The next year, at the behest of the commissioner of agriculture, representatives of the colleges met in Washington, along with delegates from state agricultural societies and boards. The college representatives and their supporters seized control of the meeting, volubly exploring the problems and potential of education for farmers and proclaiming a need for more land grants. Their plan to meet the following year failed, scuttled by the irritated commissioner. The impulse toward national organization of the Morrill colleges revived during the 1880s. Another commissioner of agriculture hoped to enhance the influence of his office, agricultural interests were renewing their political strength, and the college leaders saw united action as the path to increased federal support. There were gatherings in 1882 and 1883, both called by the commissioner.[10]

In 1885 a new commissioner convened a meeting in Washington, including both agricultural colleges and agricultural experiment stations, which had been developing with state support. He shared his worries over the lack of coordination among the Morrill colleges, especially in agricultural research. Debates concerning a pending bill for federal aid to experiment stations and other discussions revealed continuing tension over whether to emphasize the practical needs of farmers or the logic of scientific development. The meeting did not succumb to these disagreements, however. There was much to be gained by working together. The group approved not only an executive committee, but also a second committee charged with seeking further congressional support. The latter joined the drive for the landmark Hatch Act of 1887, which gave grants from public land receipts to support in each state or territory an agricultural experiment station (probably, though not mandatorily, connected with a land-grant college). With this bolstering evidence of political influence, the group reassembled in a celebratory mood in October 1887, forming itself into the "Association of American Agricultural Colleges and Experiment Stations" (AAACES). Something new had appeared in American life, a viable national association of institutions of higher education.[11]

Through inadvertence, the Hatch Act had failed to provide appropriations, threatening a year's delay in program expansion. The new organization at once busied itself with correcting this omission, calling in a body on the secretary of the Treasury and charging its executive committee with "looking after legislation affecting the stations." (Largely as a result of these efforts, a highly unusual corrective appropriation bill passed Congress in February 1888.) As at earlier gatherings, there were scientific papers and consultations on administrative procedures, but the catalyst of successful organization was unmistakable. The federal government had once again shown willingness to grant modest financial support to agricultural science and learning.[12]

The association, strengthened by the elevation of the Department of Agriculture to cabinet status in 1889, set to work to win more federal aid for the colleges themselves, a goal that had eluded continuing efforts by Senator Justin Morrill since 1872. Leaders of the AAACES were dominant in framing a new bill, mounting arguments in its favor, and accepting necessary compromises. (One of these, providing that no state should restrict the race of students benefiting from the act but allowing separate institutions for blacks, was a fateful beginning of the "separate but equal" doctrine.) The Morrill Act of 1890 required more carefully drawn reports from the colleges and provided a modicum of federal supervision. The secretary of the Interior was to certify to the Treasury that conditions of the act had been met by individual institutions. By stirring state governments to greater support of the land-grant colleges, the act gave them further stability and confidence. With the new prosperity among members of the AAACES and its demonstrated effectiveness in Washington, there was good reason to think that this new association with the cumbersome name had a future. When in 1907 AAACES president Liberty Hyde Bailey rejoiced in the "great cooperative and associative volunteer system of American education," it was with a keen awareness that his association had a special function in that system.[13]

The Slow Start of the
National Association of State Universities

In usual educational parlance, *land-grant* has come to mean receiving aid from the federal government under the Morrill Land Grant Acts. It is generally overlooked that many state universities had earlier been founded with the aid of federal land grants, usually of two townships, made when the new state was admitted to the Union. When Mississippi became a state in 1817, however, it received only one township for "a seminary of learning," rather than the usual two. And thereby hangs an associational tale.[14]

This anomaly was rediscovered by Robert B. Fulton when he took office as chancellor of the University of Mississippi in 1892. Born in the Black Belt of Alabama, Fulton was educated first by private tutors and then during the Civil War in a private classical school. Twelve years old when the war began, he did not become a combatant. He ranked first of twenty-one in the class of 1869 at the University of Mississippi and, after some secondary school teaching, returned there in 1871 as tutor in physics and astronomy. That same year he married a daughter of Landon C. Garland, professor of physics and astronomy, whose departure to head the new Vanderbilt University in 1875 conveniently opened the professorship for Fulton. His rapid promotion came partly in recognition of his role in setting up a physics laboratory, obtaining an equatorial telescope, and establishing an electrical engineering course. Though his reputation was local, that was enough to elevate him to the chancellorship of the university. Abolition of the preparatory department, one of his first steps in that office, improved the institution's academic status, and a system of certification of Mississippi high schools soon increased its enrollment.[15]

Fulton persuaded his trustees to petition Congress to rectify the alleged injustice of 1817 by granting Mississippi a second township.

Passage of the desired legislation in June 1894 raised morale at the university and inspired Fulton to seek a national role in education. A month later, at his instigation, a group of about eight state university presidents met for discussions during the annual meeting of the National Education Association (NEA). At the NEA meeting of 1895, a similar group took the name "National Association of State Universities" (NASU) and elected Fulton president.[16]

The NEA had had a Department of Higher Education since 1870, but the department's subordination in so inclusive an educational organization and its representation of both private and public higher education seemed serious drawbacks to Fulton and his associates. Although the NEA, founded in 1857 as the National Teachers Association, had grown out of a call from leaders of ten state teachers' associations, it became not a federation but an organization for individual members. Unlike the NEA, the newly founded NASU was to be an institutional association. Only one vote per university could be cast, and it was understood that universities would generally be represented by their presidents or chancellors.[17]

The University of Mississippi, a small institution in a poverty-ridden state lately in rebellion against the central government, seems an unlikely source for national leadership in higher education. But Southernness may actually have enhanced Fulton's suitability for the role of NASU founder. Some of the special appeal that attaches to a reconciled former enemy may have helped him. It was easy to trust this courtly person, who could offer evidence of recent success in dealing with Congress. Federal aid to higher education had been one of the earliest steps on the road to reunion. Congress had extended the deadline for accepting grants from the Morrill Act of 1862 so that states formerly in the Confederacy could participate. Controls were so minimal as scarcely to ruffle the most extreme advocate of state's rights. The Second Morrill Act in 1890, whose advocates included southern agriculturists, provided for sustained aid severely needed in their impoverished region, and that law struck a compromise on the matter of race.

Mississippi had from the beginning divided its Morrill funds between the state university at Oxford, for whites, and Alcorn University, for blacks. Agricultural courses at the University of Mississippi were, however, a failure, and farmers, newly organized in the Grange, denounced the program as a farce. In 1878 they managed to have Morrill funds shifted to a new institution. As a young faculty member, Fulton could hardly have missed these lessons in the importance of federal grants and the power of a determined lobby.[18]

Fulton and his colleagues in the NASU promptly turned their attention to ways of getting aid from Congress. Certain state universities had been made recipients of Morrill grants, but most had not, and some of the latter had tried unsuccessfully to be included in the Morrill Act of 1890. In his efforts to get the association started, Fulton declared that he had in mind "the urgent need for increased resources." In December 1895, the NASU submitted a memorial to Congress calling for grants of public lands to each state university. Mississippi's Senator Edward C. Walthall introduced an appropriate bill. For several months, Fulton and his associates pressed the attack, trying to get newspaper endorsement of their cause. In Washington to present their case to the Senate Public Lands Committee, Fulton and others received encouragement from Secretary of the Interior Hoke Smith; however, the bill became entangled in quarrels over the proposal for a national university, with some well-connected eastern universities resisting both forms of federal involvement in higher education. As the animosities of the 1896 election mounted ("you shall not crucify mankind upon a cross of gold"), Fulton chose to "lay low." Fitful efforts to revive the bill were made in 1897, but the death of Senator Walthall in 1898, which could scarcely have stopped a strongly based legislative drive, was taken by the NASU as rendering passage of its bill hopeless. The group lapsed into casual gatherings at NEA conventions, with no formal business transacted.[19]

Fulton's ineffectuality probably helped enervate the NASU, where he clung to the presidency. Meanwhile, his inaction contributed to the collapse of plans for another institutional association. In 1898 he headed a committee appointed to pursue the suggestion made in an address before the NEA's Department of Higher Education that a national federation of colleges and universities be formed. Professor Burke A. Hinsdale of the University of Michigan had imagined a noncoercive, discussion-centered association that would tend to raise standards and prevent duplication. Perhaps the plan lacked the urgency of the earlier proposals for the AAACES and the NASU, which had emphasized access to government for the benefit of the associating institutions. Perhaps, too, an all-inclusive organization of colleges and universities lacked the motivation of administrators thinking of themselves as representing a certain category of educational institutions with distinctive needs and possibilities. In any case, the committee formed to create such an association never reported.[20]

The quiescent NASU awakened during 1901, holding two meetings stimulated largely by another question of federal aid. The Mining School Bill, seemingly on the verge of passage, had been drawn in a way that offered no benefits to state universities not receiving Morrill land grants. With an unprecedented twenty-one state universities represented, the association adopted strategies for modifying the bill, and in Washington NASU leaders obtained its revision in the House committee. The bill failed to reach the House floor, however. Meanwhile, George E. MacLean, president of the State University of Iowa, initiated efforts toward some form of federation with the AAACES, the "older and stronger association," hoping to develop ways for state universities lacking Morrill grants to "even up with the colleges of agriculture in securing national co-operation and pecuniary support." Suspicions on both sides, heightened by the Mining School Bill controversy, blocked steps toward coordination. The NASU delegates, although at first welcoming the proposal to meet at the same time as the AAACES and hold some joint sessions, later downgraded the scheme to "merely an incident in the general plan of this Association" and withdrew a suggestion for a joint committee. Indeed, resistance to the better-established AAACES may have played a role in the stirrings that led the NASU to begin printing its proceedings. In 1903 the reinvigorated NASU replaced Fulton with MacLean, who called the developing organizational self-consciousness "a new lease on life." Subsequent presidents were elected annually.[21]

CHAMPIONS OF THE PH.D.:
THE ASSOCIATION OF AMERICAN UNIVERSITIES

The recent formation of a third association of institutions of higher education may have played a role in the new liveliness of the NASU. A group of "those which are willing to admit that they are the best" had emerged in 1900. It included only three state universities—California, Michigan, and Wisconsin—none of which felt it necessary to attend the NASU's 1901 meeting. Whereas the grounds for membership in the AAACES and the NASU were generally unexceptionable, based as they were on relationship to federal or state governments, no such objective criterion accompanied the founding of the Association of American Universities (AAU).[22]

Exclusiveness characterized the AAU from its beginning. The call for the first conference was issued by the presidents of Columbia, Harvard, Johns Hopkins, the University of California, and the University of Chicago. Representatives of eleven universities attended the first meeting, and the constitution they drew up listed fourteen potential members, all of which soon joined. Considerably more than fourteen institutions in the country called themselves universities, and forty-eight had granted nonhonorary Ph.D. degrees during the previous year (table 1). The issue of exclusion was to haunt the new organization.

Table 1
Doctor of Philosophy Degrees Granted and
Requirements Therefor, 1898–1899

According to the reports for the scholastic year 1898–99 received from the universities and colleges of the United States, the degree of doctor of philosophy was conferred during the year on 336 persons. Of this number 325 persons were granted the degree for work done under the direction of the several institutions, and the honorary degree was conferred on 11 persons. The institutions that conferred the Ph.D. degree during the year, together with the number of men and women upon whom the degree was conferred, as reported to this office, are as follows:

Ph.D. degree conferred in 1898–99 on examination

Institutions	On men	On women
*University of California	2	1
University of Colorado	2	0
*Yale University	28	2
Georgetown University, Washington, D.C.	5	0
Illinois Wesleyan University	11	0
*University of Chicago	23	8
Northwestern University, Evanston, Ill.	1	0
McKendree College, Lebanon, Ill.	4	0
Wheaton (Ill.) College	1	0
Taylor University, Upland, Ind.	14	0
Highland (Kans.) University	1	0
University of Kansas	1	0
Kansas Wesleyan University, Salina, Kans.	3	0
*Johns Hopkins University	42	0
Loyola College, Baltimore, Md.	1	0
New Windsor (Md.) College	1	0
Boston University	7	0
*Harvard University	23	0
*Clark University	4	0
*University of Michigan	3	1
University of Minnesota	1	2
University of the State of Missouri	1	0
Westminster College (Mo.)	1	0
Washington University	2	0
University of Omaha	1	0
University of Nebraska	1	0
St. Peter's College, Jersey City, N.J.	1	0
*Princeton University	2	0
*Cornell University	5	2
*Columbia University	32	2
New York University	7	1
Syracuse University	1	0
Mount Union College, Alliance, Ohio	1	0
Ohio Wesleyan University	3	0
Oxford (Ohio) College	0	1
Richmond (Ohio) College	5	0
Wittenberg College, Springfield, Ohio	1	0
University of Wooster (Ohio)	6	0

TABLE 1 *continued*

Institutions	On men	On women
Bryn Mawr (Pa.) College	0	3
Lafayette College, Easton, Pa.	3	0
Franklin and Marshall College, Lancaster, Pa.	1	0
*University of Pennsylvania	17	3
Brown University	3	0
American Temperance University, Harriman, Tenn.	3	0
University of Virginia	3	0
Washington and Lee University, Lexington, Va.	1	0
Gale College, Galesville, Wis.	15	0
*University of Wisconsin	5	0
Total	299	26

Honorary Ph.D. degree conferred in 1898–99

Hanover (Ind.) College	1
Amity College, College Springs, Iowa	1
Kansas Wesleyan University, Salina, Kans.	1
Rust University, Holly Springs, Miss.	1
North Carolina College, Mount Pleasant, N.C.	1
University of Wooster (Ohio)	1
Grove City (Pa.) College	5

The 325 degrees conferred for work done were granted by 48 different institutions in 21 States. A number of the institutions included in the foregoing list and conferring the Ph.D. degree do not provide instruction leading to that degree, but allow students to pursue the prescribed courses in absentia and to pass examinations at their homes under the supervision of a sentinel. With the exception of the institutions offering nonresident courses of study the general requirements for the Ph.D. degree may be stated as follows:

1. The candidate must have a bachelor's degree from a reputable college or university or must show that he has pursued a course of study equivalent to that for which the bachelor's degree is conferred. Each institution determines for itself as to the fitness of the candidate to become an applicant for the degree.

2. A knowledge of French and German sufficient for purposes of investigation. A reading knowledge of these languages is generally deemed to meet the requirements.

3. The pursuit of advanced study and research at some acceptable institution for not less than two years (in most cases not less than three years), the last of which must be spent in residence at the institution by which the degree is to be conferred.

4. The studies pursued must consist of one major or principal subject and, as a rule, two minor or subsidiary subjects.

5. A thesis upon some approved subject connected with the major or principal subject, which must give evidence of the candidate's ability to do original work, must be a contribution to human knowledge and must be accepted by the faculty. Some of the institutions require the thesis to be printed (or its printing guaranteed) before the degree can be conferred.

TABLE 1 *continued*

6. Examinations in all the studies pursued by the candidate.

7. The degree is given not for the mere reason of faithful study for a prescribed time or in fulfillment of a determinate programme, nor for miscellaneous studies, but on the ground of long study and high attainment in a special branch of learning.

Source: *Report of the Commissioner of Education for the Year 1898–99* (Washington, D.C., 1900), 2:1564–66.

*Institutions marked with an asterisk were original members of the AAU. Two original members, Catholic University of America and Stanford, appear not to have given any Ph.D.'s in 1898–99.

The call of January 1900 took as its point of departure the question of relations with foreign universities, notably the admission of Americans studying abroad to examinations for higher degrees. Two problems were identified. Students who had already done advanced work in American universities rarely received credit for it abroad, a difficulty of particular importance for American Ph.D. candidates at the University of Berlin, which required three years of course work. On the other hand, some European universities granted Americans a "cheap" Doctor of Philosophy degree, using standards lower than those applied to native students and lower than those in "our own universities of high standing." Both policies indicated unflattering opinions of American higher education. University leaders, proud of the complex new institutions they headed, were sensitive to evidence of a lingering European view of America as a cultural wilderness, scarcely relieved by a scattering of sectarian colleges.

Problems of international academic relations would in many nations have been treated by a ministry of education. In the United States, where the Bureau of Education (USBE) was restricted to gathering and dispensing information, these issues suggested the formation of a voluntary association. Aside from a wish to "raise the opinion entertained abroad of our own Doctor's degree," the call cited two other hopes for American universities: greater uniformity and the elevation of standards "of our own weaker institutions." There were reasons to seek the last two quite apart from foreign opinion. After all, the wealthier, more demanding universities had something to lose if Ph.D. degrees became easily accessible and widely held. Gale College in Wisconsin, a modestly staffed institution, had granted fifteen Ph.D.'s in 1898–99, more than had eight of the original AAU members. Some institutions allowed Ph.D. candidates "to pursue the prescribed courses in absentia and to pass examinations at their homes under the supervision of a sentinel." Worse still were the utterly fraudulent degree mills, which seemed to be proliferating. Protection from cheaper competition by means of organization and mutual credentialing was a relatively new procedure in education, but the North Central Association of Colleges and Secondary Schools had been following this path with some success since its founding in 1895.[23]

The founding meeting of the AAU, held at the University of Chicago on February 27–28, 1900, heard first from Berkeley's Associate Professor of Astronomy Armin O. Leuschner. The call for the conference apparently originated with Leuschner, who had reason to be particularly sensitive to international academic relations. Born in America of German ancestry, he had graduated from a German gymnasium and the University of Michigan and then had earned a Ph.D. at Berlin. Although the call had said nothing about forming a new association, the meeting authorized a committee on permanent organization, which promptly brought in a constitution of attractive brevity and generality. Except for insertion of the words "and research" in the passage on matters to be considered, the constitution remained unamended until 1948.[24]

President Benjamin Ide Wheeler of California recalled that a more modest sort of organization, a committee or commission, had been in his mind when, in the hope (presumably inspired by Leuschner) of coordinating graduate schools in a way that would ease certain perplexities at Berkeley, he had initiated matters by corresponding first with Harvard's President Charles W. Eliot and then with others. Eliot soon took a main role in planning for the conference, which he chaired. Particularly in his exchanges with Nicholas Murray Butler of Columbia and William Rainey Harper of Chicago, important decisions were made on form, location, and participants.[25]

For these academic entrepreneurs, the new association was a creative response to an opportunity. They were not new to institutional coordination. Eliot had joined in the formation of the New England Association of Colleges and Preparatory Schools in 1885. Butler, dean of the School of Philosophy and heir apparent to the presidency at Columbia, had been president of the NEA in 1894–95, taking the lead in creating committees that set precedents for nationwide standards, and was also involved in 1900 in founding the College Entrance Examination Board. As for President Harper, host of the initial meeting, he had long displayed an intense concern about rational organization and had sought through a program of "affiliation" to exercise control over colleges in the Midwest and reduce the weaker ones to two-year institutions. As early as 1895 a professor at his university had forecast concerted action among universities to remedy low standards in graduate work.[26]

Although significant as a catalyst in the formation of the AAU, concern over graduate student migration did not last long. The founding meeting included a sympathetic discussion of graduate students' complaints about their treatment in German universities, and an emissary from the Federation of Graduate Clubs addressed the assembled presidents. Representatives of the students were also permitted to attend the second and third conferences; at the fourth, however, the association voted not to renew its invitation. Graduate study in Germany by Americans was in fact declining, and university presidents, while not averse to foreign study, cared most about establishing the soundness of American doctorates. As for students' wishes to ease movement among domestic graduate schools, this matter was occasionally discussed by the AAU without the emergence of any general policy.[27]

Besides winning recognition for advanced study pursued in American universities, the founders of the AAU hoped to indicate that some institutions provided it better than others. Omitting certain universities that gave the Ph.D. might motivate them either to drop their programs or to demonstrate qualities that merited admission to the association of "leading universities." Analogies with cartelization in industry were readily made, and Chicago newspapers labeled the new organization "the Ph.D. Trust."[28]

It was not simply the doctorate and graduate study that needed protection. The very name *university* was at risk. Under the multiple chartering practices of states, territories, and (notoriously) the District of Columbia, that name had been given in response to nothing more than considerations of convenience or high institutional ambition. Now interested persons could at least inquire whether or not a certain university belonged to the AAU.

Founders of the AAU may have been partly motivated by the appearance of the term *university* in the name of the NASU. It would be a misfortune, they may have reasoned, if that organization were thought to be the proper representative of American higher education in its relations with European educational authorities. Among those eligible for NASU membership were the academically shaky University of Nevada, the politics-ridden University of Oklahoma, and West Virginia University, a school established to utilize Morrill land grants. The AAACES was less worrisome, since it linked itself to applied learning and used the more modest term *college* in its title. Presidents whose institutions belonged to more than one of these associations found themselves queried at meetings about what the others were up to.[29]

Defending a Tradition:
The Association of American Colleges

The traditional American liberal arts colleges were not involved in these earliest national institutional associations. Perhaps the colleges were satisfied with support from local or regional clienteles. Some probably feared close comparison with other colleges. At the turn of the century, regional, state, and denominational associations seemed to provide sufficient organizational support. By 1915, however, a growing awareness that higher education was being nationally systematized brought into being the Association of American Colleges (AAC).

Although the Council of Church Boards of Education (CCBE), established in 1911 by the general secretaries of several denominations, continued to gain members, it proved inadequate for some of its avowed purposes, notably defense of the liberal arts college. At the suggestion of the CCBE's executive committee, a group of denominational college presidents met at the July 1914 convention of the NEA, which once again proved a seedbed for new educational associations. The presidents discussed possibilities for a new organization, and ten of them issued a call. In response, some one hundred fifty college officers met in January 1915 in Chicago and adopted a constitution for the new "Association of American Colleges."[30]

The founders' mood was largely one of resistance to threat. Their comments suggested that these traditional institutions felt isolated, imperiled, and ill prepared for common countermeasures. The multiple dangers often came from other educationally concerned institutions. The much-touted Carnegie pension program had omitted most church-related colleges, branding them sectarian institutions, and the Carnegie Foundation had openly disparaged such "dissipation of energy" as was entailed by the existence of six Methodist colleges in Iowa. Shortly before the creation of the AAC, more animadversions on the oversupply of small colleges appeared in the first report of Rockefeller's General Education Board.[31]

State institutions offered more and more powerful competition, given their support from the tax base, widening curricula, and new reputation for social service. At the AAC's first meeting, one president enviously cited the success of the NASU in sharing ideas and inside information, activity that presumably assisted its members in raiding "the money providing power, the legislature." It had not been unusual to find businessmen and farmers belittling the role of liberal arts colleges, but now such critics were being joined by the new vocational experts. Through the AAU, universities had begun declaring which colleges worthily prepared students for advanced work, and the list was short. Among AAU chieftains, the late William Rainey Harper had published a devastating little book, *The Prospects of the Small College*, full of proposals for reordering the system of higher education, plans that college leaders took as a gloomy prophecy of shrinking influence, declining enrollments, and possible demise.[32]

Some high schools, through postgraduate courses, were aggressively projecting themselves into what had once been considered college work, and the process had gained support from a recent report of the NEA's Committee on Economy of Time in Education. Joliet, Illinois, identified its program as a "junior college"; as this institutional form spread, traditional colleges feared loss of students. Graduates of six-year high schools or junior colleges who wanted further education might well bypass the older colleges entirely, having heard the argument that for juniors and seniors specialized work was more readily available in universities.[33]

A new systematization of American education was well under way, and the colleges had to choose whether to let their role be shaped by others or to begin themselves "playing in this larger national game." "If it is not too late . . . ," one president advised, "the distinctively American colleges should get together in an organization which will make clear to them their distinctive mission and to the public their permanent value." One positive thinker at an early AAC meeting insisted that the colleges all had cordial relations with "the institutions not of our order; High schools, Normal schools, Technical schools and Universities, State and Non-State," but his litany could be heard as an anxious evocation of the "others" that were robbing colleges of students and status. At the very least, cordiality should no longer be taken for granted. There was demonstrable need for colleges to seek a common national voice.[34]

As its first president, the AAC chose Robert Lincoln Kelly, the animating force in the decision to move beyond the CCBE to a broader college association. Kelly's family traced back to South Carolina Quakers who had left slave territory for the Old Northwest, where his father, a newspaper publisher, became a member of the Indiana state legislature. Graduating in 1888 from Earlham, the Quaker college nearest his home, Kelly at once entered educational work, first serving as a town superintendent of schools and then heading successively two Quaker academies. In 1898 he began graduate study at the University of Chicago, where he earned a master's degree and developed his interest in measurement at its Dewey School. After a year as acting president of William Penn College in Iowa, he returned to his alma mater in 1901 in the triple role of professor of philosophy, college pastor, and dean, increasingly assuming duties of the ailing president, whom he succeeded in 1903.

Part of the change that the Kelly years brought to Earlham sprang from his exuberant personality. Students there, who had never before called a president "Prexy," felt free to print satirical comments on his baldness and verbosity. Student activities previously forbidden, such as music and dramatics, began to flower, though dancing and smoking remained banned. In opposition to the quietest tradition within Quakerism, Kelly supported students and faculty who entered local good-government campaigns. In fact, Kelly's sense of what it meant for Earlham to be a Quaker institution was broadly permissive. He believed that Quaker ideals, such as civic responsibility, gender equality, and silent worship, were "becoming the common possession of the Christian Church." Although willing to call Earlham "denominational," he insisted it was "nonsectarian."

During 1914–15, Kelly became involved in an academic struggle reminiscent of that at Princeton between Woodrow Wilson and Dean Andrew F. West. As at Princeton the disputed location of a building for the graduate college had brought many other tensions to the surface, so at Earlham the question of whether a new Quaker meeting house should be on or off campus unleashed the demons of academic battle. Though like Kelly a liberal Quaker, Elbert Russell, Earlham's popular professor of Biblical literature, believed the college should strive harder to develop students into loyal members of Quaker communities. Offended by Kelly's aggressive institutional modernism, Russell objected that the president favored the dean over the college preacher (a post held by Russell himself). Russell found inadequacies in the new system of student government, citing disorders in the men's dormitory and laxity about required student attendance at Sunday worship. He charged also that Kelly's idea of "standards" was set by state universities and philanthropic foundations. In short, the president stressed the college's business side over its religious and moral interests.

Although the trustees gave Kelly a vote of confidence, they first conducted a formal three-day investigation. The resulting report sought compromise, suggesting fuller consultation between president and faculty, improvements in student behavior, and attendance by all faculty at daily chapel. Greater denominational control, which seems to have been one of Russell's goals, was not recommended, and his supporters called the investigation a whitewash. The conflict, which extended into the first election of alumni trustees, scarred both men.

Russell resigned in 1915, later becoming dean of Duke University's School of Religion. Kelly left Earlham two years later.

Kelly was among the first to see the possibilities of an academic career at the transinstitutional level and, in a sense, created the very position to which he moved. Alert to interinstitutional developments and the movement for national standards, he had arranged for Earlham to modify its entrance requirements in line with new NEA recommendations. He had announced proudly in his 1914 annual report that a survey by the United States Bureau of Education had brought praise to Earlham and that it appeared on the first "approved list" of the AAU. As chairman of the Friends' national Board of Education, he pursued interdenominational cooperation by helping create the Council of Church Boards of Education. In 1917 he assumed its new executive secretaryship, a position that, he observed, meant "a pronounced increase in salary," and early the next year he became also the (unsalaried) executive secretary of the AAC.[35]

At the AAC's founding meeting and in his presidential address of 1916, Kelly had made a strong case for the new organization. He harked back to Franklinian federalism with its warning of hanging together or else hanging separately. He called for substituting "the abounding courage of the group for the faltering hope of the individual." It was time "to wipe off the map any such things as an educational north, south, east or west." He countered objections that colleges were too diverse to form an effective body with analogies to national achievements in ethnic, religious, and political pluralism. Nevertheless, creators of the AAC found themselves hampered by persisting regionalism. One Yankee college president saw the national effort as unnecessary inasmuch as New England already had an association of colleges. Although the first 204 member institutions included 8 from the Pacific Coast states, 11 from New England, and 32 from the South, midwestern dominance was evident. There were 20 from Iowa alone.[36]

The AAC's constitution hewed close to the pattern adopted by the other institutional associations, including the same officers and executive committee, the same yearly meeting, the same voting by institution. But the new association varied in important matters from the earlier ones. Although it admitted nondenominational colleges from the beginning, the association had a decidedly Christian aura. It continued to share offices and personnel with the CCBE, and the two groups held their annual meetings successively in the same city. Kelly's presidential address included a call for college executives "to bear one another's burdens and so fulfill the law of Christ." Dissipating with the years, this aura never left the association completely, perhaps because many member colleges continued to justify their existence by their religious connections.[37]

The AAC had at least three times as many members as the largest of the older institutional associations, and size contributed to its early decision to create a staff rather than rely entirely on elected officers preoccupied with full-time academic positions. The AAC was the first of these associations to establish a separate office of executive secretary, and Kelly with his religious ecumenism, administrative verve, and national perspective fit its requirements admirably. He remained the AAC's chief executive officer until 1937.

Associating the Associations:
The American Council on Education

Even before Wilson's war message on April 2, 1917, meetings on the nation's campuses had been voting to adapt academic activities to the purposes of the embattled state. Many administrators had already embraced the doctrine of military preparedness. Protestations of readiness for academic sacrifice grew more fervid after Wilson's address and the formal declaration of war. It proved very difficult, however, for institutions to discover government policies or learn what part they could best take in the struggle. Although President A. Lawrence Lowell insisted that Harvard was "in no perplexity about what we had better do to assist the Government," representatives of other institutions journeyed to Washington for guidance, only to receive contradictory advice from various agencies.[38]

The motives of academic leaders were not simply patriotic. They were understandably worried about institutional welfare amid wartime dislocations. Would students keep coming? Would income be curtailed? Would it be necessary to close? Given the new urgencies, the national educational associations seemed underorganized and awkwardly overlapping. Higher education proved to have very little leverage on the new centers of power in Washington. Particularly frustrating were efforts to get the War Department to allow deferment of students in scientific and technical training. Here the AAU found its overtures to the secretary of war rebuffed, and after hearing complaints, particularly from state university presidents, it called for coordination of the various educational associations.[39]

As head of the AAU, Indiana University's William L. Bryan initiated a planning meeting of several association representatives, timed to coincide with the AAC convention in Chicago early in January 1918.[40] Two meetings in Washington followed within the month, the second attended by delegates from the executive committees of eight educational associations. Formal organization came at a March meeting, under the name "Emergency Council on Education" (ECE), and a draft constitution was issued. The ECE leased an office near the White House in the Munsey Building, already the location of two influential new groups, the National Research Council and the Council of National Defense. Donald J. Cowling of Carleton College, president of the AAC, became ECE chairman, and Prince L. Campbell of the University of Oregon, representing the NASU, became secretary-treasurer. The AAC moved its new central office from Chicago to Washington, and Robert L. Kelly, its executive secretary, undertook many chores for the new council. His efforts to involve colleges and universities in ECE programs shared the booster enthusiasm of other wartime drives.[41]

Significantly, the council's earliest activities included lobbying for a federal Department of Education, a potential center for coordination and indicator of prestige. At the same time, the group pressed the case against an uncontrolled drain of students through the draft and enlistment. Although offered in the name of long-term national strength, the associations' "manpower" proposals revealed hard-headed institutional self-interest. The presence of the council probably hastened creation of the War Department's Committee on Education and Special Training (CEST) and its civilian advisory board. War Department representatives shared their plans at the third January meeting and invited nominations for the advisory board. During the summer of 1918, the ECE devoted much of its activity to attracting students into the pending CEST programs.[42]

Officials of the Bureau of Education cooperated in the creation of the new council. Commissioner Philander P. Claxton gave it his blessing, but another USBE official, Samuel P. Capen, turned more energetically to council development. Capen exemplified a personality, newly emerged in the Progressive Era, which Robert D. Cuff has described as demonstrating "a peculiar mixture of managerial technique and entrepreneurial spirit that perfectly suited the bureaucratic individualism of wartime Washington." Some of these go-getters were dollar-a-year men drawn from industry. Others had backgrounds in the nonbusiness, nongovernmental realm that includes universities and private associations. Members of both groups reappeared in the developing federal agencies of the 1920s and 1930s. More than any other of these wartime organizers, Capen was to gain and keep influence in American higher education.[43]

No one could brand Capen an interloper in academia. He was born (1878) the son of one college president (Elmer H. Capen of Tufts) and became (1908) the son-in-law of another, Carroll D. Wright of Clark College, the separately organized adjunct of Clark University. Four years after his graduation from Tufts, he took a Ph.D. degree at the University of Pennsylvania, having pursued graduate study also at Harvard and Leipzig. He promptly accepted a position teaching modern languages at the newly opened Clark College. With no great dedication to original scholarship, Capen displayed a strong organizational bent. He became president of Worcester's Public Education Association and a member of the city's Board of Education. In Clark University's graduate program, he began to offer courses in educational administration. Presumably he learned something of Washington bureaucracy from Wright, who had been U.S. commissioner of labor before coming to head Clark College. In 1910 Capen campaigned actively but unsuccessfully for the new USBE position of specialist in higher education, a position he won after a second try in 1914. Strikingly tall, his angularity was emphasized by his goatee, but he was far from a forbidding figure, with his ready smile and his hands thrust casually into his pockets. A regular at the Chevy Chase Country Club and the Cosmos Club, he socialized eagerly in the Washington establishment, aided by his ambitious wife. Their dreams were early directed toward some university presidency, the one in Berkeley being a special favorite.[44]

About the time he moved to Washington, Capen joined the Society for the Promotion of Engineering Education (SPEE), which had sprung from the World Congress of Engineers at the Chicago Exposition of 1893. Founded by engineering educators, the SPEE soon came to include many practicing engineers and business managers. It increasingly sought adaptation of engineering education to new corporate industrial forms, meanwhile encouraging business recruiting on campus. Somewhat awed by the panache of the SPEE activists, Capen liked to think of his new work at the USBE as "a kind of efficiency engineering."[45]

Although legal limits on federal involvement in education often hampered the USBE, its new specialist in higher education managed to undertake a wide range of influential projects. Joining the survey movement then at full tide, he issued reports on higher education in several states, reports that condemned duplication while offering guidelines for expansion. Treading carefully, Capen also sought to use the USBE as an agency for classifying institutions and thereby encouraging standardization. He was splendidly located to take a leading role in the wartime reordering of higher education. Although he was not its initiator, no one should have been surprised to find him active in giving form to the new council of associations.[46]

For those envisioning a more centralized, coherent, rationalized society, the war offered an opportunity to line up colleges and universities under the aegis of the War Department's educational program. Some participants in the effort hoped for long-term results that would promote the health of corporate capitalism. Although often their ally, Capen is more accurately viewed as a talented person in midcareer who had been applying his rage for order to educational institutions and now felt the heightened emotions of a society at war. The association officers who worked in Washington are not accurately depicted as coopted yes-men. A strong impulse toward order and standardization had already been demonstrated by the associations. The new council came into existence because of their dissatisfactions with government unpredictability in wartime. The most important leader in establishing the American Council on Education (ACE) was Carleton's Cowling, a Baptist minister, dedicated to the small-college liberal arts tradition, who shared the hopes for coordination that had inspired the creation of the AAC. He and Capen became enduring friends and collaborators.

Since the formation of an umbrella association expressed familiar organizational impulses, there was little surprise in the conclusion of its creators that it ought to outlast the war. In July 1918, they changed its name to "American Council on Education" and elevated Cowling's title to "president." Shortly after the war's abrupt end, a provisional constitution was approved.[47]

Aware that an association of associations risked looseness and impermanence, the ACE decided to establish a central office under a salaried "director." Offered this post after Cowling declined it, Capen insisted on perquisites similar to those he enjoyed at the USBE. It was agreed in December 1918 that the ACE would seek pledges totaling at least $20,000 a year for a trial period of of five years. To attain that amount, the ACE moved beyond the associations (identified as "constituent members") and provided also for direct membership by colleges and universities ("institutional members"). Cowling campaigned among the institutions, urging anew the benefits of alliance, but the drive did not meet its July 1, 1919, deadline. Some institutions had bitter memories of their recent involvement with distant authorities and yearned to be left alone, and many were under financial pressure from inflation and rising enrollments. By mid-November, however, the needed sum was pledged, and Capen took office December 1, at an annual salary of $7,500.[48]

Even without a war, the existence of diverse institutional associations was bound ultimately to suggest some sort of umbrella group. The idea drew on educators' mounting conviction that, in a complex society of increasingly powerful national organizations and increasing activity by government, education and those concerned with it must not be left to flounder amid local interests and uncertain leadership. To varying degrees such thinking had also motivated the founders of the AAACES, the NASU, the AAU, and the AAC. In 1919 Capen could claim that every national association of institutions of higher education belonged to the ACE.[49]

American academics, having looked with veneration at European higher education in the nineteenth century and striven to import European scholars and standards, believed as World War I ended that they were ready for a new role. Their sense of Europe's devastation was matched by pride in America's readiness for intellectual leadership. Europe could look to the United States, not just because it had escaped the brunt of the war, but because it had created, out of the welter of forty years before, institutions alive with the spirit of learning. Through their institutional associations, none of which had existed before 1887, these colleges and universities could share their sense of accomplishment and their strategies to make the most of new opportunities.

The Land-Grant Association Goes West, 1895

•

VENTURING beyond the Mississippi for the first time, the Association of American Agricultural Colleges and Experiment Stations held its ninth annual meeting in Denver. By agreeing to a July rather than the traditional October or November meeting, the group had obtained preferential railway rates identical to those negotiated by the NEA. Although distance reduced the number of persons attending, the institutional representation was about three-fourths of the membership, nearly as high as ever.

The host mayor and governor personally delivered their welcomes at the opening session, Tuesday morning, July 16, 1895, in the ordinary of the Brown Palace Hotel. The Denver press was there in force. The *Rocky Mountain News* praised the delegates as "toilers of the hardest kind" and printed line drawings of some of them. Among the overabundant local offers of entertainment, that from the Chamber of Commerce for a streetcar tour of the city was accepted.

The executive committee had been active during the past year, and its report was the first order of business. Chairman Henry H. Goodell, president of Massachusetts Agricultural College, told the delegates of several failed initiatives. The effort to have Congress publish the results of the Chicago Exposition tests of dairy cattle breeds had been blocked, partly by counterpressure from the Holstein-Friesian Association. The depressed economy had made it a poor time to get federal appropriations for uniforms and equipment for the colleges' military programs. There was no recent word from Preston Powers in Florence, who had contracted for a marble bust of Senator Morrill (with plaster replicas promised for members ordering them). In a year of little achievement, at least the committee had not been extravagant. True, its bills accounted for most of the $551 of expenditures, but receipts had totaled $1,117 (principally from the $10 dues of colleges and experiment stations).

That evening featured the annual address of the president,

this year Henry E. Alvord, one of the founders, who had been active on the executive committee. A leader in the cause of agricultural science, Alvord had headed Maryland Agricultural College from 1887 to 1892 and had just become chief of the U.S. Department of Agriculture's new Dairy Division. Hoping particularly to inform westerners who had not attended earlier meetings, he used his address for historical reflection and stocktaking. He sought to undercut charges that the association's dealings with the federal government constituted excessive lobbying, even as he defended the group's effectiveness in Washington.

Proud of the association's record, Alvord also had an agenda for its future. He wanted missionary work to bring in nonmembers among eligible colleges and experiment stations. "Every eligible institution must admit that the Association has been its servant and helper, doing things which it needed, better, easier, and cheaper than it could have done them alone." He recommended increased supervision of experiment stations by the Department of Agriculture. Criticizing colleges that were offering only secondary school work, he expressed doubts about the legality of using even part of the Morrill funds for preparatory departments. He called for institutions to be headed by experienced men of affairs rather than those who were merely men of letters, successful teachers, or good investigators. When Alvord concluded, the group called for a committee to frame his suggestions as motions for later action.

The "sections" met in afternoon and late evening sessions. By constitutional proviso, these were five: Agriculture and Chemistry (clearly considered most important), Horticulture and Botany, Entomology, College Work, and Mechanic Arts (the poor relation). Here members heard specialized papers and engaged in more casual exchange than was allowed at the plenary sessions. A particularly spirited discussion at the Agriculture and Chemistry section followed a paper on practical methods of maintaining soil fertility. At the Mechanic Arts section, the failure of an author to appear led to informal discussion on the education of Negroes and Indians, presumably viewed as good candidates for manual training. Some sessions grew tedious, but delegates could slip away.

The work of the sections was carefully integrated into the general sessions. Sections twice gave reports, first on their undertakings during the past year and later on their just-completed sessions. The section on College Work shared results of its recent inquiry on developments at member colleges. (Kentucky exempted seniors from military drill, Minnesota now had a department of domestic economy for women, and Texas A&M sought to increase agricultural enrollment with a paid-student-labor system.) Papers selected from three sections were presented to the full assemblage. Thus, all had the opportunity to hear California's Eugene W. Hilgard report findings of the Tulare station on alkali soils and President Alston Ellis of Colorado Agricultural College on the proper studies for the four-year B.S. course. Plenary sessions also included a panel on agricultural teaching methods, followed by discussion from the floor, and a paper, illustrated with stereopticon pictures, on the mouths of insects.

As the three days passed, an increasing number of resolutions came before the group. Some of these had been held over from the previous year (a proposal for changing the association's name was further postponed). A motion to endorse the metric system was tabled, as was one that reflected westerners' desire to establish a new section on irrigation. The meeting voted several resolutions formalized from suggestions in the president's address and that of Alfred C. True of the USDA's Office of Experiment Stations. These provided, among other matters, for codifying legislation from earlier meetings, continuing to press Congress for an office of land-grant colleges in the Bureau of Education, and warning the stations against diverting Hatch Act funds from research. Other resolutions urged that the stations report tests of dairy cows in terms of butterfat and sought increased compensation for postmasters who handled the stations' numerous free mailings. Two recently deceased founders of agricultural colleges were duly memorialized, their organizational abilities praised along with their intelligence and humanity.

The association evinced strong confidence in committees. The Committee on Entrance Requirements was continued with fuller instructions, after reporting that it had abandoned its planned questionnaire because the newly active Society for the Promotion of Engineering Education and the commissioner of education had similar investigations under way. New committees were named, including one on instructional methods in other countries and one on uniformity of nomenclature in station publications. Besides the constitutionally mandated executive committee, eight others existed by 1896.

On the whole, sessions moved along briskly. As Alvord cheerfully observed, "Now and then there seems to be some waste of time, but less than might be expected." It was voted, for example, that although each state would report on its legislature's actions for the control of bovine tuberculosis, there should be no discussion. Although debate seemed free of acrimony, there was a sharp dissent from True's plea that station officers refrain from giving testimonials for commercial products. One delegate saw no reason to conceal the brand of separator that did such good work at his station's creamery.

Just before final adjournment on Thursday evening, President

Alvord congratulated the group. Fears aroused by the unaccustomed location and timing of the meeting had proved ill founded.
"We have done more solid work, and work of a higher grade,
than at any previous meeting. I think we may resolve ourselves
for a moment into a mutual admiration society." As the delegates
departed, some to accept the invitation to visit Colorado's Agricultural College at Ft. Collins, the executive committee met to
begin its planning for the coming year.

CHAPTER 2

Shared Ideology, Diverging Missions

THE MAJOR institutional associations that had emerged by 1920 shared a common interpretation of the role of voluntary organizations in a democratic society. At the same time, they sought differentiation from one another, since each had to justify its separate existence. All exalted the contribution of higher education to social advance, but each stressed a different aspect. Although recognizing that they partook of a broad pattern in American society, the leaders of higher education considered their own associationalism different in important ways. Notably, they claimed to be more altruistic than most others who organized—to seek, beyond the good of their members, the good of all Americans, even of all humanity. Before examining particular associations, it is appropriate to recall the longstanding celebration of group life on which they relied.[1]

Voluntary groups, seen as forming an important middle way between Thoreauvian solitude and domination by too powerful a government, have long been admired in the United States. The interpretation of Alexis de Tocqueville, vigorously revived in the wake of World War II, portrayed American associationalism as a major defense against centralized power and majoritarian tyranny. In the heyday of pluralistic theorizing, the many national organizations with their offices in Washington, D.C., were thought to exhibit the health of the society and the beneficial clash of interests. It was only later that a David Stockman could brand them part of "the permanent government." That term, as William Greider put it in a famous article,

> meant not only the layers and layers of federal bureaucrats and liberal politicians who sustained open-ended growth of the central government but also the less visible infrastructure of private interests that fed off it and prospered— the law firms and lobbyists and trade associations in rows of shining office buildings along K Street in Washington;

the consulting firms and contractors; the constituencies of special interests, from schoolteachers to construction workers to failing businesses and multi-national giants, all of whom came to Washington for money and for legal protection against the perils of free competition.

No association leader could relish inclusion in such a sinister depiction.[2]

Indeed, when groups seek favors from government, they lose some of their ideological purity and become "special interests" or even "selfish special interests." And if they become themselves little governments, speaking with authority and acting to coerce, resentment against them mounts. For many years groups in what has come to be known as the "third sector" (i.e., neither business nor government) have benefited from a favorable public image. Since they were not profit seeking, they were socially benevolent; since they were not armed with governmental authority, they were noncoercive. Recently both assumptions have been challenged.[3]

When the leaders of an association sought to specify its missions or attract membership, they did not often stop to delineate the associationalist ideology. They were relying on it nonetheless. When "members" with a special interrelationship banded together, associationalism justified and guided their shared behavior. The association properly helped them influence each other. Since to some extent they were competitors, the association set rules of the game, but it also encouraged mutual improvement. Knowledge, status, wealth, and other goods could be gained through joint effort.[4]

Associationalism asserted that a proper government was limited in its powers. A society with such a government allowed ample room for other centers of authority. Associations were not just tolerated, they were needed to watch government and make sure it did not extend itself illegitimately. One way that associations reinforced limits on government was by themselves performing socially necessary tasks. Even when they set norms and penalized violations, however, the associations usually presented themselves not as wielders of power but as exemplars of mutual aid. Yet sometimes an association leader admitted its quasi-governmental role. In 1895 the president of the land-grant group urged college officers to recognize that the organization was more than a convenience and should be granted "some measure of authority as a legislative and administrative body concerning matters not regulated by law."[5]

The institutional associations began at a time when the decline of traditional party loyalty opened the way for pressure groups independent of party. Associationalist ideology envisioned the new pattern not as a free-for-all with rewards given to interest groups with electoral or financial clout, but as a rational method of change in a complex society. Often occupational grouping with individual membership was assumed to be the most legitimate basis for an association. Seeking to justify unionization of millworkers, a South Carolina state senator declared in 1901, "There are associations in every calling and profession in life: doctors, lawyers, merchants, farmers—yes, and mill presidents associate themselves together to better their condition. Is there any reason why factory hands cannot do the same? Organization gives dignity to every calling and profession in life." But the version of associationalism most useful to college and university administrators presented higher education not as an occupation but as a fundamental social function and linked it not to individual careers but to institutional development. With this approach, the president of the land-grant association could answer accusations that its objectives were selfish by insisting, "This is not an association of individuals, but of institutions, . . . united for the purpose of mutual aid and the promotion of common interests, which are public interests."[6]

Much of the enduring appeal of associationalism came from its moderation. Americans had long taken pride in their New World escape from European autocracy. By the late nineteenth century, however, an American excess—rampant individualism—began to be cited as a parallel danger. A middle-of-the-road approach offered order and action that derived from centers of power other than the state. Herbert Hoover was closely identified with the associationalist method, and his defeat in 1932 indicated that the electorate was ready for a more activist government, but the shift was hardly radical.[7]

In education, the reluctance to abandon associationalism was shown in the ideological pronouncements of George F. Zook, a Democrat and, for a brief time, FDR's commissioner of education. Shortly before he became director of the ACE, Zook declared, "Nowhere in America does the voice of individual or institutional freedom carry the same vigor or the same conviction as a century ago." Although the context for his statement was the work of accrediting agencies, his moderate ideology expressed the basic rationale for the institutional associations with which he was to become increasingly involved. Zook saw voluntary efforts for control as representing "on the one hand, a revolt from the unprogressive and autocratic manner in which government frequently deals with all things in evolution, and on the other an attempt to prevent the cause in which the members are interested from falling into confusion, low standards, and ill repute." The safe route between autocracy and anarchy was associationalism.[8]

Membership was not free. In 1926 the University of Illinois showed

TABLE 2

Organizations to Which the University of Illinois Belongs (1926)

Organization	Dues
General	
American Council on Education	$500.00
Association of Land Grant Colleges	110.00
Association of American Universities	50.00
National Association of State Universities	25.00
North Central Association of Colleges and Secondary Schools	
(for University)	10.00
Departmental	
Association of American Law Schools	40.00
American Association of Colleges of Pharmacy	35.00
Association of American Medical Colleges	50.00
American Association of Dental Schools	50.00
Association of Collegiate Schools of Architecture	10.00
Purchasing Agents' Association of Chicago	15.00
North Central Association of Colleges and Secondary Schools	
(for University High School)	2.00
Association of Collegiate Schools of Business	25.00
Association of American Library Schools	10.00

Source: David Kinley Papers, Subject File, box 3, University of Illinois Archives.

enough concern about the expense to total up its dues for the twelve associations to which it belonged (table 2). Even with the financial stringencies of the 1930s, however, most colleges and universities remained loyal to their associations. In 1938, President Clarence A. Dykstra told the AAU that the University of Wisconsin had dropped several institutional memberships. Top administrators at the University of California, however, backed down from a decision to discontinue membership in four associations after the head of the affected department protested. In the early 1930s, the University of Michigan alumni magazine prominently listed fifty-six organizations to which the university belonged, smugly declaring that "in each case . . . some definite advantage accrues to the University from its membership— otherwise it would not belong." So many categories of academic administrators had formed associations by 1936 that Miami University's Upham wondered what functions were left for an organization of "mere presidents."[9]

Consider college officers who decided that it was worthwhile to send in the dues, or journeyed to annual meetings, or inquired about proper institutional policies. These persons' motives included concern for institutional prestige, hope for relief from administrative perplexities, and sometimes most urgently of all, personal desire for comradeship, professional status, and upward career mobility. The needs of institutions and their representatives were the matrix for associational growth. Note also the officers and permanent staff of an association. They came to think of it somewhat differently, as an entity with its own purposes and justifications. It served the advancement of learning. It made for a more rationally ordered society. Meanwhile, as it developed, it offered new careers. The purposes worth examining are not just those of member institutions or those that were high-minded.[10]

CONTROVERSY WITHIN THE LAND-GRANT ASSOCIATION

Active pursuits diverged from avowed mission during the earliest years of the AAACES. Its constitution suggested a group whose primary purpose would be to talk: "the consideration and discussion of all questions pertaining to the successful progress and administration" of member institutions. But the meeting that adopted the constitution determinedly pursued another goal: winning additional federal aid for beneficiaries of the Morrill and Hatch Acts. The language of the constitution barely hinted at the large role to be given research. Annual meetings, divided into sections on the model of the American Association for the Advancement of Science, did not ignore administration and instruction, but most of the papers dealt with investigative work of faculty and staff. The reference in the constitution to the duty of each institution to give at each meeting "a brief report of [its] work and progress" had not implied such elaborate scientific content.

Desire for greater independence from the presidents, not any inadequate attention by the association to research, explains the long struggle of the experiment station heads for a section of their own. The matter came to a head in 1902. Despite decorum at recorded meetings, hotel lobbies seethed as delegates considered a possible split in the association. A compromise formally adopted in 1903 divided the association into two sections, one for the experiment stations and one for college work and administration. The balance of power was reflected by giving two positions out of five on the executive committee to the experiment stations. The station directors welcomed the new arrangement, which as Roger L. Williams has observed, gave them the opportunity to discuss professional concerns without presidential participation. They vowed to use their new section for administrative rather than technical discussions, for which disciplinary societies seemed more appropriate.[11]

The constitution was misleading also in its designation of college members as "agricultural," since the Morrill Act had directed creation of colleges whose teaching related to "agriculture and the mechanic arts." The inclusion of the federal Department of Agriculture as a member of the association increased the imbalance. There was much quarreling over the name, but early efforts to change it by adding "mechanical" or using the designation "Morrill" or "land-grant" all failed.[12]

Favoritism toward agriculture appeared in the failure of the *Proceedings* to include the engineering papers read at annual meetings. Engineering faculty felt less and less at home in the association, and in 1912 the engineering deans organized a separate "Land-Grant College Engineering Association." A joint meeting of the two associations in 1915 began a gradual rapprochement, culminating in full reunion with a renaming of the original organization. In 1919 it became the "Association of Land-Grant Colleges" (ALGC), adding "and Universities" (ALGCU) in 1926. The association showed its broadened concern by supporting a quarter-century drive for federal grants to engineering experiment stations. Although unsuccessful, this effort indicated the most sustained mission of the land-grant association: to protect and increase federal support for its members, while minimizing federal interference.[13]

By its structure of separate committees and separate sections at its annual meetings, the land-grant association satisfied representatives of engineering and home economics schools. The proper relation to liberal arts, undergraduate and graduate, was more troublesome. The association's first president, Penn State's George W. Atherton, had strongly advocated development of its members into comprehensive institutions that included nonvocational studies. Other land-grant college representatives also reminded their associates of the reference to liberal as well as practical education in the original Morrill Act, and some quoted definitions of liberal education that allowed for utilitarianism. But there was a degree of skepticism about such expansion of the association's domain. The provost at the University of California judged useless or worse reports of the ALGCU's committee on instruction, especially when they ventured into nonapplied fields. He saw such topics as honors courses and comprehensive examinations as belonging properly with the AAC. The similar argument that the land-grant association "cannot speak for a university-wide range of interests" was made in 1943 by a president of the rival NASU, whose own institution (Indiana University) did not receive Morrill grants. The ALGCU seemed determined, however, to follow the route of inclusiveness, an approach that suited the increasing complexity of member institutions.[14]

CONGENIALITY AND BEYOND: THE NASU

If the NASU's mission simply imitated the land-grant association's pursuit of federal grants it would have little reason for separate existence. The state universities that were also Morrill-grant institutions did not share the interests of the "separated" state universities in making sure federal programs were not tied to Morrill status. The University of Minnesota, in the former category, did not have problems such as those of the University of Kansas, which found itself often in competition with Kansas State. In this light, symmetry suggested an organization not of all state universities but of those not assigned Morrill funds, and such an organization did exist from as early as 1925 until 1963. Despite the muddle, the NASU managed to coexist with the older organization, sometimes competing, sometimes cooperating. The large overlap of membership helped remove suspicions.[15]

With a smaller membership and inclusion of some genteel presidents of southern state universities that did not teach agriculture or mechanic arts, the NASU developed into the most congenial of the institutional associations. In fact, the early NASU experienced a tug-of-war between those who were happy to think of the association as a club and those more ambitious for it to improve member universities and confront external challenges. For some time the clubmen generally triumphed. Under their influence the NASU expanded to admit as special members without vote "men of distinction or who have retired from presidencies or professorships in the institutions which are members of the Association." Hence the seeming anomaly that the president of Swarthmore College attended NASU meetings: he had earlier been president of Indiana University and his fellowship was valued.[16]

The advantages of membership in the NASU were apparently great enough that those who by one interpretation or another might be eligible did not want to be left out. Confusion about what constituted a state university, however, rendered some institutional applications problematic. Although admitted in 1931, Pennsylvania State College, a Morrill-grant institution with allegedly ambiguous relations to its state government, was refused admission in 1914, as was the University of the State of New York, a supervising and coordinating, rather than a teaching, institution.[17]

Despite some programmatic elaboration, the NASU retained its character as a club of university presidents, as was observed with satisfaction by both the retiring and incoming presidents in 1909. The latter called the annual meetings "the most important event of the whole year to me." The elaborate social schedule of the NASU meeting in Berkeley in 1915, including a day trip by special train to Phoebe Hearst's estate, gave satisfaction by drawing the group yet closer.[18]

Socializing did more than reinforce egos. It shifted readily to current problems of academic leadership. An after-dinner account of "My Most Amusing Experience" might do nothing except aid digestion, but presidents exchanged many ideas that affected practice in their home institutions. How did one counteract some legislators' crude per capita estimations of a university's productivity? What benefits came from visiting artists and writers? How would the Rhodes scholarships be assigned? How should one react when a student sued after being dropped for low grades? Mutual trust allowed these and more sensitive matters to be discussed "freely and confidentially."[19]

Beginning in 1905 with its work for standardization, the NASU evinced a new activism, seeking by various means to enhance the prestige of state universities. When John Hoyt, first president of the University of Wyoming, asked for support of his often-proposed plan for a national university, the NASU did not reject it as the stale hobby of one individual. Instead the association cooperated to create a version of the plan which would have established a new center for research and graduate education, at the post-Master's level, but one which did not grant degrees. State university presidents would have constituted an advisory council. A NASU committee pushed the plan and won endorsement for it from the AAACES and the NEA, though the resulting bill made little headway in Congress. When the Carnegie Foundation excluded state universities from its pension program, the NASU made itself heard in opposition and won a partial victory. More ambitious proposals, such as those of President George A. MacLean of Iowa that the NASU lead a federation of all tax-supported educational institutions and take charge of academic foreign relations, proved beyond the reach of the organization.[20]

Although some of its members were in fact small and elitist, the NASU embraced "the state university idea," a model that combined support by public revenues with wide access and practical social service, including guidance of a state's public education system, an obligation noted at the formative meeting of 1895. This identification helped mark one distinction between the land-grant association and the NASU. Only the latter could appropriately plan the elaborate "State University Day" for the St. Louis World's Fair of 1904, and state university leadership in public education was the chosen theme of the 1939 NASU meeting. In contrast with the land-grant association, the NASU looked less to the federal government's than to the states' resources and needs, including those of local schools.

The land-grant group was, however, undeniably bigger, richer, and more effective than the NASU. Even most of the presidents of non-land-grant state universities, though they might splutter about raids on the national treasury, wanted the two groups to stay in touch. An effort to decouple the NASU convention from that of the ALGCU in 1936 was blamed for an embarrassingly low NASU attendance, and the two executive committees tried joint meetings in the late 1930s.[21]

In the crisis of inflation and surging enrollments after World War I, President Myron L. Burton of Michigan thought that the association should consider suicide. It was not "getting at the problems that we ought to get at as an association. Now, our discussions and our papers and all the rest of it are delightful . . . but . . . we are not touching the things that are of paramount importance to us in our administrations." His prescription, however, was surprisingly mild: self-surveys and common statistics. Sixteen years later, in the midst of the Great Depression, President Upham of Ohio's Miami University sardonically parodied the NASU as a congenial club with members given to "assembling in easy chairs, . . . cocking up our feet in sunlit windows, . . . pointing with pride or viewing with alarm, and then dispersing to our homes. We might be moved to write a letter to the London 'Times.'" One officer observed more positively, however, that, although ill equipped to undertake investigations and incapable of taking stands that bound its members, the NASU often attained "a good deal of conformity in action."[22]

Although the NASU never declared itself a professional association, it did occasionally play that role, as when it investigated cases of dismissed state university presidents. None of these ventures led to formal condemnation of a governing board, however. Characteristically, the NASU concluded that the American Association of University Professors or the relevant regional association would be better situated to pass censure or take disciplinary action on violations of academic standards. It was difficult to think of the university presidency as a discrete profession that should give guildlike protection to its members' prerogatives. Incumbents arrived in office by many different routes. Their tenures were dependent on political considerations often hard to counter with claims of academic freedom. Although they clearly relied on special skills and faced ethical requirements, most presidents did not think of themselves as administrators by calling.[23]

THE ELITISM OF THE AAU

Whereas membership in the AAACES or the NASU required certain connections to federal or state government, the AAU had no such

touchstone. Unending concern over the membership question enhanced its clubbishness but at the same time gave it some of the
functions of a standardizing agency. The executive committee sought
to clarify the question of the association's mission as it wrestled with
membership criteria:

> Is our body an organized association, intended to take in
> all who reach a certain grade of merit, and charged with
> the duty of establishing an objective grading and standing
> among universities? Or is it a club for mutual improvement
> and enjoyment, which can exclude members not likely to
> increase this improvement or enjoyment, without the ne-
> cessity of telling them the reasons for this exclusion in a
> form available for publication?[24]

The choice was in fact not so sharp, and the AAU continued to have
it both ways. It increasingly subjected candidates to examination of
the quantity and quality of their graduate work, though without ever
publishing the names of those rejected or setting explicit standards.

At their February 1901 meeting, word reached AAU members of
anger among some omitted institutions, and resentment came to a
head when faculty members at New York University (NYU) were
invited to attend a dinner held in connection with the AAU meeting
at Columbia University in December 1902. An elaborate denunciation
of the AAU, signed by twenty-three faculty members, refused the
invitation and questioned "the academic expediency and the moral
right" of a few universities to set themselves apart with an exclusive
title without clear membership standards. The letter called AAU methods suggestive "of the commercial combines of our day (against which
the Government is now proposing to move . . .)." Shortly after this
attack, NYU's Chancellor Henry M. MacCracken withdrew his university's application, declaring his institution "unwilling to ask membership in the association until it frankly announces worthy conditions
by the fulfillment of which any American University may become
entitled to membership." Perhaps the intensity of the NYU attack
owed something to its persisting competition with Columbia, a founding member of the AAU. Both institutions had moved resolutely into
Ph.D. programs in the 1880s. MacCracken objected to elitism, not
interinstitutional cooperation: he took the lead in 1905 in calling a
conference that led to formation of the National Collegiate Athletic
Association.[25]

The original AAU institutions remained split on the membership
question. Those favoring expansion spoke of injustice to the excluded,
hoped to uplift the weaker, and hinted that a rival organization might

be formed. Others saw small size as enlivening discussions and argued that the association would influence the country's educational system more effectively if membership increased only slowly. The door opened briefly in 1904 with the admission of the University of Virginia. It had granted thirty-five Ph.D. degrees since 1885, and the absence of any southern institution among the original members probably helped its case.[26]

Granting that the gatherings were not profoundly important, Wisconsin's Van Hise still urged James B. Angell of Michigan in 1905 to have his university represented at the upcoming AAU meeting. State universities should do all they could to develop advanced work and should help each other attain AAU membership. Negative reactions to the pretensions of the AAU were expressed at meetings of the NASU, which spent hours debating its own steps toward defining the "Standard American University." In turn, the AAU bestirred itself, appointing a committee on "aim and scope" and in 1908 adopting its recommendations. Thenceforth a university was eligible for AAU membership if it had both a creditable graduate school and, at a minimum, one professional school that required at least a year of collegiate work for admission, with the professional degree taking not under five years. With these criteria the AAU admitted seven more institutions in 1908 and 1909, all midwestern state universities. These changes allowed some defense of the AAU when at the NASU meeting of 1912 President James Baker of the University of Colorado led a renewed attack, stressing the special privileges granted abroad to students from AAU member institutions.[27]

In keeping with its avowed purpose of strengthening graduate programs in nonmember institutions, the AAU created something of a halfway house in 1922 by extending its "approved list" to include the category "Universities of Complex Organization, Usually with Graduate Schools and Certain Professional and Technological Schools." Asterisks unsubtly indicated which of these institutions belonged to the AAU. The eight unasterisked institutions on the list seemed identified as "approved" but inferior. Still, their position was preferable to that of Ph.D.-granting institutions not on the list at all.[28]

When justifying its separate existence, the AAU continued to rely on members' involvement in advanced teaching, but the idea grew that their particular distinction lay at least as much in the fostering of research, whether by faculty, advanced students, or nonteaching associates. The 1929 meeting highlighted the emerging research institutes, and in 1931 the association, making the first change ever in its constitution, added to its declared purpose—"considering matters of common interest relating to graduate study"—the words "and research." The designation *research university,* however, so convenient for a later generation, was still not in general academic use.[29]

Aside from accrediting, the AAU between World Wars I and II functioned chiefly by holding meetings. Presumably its gatherings provided mutual encouragement and shared understandings important to advanced education. In fact, although the *Journal of Proceedings and Addresses* continued to appear annually, the meetings ceased to attract the university presidents. The executive committee, in the somber year 1932, seemed in a mood to render the AAU even more quiescent. It successfully recommended withdrawal from the ACE, refused to cooperate with the AAC in setting guidelines for budget cutting, and recommended meeting only every other year (although the annual business meeting tabled the last proposal). The nadir came at the 1936 meeting, when only two presidents attended, one of them from the host institution. Deans complained openly, with one hoping that the presidents would take action on the issue under discussion "in whatever organization they deign to attend."[30]

Management of the association fell mostly to the graduate deans, and session topics increasingly treated instruction, testing, and graduate school administrative procedures. To give them their due, the deans diverted some of the narrower topics into a separate conference of their own, beginning in 1911, and tried repeatedly to revive the interest of the presidents, often by urging that the association extend its province beyond graduate education. Sessions in 1929 on medical schools and on research institutes reflected such efforts. Much of the trouble lay with the format of the sessions. They began with invited addresses and even when one member was assigned to begin discussion, commentary dwindled. The association rejected a proposal in 1918 to stop publishing discussions in the *Proceedings,* a step that Harvard's President Lowell argued would restore earlier vitality.[31]

During his presidency of the association in 1937, Ray Lyman Wilbur of Stanford launched an inquiry seeking to revive presidential interest. Yale's James Rowland Angell responded discouragingly that many associations exhaust the most lively topics during their first few years and let meetings become routine. Conant of Harvard desired neither to prepare an address for the AAU nor to listen to one from a colleague. He recalled that as a new president he had dutifully attended the AAU meeting of 1933, only to be disappointed. AAU meetings struck him as far less satisfactory than those of "a small informal group of heads of certain New England colleges and universities" (presumably the fourteen-member Association of Colleges in New England) whose off-the-record annual meetings allowed the presidents to "pitch into each other." With Wilbur's encouragement, the presidents began to meet in at least one session separate from the deans. In 1939, deans and presidents agreed that the AAU had been effectively serving its original purpose of promoting graduate work but that, since "the stronger endowed and state-supported universities" were united in the AAU "as in no other organization," it should widen its scope.[32]

The symposium at the 1939 meeting on the relation of the federal government to higher education, conducted by two presidents, a professor, and a U.S. Office of Education (USOE) official, revealed both a more promising format and one direction of widened involvement. The next year, dropping the policy of allowing guests at its sessions, the association sought "to insure that the subjects set for discussion would be considered with complete freedom and in full detail." The new war in Europe would rapidly focus the AAU's interests on refugee scholars, the effects of the draft on enrollment, and military research. Whether or not this particular association could, as some wanted, assume leadership of American higher education was harder to discern.[33]

THE AAC AND THE SUPPORT OF LIBERAL EDUCATION

Like earlier associations the AAC tried to set a group of institutions apart as a distinct category. At its founding meeting, college presidents urged the importance of distinguishing their institutions from others. John H. T. Main of Grinnell saw danger of the colleges' being overwhelmed by the universities. "The present-day college must show that it is doing a work that is not done and cannot be done by the university"; otherwise, "as sure as the railroad succeeded the stage coach will the college have to close its doors." In Main's view, colleges could embrace Cardinal Newman's vision of liberal education in a way universities could not match. A college implied "living together, aspiring together, achieving together as a community." Although granting that some eastern "university colleges" like Yale might meet the ideal, he asserted that as a rule only the separate college could be a community liberally preparing its students for citizenship. The college, unlike the university, was "not confused in its purpose by the affiliation of professional schools; or by the over-emphasis on vocational, wage-earning, ends."[34]

Lower schools also cast a shadow. Stephen B. L. Penrose of Whitman College urged disbanding college preparatory departments, which inevitably influenced "the life and methods of the college." The public must be shown that the college was "an institution distinct in its aims and methods." Whitman's recent abandonment of its academy had brought happy results. High schools no longer saw it as a rival, and its discipline problems had been eased.[35]

As to the "junior college," one AAC founder urged legislation to forbid the term as an abuse of the "historic and honored designation" of "college." But the matter was tabled, and junior colleges were allowed in under the constitution as "associate members." The few that joined, however, soon dropped out, and constitutional revision in 1926 omitted the provision for associate members.[36]

At first, membership required meeting a standard, set in the bylaws, of fourteen units for freshman admission and 120 credit hours for graduation, and in 1920 the executive committee was directed to investigate applicants for membership. In a loose sense, then, the AAC was an accrediting agency. As accrediting lost some of its appeal, however, such an identity began to be regularly denied by the executive committee, a denial specifically voted by the association in 1926. The association was rather, the committee told an inquirer, "an organization for mutual improvement." Still, the association remained alert to competition from fraudulent institutions. Encouraged by the head of the Federal Trade Commission, the AAC in 1929 agreed to refer cases of suspected fraud to the regional accrediting associations or to appoint an investigative committee of its own.[37]

Like the trade associations, the AAC tried to limit entry into its field even of "legitimate" newcomers. In 1921 it issued a study of the distribution of colleges which, not surprisingly, favored strengthening existing colleges over the founding of new ones. No college should be established without conclusive demonstration "that existing colleges cannot solve the problem." It was doubtless sensitivity to possible competition that led the AAC's executive committee to cast a cold eye on a plan for the New Deal's Federal Emergency Relief Administration to establish "emergency colleges."[38]

After World War I broadened associational activities, the AAC's 1918 meeting spelled out its mission in a mandate to the executive committee. The directive spoke boldly of power, money, control through information, and bureaucratic rationalization. In language far more specific than the borrowed phrases of its constitution, the association asserted its determination

> to formulate plans and construct machinery with a view to strengthening the position and extending the influence of the American College through articulation with government agencies, through legislation, through the securing of data regarding college teachers, through surveys, through co-operative publicity, through the consideration

of some possible system of co-operative use and purchase of supplies, [and] through securing information as to the best types of investments of college funds.[39]

This evocation of organizational modernism echoed ideas of the executive secretary. A pioneer in the study of higher education administration, Kelly, whose *Tendencies in College Administration* appeared in 1925, became part-time lecturer in that field at Columbia's Teachers College and NYU. In his view, links to professional study could help the AAC advance the status of college presidents. He defended an increase in dues by attributing it in part to the extensive "business of the Association in developing a science of college administration." Seeing no anomaly in identifying new graduate departments of college administration as a phase of the liberal education movement, he praised them in the executive committee's report for 1926. The display at the 1930 annual meeting of a "college president's library," dealing primarily with "the professional and technical problems of college administration and teaching," also suggested the AAC's role as a professional association for college presidents. But administrative skills did not become a major subject for AAC meetings. The many college presidents who had reached office through the ministry or teaching could hardly welcome the implication that there was now specific professional training available for their positions which they had not undergone.[40]

Although concerned to conduct a modern organization, the leaders of the AAC early identified it with a venerable purpose, the advancement of liberal education. Beyond its missions of defending threatened institutions of a certain type and strengthening a new profession, the AAC advocated an educational philosophy. As attention to undergraduate education swelled after World War I, Kelly and his associates imagined their organization in the vanguard of an academic movement. In 1928, soon after President Lowell was invited to give the major address at the annual meeting, Harvard became a new AAC member, along with five other New England institutions. The AAC gradually gained recognition as the nation's leading organizational advocate of liberal education.[41]

This broader function gave additional point to the AAC's announced policy of inclusiveness. Although a reference to "independent and denominational colleges" in its original constitution might have seemed to bar public institutions from membership, several had already slipped in before the restriction was formally revoked. Nor were complex universities ever effectively barred. Northwestern and Stanford were among the original members, and by 1924 the executive secretary was beckoning to deans of liberal arts colleges within universities. The executive committee tried to make clear that the undergraduate colleges of liberal arts became members, not the universities of which they were a part, but the matter remained ambiguous.[42]

It is questionable whether the AAC advanced its institutional health by its inclusive membership policy. One participating dean recalled its membership as "a very mixed bag." The AAC did indeed have a common denominator in "dedication to undergraduate education in the arts and sciences," but he found that "problems and solutions were rarely the same for all of us and it was often difficult to find a common language of discourse."[43]

THE ELUSIVE DISTINCTIVENESS OF A PEAK ASSOCIATION

When discussions of postwar student exchange were under way at the AAU in 1918, several speakers downplayed organizational apparatus, urging that the program be left up to individual institutions. Donald J. Cowling, present as a representative of the new American Council on Education, voiced superficial agreement, but his remarks showed his growing respect for organization. Though properly kept secondary, "mechanism is universal," he observed, declaring himself persuaded of the need for "some central agency which shall act as servant of all in order that the needed adjustments may be made." He also contrasted the categorical limitations of the AAU and the NASU with the comprehensiveness of the ACE. Beneath the mildness of the phrases appeared a potential role of coordination for the ACE which would constitute a sort of government.[44]

By intensifying the sense that the highest stakes were now being wagered in a national game, war had precipitated the formation of an apex association. Few were more alert to social reordering than Samuel Capen, who declared that the war had "ruthlessly exposed certain great national weaknesses"—physical unfitness, illiteracy, and nonassimilation of aliens. These, it was now clear, could not be overcome "by local remedies spasmodically and unevenly applied." Understandably, Capen has been identified as an exemplar of the corporate centralizers and classifiers. Both Capen and his successor, Charles Riborg Mann, urged business to specify its labor needs so that educators could adapt to them. Rather than referring to control, however, ACE spokesmen evoked the national tradition of voluntarism. The founders took for granted, the ACE's first chairman explained (perhaps because he had heard insinuations to the contrary), "that this unifying federal organization would assume no coercive powers, and would require no such powers to secure the desired results."

Moreover, its coordinating mission gave the ACE immunity from charges that too many associations were being created. It could help counteract overproliferation. A later chairman defended the ACE as a selecting and assigning body, able to start projects and then divert them to other agencies.[45]

Growing visibility, enhanced by a well-chosen name, gave the ACE potential as a molder of public opinion. In his first annual report, Capen declared that the ACE must provide authoritative interpretations to "the public upon whose comprehension and sympathy every educational institution depends." Its broad membership helped the ACE in this function, since it did not speak for only one group within higher education. It could reach the press, foundations, and businesses on behalf of general educational purposes, but it had to choose its positions carefully. Members had conflicting interests.[46]

When it set up special research commissions, the ACE generally presented itself as facilitator and publisher, keeping a certain distance from any particular finding or policy recommendation. An early spokesman had declared that the ACE could serve as a "bureau of investigation and information" even on controversial matters where it should not take a stand. As a catalyst in mutual improvement, the ACE could bring several institutions into a project, making them "members of a seminar where they educate each other by making experiments and comparing results." In the mid-1930s the ACE raised hopes that it would imitate the system of research fellowships administered by three other councils—the American Council of Learned Societies (ACLS), the National Research Council (NRC), and the Social Science Research Council (SSRC), but no such program developed.[47]

Its origins during World War I, a time of extreme federal impingement on higher education, forecast the ACE's mission of liaison between the government and academia. Its constitution pledged "patriotic service," but the ACE also protectively monitored federal actions bearing on education, whether grants or controls or inadvertent influences. The council would provide close attention to pending educational legislation, Capen promised, some of which was dangerous.[48]

Founded in a period when "service" had become a cliché of both business and the nonprofit sector, the ACE joined in ritual use of the term. Still, the council credibly presented itself as ready to help institutions with individual problems, offering, for instance, financial advice and investigation of troubled curricular programs. Such direct benefits, in contrast to serving only the general interests of a group of institutions, help remove the temptation for an institution to remain a "free-riding" nonmember.[49]

Trying to work in the international field during the 1920s, the ACE encountered typical problems of interorganizational confusion. It was not principally the AAC or the AAU that a member of the ACE executive committee had in mind when he complained in 1923 that "foreign friends naturally find it difficult to choose among our manifold agencies." A more troublesome competitor in the effort to manage academic foreign relations was the American University Union in Europe. Created during the war to provide counsel and comfort to alumni serving in Britain or France, it boasted a distinguished list of trustees and patrons. After the armistice, the union continued to function, helping Americans who desired to teach or study in Britain and France, many of whom were encountering foreign institutions for the first time.[50]

Even more threatening to the centralizers at the ACE was the New York-based Institute of International Education (IIE), established in 1919 and funded by the Carnegie Endowment for International Peace. It was a delicate matter to dispute the wisdom of Carnegie administrators, but leaders of the ACE felt that the IIE had been founded without adequate consultation. They warned in the pages of the *Educational Record* that the international field was overcrowded and chaotic.[51]

Frustrated by multiple agencies with overlapping functions (and overlapping appeals for funds), the advocates of coordination set to work and created a concordat in 1924. After a period of informal cooperation, the ACE absorbed the American University Union in 1924, though its endowment remained under independent trustees. At the same time, the Institute of International Education became a constituent member of the ACE, which was reciprocally given a role in nominating IIE trustees. This uniting of international academic agencies was supported by Rockefeller and Carnegie grants. The settlement raised morale at the ACE, which pledged to find new money for international programs, doubled its dues, and sought to increase membership. Already in charge of a program of scholarships for foreign study by American undergraduates, the ACE did much to popularize the "Junior Year Abroad."[52]

The ACE fell far short of its ambitions, however. In 1927, under Carnegie pressure, the ACE's foreign scholarship program and the work of the University Union were surrendered to the IIE. Although it remained a constituent member of the ACE and the ACE still nominated part of its trustees, the IIE was in fact set on an independent course. The ACE hierarchy tried to see the bright side. Having rid itself of "a large administrative job it is not equipped to handle," the ACE could now turn its energies to studies of higher education "at home." Meanwhile, the ACE's study of the teaching of modern languages, a five-year project with Carnegie Corporation funding, had ended. The resistance to "large administrative jobs" suggested that the ACE was refining its goals.[53]

Like other associations, the ACE sought rationally to connect its mission and its membership policies. In 1919, as previously noted, it claimed to include every national association of institutions of higher education. The decision that year to admit colleges and universities as well as associations, besides generating income, offered protection from charges that the ACE was too insulated from actual institutional problems. At the same time, however, inclusion of such members opened it to charges of duplication.

Membership for institutions as well as associations blurred the ACE's identity as a peak organization. Rather confusingly, institutional members of its member associations were also members of the ACE. If the AAU and the AAC represented Stanford in the council, why did Stanford need to belong? What in the ACE's mission made direct institutional membership appropriate? Could it convincingly offer superior service to institutions or help them significantly through its headquarters in the nation's capital? Perhaps the ACE needed its institutional members more than they needed it. Although rules that limited voting and office holding to representatives of constituent members were gradually changed, institutional members continued to complain of second-class status.[54]

Besides the peculiarities of having both associational and institutional members, the ACE had greater institutional breadth than any other association. Like the AAU, the ACE included research universities, and like the AAC, liberal arts colleges. It included land-grant colleges, state universities, and combinations of the two. In 1927 it opened its doors to regionally accredited teachers colleges and junior colleges. This range, although it suggested special missions for the ACE, caused problems. The president of a New England college that dropped its membership imagined the ACE as "a pure trade association which attempts to amalgamate in one group a large number of institutions which have little in common." College or university, public or private—in fact, every higher education variant except degree mills was supposedly helped by the ACE. But, to repeat, different types of institutions had conflicting interests. Although at its best the ACE could rise to this challenge by providing mediation, it could also find itself paralyzed.[55]

Did the ACE represent all of American education or only higher education? Either answer might be correct, depending on the time and the issue. The ACE attended most directly to lower schools in the 1930s. In 1935 it admitted state departments of education and city

school systems. Two years later, it admitted "twenty-five special institutions and private secondary schools of distinctive type," and in 1940
town school systems. Beginning in 1926, the ACE had included as
institutional members some business corporations and trade associations, including, for example, the Retail Research Association. Their
admission stretched thin the concept of education and further confused the ACE's identity.[56]

Inclusiveness, while it could cause problems, was the most credible
ground for specifying the missions of the ACE. During its first quarter
century, spokesmen had variously promised coordination, mutual
counsel, public relations, research, representation to the federal government, and direct service to members. Accompanying these alleged
benefits, however, was a persisting challenge springing from the ACE's
dual role as a federation of associations and an association of institutions. The council needed to demonstrate that it was neither self-
contradictory nor redundant.

IDEOLOGY, MISSION, PROGRAM

In their controlling social philosophies, all of the institutional associations embraced a mixture of governmental and private action. They
strongly affirmed voluntarism and local initiative. At the same time,
as evidenced by their very formation, they called for coordination of
the institutions created out of this welter of uncoerced effort. Recognizing that the states under the federal system were the locus of
power over public education, the associations still maintained that the
states should allow a large measure of institutional autonomy. As to
the federal government, its role ought to be particularly restrained
in educational matters. National coordination was better left to voluntary associations. Repeatedly, the groups into which colleges and
universities formed themselves declared their allegiance to the associational ideology.

Linked to post–Civil War farmers' organizations, the land-grant
college association shared some of their sense of threat to an economic
sector declining in importance for national wealth. The AAACES was
far more than a farmers' interest group, however. The leaders in its
councils were agricultural scientists, with their own agenda and need
for support. As engineering and other fields gained recognition within
the association, its dominant mission was clarified: making sure that
the federal government continued financial support for a favored
group of public institutions, without excessive federal control.

Although the NASU also began with a claim for federal grants, its
failure in that effort altered its mission. It would be in part a profes-

sional association for university presidents, almost coincidentally those who headed state universities. Through shared information the NASU would encourage the states to embrace an ambitious version of publicly supported higher education, and it would keep the national government aware of the importance of non-Morrill-grant universities. The group also sought to keep public universities comparable in quality to endowed universities. The sought-after mix of financial supporters—state and federal governments, foundations, and individual benefactors—had to be carefully pursued in order not to diminish the central responsibility of the state and the claim on state pride.

On the originally rather shaky basis of mutual recognition, the AAU stood for high standards, and it took the graduate school (and to a lesser extent professional schools) as the essential locus of university quality. Beyond the approval it gave its own members, the AAU gradually became a widely recognized and quite demanding approver of undergraduate programs. Failing as a satisfactory presidents' club, it gave graduate school deans an arena for mutual support, debate, and information sharing, and it set limits to the variation among Ph.D. programs.

With a more diverse membership than the older institutional associations, the AAC declared a multiple mission that included promoting administrative professionalism and supporting research projects. But its origin among embattled church-related colleges set a permanent pattern. It would advance the interests of undergraduate liberal arts programs, especially as these existed in small colleges. In addition, it would encourage religion in higher education.

Leaders of the ACE were especially prominent in stating the associational ideology. After all, their peak organization came closer than any other to being a quasi government and hence a protection from excessive federal control. But federal relations were far from dominant in the early ACE. It made much of being a council, a means for sharing views, experiences, and experimental results. When higher education needed a single voice, the ACE would presumably provide it. Difficulties came, however, when public and private sectors were advocating different policies and the ACE had little choice but to equivocate. Its claims, expanded after 1934, to represent American education of all levels further blurred its mission. The ACE's most promising claim to a clear purpose was that its very inclusiveness let it act as coordinator and mediator among various educational bodies.

The broad implications of associationalism allowed plenty of room for differing missions among leading American institutional associations. When missions gained the specificity of programs, the result was a plethora of studies, projects, reports, guidelines, handbooks, committees, commissions, and even spun-off new organizations. Some programs were stillborn; others had the complexity and importance that invites scholarly investigation well beyond this volume's concern with their associational matrix. A random list suggests how diverse these programs could be. The land-grant association created a summer graduate school of agriculture (1902–19), taught by representatives of various member institutions and shifting its location annually. The NASU, sometimes by telegraph, gathered comparative statistics on legislative appropriations to member universities. The AAU set April 15 as a shared deadline for candidates' acceptance of graduate fellowships. The AAC sponsored brief campus visits by artists and musicians. The ACE distributed intelligence tests.[57]

The very multiplication of projects raised problems of governance that led to centralization within the associations, to development of elites in executive and other committees, and eventually to a bureaucracy of permanent staff. Outside the associations' own governance mechanisms, power to determine which projects they would pursue shifted increasingly during the 1920s and 1930s to philanthropic foundations. The definitive associational project was the creation of an American higher education system independent of governmental decrees. By pursing accreditation programs, announcing standards, and forming new interassociational coordinating bodies, the institutional organizations responded to disquiets about educational disarray similar to those that had motivated their founders. Sometimes, however, the associations resisted such steps, uneasy about dangers to institutional variety and freedom. The associational ideology invited such tension.

Increasingly and ultimately to a point where it seemed their very reason for being, the associations focused their attention on the federal government's relations with higher education. This involved not only the making of laws, but their enforcement through executive agencies and their judicial interpretation. The nation's military program impinged significantly on colleges and universities, and during World Wars I and II it became the dominant concern for most of them. The onset of the Cold War set patterns that carried government involvement to a degree undreamed of by the grant-seeking founders of the AAACES in 1887. By the time of the Korean War, the associationalist philosophy still underlay the work of the higher education organizations, but the deepening influence of government on their members had raised new challenges. Banding together seemed more important than ever.

The NASU Gathers in the Nation's Capital, 1905

•

FOR the fourth time in its ten meetings the NASU gathered in Washington, D.C., in 1905. Partly because the land-grant association, with which NASU membership overlapped, was convening there on adjacent November dates, attendance was good—thirty-seven, up from thirty in Des Moines the year before. Public universities with mining programs were uniting to seek aid from Congress, and the NASU's evening session on November 13 was delayed to allow members to attend a meeting on lobbying strategy.

Unlike the larger land-grant association, the NASU kept all attending members together to hear all presentations, starting with the presidential address. The year's president, E. Benjamin Andrews, had led private universities (Denison and Brown) as well as public (Nebraska, where he was now chancellor). The title of his talk, "Current Criticisms of Universities," did not differentiate private and public, and the bogies he derided— "the infidel, the 'rake,' the 'dude,' the shaggy athlete, the spectacled pedant, the pale recluse"—were not associated only with state universities. Still, he contrasted students at state universities favorably with those in "effete regions" and in "cologne water colleges." Coeducation, more characteristic of state universities, was praised as a source of democracy. Perhaps recalling the effort of Brown's trustees to silence his free silver opinions, he singled out state universities as "more than any others bound to stand for academic liberty." He rejected the view of a University of Chicago professor that research and teaching were incompatible. The trouble was scholarly narrowness and resistance to conscious improvements in pedagogy, and here state universities might make a difference. Andrews's peroration, however, was a message of uplift for the entire "university system of America," not just state universities.

The ten topics for papers and discussion had grown from responses to an inquiry circulated by the longtime secretary-treasurer, Maine's George E. Fellows. Desire for national standards set the tone of papers on graduate work, admission programs, and undergraduate degrees. Concern for living conditions of students and faculty appeared in talks on dormitories, student loans, and professorial pensions. The concluding address, by Wisconsin's Charles R. Van Hise, though it did not use the term "The Wisconsin Idea," told how innovatively his university was making "its work and opportunities known."

Since all sessions were plenary, members could slip motions into interstices in the discussions without waiting for a business meeting. David R. Boyd of Oklahoma moved for harmonizing the schedules of the NASU and the land-grant association. Frank Strong of Kansas urged that no state university grant more credit for normal school work than was allowed by its home state university. George E. MacLean of Iowa, distressed by the foreign recognition given exclusively to members of the AAU, sought a committee to report on standards for universities and for degrees. A specially appointed committee proposed that the regional associations jointly set up a body to establish and interpret college admission standards. James H. Baker of Colorado asked for a committee to pursue the possibilities of a University of the United States. All these motions passed.

The only defeat came for William O. Thompson of Ohio State, whose motion "on the subject of athletics" was killed by tabling. Football deaths and injuries were very much in the news, and a tangle of conferences presaged creation of the National Collegiate Athletic Association. Perhaps the presidents spotted a thicket they hoped to avoid. The meeting included no committee reports (except auditing and nominating), but several motions involved the appointment of committees, foretelling a different pattern.

So courtly were the discussions that Alston Ellis of Ohio University objected. Those present were "throwing each other bouquets." Hoping to provoke a little controversy, he contradicted Andrews's case for giving the A.B. without Latin or Greek, even though Ellis felt his own institution would probably "follow the crowd." But cantankerousness was the exception. Two speakers in succession announced that they had no wish to prolong the discussion—before doing so. The gathered executives tolerated each other's loquacity and platitudes and slogans. They shared a joke about accepting "tainted money." Daniel B. Purinton of West Virginia, who saw a religious parallel to the NASU's "educational experience meeting," recounted his institution's sponsorship of a School Improvement League. The only dean present, William M. Thornton of Virginia, was assured that he had full rights to debate and vote. The chair resisted as against tradition—and perhaps as needlessly divisive—a request for a poll on the desirability of dormitories. At the end of the final session,

Andrews called on the few who had not spoken for "just a word of cheer." Their remarks were pedestrian but collegial.

This personal and professional bonding supported persistent assertions of the need for national unity. Most of those present had been alive during the Civil War. Some had fought in it. All could remember the regional antagonisms of the Populist era. Although a few eastern seaboard states lacked state universities, all regions were represented. Presidents of the Universities of Washington, Arizona, North Dakota, and Alabama had made the trip. MacLean of Iowa complained that eastern university leaders "do not travel amongst us to catch the light of the setting sun which now, in the new world, is also the rising sun." In an era of "co-operation and combination," with improved transportation and communication, increased interstate migration, and new foreign involvements, MacLean called for "the recognition and development of a national system of education." William L. Bryan of Indiana declared that dispersal of gifted researchers across the nation was good educational statesmanship. A eulogy for the NASU's late vice-president, William L. Prather of the University of Texas, personified the ideal of interregional concord, identifying him with the faith that state universities were centers of national unification. Steeped in national pride and optimism, the association adjourned after a day and a half, fittingly to be received at the White House, along with the land-grant association, by Theodore Roosevelt.

CHAPTER 3

From Voluntarism to Bureaucracy

As LEAGUES or confederacies, the institutional associations provided little top-downward authority for officers, and coercion of members was explicitly abjured in constitutions and statements of purpose. Members were, after all, institutions with their own income, clientage, and prestige. In arrangements for governance, however, these associations resembled those with persons as members. Forms were readily borrowed from the NEA, the American Social Science Association, or agricultural betterment organizations. Formal structures, of course, provide no sure guide to the location of power and influence.[1]

OLIGARCHY AND PARTICIPATION

In the formative period of an association, officers tended to withhold decisions until the gathered membership could consult at annual meetings. Floor debate, spontaneous motions, and amendments to committee proposals marked the period before World War I, as when the assembled members of the NASU watered down an executive committee plan to coordinate annual meetings with the land-grant association. Still, as membership grew and agendas lengthened, decisions were more and more likely to be left to executive committees, which in most associations showed distinct tendencies toward oligarchy.[2]

Formally, the annually elected president (sometimes renamed "chairman") headed the association; often, however, holding that office was an honor with little responsibility beyond maintaining the dignity of the association and inspiring colleagues with a featured address at the annual meeting. Some officers were simply taking their turn in performing the modest chores that keep a club together. When presidents held such attitudes, the way was open for someone else to initiate new measures and direct the organization. This might be the chairman of the executive committee, a position that, in the case of the land-grant association, gave leverage on government agencies in Washington and an avenue for communication with members. The incumbent chairman tended to be re-elected. Raymond A. Pearson held the office from 1919 to 1935, his effectiveness only enhanced by a move from the presidency of Iowa State to that of the University of Maryland, within hailing distance of Washington. In 1935 the executive committee was authorized to employ counsel and to decide whether to raise dues. The president of the association did not even serve on the executive committee until that year.[3]

The increasing power of an executive committee was shown in the fate of two unexpected initiatives at the 1924 meeting of the AAC. First, a former dean of Beloit College proposed that the AAC sponsor a new study of colleges and accompanied his address with a four-page mimeographed outline of potential benefits. The floor was promptly taken by Samuel Capen, whose recent accession to the presidency of the University of Buffalo had not lessened his interest in associations. He urged that nothing be done about this abruptly made proposal till the appearance of a current related study sponsored by the Commonwealth Fund. The matter was referred to the executive committee with power. Even more disconcerting for the officers, the president of Union College offered a resolution disapproving the pending bill for a federal Department of Education. Others spoke in opposition and the motion was tabled. In alarm, the executive committee obtained passage of a new bylaw to establish a filtering Committee on Resolutions at each annual meeting. The new committee proved able to keep meetings in line. In 1929, resolutions backed by the committee were unanimously adopted, whereas a request from the floor for a pronouncement on anti-evolution teaching laws, referred to the committee, quietly died there.[4]

Executive committees were not always powerful. Perhaps because of its persisting smallness, the AAU could settle many matters at its annual meetings (called "conferences"), initiating new projects and reviewing old ones. Although affairs could be referred to the executive committee, in some years it met only at the time of the annual conference. It did, however, guard one of its functions closely, the right to judge candidates for membership.[5]

Long-term experience of the associations supports Robert Michels's theory of elites with its claim that power tends to devolve from the group in whose name it is exerted into the hands of a few. The executive committee overlapped a small group of presidents or deans within each association who exerted disproportional influence. Regular attendance and engagement in debate, circulation through various offices and committee posts, and sheer accumulation of seniority all contributed to inclusion in an informal oligarchy.

Some of the oligarchs were forceful and ambitious persons who, precisely because their home institutions were otherwise undistinguished, sought institutional (and personal) recognition through participation in national bodies. Such appeared to be the case with Howard Edwards, president of Rhode Island State College, who was highly active in the AAACES, and John C. West, president of the University of North Dakota, in the NASU. Others among the influentials, such as Yale's Arthur Twining Hadley at the AAU, drew on the prestige of their home institutions, sometimes the revered alma maters of other presidents. An administrator who united high institutional status and unusual personal force, as did Cornell's Jacob Gould Schurman, could decisively shape meetings and projects of associations. Another avenue into the associational elite lay through a foundation or government agency involved with higher education. The head of the Carnegie Foundation for the Advancement of Teaching, the U.S. Commissioner of Education, and the chief of the division of higher education at the USBE all participated in annual meetings and were sometimes elected to membership under special arrangements. Capen followed this route to influence after 1914.[6]

In the NASU, where the executive committee normally convened only at annual meetings, it was understood that the secretary-treasurer held the association together. Although subject to annual election, this office was occupied for long stretches by the same university president: George E. Fellows of Maine, 1904–10, Frank L. McVey of Kentucky, 1915–22, and Alfred Horatio Upham of Miami University, 1927–35. In a revealing jest the president of the NASU in 1920 referred to himself as "easily bossed" by the secretary-treasurer, who actually controlled the organization. But to be the chief officer of the NASU was in any case no great burden. "One of the delightful features of our Association," a participant observed, "is the simplicity and informality of its organization. There is not a superfluous officer, rule or piece of machinery. This helps to give the Association much the spirit of a club, made up of congenial members."[7]

The only office of the AAU that did not change annually was the secretary-treasurership, generally held by the same individual, usually a graduate dean, for four to six years. This was also the only officer whose name was given in the *Proceedings*, the fiction being maintained that member institutions, not individuals, held office. Persistence of graduate deans in the secretary-treasurership contributed to their growing influence in the association.

Besides the officers and the executive committee, other committees were potential locations of personal or oligarchic power. Committees were often defended, however, in the name of wider participation. They meant, it was said, sharing the work of the organization and giving visibility to a larger number of members. Yet committees were also a way of resisting broad membership involvement. Undeniably, there were difficulties to investigation, discussion, and action at unwieldy meetings of all members. To form a committee curtailed meandering debate, while still allowing development of promising ideas and gentle deflation of unpromising ones. Forming committees was, of course, an institutional habit, but often a useful one, especially to those who feared the unpredictability of annual meetings.

When annual meetings called on each and every committee, as was long the custom, the strongest impression was often one of ineffectuality. Some had important business to report; others did not. An alert committee could protect the general membership from tedium by stifling a wordy, pointless draft report, as the ACE's Committee on Education for Citizenship did in 1922. The ALGCU's Committee on Negro Land-Grant Colleges rarely met or reported, being essentially a sop to excluded Morrill institutions. At the NASU meeting of 1920 the secretary-treasurer bluntly admitted that committees did very little work. "Most of us know what happens when we are appointed to a standing committee," one presidential wit averred. "We stand."[8]

Since it was easier to vote committees into existence than to terminate them, longevity did not necessarily mean power or effectiveness. After a "very weak, not to say useless, report" of the Committee on Instruction in Agriculture, Home Economics and Mechanic Arts, one critic in the land-grant association suspected that this standing committee felt compelled to make an annual study simply to "justify its existence." Committees could be abolished. In 1936, however, when the ACE executive committee terminated three (on Personnel Methods, Manual of Examinations, and the Study of Pharmacy), it simultaneously created four (on Editorial Policy, Measurement and Guidance, Motion Pictures in Education, and the Financial Advisory Service). Even when chairmen begged for committees' discharge, associations sometimes declined the request. Still, a committee could be scuttled by its chairman, as in the case of President Lowell, who had never much liked the idea behind the AAU's Committee on Economy of Time in Education, with its threat to four-year undergraduate programs. By not calling meetings and by reporting no progress, he managed to kill the committee in four years. Although he could not stop James H. Baker of the University of Colorado from pushing his efficiency ideas through other associations, Lowell deprived Baker of the prestige of AAU support. Even inert committees could in fact be instruments of power.[9]

A new source of control arose as associations matured and central offices with salaried staffs emerged. Most of this development came after World War II, but its beginnings can be found earlier in two of the associations.

THE CENTRAL OFFICE OF THE AAC

The AAC established an executive secretaryship in January 1918 and, as already noted, immediately elected Robert L. Kelly, chief mover in the founding of the association. The incumbent would hold the same post in the Council of Church Boards of Education, and it would pay his salary. His office was located with that of the CCBE in Chicago, which, given its convenient centrality to the college belt, was for a time designated as the site of all AAC annual meetings.

It is worth exploring why the association of liberal arts colleges was the first to have a central office. There is a revealing parallel in the case of the automobile parts standardization movement that began about 1910. The drive's leader, Howard E. Coffin, represented one of the smaller automobile manufacturers, and it was other small companies that first joined with him. They had more to gain by the predictability and economy of such coordination than did the bigger, more nearly self-sufficient companies. Working through the Society of Automobile Engineers, Coffin's approach was not coercion but data gathering, centralized administration, and publicity.[10]

More than timing linked automobile parts standardization and the development of the AAC. The AAC included smaller institutions, some with their existence in jeopardy. With the largest membership of any institutional association, it was also highly diverse. These characteristics suggested special needs for coordination and for sharing of information, standards, and public relations programs. All these called for the continuing involvement that an executive secretary, freed from obligations to a single institution, could give.

Although the matter has been little studied, it seems clear that the CCBE had already worked out patterns of central control which the AAC borrowed. The CCBE itself drew on methods used within the denominations to try to bring order to their various colleges, boarding schools, and Sunday schools. Efforts for interdenominational organization went back at least as far as the Society for Promotion of Collegiate and Theological Education at the West, founded in 1843, but they had lately become more sophisticated. It was the CCBE that arranged for the creation of the AAC, and the same burst of creative endeavor included a fund drive and a call for "permanent establishment of a central office for the college world." Kelly had already been executive secretary of the CCBE for half a year when he was elected to the AAC's parallel office. Holding the positions simultaneously, he "thought of the AAC for most practical purposes as if it were the college division of the CCBE."[11]

The central office of the AAC began as a bureaucratically modest affair and gave evidence of the dominance among its members of church-related liberal arts colleges. Kelly's communications to members were frequently verbose and determinedly inspirational. Even though the more overtly religious activities and fund drives tended to appear under auspices of the CCBE, the AAC itself often discussed religious education. Both groups affirmed Christian uplift. But both also called for the exercise of new managerial techniques, and Kelly created frames of action similar to those emerging in other national associations. Kelly's organizational and promotional skills were readily shifted from religion to war. For an exhilarating five months, from July to December 1918, he operated his office from Washington, D.C. There he had an extra expense account and some pretensions to being executive secretary of the ACE (though no such office formally existed).[12]

Sharing the euphoria of the Interchurch World Movement (IWM), a pan-Protestant missionary drive launched in the wake of World War I, Kelly called on the AAC for full participation. Excited by his appointment as head of the IWM's educational division, he devoted his 1920 AAC report to explaining the IWM's promise of information gathering, publicity, and fund raising for church colleges. The movement's failure indicated how much had changed for Protestant progressivism. In part because of resentment against its penetrating study of the Steel Strike of 1919, the IWM received nothing like the projected financial support and collapsed in the summer of 1920. Still, some of Kelly's educational analyses were published and his work with the IWM deepened his acquaintance with philanthropic foundations. Partly to be closer to them, the joint CCBE-AAC headquarters was moved from Chicago to New York in 1922.[13]

The IWM debacle was rarely mentioned in AAC circles, and the association grew less explicitly Protestant. Sharing the current economic optimism, the AAC in 1929 doubled its dues to $50 a year, replaced the CCBE as the source of Kelly's salary, and added a department of educational research, headed by an associate secretary. Disbursements for the executive secretary's office rose from $5,850 in 1928 to $14,180 in 1929, and in 1930 office facilities were expanded, with a library and an architectural bureau included. Under the impact of hard times, however, the new position was discontinued in 1934. The association considered moving out of New York to save money and did find a more modest office there in 1935.[14]

With his salary now paid by the AAC, Kelly could safely assent when its executive committee resisted an ill-timed burst of money raising from the CCBE. When amid much ballyhoo a group of college presidents and church education board secretaries launched a "concerted appeal" under the name of "the Liberal Arts College Movement," the AAC carefully distanced itself. Although willing to provide accurate data, it declared that its mission was not to promote such campaigns or advance their publicity. Since the CCBE now seemed to emphasize promotional work over education, the two organizations slowly disentangled their affairs.[15]

With only six staff members in 1931, at least some employed jointly with the CCBE, the AAC can scarcely be considered a complex organization. Still, Kelly had to deal with a membership that rose from two hundred to five hundred during his tenure. He arranged the annual meeting, edited the *Bulletin,* encouraged the work of commissions and committees, and sought aid for various projects. He liked to refer to "the Headquarters staff" and crisply reminded his counterpart at the ACE that most of the "actual business" of the AAC was conducted by the executive secretary and not the annually elected president.[16]

Although the direction of its projects was often determined by foundation decisions and the executive committee increasingly assumed power, the AAC kept a strong personal identification with Kelly. Recognizing how much of the organization lay in the thought and habits of one person, the executive committee directed Kelly as his retirement neared to prepare a book of procedure and an "audit of experience" for his successor. The two documents reveal the bureaucratic mentality at work, emphasizing authorization and precedent while noting and tolerating exceptions and the role of traditional usage. But to remember Kelly as primarily a bureaucrat would be a distortion. His presentation of the cause of liberal education, as well as his gregariousness and volubility, identifies this founder of a pioneer central office as predominantly a developer of public relations and propaganda. A practitioner of efficiency, his passion was for uplift.[17]

The AAC Board of Directors (the recently renamed Executive Committee) offered Kelly's post to Levering Tyson. This former alumni secretary at Columbia had been active in developing national associations of alumni secretaries and editors of alumni magazines. After heading a study on radio and adult education for the Carnegie Corporation, he had become director of the National Advisory Council on Radio in Education. Although his career well suited the requirements for executive director (as the post was now named) of the AAC, Tyson preferred to accept the presidency of Muhlenberg College. The board turned to the obvious backup candidate. Guy E. Snavely had attended every AAC meeting since 1920, serving as president in 1929–30. As executive director of the AAC, he showed no inclinations toward bureaucratic expansion. Central office administrative expenses, at $19,130 ($10,000 of it his salary) in 1937, the year he took office, had reached only $25,750 by 1950. Controlling for inflation, this was a decrease of nearly 20 percent. His staff of a bookkeeper and a secretary seemed to him adequate. Usually one or two active AAC commissions or projects shared the headquarters, but they required little supervision.[18]

Plain-faced and bespectacled, Snavely somewhat resembled Harry S. Truman. He made friends easily. He remembered names. Under his leadership the *AAC Bulletin* often read like the society column of a small-town newspaper, and he planned for both the *Bulletin* and the annual meeting to give inspiration as well as information. Activism in the organizational empire of the Methodist Church had developed skills that brought him success in academic life. His irrepressible sociability masked a persistence that verged on stubbornness. Like Kelly before him, he remained in office till he was seventy-two.

Born and educated in Maryland, Snavely had a border-state capacity for compromise. A precocious undergraduate at Johns Hopkins, he also earned a Ph.D. there in Romance languages. At Allegheny College he was registrar as well as professor, and when he was rejected for department head at NYU—because, he recalled, he had mispronounced a French word during a crucial interview—he shifted to full-time administration. Elected president of Birmingham-Southern College in 1921, soon after it had been created through the merger of two small Methodist institutions, he met pressing needs by raising money and attracting students. He also became a trustee of Birmingham's Miles College, an institution for African Americans, and helped get it grants from foundations.

Snavely seemed well aware of the AAC's pluralistic tradition. At his suggestion, nearly every commission included representatives of both Roman Catholic and traditionally Afro-American colleges. He heaped encomiums on the two women presidents of the AAC during his tenure, Meta Glass and Mildred McAfee Horton. Yet he had little insight into the social class barriers in higher education. Having worked his own way through Johns Hopkins, he insisted that ambitious and needy students could readily find ways and means to attend college. The GI Bill was acceptable to him, as were National Science

Foundation fellowships. But any "blanket subsidy" to college students, according to this lifelong Republican, could breed welfare-state thinking.[19]

THE ACE CENTRAL OFFICE UNDER CAPEN AND MANN

In his first two months as director of the ACE, Samuel Capen showed how many functions a central office with a full-time head could perform. He wanted to forestall any suggestion that the armistice had rendered the ACE superfluous. Besides creating the quarterly *Educational Record,* he attacked dues delinquencies, launched plans for a study of liberal arts colleges, and erected machinery for uniformity in American treatment of foreign degree holders. The nine-member executive committee, trusting his discretion, referred to him the matter of how to meet Vassar's complaint about inadequate attention from the ACE to women's education. Soon Capen was asking for enlargement of his staff. In his first annual report, he stressed his service in consultation, including "advising boards of trustees and institutional executives on matters relating to the budget, administrative appointments, and curriculum reorganization." A year later, he characterized his position as that of "a kind of general liaison officer for higher education."[20]

When he worked at the USBE, Capen had itched to impose a regimen that would protect officials from "clanging typewriters and the endless interrupting interviews." Once in charge at the ACE, he felt "rushed to death" and declared that the organization needed two directors, "one to travel and one to run the shop." In fact, this shop suited him far better than the USBE. His choice of Helen C. Hurley as secretary brought to the new organization a person of "high intelligence and discretion and gaiety and good will." Working in only two rooms, Capen, Hurley, and bookkeeper Grace R. Ontrich developed a cordial atmosphere for academic visitors and a task orientation that excluded clock watching. Sharing his ideas with the newly formed Association of Collegiate Registrars, Capen challenged its members to avoid narrow bureaucracy by embracing professional standards.[21]

Unhappy with the ACE's precarious finances and eager to practice the institutional administration about which he had been theorizing, Capen became a contender for various university presidencies. Although he declined the presidency of Purdue, he resigned his ACE post in 1922 to head the University of Buffalo. His inaugural there celebrated the associational ideology, approving the lack of central educational authority in the United States and praising a system of local experiments followed by selective imitation. His new office did not require cutting all his ties to the ACE. He served as its chairman in 1923, remained on its executive committee from 1923 to 1940, and was first chairman of its influential Problems and Plans Committee. Though yielding bureaucratic power, he remained in the oligarchy that dominated the organization. Perhaps he had recognized as director how much influence a knowledgeable, persistent university president could have in the association. When one such president, Henry Suzzallo of the University of Washington, turned down the vacated directorship, the search committee was "not in the least surprised."[22]

Charles Riborg Mann, Capen's successor at the ACE, who stayed four times as long, had become a member of the ACE executive committee as a representative of the Society for the Promotion of Engineering Education. Mann was not an engineer, however, but a physicist. A graduate of Columbia University, he earned a Ph.D. in 1895 at the University of Berlin, with a dissertation on magnetic induction published in both Germany and the United States. He returned to a post as Albert A. Michelson's assistant at the University of Chicago, where he steadily won promotions. In the 1906 edition of *American Men of Science,* Mann was among the 150 physicists starred to signify those "whose work is supposed to be the most important." He did not in fact become a productive researcher, but he published widely—translations of German work in optics, textbooks, laboratory manuals, and commentaries on education. About 1906, when articles by him began to appear in the *School Review: A Journal of Secondary Education,* he underwent a decided change in his sense of vocation. His role as secretary of a committee that helped liberalize the University of Chicago curriculum contributed to his new pedagogical interest. So did his confidence that education, though less developed, was as much a science as physics. Like other Progressive educators, Mann wanted subjects taught in ways that linked them to students' daily lives, and he cited, as a corrective to Herbert Spencer, John Dewey's insistence that science as method was anterior to science as subject matter.[23]

Still at the rank of associate professor, Mann in 1914 began a leave of absence to conduct a study of American engineering education, funded by the Carnegie Foundation. His report distilled much of the thinking developed within the SPEE since 1893, ideas with which Mann increasingly identified himself. During his investigation, he worked closely with a committee representing the SPEE, five other engineering societies, and the American Chemical Society. The report, published in 1918, sought to strengthen engineering's status as a profession and argued that beyond its function in physical construction, engineering should be a source of industrial and social leadership.[24]

This Carnegie venture into reform of education for a profession did not match its 1910 report on medical schools. A thoughtful critic of prevailing educational performance who made moderate recommendations, Mann lacked Abraham Flexner's muckraking intensity and intellectual incisiveness. Still, A *Study of Engineering Education* revealed a great deal about current practices, much of it uncomplimentary. Discovering that less than 40 percent of entering engineering students completed the course in the alotted time, Mann called for countermeasures, particularly greater use of objective tests in admission and grading. Here he drew on ideas of the Columbia University psychologist Edward L. Thorndike, who had participated in the study. Strongly tinctured by the ideals of scientific management, the report depicted engineers as peculiarly well suited to link not only pure and applied science, but also material and social organization. Accordingly, it called for required study in humanities and social sciences. Mann wanted foreign languages dropped from engineering curricula, but he praised MIT's required two-year English course for engineers, in which "the aim is to raise questions which it may take half a lifetime to answer, but the thoughtful consideration of which will give a saner outlook on life and on [the student's] profession." Adoption of his recommendations, Mann maintained, would build character in engineering students and render unnecessary any collegiate liberal training before admission to engineering school. Attracting little public attention, partly because it was released amid wartime excitement, Mann's report had negligible influence on engineering schools. It did, however, provide the themes that dominated his statements as director of the ACE.[25]

Mann never resumed his duties at the University of Chicago. In 1917 he became professor of education and director of educational research at MIT, where as head of a new faculty committee to improve methods of instruction he was himself virtually free of teaching obligations. Although he pursued his later career chiefly through the new professional and institutional associations, Mann like Capen also held government posts. During World War I he chaired the civilian advisory board for the War Department's Committee on Education and Special Training, where Capen judged him a mastermind who deserved a monument. In 1919 he left his MIT professorship to become full-time adviser on education and recreation to the Army's General Staff, emerging as a strong advocate of universal military training. He retained his War Department post part-time until mid-1925, combining it with his new duties at the ACE. On assuming the ACE directorship, Mann declared himself inspired by Capen's administrative control in the ACE office, as evidenced by its rationally ordered and comprehensive files. Yet for all his engineering and military involvements, for all his support of objective tests and admiration for Capen's managerialism, Mann impressed his co-workers not as hard driving or determinedly bureaucratic, but rather as paternal and philosophical.[26]

Mann used his new position to invite certain business and trade associations to become ACE members. In his eyes only false distinctions would have barred them. "Cooperation with the United States Chamber of Commerce and other business and industrial organizations is proving the most fruitful of all [the ACE's] activities," he wrote. "Education is not thereby becoming commercialized. Rather, the day's work is becoming a vital means of education." His belief that the clearest mission for the ACE lay in addressing "the major personnel problems of appraising abilities and defining objectives" led to a Cooperative Test Service, which throve, and a Personnel Service designed to list available college teachers, which proved unduly expensive and was discontinued in 1929.[27]

Under Mann, ACE files and staff expanded. An assistant directorship with responsibility for international relations, created in 1924, went to David Allan Robertson, a dean at the University of Chicago whose associational experience included having been secretary of the AAU and for a time its paid college inspector. When Robertson resigned in 1930 to become president of Goucher College, the ACE post was elevated to an associate directorship and given to John H. Mac-Cracken, former president of Lafayette College. Evidently the new salaried offices at the ACE were at least loosely comparable to those in colleges.[28]

The directorship of the ACE promised its incumbent increasing influence. The location of his office in Washington deepened his knowledge of the federal bureaucracy. Mann was able to assure an inquirer that the Federal Trade Commission was "a highly respectable and very valuable organization" that cooperated closely with the U.S. Chamber of Commerce in suppressing unfair business practices. As a full-time executive the director generally knew more about the association's activities than did its elected officers or appointed committee members. On at least one occasion a chairman virtually asked Mann to write his committee's report for him. Expenditures under Mann (excluding those from foundation grants for special programs) grew from $31,000 in 1923–24 to $65,000 in 1928–29, and his salary rose from an original $9,000 to $11,400 (at a time when the president of the University of Missouri earned $12,500 a year.)[29]

Although staff expansion suggested increasing approbation, the

ACE central office did not escape criticism. To Berkeley's President William Wallace Campbell and Harvard's Lowell, it was an undesirable relic of exaggerated wartime efforts at coordination, and Mann heard that President Lotus D. Coffman of the University of Minnesota found himself hard pressed when asked by his trustees to justify the dues paid to the ACE. A challenge to Mann's power came when the ACE created the Problems and Plans Committee in 1930, giving institutional presidents and deans an important new means to set the agenda of projects and assess the director's stewardship.[30]

Taking his turn at shaping the new role of Washington-based head for a national voluntary association, Mann liked to share his reflections on the emerging organizational arrangements. He praised localism and voluntarism in education while stressing the need for a central agency to coordinate scattered efforts. A friend and supporter of Herbert Hoover, Mann liked to trace the development after the war of "a novel technique of forcing self-discipline through voluntary cooperation," a process to which he attached the rubric "decentralized responsibility with centralized cooperation." Engineers were particularly effective at this, he claimed, adding that nowhere was it closer to attainment than in Hoover's Department of Commerce. In 1929 Mann became chairman of President Hoover's National Advisory Committee on Education (NACE), and its staff was housed conveniently near the ACE headquarters. For a time the NACE made Mann a conspicuous national educational leader, but it also exposed his weaknesses to members of its active inner group, the "Conference Committee," most of whom were also influential in the ACE.[31]

After the arrival of the New Deal, Mann opposed congressional educational aid bills on grounds that they did not insist on proof of need and local economizing measures. It was not so much his position on federal power that undercut Mann, however, as resistance to his continuation in office by foundation executives and members of the ACE's elite who increasingly found his administrative capacities inadequate. These educators, men like Capen, Coffman, and Charles H. Judd, professor at the University of Chicago, had developed a new base of influence through the Problems and Plans Committee. Supported by the Julius Rosenwald Fund from 1930 to 1935 and given constitutional status in 1933, the new group met as often as four times a year, sometimes with foundation representatives present. The committee's discussions, including the possibilities of reorganizing the council itself, rivaled in significance those of the executive committee, with which its membership overlapped.[32]

Foundation officers suggested in 1933 that the ACE extend its responsibilities to all levels of education, but an effort to change the constitution for that purpose initially failed. A group, alleged to be Mann's supporters, managed to retain constitutional language that emphasized higher education. The expansionists persisted, however, and, at a special meeting of the ACE in February 1934, they succeeded in amending the constitution to declare it the object of the organization "to advance American education in any or all of its phases." Meanwhile, in its meeting of October 1933, with the new U.S. commissioner of education present, the Problems and Plans Committee explored possibilities for federal aid to schools, aid potentially of the sort Mann had anathematized.

To influential members of the ACE, as to certain foundation executives, Mann seemed mired in a bygone era. He was, moreover, nearing sixty-five, increasingly viewed as retirement age. Contrary to usual practice, William F. Russell, dean of Teachers College, Columbia, stayed in the ACE chairmanship for two terms, 1933–35. Intimate with New York-based foundation officers, he proved himself effective in both justifying the ACE's constitutional shift and conciliating the losers. Mann, declaring that he favored the changes, was eased into the face-saving role of director emeritus and provided with salary, office space, and control of a few pet projects, such as one devoted to character training in the public schools. His philosophical musings continued to appear in the *Educational Record,* though no longer as annual reports of the organization's chief operating officer.[33]

The Zook Era at the ACE

Getting George F. Zook as its new director in 1934 was something of a coup for the ACE. U.S. commissioner of education since 1933, Zook's earlier career had been an instructive alternation of institutional and federal positions. A professor of history at Pennsylvania State, with a Ph.D. from Cornell, he was drawn to government work during World War I through the Committee on Public Information, for which he prepared a widely used series of slide lectures. After the war he taught again briefly at Penn State, but he returned to Washington from 1920 to 1925, holding Capen's former position as chief of the USBE's division of higher education. He left for the presidency of the University of Akron, at a time when urban universities constituted a new educational frontier. By 1933 the Depression had frustrated many of his plans there, and admirers like Capen and Henry Suzzallo, president of the Carnegie Foundation, worked to get him the commissionership, aided by the fact that he was a Democrat. He found that position constricting, however, and concluded that the higher-salaried headship of the ACE offered a wider field of action.[34]

An associate who identified Capen as "diplomat" and Mann as "philosopher" chose the label "organizer and administrator" for Zook. "A hard, meticulous worker and consummate bureaucrat," he inspired staff members by his stamina and somewhat intimidated them by his reserve. Occasional references to him as "the soft underbelly of American higher education" accurately reflected his girth, but not his personal forcefulness or his reputation as an empire builder. One university president recalled thirty years later the stubbornness of Zook, who "tackled" him to warn against a proposed merger of testing organizations. In a characteristic reaction to dead-end reports, Zook called for "implementation" and defended the term against charges of being mere jargon. It meant, Zook said, "getting something done about the results of studies and investigation." Zook's annual reports were lucid and cogent and, while including some personal views, did not ride hobbies as Mann's often had.[35]

"The Council at Work," a new section in the *Educational Record*, captured the Zook spirit. As the ACE busily sought new projects in keeping with its broadened declaration of aims, Zook found his strongest support in the Problems and Plans Committee. This elite body, through a series of ad hoc subcommittees, explored possibilities for large-scale research projects. Approval of its recommendations by the executive committee was virtually automatic, and the General Education Board and Carnegie Corporation repeatedly granted the requested funding. But functions changed during World War II. Declaring that operations and administrative oversight were the responsibility of the executive committee, the Problems and Plans Committee gradually detached itself from the design and supervision of projects. Although its pronouncements, such as one on universal military training, gained national circulation, the newly named "Problems and Policies Committee" lost much of its innovative force within the ACE.[36]

In 1935 the ACE halved its dues for institutional members (to $50) and admitted teachers colleges, state departments of education, and city school systems. Within a year, institutional membership rose 45 percent, and dues income for 1935–36 (at $21,590) was nearly double the budget projection.[37] Reduced dues and widened eligibility doubtless contributed to the rapid gains in membership, but there were other causes as well. New federal programs made representation in Washington seem more important to educators. The new activism of the ACE made it better known. Though kept somewhat separate, the American Youth Commission (with its grants of ultimately over $1,250,000 from the General Education Board) gave a sense of renewal to the entire council. With foundation grants, the council carried out programs under at least two federal agencies, the Works Progress

Administration (WPA) and the Bureau of Indian Affairs. Some projects developed their own staffs, loosely supervised by special ACE committees, and operated from the home university of the project director. Such was the case with the Cooperative Study in General Education, under Ralph W. Tyler at the University of Chicago. Zook reported with equanimity in 1940 that some of the ACE's projects had bigger bank accounts and wider reputations than the parent council.[38]

Each year's annual report conspicuously listed those newly admitted to the ACE. From 1935 to 1941, institutional members increased from 225 to 445 and constituent members increased from 26 to 43. Zook courted the constituent members in particular. Such associations, although in certain ways competitors, had founded the council in the first place. Some of them had drifted in and out of membership. The delegate from the land-grant association had inquired after a year of inactivity if he had any responsibilities at all. Mann had assured him that he need only attend the national meeting, though occasionally his association's views might be requested by mail. Such casualness disappeared under Zook, who in 1936 launched a series of regional conferences with delegates from constituent members, reporting on current ACE activities and seeking suggestions for fresh ventures. In 1943 there was renewed attention to the special role of constituent members, who gathered that year (because of the war) in replacement of the usual annual meeting. These associations, which had once been the only voting members of the council, now pressed for a more distinct place in its work, hoping to turn the council into a more satisfactory coordinator of member associations. As a result, separate meetings of the constituent members continued after the war.[39]

Determined to find new activities, the ACE rapidly added committees and commissions. Some ineffective groups were terminated, but with over thirty standing committees in 1945, the officers discussed streamlining. Zook resisted, arguing that lack of special financing should not doom a committee and that having numerous committees widened the influence of the ACE by involving more individuals in its work. Also, he had confidence in the integrative capacity of the central office staff.[40]

The ACE bureaucracy had reached such complexity by 1938 that the annually elected chairman could describe his office as "a mere minor gadget attached to the governing mechanism." Running down the list of appointed, salaried officers, he called them "not only . . . the power behind the Council throne, but . . . the throne itself." In fact, the change had been far less in staff size than in procedural rationalization. The well-ordered files left by Capen were dwarfed by those created during the Zook years. In 1939, as an innovation in central office organization, a publications division with a revolving fund and a separate budget was established. Reducing its reliance on commercial publishers, the ACE began itself to issue the books that resulted from its various projects, handling all promotion and distribution. The editorship of the *Educational Record* was held by Capen, Mann, and Zook in turn. It shifted in 1937 to the vice-president, who supervised all publications for a time. In 1945 a new staff position of "editor" was created, joined a year later by a higher-ranking "manager of publications." The central office budget rose from $51,000 in 1934–35 to $94,000 in 1940–41. By 1949–50 it had reached $126,000. Salaries regularly constituted about two-thirds of the total.[41]

In November 1935, the ACE made a status-seeking claim that it had eight "executive officers." This exaggerated the size and stability of the central office. Two of those on the list functioned outside Washington. Ben D. Wood, director of the Cooperative Test Service, was located at Columbia University, and Lloyd Morey, chief consultant of the Financial Advisory Service, at the University of Illinois. Although located in Washington, Homer P. Rainey, director of the American Youth Commission, operated with a separate board and a foundation-derived budget of limited duration. More accurately, the central office consisted of Zook, Mann as president emeritus, Clarence Stephen Marsh, and Donald J. Shank. Marsh, who had followed a mixed career line similar to Zook's, having been a dean at the University of Buffalo and head of education for the Civilian Conservation Corps, was appointed "director in the field of higher education" in 1935. He shortly took the title "associate director" and then, in 1936, "vice-president," in conformity with the elevation of Zook's title from "director" to "president." Shank's position, assistant to the president, was especially revealing of the central office trend toward hierarchical elaboration above the level of secretaries and clerks.[42]

As he left the ACE in 1950, Zook took pleasure in thinking of his staff as "large enough to be effective but small enough to be a family." Over the years, however, he had repeatedly urged its expansion. In 1939, he complained of the enlarged program's being accompanied by only two additions to the staff. Adequately to inform members about national legislation, he said, would require another full-time person. Similarly, Zook linked the plan of 1943 to give the Problems and Plans Committee a stronger policy role with a request for an additional staff member.[43]

In light of later growth, the Zook central office seems surprisingly small, especially given the increasing number of projects, publications, pronouncements, and conferences. Yet there was significant personnel increase. Evidence of this expansion appeared in the salary expenditures for "assistants," which rose from $13,000 in 1934–35 to $35,000 in 1938–39 to $51,000 in 1949–50 (the last full fiscal year under Zook). These figures included all employees except the president, vice-president, and president emeritus.[44]

Although expenses for "assistants" rose, the number of staff members listed as "executive officers" changed little under Zook. Reversing his original practice, he began to distinguish central office staff from heads of projects, perhaps to emphasize the smallness of his bureaucracy. Presumably the General Education Board was concerned to have a lean central apparatus for this body that it was supporting, and dues-conscious members may also have exerted restraining influence. Never himself receiving a raise from the ACE, Zook doubtless took some pride in economical performance of the growing tasks of central administration. Such expansion as occurred often came through temporary borrowings from member institutions. Associates arrived for projects, brought something fresh, did their work, and departed. In at least one case, however, such a borrowing led to a permanent staff addition. Francis J. Brown was originally "lent" by NYU, for a time even drawing sabbatical salary, but he never returned to the university, remaining at the ACE as a highly influential staff associate.[45]

Of titles used for offices below the rank of vice-president, "assistant to the president" was notably persistent. Helen C. Hurley, who as secretary had helped Capen start the central office, succeeded to that position in 1945. Earl J. McGrath's original title of "specialist in higher education" did not endure. The increasing use of "research associate," "administrative associate," and "staff associate" suggested flexibility in task designation, the ad hoc assigning of budding projects to whoever could best fit them in.

The rather unspecific titles of ACE officers as well as the limited size of the central office invite an interpretation that downplays rationalization and functional differentiation. For all his talk of "family," however, Zook was remembered primarily for his skill as a bureaucrat. His staff respected him and followed his example of brisk, goal-oriented work. As the ACE grew, probability mounted that leaders of member associations and institutions would think of it as a rather distant center of services, an entity looked to for efficiently representing a general academic interest and not as an arena for decision making by its members. Gradually, the council came to take its institutional character from a centralized office whose personnel identified themselves with the organization rather than its members.

As organizational life grew more complex, the idea of administration gained prominence. Business administration and educational administration became the names for textbooks, courses, schools, and careers. Some advocates argued that administration was properly the fourth branch of government. Limited size, limited programs, and emphasis on comradeliness long made elaboration of administrative apparatus seem inappropriate in some of the institutional associations. Two of them created central offices in the 1910s. Modest initial Washington offices were established by the land-grant association in 1939, the NASU in 1955, and the AAU in 1962.[46]

When an association created a permanent staff, it hoped that its program would be better managed. A central office promised a readily accessible institutional memory, regular information gathering, rapid consultation, and responsible adaptation of policy in unforeseen situations—all elements of the increasingly admired science of administration. Although presumably the willing servant of the association and its officers, the full-time head of a central office was well positioned to accrete power. Students of administration have long recognized that those applying a law often have power that is largely immune to control by supposedly superior governing bodies. To be involved with a matter daily, to interpret imprecisions or gaps in the rules, to move aggressively or grudgingly on an issue, to put a document on the top or the bottom of the pile—power inheres in all these actions. Such power was indicated by the gradual elevation in title and status of chiefs of central offices.[47]

INTERLUDE

The AAU Comes to the Fair, 1915

•

OF MORE than nine hundred conventions held in conjunction with the Panama-Pacific International Exposition, the AAU's was among the less conspicuous, its sessions held quietly across the bay at the University of California in Berkeley. Although Cal's President Benjamin Ide Wheeler had urged June as more agreeable, allowing side trips before the country became "dried up and dusty," and had been supported by a straw vote at the previous meeting, the executive committee had settled on August 27–28.

In his welcoming address, Wheeler joked about the climate, generalized about the Californian character, and gave a bit of AAU history which identified Berkeley as its place of origin. In fact, the weather cooperated, and Wheeler had no trouble showing off his adopted state. The delegates sat on the stage during an all-campus meeting in Berkeley's Greek Theater, where two of them made some genial remarks. The proceedings were interspersed with songs and cheers. One delegate admired the gathered students as "young gods and goddesses." Wheeler introduced selected members of his faculty at a reception for the visitors, one of whom found the presidential residence the best part of the affair, telling his wife it was "not so large as Princeton's but far more gorgeous, set on a height on one side of the campus staring the Golden Gate in the eye."[1]

At this 1915 meeting, the AAU was a "presidents' club" from which presidents were conspicuously absent. Of twenty-two member institutions, only four were represented by their presidents and four sent no representative at all. Still, the attendance percentage was up from the AAU's California meeting of 1906. The West Coast location explained some of the dearth of presidents, but conference content indicated that the group was drifting to the interests of a new tribe of graduate school deans and, to some extent, deans of professional schools. A few professors who were not administrators attended, however, and they proved far from reticent.

Earlier in the year faculty members had formed their own professional organization, the American Association of University Professors, an event recognized in Wheeler's welcoming address. He hoped the new AAUP would establish "a standard" in the academic profession and help purge faculty life of misstatements (such presumably as the attacks on university presidents in which James McKeen Cattell had taken the lead).

Remarks by the president of the new professors' association, John Dewey, dominated the first AAU session. Though not present, Dewey had prepared a paper on "Faculty Share in University Control," a title echoing that of Cattell's recent book. Far gentler in approach, Dewey justified faculty discontent over lack of participation in governance but put more blame on structure than on presidents, with whose dilemma-ridden position he sympathized. He recommended that each university establish a faculty-elected committee to confer on matters of legislation and policy with a parallel committee of trustees. Flattering the AAU as "the older and more experienced body," he hoped for cooperation between it and the AAUP.

Discussion of the paper spilled over into a second session. Professor Arthur O. Lovejoy of Johns Hopkins, a leader in founding the new association, reported that rejection of a plan like Dewey's had contributed to the recent academic freedom scandal at the University of Utah. A new committee there now had recommendatory power in areas previously controlled solely by the president. William Howard Taft, giving testimony as a former member of Yale's Corporation and a present professor in its law school, maintained that, despite its reputation for being "conservative and reactionary," Yale was quite progressive in its degree of faculty power. What the corporation did was "largely a matter of registration." Henry S. Pritchett of the Carnegie Foundation had not heard the paper, but that did not keep him from commenting that charges of presidential autocracy were exaggerated or from likening academic problems to those in the worldwide struggle to attain democracy and efficiency simultaneously. Missouri's President A. Ross Hill had found that faculty sometimes ducked the opportunity to participate in budget and promotion decisions, and Dean Frank W. Blackmar of the University of Kansas suggested that busy faculty members referred matters to administrators but then complained of undemocratic procedures. Professor James E. Creighton of Cornell passionately defended a plan under consideration there to add faculty to the board of trustees, a reform that he saw recognizing faculty status as "organic members of the university," not simply employees. Hill, a Cornell alumnus, was skeptical, partly because he felt that adding alumni trustees there had made little difference. Even more strongly against the Cornell plan, Lovejoy insisted on distinct provinces, with educational policy left to the faculty and conferences with the trustees arranged when educational and financial questions overlapped. Calling for "clear definitions of the tenure of office," with judicial processes before dismissal, he indicated that presidents could also benefit from such protection. The discussion tended toward defense of the status quo, but Creighton's and Lovejoy's remarks brought unaccustomed controversy to an AAU debate.

A blander response met the paper at the second session, California's Dean Armin O. Leuschner's exploration of graduate school organization. Detailing Berkeley's various arrangements since 1895, he praised its recent turn to centralization. A large Committee on Higher Degrees, which he labeled an "interlocking directorate," set policy but left much power in the hands of the graduate dean (himself). Even professional degrees were to come under the new committee, which had blocked the establishment of some proposed new doctorates. The new name "Graduate Division" distinguished the committee and dean from the "Schools." With these new powers, Leuschner and his committee had taken steps to serve both order and freedom, ending credit for unattended courses but removing barriers to programs that cut across professional school boundaries.

Leuschner's report, to a historian's eye a valuable record of how an organization linked strategy and structure, probably proved less engaging for delegates who had traveled to exotic California and hoped to see more of the world's fair. Still, with a little prodding from the chairman, they commented and testified at length. Objecting to the new doctorate of public health, Pritchett protested that there should be fewer distinctions in degrees, not more. Dean Herman V. Ames of the University of Pennsylvania, currently secretary of the association, pushed hard for separate budgets that could extricate graduate schools from "leading-strings to the College." Lovejoy recommended keeping graduate and undergraduate classes separate, a practice that at Johns Hopkins developed an esprit de corps that prepared graduate students "for the career of the professional scholar." His Hopkins colleague Jacob H. Hollander also saw a threat from undergraduates: their growing numbers could reduce resources needed for graduate work.

The AAU executive committee had held two brief meetings during the course of the conference, arranging business for the closing session. There, without naming the institution, the leadership declared that the single petitioner for AAU membership lacked "a sufficiently strong graduate department." As approved by the executive committee, a project to rationalize university publishers' catalogues through common style and format won the meeting's acceptance.[2]

Following recent practice, the graduate school deans had met separately before the formal sessions began. From their discussions had come a motion to reaffirm the AAU's position that the master's degree should require at least one year of bona fide graduate study and full equivalency when summer programs were used for graduate credit. This recommendation brought more debate than anything else at the business meeting. With votes cast as always by institution, those who wanted fewer strictures on summer work were bested by those who wanted more, President Hill winning adoption of his amendment to increase from four to five the recommended number of six-week summer sessions required for a master's. Had delegates crossed the continent for this exercise in unenforceable legislation? In response to deans who sought restriction of the master's to "academic work," excluding such fields as architecture and forestry, the business meeting established a new committee. The deans' request for a formal endorsement of the metric system, however, was rejected as beyond the objectives of the association. Iowa's offer to host the next year's meeting was declined so that East-West alternation could be maintained. Perhaps as consolation, the association's presidency went to Iowa.

The federal government seemed of little concern. An invitation from the State Department to participate in a pan-American scientific congress was accepted, and a delegate reported on the USBE's latest effort to classify colleges. Though Samuel Capen of the USBE, chief instigator of this project, was present, he made no contribution that was included in the formal minutes and wrote his wife that he felt very young among the "university Brahmins." The war in Europe played virtually no part in the debates. In California it seemed even further away, and academics were still divided about the two sides.[3]

There is evidence that only a saving remnant heard Stanford's Professor Charles D. Marx discuss outside remunerative work by faculty members. Relying on his own experience in engineering, foundation reports on medical education, and law review articles, he recommended such work for engineers, doubted its appropriateness for physicians, and took no stand about attorneys, where he found opinion evenly divided. His fellow engineer, Harvard's Arthur E. Kennelly, suggested the alternative of leaves of absence and branded any total bar to outside professional practice "a grave infraction of academic freedom." The conference thus ended as it had begun, with recognition of newly invigorated faculty professionalism.

The very last action before adjournment recalled extramural pleasures. A resolution thanked, among others, Mrs. Phoebe Apperson Hearst, benefactress of the University of California, who had followed her custom of entertaining distinguished ac-

ademic visitors at her ranch. A special train and a fleet of au-
tomobiles had brought the visitors to her Hacienda del Pozo de
Verona. For about four hours, Capen reported, they had reveled
"in the 'objects de vertu' the palms and flowers and glorious
views." Forty-six sat down for a luncheon "as magnificent as the
house and the guests." His hangover, he declared, was worth it.[4]

CHAPTER 4

Toward System

FOR ACADEMIA, the years 1895 to 1920 can aptly be designated "The Age of Standards." During those years, regional associations strengthened their work in accrediting secondary schools and began accrediting colleges. Professional associations began to declare what was acceptable in schools that trained physicians, engineers, and lawyers. A new private foundation used its pension program to gain leverage in regularizing the nation's institutions of higher education. The U.S. Bureau of Education attempted to rate the nation's colleges and, although blocked, went on to publish elaborate data on institutions. In revealingly diverse ways, the institutional associations became part of this drive for standards or, as leaders often phrased it, for a system of American education.[1]

"The Age of Standards" stretched old terms and created new ones. *Standard,* for instance, characterized consensual common units of measurement ("a credit hour"), or terms (calling graduate programs by the name *school* and not *college*), or devices (the regular issuance of catalogues). But *standard* readily took on stronger valuational connotations and could mean an acceptable minimum, a requirement for respectability. To be a "standard college," one association determined, an institution must require (among other things) 120 credit hours for the bachelor's degree. The term *system* could be used to indicate whatever educational forms happened to exist. Increasingly after 1895, however, *system* meant that (through the operation of some authoritative body) institutions met common standards, could identify each other by type, and connected with each other in rationalized ways. *Accreditation* meant authentication of an educational unit by an external authority as meeting certain standards and (at least by implication) thereby fitting into a system.[2]

In their earliest gatherings, associations presented themselves as free institutions loosely grouped to seek limited purposes. But the rhetoric of these new organizations increasingly stressed higher education as a rational system, at least an emerging one, into which the association and its members fit. There was, however, no desire for a centralized national pattern like the one developed in France. Academic leaders were trying to create a system with multiple, nongovernmental centers of authority. This pluralistic, systemic approach allowed for differences among categories of institutions, each good in its place.

There was something talismanic in the frequent use at association meetings of the word *system,* with its denial of untidiness, its implied negation of mere persistence in traditional or locally determined practice. The NASU sometimes defined its members as capstones of state systems, but the AAACES, the only association with members in every state, had its own special claims as a national body. The AAU sought to regularize distinctions between undergraduate and graduate study, while the late-emerging AAC began with an awareness that the maturing system threatened to omit or demean liberal arts colleges. All of the associations dwelt on gaining recognition for their members. The message, though often left implicit, was not hard to discern. We are this special, acknowledged sort of institution. We connect with the other sorts. Not only is our mission plain, but it has great value to society. The foundings of two other bodies, the Association of Urban Universities (1914) and the American Association of Junior Colleges (1920), witnessed similar justifications. Although associations sometimes portrayed their membership as the linchpin of the whole, the implications of having multiple associations remained clear. With this increasing mutual acceptance and quest for coherence, it was reasonable to join in an umbrella organization like the ACE.[3]

The Land-Grant Institutions' Search for Common Identity

Although first to found a national association of institutions of higher education, the land-grant colleges had difficulties in establishing common ground. Their very spread into every state invited different practices, depending on such factors as a state's wealth and the maturity of its public high school system. But the land-grant institutions had one immense advantage in shaping an identity. In a nation that based its existence on revered founding documents, it was easier to justify an undertaking with a national charter. Again and again a retelling of the saga of the first Morrill Act marked the conventions of the land-grant college association. The fact that Lincoln had signed the act and done so in crisis times endowed the Morrill-grant institutions with a mythic quality. Besides Lincoln, the association could venerate Justin S. Morrill as a founding father. Remaining in Congress until his death in 1898, Morrill was long a spokesman for the new institutions and a fount of democratic aphorisms. After his death, recollections of his wisdom lent a special aura to institutions that benefited from the laws he had promoted.[4]

Given difficulties in attracting students and the primitive state of agricultural science, there was danger that some early Morrill-supported institutions would be mistaken for high schools. In 1888 South Dakota State College required for entrance only one year of preparation beyond the eighth grade. Only after 1913 did Connecticut Agricultural College require high school graduation. In 1896 the association accepted a committee's recommendations for more nearly uniform entrance and graduation requirements, with a strong general education component, but one-fourth of the members voted against the plan and nothing was made mandatory.[5]

Another problem of identity for the Morrill colleges was connection to state universities. Was it better to be part of a larger, more complex institution? As membership in both the AAACES and the NASU by the University of Kentucky, the University of Illinois, and others demonstrated, land-grant college and state university were not mutually exclusive categories. At times this overlap was awkward for the system-minded, but neither association wanted to sacrifice its special role. For over sixty years the presidents tolerated increasing redundancy in the activities of the two groups. Members came to the defense of whichever arrangement they were associated with. For William Oxley Thompson of Ohio State, the unified institution prevented antagonisms and broadened student perspective, but Albert Boynton Storms of Iowa Agricultural College insisted that creating colleges of agriculture and mechanic arts independent of state universities was wiser pedagogically and truer to the spirit of the Morrill Act. The president of Mississippi Agricultural College could testify that, when the state university had received the Morrill funds (until 1878), agriculture had been scorned and neglected.[6]

The term *agricultural* in the association's title proved a handicap to the ambitions of its members. It was narrower than the curricular mandate of the Morrill Act, which also named "mechanic arts," as well as scientific, classical, and military studies. Because of its link with agriculture, the land-grant association was sometimes regarded as representing a vocationally separated branch of education, as would a grouping of normal schools. The link, although giving the association a base in Washington through the Department of Agriculture, also invited constraints. President Henry Suzzallo of the University of

Washington, who wanted his state to have "one great university and one great vocational college for agriculture," condemned as disloyal to agriculture the efforts of "slyly ambitious" educators at State College to enter the state university's terrain.[7]

To be an association of "colleges" also implied limitation. In 1925, as noted in chapter 2, what was then called the Association of Land-Grant Colleges added the phrase "and Universities" to its title. If support for research was what made a university, the association could point to work in the experiment stations, which one president claimed had inspired the adoption of research in older private universities. Although there were comforts in being precisely placed within a category within a system, institutions tended to expand their functions beyond categorical boundaries. The example of complex research universities with their prestige and wealth was a magnet hard to resist.[8]

External acknowledgment was necessary if the group's identity was to be firmly established, and for some time the AAACES was worried about inadequate recognition. In 1900, after much correspondence, the association managed to get a place on the NEA program "in order to present the mission and scope of the land-grant colleges in the American system of education." By 1907 it was possible for a member of the executive committee to declare, "The land-grant colleges stand before the public as a well-defined group of institutions."[9]

But a year later, Henry S. Pritchett, the influential head of the Carnegie Foundation, criticized the group for relying thoughtlessly on the term *land-grant* and avoiding shared standards. The association thereupon resumed its interest in categorical clarification, including reconsideration of entrance and graduation requirements. The president of Iowa Agricultural College insisted in 1909 that "decent self-respect" required four years of secondary preparation, thus meeting the "standards established by long experience for classical and liberal arts schools." Another president recommended as a route to coherence the identification of members as "national" institutions, united by "national legislation, by the fact that they are to a certain extent under national control, that they are beneficiaries of the national fund, and that they represent a truly national spirit."[10]

Those pressing for uniform standards and a shared national identity encountered objections from others who emphasized the value of special adaptation to the needs of each state. During a reconsideration of entrance requirements following Pritchett's castigation of the association, Winthrop Ellsworth Stone of Purdue maintained that land-grant colleges properly had many students who were not degree candidates. Besides, he insisted, "the whole problem of college entrance requirements is . . . something which can not be standardized for the whole country. . . . There are state problems, local problems." Such a view had earlier helped bring the tabling of a plan to invite annual inspection of land-grant institutions by the Bureau of Education.[11]

THE AMBITIONS OF STATE UNIVERSITIES

Like the land-grant association, the National Association of State Universities, with a highly diverse membership, felt pressure to clarify member institutions' place within a system. The younger association urged recognition of the state university as a fixed part of American education, dismissing the lack of this institution in a few eastern states as a regional oddity that probably would not persist. Unlike the AAACES, the NASU did not have representation from every state. In 1918, it had no members from four New England states (Connecticut, Massachusetts, New Hampshire, and Rhode Island) or from four middle states (New Jersey, Pennsylvania, Maryland, and Delaware). Drawing on arguments developed to gain support for tax-supported, graded, free schools, the NASU emphasized the state university's place on an educational ladder of public education. The vital matter of learning for a democratic people should not be left to the efforts of competing religious denominations or to "the caprice and uncertainty of private generosity." Nor should public education lack comprehensibility and order. Such order was promoted when state universities set standards for other institutions, notably through undergraduate and graduate admission requirements that impinged on high schools and independent liberal arts colleges. At NASU meetings Kentucky's James K. Patterson shared horror stories about a high school in Louisville authorized to give the B.A. and a one-year degree program at "National University" in Lebanon, Ohio.[12]

The Carnegie Foundation for the Advancement of Teaching (CFAT), aggressively concerned with the educational system, had done much to sharpen interest in standards among the major institutional associations. About the time of the CFAT's founding both the NASU and the AAU set up committees on standards. When the NASU's Committee on Standards of American Universities, established in 1905, proved slow in reporting, it was urged not to dally. The state university presidents were clearly worried that some other body might preempt important functions within the emerging national system. George E. MacLean of Iowa warned that agencies lacking the NASU's breadth, such as national professional associations, were beginning to set standards. There was particular concern over the vigorous interest in defining a standard university displayed by "the so-called Association of American Universities," as the president of the University of Illinois, not yet a member of the AAU, phrased it.[13]

When the committee reported in 1908, it foresaw development of "a typical institution of learning which we may not improperly call the Standard American University" and called for quantifiable criteria: completion of sixty "year-hours" for the bachelor's degree, two undergraduate years of preparation before admission to professional courses, and Ph.D. programs in at least five departments. But the application of the definition should not be mechanical. In recommending an institution, an examining body should weigh "the character of the curriculum, the efficiency of instruction, the scientific spirit, the standard for regular degrees, conservatism in granting honorary degrees, and the spirit of the institution." The committee suggested that the NASU might issue certificates to nonmembers adhering to its standards. Partly because the recent admission of more state universities to the AAU had moderated interassociational antagonisms, the NASU drew back from the more ambitious plans of its committee and directed it to cooperate with a parallel AAU group. Between 1911 and 1913, Kendric C. Babcock of the USBE conducted inspections at the NASU's request, but these were limited to state universities. Reporting the NASU's criteria, a journalist foreshadowed later resistance to standardization by derisively suggesting that American universities were already more alike than they ought to be.[14]

During this assertive period the NASU had taken the lead in national efforts to coordinate standardization programs. It called the original meeting (1906) of the National Conference Committee on Standards of Colleges and Secondary Schools, familiarly known as the Williamstown Conference after the site of its early meetings. Here, in conjunction with regional accrediting associations and the College Entrance Examination Board (and shortly also the CFAT and the U.S. Commissioner of Education), the representatives of the NASU promoted a full system of regional accrediting bodies, common admission requirements, and common terminology (most influentially, the definition of a *unit* as "a year's study in any subject in a secondary school, constituting approximately a quarter of a full year's work").[15]

A pioneer in amassing educational statistics, the NASU began about 1905 compiling data on all state universities and land-grant colleges. Later it redesigned its questionnaire in consultation with Pritchett of the CFAT. The assembled information allowed creation of "practicable standards" and development of statistical comparisons that proved useful in influencing state legislators. Complaints about overdetail in questionnaires began jocularly; as their number multiplied, however, beleaguered administrators called for simplification and centralization. There was some relief when the USBE, advised by a committee that included institutional associations, began in 1915 to publish elaborate data from colleges and universities.[16]

The NASU never lived up to the expectations held by its more ardent members for influence as a system-maker and standardizer. Even colleagues who voted for their programs expressed doubts, one warning that future crystallization would turn the elevation of standards into tyranny and arguing that, to serve its constituency properly, each institution needed strong individuality with "a large freedom as to the method of its organization and work." In the Age of Standards, some educators made the case for diversity, even if it was branded provincialism.[17]

Against Confusion: The AAU

In 1908 the AAU declared its intention to undertake "the standardization of American universities" by insisting that those admitted to membership not only have a strong graduate department, but also require at least one year's undergraduate work for admission to professional programs. At the same time the association expressed its interest in the standards of American colleges, reasoning that since it called for undergraduate work as prerequisite to graduate and professional study, it ought to identify genuine colleges. Moreover, since some foreign universities recognized bachelor's degrees only from members of the AAU, it behooved the association to inform the world that other institutions provided equivalent undergraduate education. The program of college recognition already under way by the Carnegie Foundation won AAU praise, and Pritchett was named a member of the association's committee on standardization.[18]

For a time the AAU hoped that the USBE would perform the desired college-accrediting function. In 1910 Kendric C. Babcock, newly added to the bureau as Specialist in Higher Education, attended the AAU meeting. Although what Samuel Capen called his "cold-blooded cocksureness" had turned some officials against him, the graduate deans praised his provisional classified list of colleges, findings its criteria well suited to help graduate-school admission decisions. But after this list of 344 institutions, hierarchized into four groups, reached the newspapers, representatives of institutions not placed in Group I raised vigorous objections. Chancellor James R. Day of Syracuse University charged unfair procedures and misleading results, hinting that Babcock, "an obscure man" (he had in fact taught at Minnesota and California and been president of the University of Arizona), was the tool of others. Day named Boston University, New

York University, and the University of North Carolina as similarly dissatisfied. Like Syracuse, these had been barred from the honors of AAU membership. Early in 1913, President Taft ordered publication of the list halted, and the AAU's efforts to have President Wilson reverse the decision failed.[19]

Insulated from democratic politics, the AAU decided to perform the task itself. Through a committee chaired by Babcock, who had left the USBE for the University of Illinois, the AAU in 1913 issued its own list of approved colleges. More precisely, it adopted the Carnegie Foundation list (including colleges barred from the Carnegie pension program only because of religious connections). The AAU's approved list, justified as giving evidence of readiness for graduate study and not expanded until 1917, was recognized as more conservative than those of the regional associations, the first of which, from the North Central Association, had also appeared in 1913. Indeed, such lists were becoming something of a fad, and the AAU was not immune. In 1907 it had drawn up a list of Latin American universities "of approximately equal rank to each other."[20]

Babcock described AAU accreditation as "purely a voluntary act of a voluntary Association," but in fact the process coerced institutions not on the list to strive toward the AAU's standards. Without the prestige of certain of its members, the association could hardly have succeeded in asserting such quasi-governmental power. Soon catalogues of some colleges on the list were prominently mentioning their authentication by this national authority. Although other bodies also served accrediting functions, the AAU's list was particularly visible. Its undertaking became far more elaborate after 1924, when its Committee on Classification began visiting institutions. The dropping of Fordham University from the list after inspection in 1935 precipitated a contretemps between the institution's defensive president and the educational *commissarius* recently appointed by the Jesuit General. Acceding to recommended changes, Fordham regained the list a year later. Financial support came from the inspection fees and from the Carnegie Corporation, with the understanding that the AAU was continuing the classification program begun by the CFAT. Between 1923 and 1924, AAU expenditures had more than tripled, with two-thirds of the total resulting from the new inspection visits. In fact, the program required the AAU for the first time to have a salaried employee.[21]

The accrediting function caused the AAU many difficulties, nicely summarized by William K. Selden:

> It underwent the agony of establishing standards for educational institutions, of sending teams to visit colleges, of deciding what types of institutions should be included, of

re-evaluating colleges, of warning and removing colleges
from its list, of obtaining sufficient funds to conduct these
operations, of responding to reams of correspondence, and
of defending its decisions against innumerable criticisms.

In the late 1930s the AAU was caught by a wave of resentment against
accrediting bodies. Within its membership, some were complaining
of the high-handedness of professional associations that sought to
accredit universities, while others were defending the AAU against
insinuations that its accrediting program was arbitrary and elitist.
Despite evidence of weakening resolve among the membership, the
AAU continued its program.[22]

Degrees, the academic currency in most general circulation, could
hardly escape the attention of standardizers. The thought of confusion
over American degrees in Europe, where education was so much more
systematic, as well as the fear of charlatans and degrees mills, doubtless
encouraged this part of the AAU's activities. To base institutional
identification on degrees granted promised an orderly comparability
and some semblance of system.

From its beginning the AAU had concentrated on the Ph.D. degree,
the standards for which had virtually determined the original choice
of members. Concern about the proliferation of ill-defined professional degrees, especially those that represented no more than four
years of undergraduate study, led the AAU in 1915 to set up a "Committee on Academic and Professional Higher Degrees," chaired by
Dean Armin Leuschner of the University of California. Leuschner
had shown interest at the time of the AAU's founding in extending
the associational impulse to professional education by creating "separate sections in all the learned professions, including the technical
sciences." He won acceptance for neither this suggestion nor his companion proposal that the association seek "federal or uniform state
legislation for the upholding of the standard of the various professions." After meeting with representatives of professional associations
and gathering data on current practices, the committee reported that,
whereas "the academic Masters' and Doctors' degree have assumed a
somewhat definite significance through the co-operation of this Association," there was an alarming proliferation of professional degrees.
Among the members of the AAU alone, over 130 differently named
degrees had been granted between 1914 and 1916. The committee,
whose reports became a staple of the annual meeting, continued to
confer with representatives of the professional associations, urging
fewer degree designations and higher standards.[23]

In 1920, the committee was authorized to formulate clearer standards for the Ph.D., to set it off even more sharply "as a research

degree, as distinguished from professional Doctors' degrees." In this matter, efforts were largely successful. The Masters' degree, however, seemed hopelessly diverse. The bedrock of institutional categorization remained the Bachelor of Arts as the degree expected of colleges, and its definition had been firmly established by 1920 through efforts of the regional accrediting associations and the CFAT, with the AAU playing a role through its "Approved List." As to systematizing professional education, this the AAU sought through collaboration with other associations. It accepted the rationale of medical and other professional doctorates, but carefully reserved the Ph.D. as a symbol of achievement in research, a function increasingly identified as the sine qua non of a university.[24]

Standardization is too strong a word for some of the means by which members of the AAU came more closely to resemble each other. Often discussion raised a question of practice, and the administrators present freely exchanged information. Member universities could at least learn if they were unusual in their handling of such matters as department headship, salary differentials within ranks, or the teaching load of assistant professors. As usage spread through imitation, anomalies dwindled. Similar exchanges went on in other institutional associations, but the relative smallness and elitist ethos of the AAU bound its members with unusual closeness. Sometimes, of course, an institution took pride in being different. After describing the Harvard custom of mingling undergraduates and graduates in the same courses, Eliot declared this atypical arrangement to be delightful evidence of nonstandardization. The trend, however, was in the other direction.[25]

The drive for statistical conformity found an early champion in Frederick P. Keppel, then secretary to the president of Columbia. In his 1902 paper for the AAU, "Uniformity of University Statistics of Enrolment and Expenditure," Keppel advocated the department as the primary unit in both expenditure and enrollment statistics, providing the basis for calculations of cost per student. In pressing for fuller and more uniform tables of income and outgo, he admonished the gathered administrators: "We cannot expect an institution to announce that it is spending one hundred thousand dollars a year for, say, conchology, simply because it is conchology or nothing with some particular benefactor; but there is no reason why an opportunity should not be given to read the fact between the lines." Keppel's suggestions led some institutions to modify procedures, and Eliot praised his work as an aid in preventing padding of enrollment figures in catalogues.[26]

The hope for standardized nomenclature, with its expected benefits to interinstitutional communication and comparison, brought the creation of a special AAU committee in 1908. Citing wide divergences, the committee argued that "the institutions which are supposed to systematize and advance knowledge, which ought to illustrate the principles of education in their organizations as far as practicable, have permitted without protest a hopeless confusion of nomenclature which would not be tolerated in any of the sciences." With this rationale, the committee proposed standard meanings for the terms *department, course, college,* and *school.* In a spirit of interassociational comity, aided by overlapping membership, the NASU shortly agreed to accept these definitions. In making the case for all this regularization, the convenience of student transfers was rarely emphasized. Perhaps easing the departure of students was not a particularly good selling point to institutional leaders.[27]

In the wake of World War I, during which institutional variations had made national "manpower" programs harder to administer, representatives of the University of Wisconsin urged the AAU to consider the adoption of uniform opening and closing dates in higher education and a common decision as between semesters and trimesters. But wartime urgency had ebbed. The resulting committee never reported and was discharged after two years.[28]

The Ambivalence of the AAC

Early meetings of the AAC revealed members' anxiety over the processes of standardization already affecting them. Particularly worrisome was the labeling by the U.S. commissioner of education of some colleges as "sectarian." Colleges had, in fact, been barred from the Carnegie pension program because of this identification. The first AAC meeting urged the commissioner to change classification by control from "state-controlled, sectarian, and non-sectarian" to "tax-supported and non-tax-supported," with the latter divided into "church controlled, church affiliated, and independent."[29]

Although unsuccessful in this effort, the new association remained in close touch with the bureau, which had sent its specialist in higher education to the opening meeting. Capen gave words of comfort to presidents of institutions beleaguered by standardizers. It would be unwise to define a "standard college" just now, he declared. "After all most colleges are local institutions." Why should there be only one type? Williams and Reed need not be the same. A college had no obligation to commit suicide because some agency had set standards impossible for its local or regional constituency. Still, Capen justified certain classifications and urged that private colleges open their records as public institutions were obliged to do. In a cooperative spirit the AAC joined Capen's recently founded "Committee on Higher Educational Statistics" at the USBE, as did several other associations. The committee's work indicated limits to toleration of local variation. Although there was no classification, the first report followed its statistics on colleges with the declaration, "To the eye of the initiated the entries in this table tell their own story." The report included thirteen "Suggested Requirements for a Successful College of Arts and Sciences."[30]

Only by admitting an institution to membership did the AAC in any sense serve as an accrediting body. It lacked the authoritative self-confidence that allowed the AAU to publish rankings of nonmembers. Reluctant to sit in judgment, the AAC rejected an early proposal that it evaluate credits offered by transfer students. As the only national association of colleges, however, the AAC joined in the definitional movement already under way. One of its earliest committees drew up criteria for a "minimum college" and for an "efficient college," criteria designed, it was said, to be helpful in institutional self-analysis. At first, AAC membership was to be limited to those meeting the minimum, but waivers were soon allowed. Legislatures, noting the minimum criteria, were expected to "retard the birth rate of institutions with vastly inferior standards." As with trade associations, limiting competition was an AAC goal, a goal aided by the sometimes irritating standardization movement.[31]

Some AAC members were familiar with external appraisal through the work of church boards of education, whose programs of inspection had begun, in the case of the Methodists, as early as 1893. The council of these boards, the CCBE, it will be remembered, was the matrix in which the AAC originated. Like the AAC, the CCBE was interested in both uplift and efficiency. Its "Forward Movement" campaign of 1916 was designed not only to promote students' religious life but also "to assist in defining the function of the independent (non-tax-supported) college in America, and to assist in securing more definite recognition of it as a natural and permanent part of our developing system of education."[32]

Although they gave prominence to spiritual aspects of college education, the AAC leaders still urged the case for standard definitions and shared statistics. The AAC participated in an interassociational Committee on Standard Reports, which emerged in 1930 from work of the CCBE. Kelly begged the presidents to adopt similar methods in their annual reports "so that significant totals and averages may be arrived at and conclusions reached of actual scientific value." Among the ultimate results might well be "a science of college administration."

A Quaker and a bureaucrat, Kelly wanted guidance from both the inner light and the lamp of classified knowledge. Like other administrative progressives, he linked hope for human betterment with a dedication to ordered institutions.[33]

THE ACE AND THE RESHAPING OF STANDARDIZATION, 1920–1940

California institutions did not belong to a regional association and the New England Association did no accrediting. The regionals were nevertheless considered by the 1920s to be the heart of accreditation in the American system. There was little complaint about their work from the institutional associations, whose own prerogatives in accreditation had been clarified. The AAU backed its prestigious "Accepted List" with elaborate criteria and inspections. Although the AAC denied that it accredited, its membership list gave institutional validation, and in 1925 the AAC turned the tables on the AAU when a committee presented ratings of graduate departments in universities as judged by college professors. The NASU and the land-grant association continued to urge standard entrance and graduation requirements, but without requiring these for membership. As for the ACE, it quickly rose to prominence in the accreditation movement, emphasizing its special capacities for national coordination.[34]

Even before he had formally assumed the directorship of the ACE in 1919, Capen forecast that it would standardize the standardizing agencies, of which a recent study had discovered no fewer than seventy-three. The council's initial venture into the field was considerably more modest, however. On the ground that it had an obligation to inform foreigners of the status of various colleges, the ACE entered what Capen called "perhaps the most dangerous of all sports" and published annually the lists of approved colleges issued by the AAU, the regionals, and the University of California. Although maintaining that it was not an accrediting agency, the ACE stood ready to answer inquiries. The response from a central national organization that a certain institution appeared on none of the approved lists was doubtless effective.[35]

But the ACE was not a passive compiler of lists. It quickly moved into a dominant position within the National Conference Committee on Standards (the Williamstown Conference), which in 1923 merged into the ACE's Committee on Standards. Beginning in 1922 the ACE issued guidelines for accrediting bodies, largely substantive criteria (such as a maximum teaching schedule of sixteen hours), which were soon adopted by various regionals, church boards of education, and state education departments. Four years later it led the exposure when some diploma mills sought to accredit each other through a fly-by-night "National Association of Colleges and Universities." Denouncing "Degrees for Dollars," the ACE's assistant director made sport of Helmut P. Holler and his "Oriental University," located in his home.[36]

In an uncharacteristic direct institutional appraisal, the ACE in 1934 published lists compiled by its Committee on Graduate Instruction which identified graduate departments with adequate or outstanding programs. The lists, based on the judgment of specialists in each field, gained extra notoriety when they were covered by the *New York Times*. The committee's work was not continued. The ACE gained little influence among professional associations that accredited programs in their fields, although some of them, such as the Council on Medical Education of the American Medical Association, became constituent members of the ACE.[37]

The idea of standards remained integrally tied to that of an educational system. The standards drawn up for junior colleges by the regionals and the ACE assumed that these institutions were part of a system through which students could move without encountering barriers peculiar to one institution. With the course credit as the medium of exchange, the United States had in fact developed an unusual if not unique system of educational "free trade."[38]

Besides promoting minimal standards, the ACE pressed for the adoption of common usage in terminology and statistics. Terms such as *semester* and *credit* were regularized to the point that noncomplying institutions had to adapt or issue defensive statements. The benefits of uniform statistics seemed plain to the system-minded, and studies sponsored by the Carnegie Foundation (1910) and the General Education Board (1922) sought to advance that cause. Without comparable figures, it was hard to test the accommodation to standards, to reward achievers and stimulate laggards, or to analyze "the system as a whole." Such views inspired the labors of the National Committee on Standard Reports, formed in 1930 by a merger of similar committees working under the auspices of the AAC-CCBE and the USOE and including representatives from associations of business officers, registrars, and teachers colleges. Its crowning work, *Financial Reports for Colleges and Universities* (1935), proposed uniformities that offered some relief to academic administrators beset by variously designed reporting requirements from external authorities.[39]

Although college and university presidents had helped launch the standardization movement, they came to have second thoughts as it exerted troublesome outside pressure on the institutions they headed. "University presidents," Harold Orlans has wryly observed, "have responded to accrediting agencies much as a dog responds to fleas—

and with as little ultimate success." The institutional associations were apt forums for expressing the presidents' rising irritation. What had originally been praised as a way to elevate standards and give systemic coherence began to evoke warnings of "a stifling of initiative and experimentation and an unfortunate crystallization of the whole educational structure." Sometimes presidential complaints seemed directed at the regionals, as when President Harry Pratt Judson of the University of Chicago protested that even the emphasis on four years of college represented inflexibility. But it was specialized, professional accrediting programs that roused militant opposition. Besieged presidents could imagine that virtually every occupation was determined to become a profession and that the chosen means was to be advanced education authenticated by accreditation.[40]

The lustrous model of the standardizer of professional schools, exemplified by Abraham Flexner with his 1910 study of medical schools, was beginning to tarnish. In the NASU, discussion of "the attempt of outside agencies to 'standardize' us" followed a 1923 address by Minnesota's Lotus D. Coffman and led the next year to passage of a resolution against the growing tendency "seriously to limit both local initiative and that freedom of experimentation which is necessary for educational advance." The president of the University of Washington returned home to fulminate against "groups of specialists having no acquaintance with general university administration who, by the threat of classification, are taking administration out of our hands and forcing us to new expenses." That the chief irritant was not the regionals became all the clearer when the NASU-authorized study of standardizing agencies appeared in 1926, focusing its attack on accreditation of professional schools. Besides undemocratically limiting the number who could enter a profession, the report alleged, the new procedures gave disproportionate leverage within a university to its professional schools.[41]

His embrace of this NASU report brought Samuel Capen to the fore as a critic of accreditation, a paradoxical role for the leading standardizer of ten years before. His apostasy owed much to his new perspective as a university president beset by accrediting agencies, but also something to his experience on committees with "persons of bureaucratic temper . . . who like to apply mechanical rules, to whom a rule becomes sacred as soon as it is adopted, persons who lack vicariousness and constructive imagination." The accreditors, he protested, used not educational standards but those of engineering, organization, or politics. Increased autonomy for institutions was the proper route to genuine advance of learning.[42]

The regionals with their accreditation of undergraduate programs did not escape the mood of counterreformation. As usual, it was the North Central Association that took the lead, beginning in 1928 with an admission that present standards failed to measure the real worth of colleges. A thorough reconsideration led to the adoption six years later of nonnumerical standards, designed to meet an institution's own sense of its mission. Shortly before it was published, the director of this study, George F. Zook, had become director of the ACE. In that office, he proselytized for the new cause: qualitative rather than quantitative standards and flexibility in accrediting procedures. Under Zook the ACE discontinued its statement of accrediting standards, many of which were quantitative. Although he encouraged various associations as they moved against mechanical or excessive standardization, he praised the voluntaristic origins of accrediting agencies and rejected suggestions for their abolition. Stimulation of institutional self-development was one of his ideals for accreditation reform; restricting practitioners' interference in professional education was another.[43]

Functioning a good deal like the regionals in accreditation of colleges, the AAU felt similar winds of change. Perhaps the AAU should itself give up accrediting to encourage similar restraint by professional associations, since those outsiders functioned "from the standpoint of aggrandizing a particular field of work and without understanding the problems of particular institutions." Such was the advice from one University of California dean to another, who was preparing a talk on accreditation for an AAU meeting. The resulting paper used medical education to exemplify problems of imposed curricular rigidity, although its author thought that newer professions with their social insecurities posed a greater threat to university freedom. The aggressiveness of pharmacists seemed particularly troublesome at the moment, and their stiff inspection fees added offense. In 1938 the AAU announced that it did not apply standards mechanically and that a course of study not measurable in quantitative units might be acceptable, but the association retained numerical criteria and continued to insist on inspection.[44]

Changed attitudes toward accreditation marked a report published in 1940 by the USOE at the suggestion of the Association of Chief State School Officers. Emphasizing state responsibilities, the report declared that voluntary associations should limit themselves to improving colleges, which could be done better if not accompanied by accrediting functions. The report skirted the issue of national comparability that had motivated much of the work of the institutional associations. Deans at the AAU received a preliminary version skeptically, but evidence was mounting that the AAU's glory days as an accrediting agency were over.[45]

As early as 1924 the NASU formally warned that the standardization movement suffered from overproliferation of accreditors and high-handedness. At the NASU meeting of 1938, simmering complaints against accreditors of professional programs erupted into a great deal of rhetoric and a plan to join other institutional associations in common action. The resulting Joint Committee on Accrediting (JCA) was intended to eliminate some accrediting agencies, simplify procedures, reduce expenses, and reclaim institutional responsibility. Praised by Zook, the venture attracted the cooperation of three other institutional associations.[46]

As a parallel effort, the ACE in 1939 and 1940 called conferences that launched projects to coordinate accrediting agencies. Some accreditation activists grew defensive. The disgruntled chairman of the AAU committee on classification charged the first ACE conference with using steamroller tactics. The principal speakers had complained of pestiferous accrediting bodies. "They implied that presidents no longer had time to manage their institutions and play golf. They further implied that it wasn't our business anyhow to ask too many questions about the intimate affairs of an institution, particularly about the coach's salary and stipends for athletes. . . . A few feeble voices were heard in protest, but they made little impression." As matters turned out, neither the JCA nor the coordinating projects begun by the ACE conferences had much success. But the distractions of World War II considerably lessened the accrediting activities that had irritated presidents and aroused their associations.[47]

THE APPRAISERS APPRAISED

The direction of academic energies into setting standards, coordinating a system, and arranging accrediting procedures reached well beyond the institutional associations, but they were central to the effort. Their national identities gave them influence that regional accrediting associations and state governments lacked. Their non-governmental status associated them with American traditions of voluntarism; in fact, the system that emerged was far less coercive than those in centrally administered governmental systems such as the French.

A variety of motives gave heart to the system-makers. They found models in other parts of society. Business was increasingly shifting away from market competition through conscious coordination, as in trade associations and price leadership. Protestant religious bodies moved in the same direction, with national denominational organizations that included specialized bureaucracies and linked themselves in interdenominational federations. The military exemplified order through hierarchy, and the republican polity was a venerated system of levels and branches. In a society so structured, it was easy to argue that higher education must not remain a congeries of autonomous local ventures.

Standardizers claimed that they had not lost sight of the individual, that in fact their control over institutions advanced the freedom of the individual. Recognized degrees, transferable credits, a clearly distinguished ladder—all of these presumably informed students and kept them out of academic cul-de-sacs. To be able to ask if an institution was accredited and by whom allowed the seeker of higher education some protection against the lures of advertisement or mere propinquity.

The benefits of system and standards for institutional association members included the blocking off of competition. Explicit criteria for "higher education" made entry of new units more difficult, while pressuring others to merge or disappear. At the same time, recognized standards and accrediting procedures helped leaders of individual institutions make the case for increased financial support and counseled them on how best to use it.

There were benefits from the standardization movement, no doubt, but it had many flaws. It began with naively numerical criteria. It gave leverage to rigid officials and not just enlightened ones. Its development by a multiplicity of regional, institutional, and professional associations brought public confusion and administrative exhaustion. It reduced institutional variety, embarrassing the idiosyncratic, undervaluing local tradition, and discouraging experimental innovation. As these disadvantages came to light, the institutional associations played an important corrective role.

Even while some participants in associations were dedicated to enforcement of standards, others used the associations as forums to raise objections and poke fun. The counterreform of the 1930s with its shift toward institutional self-appraisal and qualitative considerations began in the North Central Association, but the institutional associations advanced the process. The officiousness of the rapidly increasing professional accrediting bodies affronted institutional presidents. They had thought that universities legitimized professions. Now the process seemed reversed. The AAU began to question all accrediting programs, even its own. The other institutional associations had always denied being accrediting bodies, though occasionally acting as if they were. Now, in reaction to excesses, they were well placed to raise objections and lend support to counterreformers. The ACE, under Zook's leadership, pulled back from quantitative standards and brought accrediting officers and disillusioned institutional administrators together. No one asked for the system to be dismantled. Virtually every academic had some vested interest in it. Zook's bureaucratic meliorism set the tone for alteration.

A Confident AAC Returns
to Its Birthplace, 1925
•

ALTHOUGH it had twice held annual meetings in New York, where its headquarters were now located, the AAC returned to Chicago, originally mandated as its regular convention site, for its eleventh meeting, January 8–10, 1925. The AAC, with many midwestern members, still had strong ties to the city where it had been born amid mounting concern over the fate of small liberal arts colleges. Now a mature organization, its convention program offered a rich variety, carefully arranged. Although delegates were able to initiate measures and periods marked "discussion" dotted the schedule, evidence of planning and cental control abounded.

Scheduling the convention at the conclusion of "Christian Education Week" indicated the AAC's continuing links to religion. Denominational groups and the umbrella Council of Church Boards of Education dominated the early part of the week and held a climactic Union Mass Meeting on the afternoon of Thursday, January 8. That evening, shifting to a somewhat more secular tone, the AAC began its five sessions, which artfully combined addresses, commission reports, and items of business. Tedium was minimized, and delegates were more likely to participate in decisions than if all business had been reserved to a single, avoidable session. Perhaps the Chicago winter also helped keep delegates assembled, comfortably sheltered in the Morrison Hotel. Someone judged the pattern unattractive, however, and the following year a single business meeting was scheduled for the late afternoon of the second day.

The Friday morning session displayed the executive secretary, Robert L. Kelly, as the central organizing intelligence of the AAC. He presented not only his own report, but also those of the absent treasurer and the executive committee, the latter a brisk document with nine numbered proposals. A reworking of the constitution by the executive committee was distributed in mimeographed form, to lie over until 1926.

One initiative from the floor caught the planners by surprise. A successful motion added to the all-male list of new honorary members the name of Mina Kerr, executive secretary of the American Association of University Women. Perhaps women delegates and male sympathizers were reacting against the prejudice that had made a woman for the third time in five years vice-president, but later the nominating committee blandly selected Aurelia Reinhardt of Mills College for the increasingly traditional "woman's position" of vice-president.

Kelly's hand was evident in a later motion by a delegate from Loyola University of Chicago. This successful call for a new committee to explore current policies regarding credit for courses in religion echoed a report on collegiate religious instruction which Kelly had given earlier to the CCBE. He headed the new committee, which promptly sent out a questionnaire and published the highly mixed results within the year. Kelly welcomed religious education, of course, as he had while president of Earlham, but was concerned about uneven standards.

The executive committee had voted to reestablish the lapsed custom of an opening address for the annually elected president of the association. Calling the decision a joke on both himself and the audience, Chancellor James H. Kirkland of Vanderbilt used the occasion (the minutes insisted) to strike the meeting's keynote, "the obligation of the college to society." Actually, he simply said what was on his mind, relying on the privilege of an academic elder statesman. He hoped colleges could rescue the increasing numbers of vocationally oriented students from becoming mere technicians. He pled for inculcation of both culture and social sciences, the latter now "at the very heart of the college curriculum." After Kirkland, in accordance with the AAC tradition of including well-known outsiders as speakers, delegates heard one of the founders of the social settlement movement, Graham Taylor of Chicago Commons, who called on colleges to give their students a "vision truer to group life and the common welfare." Stressing interclass obligations, he assailed negative attitudes toward the American labor movement as well as the intolerance indicated by the new immigration laws. Listening, one could conclude that the spirit of Progressivism lived on amid retrograde social developments.

Kirkland and Taylor provided enough postbanquet inspiration to carry delegates through drier business the next morning, including a strictly pro forma letter of greeting from President Coolidge. Two reports indicated the rising strength of testing, placement, and selective admissions. Ben D. Wood, of Columbia University's Bureau of Collegiate Educational Research, was just setting out on a redoubtable career in the testing movement. Although he represented the AAC's Commission on the Organization of the College Curriculum, Wood's remarks were very much his own. By presenting more recent and more "scientific"

studies, he cast doubt on an earlier claim by Harvard's President
Lowell that an undergraduate's field of concentration had little
to do with achievement in law school. Criticizing the weakness
of Lowell's measurements, Wood called for reliance on psychological experts. He praised the College Entrance Examination
Board with its alternative to records based on "local standards
and local curricula."

Even more than Wood's remarks, those of his superior at
Columbia, Adam Leroy Jones, displayed the rise of the new
administrative specialities of admissions and placement. Jones
was shortly to rise from member to chair of an AAC commission
that would broaden its name from "Psychological Tests and
Methods of Rating" to "College Personnel Techniques." Like
Wood, Jones spoke of waste. Through careful admission procedures, orientation of freshmen, and course placement, colleges
could improve matters. While urging "suitable instruments of
measurement," Jones also recommended complex admission and
advising systems that would rely heavily on information about
students' family backgrounds. At Columbia, he announced, the
interviewing officers' predictions had been the most accurate of
all bases used to predict an applicant's academic success in college.
Clearly the emerging profession of "personnel work" went beyond merely creating and administering tests.

An intensifying professionalism also suffused the report of
the Commission on Academic Freedom and Academic Tenure,
presented by the University of Michigan's Dean John R. Effinger.
He told of important developments at a recent meeting of representatives from not only institutional associations, but also the
faculty members' ten-year-old AAUP and the American Association of University Women. The AAC had come best prepared.
It presented the statements on academic freedom and tenure
which it had voted in 1923, and in modified form they won
unanimous adoption. The document combined declarations of
high principle with many institutionally protective "unless" and
"except" phrases. Noting the minor changes to its original proposal, the AAC adopted the report as read, presumably giving
the association's imprimatur to the new versions. It was probably
not foreseen how frustrating would be the quest to get other
institutional associations to accede to the statements. (When in
1940 a modified form was finally declared in force, it was officially
adopted by only the AAC and the AAUP.)

Sandwiched between reports, an address on "Practicalizing
the Social Sciences" may have lost impact. Nevertheless, Birmingham-Southern's Dean Ludd M. Spivey was able to suggest
the vitality of Progressivism in his home region. He called for
active community citizenship that would last beyond the college
years, with students realizing that college itself was part of "real

life." While seeing the control attained through physical sciences as a useful model for social sciences, he warned against the pursuit of "better stock" by eugenicists and immigration restrictionists.

The convention planners had placed communications from three other associations in the Friday afternoon session. C. R. Mann, director of the ACE, was allowed ten minutes in which to justify his umbrella association before the gathered representatives of one of its founding groups. In a medley of metaphors, he spoke of the council as ending its infancy and beginning to show "objective returns." As proof of practical benefits, he described the workings of the ACE's register of faculty members (its "Personnel Service"), available to any staff-seeking institution but gratis for ACE members. Like Wood and Jones earlier that day, he lauded standardized tests, promising that the movement would expand entrance examinations to include instruments for placement and vocational guidance. Best of all, the ACE had succeeded in bringing together various standardizing agencies— in coordinating the coordinators. After Mann, in short order, a representative of Phi Beta Kappa reported on "interscholastic" debating (i.e., among high schools), and one from the National Council on Religion in Higher Education was granted the podium to describe new fellowships to train teachers for undergraduate religion courses.

Disappointment with the quality of teaching among those trained in American graduate schools underlay a report presented by President Raymond M. Hughes of Miami University of Ohio. Innovatively, the study ranked individual graduate departments rather than entire universities, using judgments by specialists from both colleges and universities. Hughes suggested that graduate schools could better serve future college teachers by instituting an alternative graduate degree less directed to research than was the Ph.D. and by developing "cultivated gentlemen" as examples for the cruder youths now coming to college. The usually staid association had a sensitive matter before it. Should the lists resulting from the study be published? An ad hoc committee reported back with a compromise. Hughes's address would be published in the *Bulletin*, but the controversial lists would only be mimeographed and mailed to each member institution. The executive committee was directed to take steps to have a rerating "in due time by a competent agency."

The Carnegie Corporation was determined to elevate the arts in America, and the AAC was happy to cooperate. After President Cowling of Carleton spoke for the AAC's Commission on College Architecture, the architect George C. Nimmons reviewed the work of a six-year-old joint committee of the AAC and the American Institute of Architects. In its efforts to promote the fine arts in higher education, the committee had prepared a textbook and syllabus for a "standard" art appreciation course. Such training, Nimmons argued, would develop the "good taste" that many college students now lacked because of family origins. The Carnegie Corporation's president and the inspirer of much of this activity, Frederick P. Keppel, reported his sympathy with colleges' difficulties in supporting the arts. The curriculum, he recognized, was already overcrowded, art courses tended to be snaps, and it was harder to test students "to whom the dominant appeal is through the sensibilities and emotions rather than through the intellect." But he believed that general talent for the arts was widespread and that America's ethnic pluralism gave it unique advantages in tapping a variety of aesthetic traditions. He warned against required art courses and those that divorced appreciation from performance and production. All in all, Keppel projected a freshness of thought, a moderated sense of possibilities, and an insight into his audience's institutional situations that took much of the bite out of charges of philanthropic paternalism.

Although the session had already heard from seven speakers, the major address of the afternoon was yet to come. Its assignment to Dean John Black Johnston of the University of Minnesota suggested the increasing importance of large-university representatives in the AAC. Obviously troubled by the effect of rising student numbers, a phenomenon felt most intensely at state universities like his own, Johnston discussed how to prevent lower standards, rampant vocationalism, and student anomie. Selective admission was ruled out for an institution required to admit virtually any high school graduate in the state, but measurement and guidance offered help. The ablest students could be challenged through separate senior college admission, independent study, and comprehensive examinations. Reflecting the needs of the less gifted, Johnston's espousal of survey courses and junior college divisions within universities forecast Minnesota's soon-to-emerge General College.

Friday evening's program included the sensible announcement (from Samuel Capen) that the Commission on the Distribution of Colleges had finished its work and should be discontinued. As proof of the Commission's achievement, George F. Zook of the USBE presented a study measuring college attendance within and outside students' home states as well as the proportion of each state's population attending college. It was a quintessential Zookian enterprise, offering precise data, with a careful drawing of progressive, pro-education conclusions. The report was a harbinger of change. In it, Zook reversed a generation of attacks on overproliferation of colleges. New Jersey, with the highest percentage of students leaving the state, might

well be undersupplied, as might certain other states. Some response was needed to the greater pressure on women than men
to leave their home states for college education. New England
states without state universities failed to serve a significant portion of their populations, as did southern states that lacked public
high school systems.

A report from the Commission on Athletics judged alumni
and local supporters the main sources of abuse, which strong
regional conferences and faculty control showed promise of correcting. The report struck an optimistic note, though admitting
that its data came mostly from small colleges. There were words
of approval for the National Collegiate Athletic Association, an
interinstitutional effort begun in 1905, and for the recent professionalizing movement that sought to restrict athletic coaching
to faculty members in departments of physical education.

Two Friday evening addresses shared the theme of comparative education. First came Kelly's account of his recent exchange
professorship at the University of Paris, where he had lectured
on American college administration. Though patently Franco-
philic, Kelly had been an astute observer. Compared to the
French, American higher education was a system of "mass production," tolerating high student mortality rates and examining
chiefly for retentive memory. Still, American experimentalism
and variety deserved recognition, as of course did the "unity of
effort and concert of purpose attained through voluntary associations."

In his comparison of Japanese and American higher education, the featured speaker of the session, Yusuke Tsurumi,
avoided organizational intricacies to contrast American emphasis
on personality development with the Japanese ethos of harmony.
From that ethos sprang Japan's participation in both arms reduction measures and the League of Nations. Lacing his account
with humor, he presented Japan as developing from intense
provincialism to internationalism. The audience stood and applauded.

The convention planners had found a clever way to exploit
a major policy difference within the AAC. The closing session
Saturday morning was enlivened by a debate on the now fading
Sterling bill, a six-year-old plan to create a new cabinet-level
Department of Education combined with grants in aid to the
states. The antagonists were two leaders of the educational establishment. George D. Strayer of Columbia's Teachers College
denied that the bill would impose central control, urged the duty
of wealthier states to help the poorer, and stressed recognition
for the profession. Charles H. Judd, director of the University
of Chicago's School of Education, declaring himself not against
a department, concentrated on attacking the bill as out of date,

distorted by the temper of wartime and the desires of state and city superintendents of education to get federal aid. He mocked the bill as unlikely even to get out of committee. His tilt toward private education plus his satire won him more positive audience response than Strayer received. In his rebuttal Strayer seemed a bit annoyed, even associating his "worthy opponent" with "the period of reaction in which we are now living." Although somewhat forced, the format let two supporters of a cabinet-level department present their views in a stimulating way. Adrenaline flowed, and this was one convention that did not wind down in an atmosphere of ennui.

When Kelly later described AAC annual meetings as "a revivifying agency" that developed "guild spirit," he captured their special blend of inspiration and professionalization. When the meeting of 1925 ended, a revised constitution was a step closer to adoption, and seven commissions had reported, none trivially. Addresses had come from not only presidents and deans but also distinguished outsiders, whose selection indicated abiding Progressivism among the powers in the AAC. For those who had missed sessions, virtually every address and report could be read in the pages of forthcoming issues of the *AAC Bulletin*. In fact, some speakers had mercifully abbreviated their remarks, knowing that they would be available in print. No session had run beyond a seemingly tolerable two hours and forty minutes. All in all, the planners must have been well satisfied.

CHAPTER 5

The Philanthropic Aegis

AUTONOMY was not claimed by the institutional associations. They did as their members directed, or so leaders declared. Another source of control, less often mentioned, was agencies that contributed financial support, notably philanthropic foundations, those new social institutions of immense potential that were an American innovation of the early twentieth century. Foundation influence over certain of the associations ultimately became a principal route for foundation-inspired changes in colleges and universities themselves.

Around 1910 the institutional associations sometimes provided the setting for principled opposition to foundations. When the effort to win a federal charter for the Rockefeller Foundation heightened worries about the expanding power of these private bodies, Schurman of Cornell addressed the issue before his assembled presidential colleagues. He warned of the foundations' meddlesome tendencies and their freedom from public accountability. In general, however, the establishment of foundations stirred lively anticipations of funding for association members. Only after World War I did it become clear that the associations themselves could benefit from foundation grants, through both direct support and subvention for specific projects. Apart from funding, the foundations influenced the associations as models of successful "third-sector" ventures, which could claim to be neither governmental nor profit seeking. In structure and ideology the two types of organization found much to share. Both developed central bureaucracies, claimed to be "above politics," and faced accusations of asserting illegitimate power.[1]

EARLY ENCOUNTERS

In seeking to understand the foundations, it is misleading to dwell on priorities between the ventures of Andrew Carnegie and those of John

D. Rockefeller. Carnegie, with his essays, elaborated a theory of stewardship for the age of gigantic industrial fortunes, whereas Rockefeller said little on the subject. As Roger Geiger has pointed out, however, the two men's philanthropies developed in parallel. First came aid to single great educational institutions (the University of Chicago, Carnegie Tech), then research institutes (the Rockefeller Institute for Medical Research, the Carnegie Institution of Washington), then broad educational aid through a philanthropic trust (the General Education Board [GEB], the Carnegie Foundation for the Advancement of Teaching [CFAT]), climaxing in general-purpose foundations to which the bulk of the two men's benefactions was assigned (the Rockefeller Foundation, the Carnegie Corporation of New York).[2]

Rockefeller's religiously motivated giving had begun in his youth. Less religious and disinclined to aid religious institutions, Carnegie in his early charities aimed at stimulating self-help and local initiative. In both cases, the men they chose to administer their educational trusts were not mere dispensers of charity. Rather, as representatives of a new species that later evoked the name *philanthropoid,* they launched drives for standardization that suited the current "gospel of efficiency." Admirers of "system," they wanted society to move away from laissez-faire toward greater cooperation. Rockefeller's chief advisor in philanthropic matters, the minister Frederick T. Gates, had caught the oil magnate's eye as head of the American Baptist Education Society, founded in 1888. Gates, who had sought to limit the multiplication of impecunious Baptist colleges, claimed to have introduced "the principles of scientific giving" into Rockefeller's charities. Henry S. Pritchett, having recently assumed the presidency of MIT, began cultivating Carnegie's friendship in 1901 and strongly influenced the shaping of the Carnegie Foundation, which he headed for twenty-five years. Disdaining mere alms giving, both Gates and Pritchett were determined that these philanthropic programs for education would bring order to what they considered a chaotic situation.[3]

Having originally directed its attention to the South, the General Education Board (founded 1902, chartered by Congress 1903) launched in 1905 a program of aid to higher education throughout the nation. According to Rockefeller's directive, drafted by Gates, the income from additional endowment was to be used "to promote a comprehensive system of higher education in the United States." Of the various things "system" might involve, Gates, who headed the GEB from 1907 to 1917, was particularly attentive to institutional distribution. Were colleges too close to each other to be well supported? Were some ill-placed in relation to population? The earliest report of the board, covering the period 1902–14, contains information on

colleges that were poor, scantily attended, and limited to narrow curricula, information meant to demonstrate an oversupply. Gates did
not want any grants to go to the "no less than nine so-called Christian
colleges" in Nebraska, which had sprung, he argued, from real estate
speculation and local pride. In Gates's opinion, the institutions of
higher education in the country could well be reduced in number by
three-fourths and "formed by careful selection into a system of higher
education." Arguments that weaker institutions met important needs
in sustaining a religious tradition or providing access to education for
young people nearby or that they promised future usefulness if college
attendance increased, were not given much credence in the years when
the idea of system dominated the new foundations. In their formative
period, the great foundations, like the institutional associations,
stressed the twin ideas of the need for educational order and the
unreliability of democratic government as a source for such order.[4]

In the long run, the GEB lost its more extreme ambitions for
reordering higher education. Its grants in the early 1920s to bolster
inflation-ravaged faculty salaries had more to do with the need to keep
teachers teaching than with a master plan for selective institutional
survival. But the desire for central coordination continued—in not
only the GEB's historic grants to medical schools, but also its less
conspicuous efforts to promote regularization of financial records.
Reasoning that accurate knowledge about an institution's needs and
likelihood of survival required the capacity to decipher its accounts,
the board enlisted Trevor Arnett, a University of Chicago administrator with a genius for accounting, and sent him into the field. (He
claimed to find one college president who kept receipts and bills in
his hat.) The institutional associations, having themselves urged standard statistics as early as a NASU discussion of 1904, welcomed Arnett's work, particularly his guidebook *College and University Finance*
(1922). If those at the center saw standard accounting methods as a
source of control, local administrators saw them as easing the rising
burden of questionnaires and offering financial benefits. An AAU
delegate expressed thanks for an address by Arnett which showed
how "in large industrial concerns . . . great sums of money are saved
by proper accounting systems." In 1928, the year Arnett became president of the GEB, he also served as president of the AAC, a post
usually reserved for the head of a college. His AAC presidential address advocated higher faculty salaries, a cause he believed might be
advanced by waiving the right of permanent tenure.[5]

Although the ACE had used foundation funds in its early ventures
in international educational exchange, it was not until 1921 that it
received major foundation funding for a project. In a process often

to be repeated, informal discussions among foundation officials, representatives of associations, and college administrators led to a conference that drew up a proposal for an investigation with an overseeing board and a staff to carry out the research. The investigation of college revenues and expenditures recommended in this case was to be much broader than Arnett's inquiry for the GEB. Four foundations, including the GEB and the Carnegie Corporation, supported the plan with $170,000, a figure that dwarfed the ACE's earlier expenditures. The ACE set up a commission on the Educational Finance Inquiry headed by George D. Strayer of Teachers College, Columbia. It issued a thirteen-volume report in 1924 comparing educational and other public expenses and examining the effect on education of different systems of taxation.[6]

THE CARNEGIE FOUNDATION AND THE ASSOCIATIONS

Although the GEB's matching grants to colleges exceeded $10 million by 1914, the Carnegie Foundation (incorporated 1905, chartered by Congress 1906) figured more prominently in the deliberations of the institutional associations. Developing in part because of expectations for widespread Carnegie pension benefits, this salience also owed much to the determination of Pritchett to make the foundation a "great agency" in the unification of American higher education. A figure representative of the Progressive Era's quest for system, Pritchett had been a professor of astronomy, the head of the U.S. Coast and Geodetic Survey, and a promoter of an independent National Bureau of Standards. He scarcely expected Newtonian relationships in the educational universe, but he was determined that it be mapped and standardized. Carnegie's idea of awarding pensions to professors, whom he regarded as underpaid altruists, sustained considerable reshaping under Pritchett's influence. After initial reluctance, the founder himself took pride in the foundation's "good work . . . in raising the standards of education." With the pension program absorbing more and more of the CFAT's resources, Carnegie in 1913 gave it additional endowment for a "Division of Educational Enquiry" to continue the investigations for which it was already famous.[7]

Aiding Pritchett in his undertaking were the trustees of the new foundation, nearly all college or university presidents, some of them leaders in the institutional associations. Since Carnegie's gift specified pensions for teachers in "higher educational institutions," Pritchett declared it his duty to define the type and identify legitimate exemplars through careful investigation. Of the 627 initial questionnaires sent out to putative institutions of higher education, 421 were returned.

Building on standards set earlier by the New York Board of Regents, the CFAT's pioneering national list ranked as institutions of higher education only those employing at least six full-time professors, offering four years of liberal studies, and requiring for admission four years of high school preparation (a minimum of fourteen "units"). These standards meant many exclusions. No college in the South was eligible, although Tulane raised its admission requirements in time to be on the initial list of fifty-two "accepted institutions." There was nothing particularly new in the complaint that the terms *college* and *university* lacked fixed meaning. Daniel C. Gilman had talked that way a quarter of a century earlier. But Pritchett's amassing of data about institutions that claimed to purvey higher education helped make him for two decades one of the most powerful figures in the academic world.[8]

Pritchett showed no hesitation in exerting his influence on the institutional associations. His second annual report included a rather acerbic history of the AAU, which he criticized as inconsistent in its membership standards and remiss in not defining *university* and *graduate study*. At its next meeting the AAU elected the CFAT to membership and appointed Pritchett to its Committee on Aim and Scope. President Schurman greeted the appointment with barbed wit, saying Pritchett was being asked "to assist in doing a very small piece of work which he can easily throw off, standardizing the colleges of the United States." Soon AAU committees took to meeting in the CFAT's offices.[9]

Two institutional associations promptly confronted the foundation over its decision to deny pensions to professors at tax-supported institutions, an exclusion implied but not clearly required by Carnegie's letter of gift. State universities and land-grant colleges seized the occasion to make use of their respective associations. In a series of meetings and letters, Pritchett defended his position, and he used the first CFAT *Bulletin* to discuss the controversy. Without the authority conferred on spokesmen by the existence of the NASU and the AAACES, it is doubtful that public institutions would have received so full a hearing. These two associations acted as pressure groups, sending representatives to argue before the CFAT trustees. The AAU played a different role. It provided neutral ground on which both Van Hise of Wisconsin, with the state university perspective, and Eliot of Harvard, chair of the Carnegie trustees, could explore the issues, and the discussion was broadened to include long-term effects.[10]

The controversy dragged on. Van Hise and his allies often had sympathy with Pritchett's hope to restructure American higher education, but they contended that the CFAT would gain more leverage on public institutions if they were included among candidates for the pension program. What seemed the climax came in January 1908, when Pritchett addressed a special meeting of the NASU. Shortly thereafter, he and Van Hise worked out a compromise for temporary participation by some state universities, while those institutions launched efforts to develop state-supported pension programs.[11]

At this juncture, Carnegie himself intervened, adding to the original endowment so that tax-supported universities could be admitted without time limitation. Delighted members of the NASU sent an engraved resolution of appreciation to Carnegie and elected Pritchett to honorary membership. But Pritchett, still determined to elevate and regularize academic standards, managed to apply strict eligibility requirements to the public institutions. Besides meeting the entrance and graduation criteria already set, they must have an annual income of $100,000 and demonstrate that politicians did not control their governing boards. Partly because of these standards, but also because of the trustees' growing awareness that even their expanded funds might not cover the commitments already made to private institutions, only nine public institutions were admitted to the pension program before the shift to a contributory system in 1919. The NASU nevertheless took satisfaction in its accomplishment, with one member irenically suggesting that, even if all were not included, it was still a gain that some of the state universities were deemed equal to the private.[12]

Effective in dealing with Congress, the land-grant association was not well positioned to attract private philanthropy for its members. After Carnegie's intervention but before specific tax-supported beneficiaries had been named, Pritchett addressed the AAACES. Noting that the foundation would aid only colleges limiting admission to candidates with four years of high school education, he expressed doubt that it would be wise for many of the agricultural colleges to break with their constituencies by setting requirements that high. Even as he gave such advice, unusually localistic for him, he criticized the agricultural colleges for failing to become part of a system: "You have not yet brought about in your own conception . . . any uniformity as to what your mission is, as to what your work is, as to what your relations to education are to be. This is exactly what the Carnegie Foundation desires to know." The association thereupon wishfully voted to acknowledge the foundation's "sympathetic and helpful consideration of the land-grant colleges."[13]

Debate at the next year's convention featured reactions to Pritchett's challenge, with renewed efforts made to specify the function of land-grant colleges and to reconsider their entrance and graduation requirements. There were also some sour grapes. One speaker called the CFAT's endowment "pitiful" compared to the vast public wealth on which the land-grant colleges drew. The 1910 presidential address was devoted to answering the "unwarranted disparagement" to which Pritchett had subjected the land-grant institutions in his latest annual report. Of the members of the AAACES which were not also state universities, only one, Purdue, was added to the Carnegie program after the donor's second gift. Perhaps this was a minimal gesture toward the pleas made by the association, but it was more probably intended to reward the coordination recently worked out between that land-grant institution and Indiana University, a triumph of system on the state level.[14]

Although recognizing that many colleges had begun under religious auspices, Carnegie had made clear his wish that the pension program not include "sectarian institutions," those "under the control of a sect or [requiring] Trustees (or a majority thereof), Officers, Faculty or Students, to belong to any specified sect, or which impose any theological test." Excluded institutions often protested to the foundation, leaving what one CFAT insider branded an ugly record of special pleading and sharp dealings. Reaction to this discrimination helps explain the formation of the Council of Church Boards of Education and its offspring, the AAC. If the much-touted pension program barred church colleges, then they had better begin to counsel together about their position in American education. Perhaps even more influential in the creation of the AAC were the comments in CFAT publications on the oversupply of small colleges, animadversions echoed in the first report of the GEB (1914). As discussed in chapter 4, the originators of the AAC, sharing the foundations' concern about standards, set minimum qualifications for membership and defined a "minimum college"; nevertheless, the AAC hoped to encourage weaker institutions that seemed on the right track.[15]

Threatened with bankruptcy, the CFAT in 1916 launched a study of possibilities for a contributory pension plan as an alternative to its original policy. In meeting the crisis, Pritchett took pains to involve the institutional associations. A special commission included representatives of the AAC, the AAU, and the NASU, as well as the newly formed American Association of University Professors. While the president-dominated institutional associations proved largely acquiescent in the CFAT's plans for the Teachers Insurance and Annuity Association (TIAA), the AAUP raised strong objections. Resulting changes included the addition of professors to the governing board of the new organizations, and the episode forecast a long record of AAUP challenges to positions taken by institutional associations.[16]

FOUNDATIONS AND ASSOCIATIONS IN THE INTERWAR PERIOD

The Carnegie Foundation's much wealthier sibling, the Carnegie Corporation (established 1911), had assisted the beleaguered noncontributory pension program. Although the two continued to work together, the corporation began to have an independent role in education. After Carnegie's death in 1919, the corporation gradually paid off the backlog of commitments to his favorite causes and instituted programs far more socially directive than those embraced by the founder, a quintessential nineteenth-century liberal. In 1919 the corporation gave $5 million to the National Academy of Sciences and its activist offshoot the National Research Council, soon followed by other grants to encourage development of science and scholarship. Under the presidency of James Rowland Angell, who left to head Yale University, and the acting presidency of Pritchett, the Carnegie Corporation sought to coordinate research and centralize policy formation through entities "accessible to the federal government but not controlled by it." The institutional associations, with their limited-government ideology and their position as national networks, were potential beneficiaries of this approach.[17]

The Carnegie Corporation's president from 1923 to 1941, Frederick P. Keppel, knew the workings of one institutional association well. As an assistant to Butler at Columbia he had performed administrative chores for the AAU. As an Assistant Secretary of War during World War I he had worked closely with training programs and won the intense admiration of Samuel Capen. In 1925 the board of regents of the University of Wisconsin showed its antipathy toward both the origins of foundations' wealth and their reformist pretensions by forbidding the university to accept their grants. Keppel reacted with a landmark address before the AAU. Muting the language of system, he praised the breadth of view possible for foundations and their role as clearinghouses for educational ideas. He predicted that thenceforth foundations would channel their funds less to individual institutions than to projects of general applicability, a change that promised enhanced importance for institutional associations as sponsors of foundation-funded undertakings.[18]

Unlike the other associations, the ACE and the AAC drew often and heavily on foundation largesse—and wisdom, as their leaders tended diplomatically to add. Beginning in 1921, when it won the grant for an investigation of educational finance, the ACE usually received at least twice as much yearly income from foundations as from members' dues. The grants to the AAC were relatively small when compared to those received by the ACE and were almost always less than income from dues (table 3). Still, at times the AAC seemed a captive of the Carnegie Corporation, from which it received its first grant in 1925 and in whose headquarters the AAC executive committee often met, with corporation officials present. In keeping with Keppel's special interest in advancing the fine arts, the AAC accepted Carnegie Corporation grants to conduct studies of campus architecture and of visual arts teaching, as well as grants to allow brief campus stays, including concerts and other performances, by visiting artists.[19]

Even while citing gifts from foundations as evidence that the ACE was a responsible and permanent body, Capen used the dues support from members to justify an extravagant claim that the council was "absolutely democratic, absolutely representative." Arguing that an endowment would be unhealthy for the council, he saw nothing wrong in continuing to seek project support from endowed philanthropic foundations. In fact, although it failed in efforts to get building funds from the Carnegie Corporation, the ACE quickly became the greatest beneficiary of foundation aid among the institutional associations. At the apex of other associations, it was a credible locus for foundation efforts to reform the whole of American higher education. Grants came from various Rockefeller philanthropies, the Carnegie Corporation, and the Commonwealth Fund, created in 1918 by Edward S. Harkness and his mother, widow of one of John D. Rockefeller's Standard Oil partners. The ACE benefited (as did the AAC to some extent) from having a central staff that could draw up projects and negotiate with foundation officers, sharing with them an emerging style and language.[20]

Specially created committees rather than central office staffs usually conducted foundation-supported projects, such as the ACE's programs to improve the teaching of modern languages, which the Carnegie Corporation supported, and others to promote "personnel methods" (testing, record keeping, and counseling), which had Rockefeller backing. But after 1924 the ACE sought and sometimes obtained a percentage of grants to cover "the cost of executive work." With no fellowship program for scholarly research, such as those foundations provided through the NRC and the SSRC, the ACE did little for small-scale investigations and in 1936 explicitly denied any role as "middleman between persons who have projects and foundations or other sources of financial support." A few months later, however, Zook was advising the president of New Mexico State College on which members of foundation staffs would be most likely to favor a program to improve rural life.[21]

Many avenues could turn money into influence in educational affairs. Foundations could carry out their own research projects, such

TABLE 3
Financial Receipts of the AAC and the ACE, 1918–1950

Association of American Colleges					
Fiscal Year Ending in:	*From Dues*	*% of Receipts from Dues*	*From Foundation Grants*	*% of Receipts from Foundation Grants*	*Total Receipts*
1918	$2,350	96.7	0	0	$2,430
1920	5,730	100.0	0	0	5,730
1922			(not available)		8,070
1924	7,000	94.0	0	0	7,450
1926	7,880	61.2	$5,000	38.8	12,880
1928	9,950	59.7	0	0	16,670
1930	20,750	79.7	2,000	7.7	26,020
1932	21,660	32.1	39,870	59.1	67,470
1934	23,620	80.6	1,500	5.1	29,290
1936	25,340	54.2	14,530	31.1	46,750
1938	26,400	32.1	10,500	12.8	82,190
1940	27,680	34.7	6,750	8.5	79,680
1942	29,010	42.9	19,300	28.5	67,700
1944	29,550	37.5	26,250	33.3	78,860
1946	30,710	54.0	2,000	3.5	56,820
1948	47,950	59.2	0	0	80,930
1950	49,490	63.0	0	0	78,560

American Council on Education							
Fiscal Year Ending in:	*From Dues*	*% of Receipts from Dues*	*From Foundation Grants*	*% of Receipts from Foundation Grants*	*Total Receipts*	*Receipts for General Fund*	*Receipts for Special Funds*
1918				(not available)			
1920	$23,540	98.2	0	0	$23,970		
1922	23,910	29.1	$57,500	70.0	82,190		
1924	25,270	25.3	49,720	49.7	99,960		
1926	32,780	15.3	142,390	66.3	214,890		
1928	34,070	20.3	114,450	68.3	167,460		
1930	36,240	34.1	50,870	47.8	106,410		
1932	34,650	49.6	17,190	24.6	69,830		
1934	22,670	28.5	38,510	48.5	79,450		
1936	21,590	10.1	158,560	64.3	212,930		
1938	20,980	8.5	173,700	70.5	246,510		
1940	24,110					$102,580	$854,570
1942	30,840					92,870	649,620
1944	36,240					88,180	728,990
1946	45,990					105,430	850,590
1948	84,500					140,530	758,100
1950	113,120					151,300	880,080

Sources: For the AAC, Treasurer's Report appearing in *AAC Bulletin* and, for the ACE, Auditor's Report, Treasurer's Report, or "Financial Statements of the American Council of Education" appearing in *Educational Record,* for fiscal years ending in even numbers. Notes: I have substracted the opening "cash on hand" in figuring total receipts for each year. To avoid double-counting I have deleted AAC dues allocations in 1948 and 1950

TABLE 3 *continued*

to the Arts Program and the Commission on Christian Higher Education. After 1938 the ACE Financial Statement did not separately identify receipts from foundations.

The creation in 1939–40 of an ACE Publications Revolving Fund prevents continuing a consistent series and heightens the likelihood of double-counting. I have chosen from 1940–50 to list receipts for the General Fund (which included all dues), spent mostly for central office expenses, and receipts for Special Funds, spent mostly for special projects but including such standing programs as the Cooperative Test Service. Because the central office received payments from special projects for administrative services, these two figures cannot be added together without double counting. It might be possible from archival records to determine the changing proportion of Special Funds income from foundation grants and from fees paid by governments and private bodies. I have not undertaken that chore. Note also that the Publications Fund does not appear above.

ACE receipts for special funds in 1938 were $134,620. The sharp increase in 1940 traces mostly to receipts for the American Youth Commission, the Cooperative Test Service, and the Commission on Teacher Education, the three amounting to approximately $500,000.

The ACE fiscal year shifted in 1936–37 from May 1–April 30 to July 1–June 30. The fourteen-month figures for that year do not appear in this table.

Direct contributions from John D. Rockefeller, Jr., usually from his Benevolent Fund, are counted as receipts from foundations.

as the CFAT's studies of teacher education, or action projects, such as the GEB's program to coordinate the black colleges of Atlanta. One alternative was to create new organizations, technically independent but designed to accept foundation grants, such as the Institute of Economics and the American Association for Adult Education, both established in the 1920s under Carnegie Corporation sponsorship. But sometimes foundations chose institutional associations as their vehicles. If the ACE sponsored a study, it could be "distinctly understood that the Foundations have no control of the investigation or of the publication of the results." Such an arrangement appealed to foundations in the face of persisting questions about their exercise of power without public supervision (in short, about their legitimacy), but only the naive imagined the foundations to be neutral benefactors of other organizations' programs. The highly courteous correspondence between foundations and associations demonstrated the influence that accompanied the power to give or withhold grants, to insist on redefinition of goals before a project was financed, or to fund a project in stages. In 1927 a professor warned of the threat to university autonomy if foundations were allowed to develop into a "general staff." Similar questions were raised in a statistically meticulous examination of the foundations published in 1936. Such studies, it need hardly be said, were not supported by the institutional associations.[22]

Its foundation-supported study of educational finance helped establish the ACE's viability as a national instrument for analyzing educational problems. During the 1920s foundations came to regard the council as a highly respectable donee. It was based in education, their favorite benefaction, and as an association of associations was well placed to perform a sifting function. The head of social science programs for the GEB and the Rockefeller Foundation let it be known in 1936 that the ACE "will probably have to prepare the way before any national association of school officials is likely to get a grant from any of the foundations with which I am acquainted."[23]

While performing mediatorial work in getting grants for other organizations, the ACE itself grew increasingly dependent on foundation aid. The failure of the GEB to approve successive plans at the ACE for a study of the teaching of English effectively killed the undertaking. Support for the ACE was in doubt during the early years of the Great Depression when leaders of the Rockefeller philanthropies undertook searching reconsiderations that led them to express dissatisfaction with projects that were "often unrelated to human aspiration or need." From such reappraisal grew opposition to continued support of the ACE so long as it kept to the course Mann had charted. As Associate Director John H. MacCracken had foreseen, the views of Rockefeller and Carnegie officials were controlling in decisions of 1933–34 to restructure the ACE. (See table 3 for the changing percentage of ACE receipts from foundations.)[24]

As discussed in chapter 3, Mann's vision of American education, with its principled objections to direct federal aid, was ill-adapted to times of economic crisis. Beyond that, he did not, in the foundations' view, have the administrative talents necessary for a greatly expanded program. It was more than a personnel change that the foundations sought. They encouraged the ACE to broaden its field to all of American education, judging its traditional focus on higher education unduly elitist. With the collaboration of Dean William F. Russell of Teachers College, Columbia, who was ACE chairman, the New York–based foundation executives had their way, and the ACE expanded its responsibilities to include "all phases" of American education. George F. Zook became the new ACE director, and the GEB granted $300,000 for "general expenses and cooperative enterprises" during the next five years. The council thereupon began helping the Federal Emergency Relief Administration in a student-aid program that went directly counter to Mann's antigovernment pronouncements.[25]

A second grant of a half million dollars, also from the GEB, directed the council into youth problems broadly conceived. Through its new American Youth Commission, the ACE launched studies far beyond its traditional province, dealing with lower schools and venturing into questions of unemployment and crime. Notable publications resulted, including *Youth Tell Their Story* and *Children of Bondage*. Other GEB grants to the ACE supported programs for education through film and teacher training, from the latter of which the American Association of Colleges of Teacher Education (AACTE) ultimately sprang. Both projects reflected the GEB's new interest in what it labeled "general education." In response to foundation wishes, the ACE had radically shifted course.[26]

In 1940–41 the GEB grant was up for renewal. The Problems and Plans and Executive Committees began in 1939 to devote much of their attention to the impending end of the GEB's subvention for general purposes, which had averaged roughly $50,000 a year. Zook observed that, although certain services, such as surveys, financial advising, and tests, might be partly covered by user fees, continued foundation support for even these programs would usually be needed. As to nonproject expenses, dues, which had reached approximately $22,500 a year, could cover part but not all. Zook noted with pride that among the "four comprehensive councils" created during and after World War I (all heavily reliant on foundation support), the ACE alone had drawn significantly on membership dues. (He had in mind the National Research Council, the American Council of Learned Societies, and the Social Science Research Council.) A special ACE committee under Mark A. May of Yale's Institute of Human Relations began reconsidering programs and seeking funds. The upshot was a request to the GEB for an endowment of one and a half million dollars to provide a building and annual endowment income. Less ambitious requests for term grants were also presented. The GEB opted for a two-year grant of $95,000 and set up its own committee under George A. Works of the University of Chicago to review the functioning of the ACE.[27]

A frequent appraiser of institutions, the ACE was now itself the object of inspection. The Works report urged an even stronger role for the Problems and Plans Committee, making it a source of major policy pronouncements, and called for the ACE to become yet more representative of the public elementary and secondary schools. On the whole, the report supported the ACE's standard arguments for its importance as an identifier of major educational problems and a center for coordination.[28]

In response the ACE formed a broadly representative special committee, which gathered in July 1941 in Skytop, Pennsylvania. Not surprisingly, the five-day conference produced a statement of general approval for the ACE, emphasizing its need for a strong central office. More daring was the conference's proposal to add ACE representatives to the elite Educational Policies Commission (EPC), created in 1935 by the NEA and the American Association of School Administrators (AASA). Although this proposed "National Education Policies Commission" appeared to respond appropriately to the Works committee's call for greater ACE involvement in the public schools, the plan did not meet GEB approval. This failure eroded ACE prestige, as did the NEA's successful insistence that it become joint sponsor with the ACE of a new National Committee on Education and Defense. With the merged policy commission plan scuttled, the ACE proceeded in keeping with the Works report recommendations to elevate the policy role of its own Committee on Problems and Plans, in 1944 renaming it the Committee on Problems and Policies. More important than its rejection of the new commission, however, was the GEB's agreement to provide general support for the ACE—$300,000 over a period of six or seven years. The GEB made clear that it would not extend this grant and that the ACE must develop other funding sources. The episode demonstrated once again the power of foundations over the nation's apex organization of higher education.[29]

War changed matters in ways that increased the council's autonomy. It gained a quasi-governmental role and a greater chance to aid institutions confused by federal actions. Even larger than its grant from the Carnegie Corporation to help coordinate educationally related defense programs was a payment from the War Department for development of examinations for officer candidates. There were indications that the ACE would never again be so dependent on the foundations. But foundation grants coinciding with the arrival of new ACE presidents in 1951 and 1961 indicated a continued wish to influence the ACE's direction at crucial turning points.[30]

As they took form in the early years of the twentieth century, both philanthropic trusts and institutional associations faced uncertainties about role, power, and survival. Often the foundations and associations shared common aims, such as that of systematizing and standardizing American education. Between World Wars I and II the greater power unquestionably lay with the foundations because of their ability to give or withhold money. But the associations provided the foundations with a valuable source of ideas and personnel, besides offering some insulation from public criticism. After World War II, increases in other sources of funds, especially tax support and tuition, lessened foundation influence over higher education, including the associations, which were able to raise dues sharply. The emergence in 1947 of the giant Ford Foundation, with particular concern for education, heightened the stakes but did not essentially change the relationships with foundations which the associations had already worked out. By then they were old hands at the game.[31]

The ACE Changes Helmsmen, 1935

•

AT ITS annual meeting, May 3–4, 1935, in Washington, D.C., the ACE welcomed a new executive officer, honored his predecessor, celebrated new support from foundations, and associated itself more closely with New Deal programs. The meeting's theme, "Unoccupied Areas in Education," reflected new organizational ambitions that carried well beyond higher education. The attendance of 157 delegates marked a new high for the annual meeting. As if to signal that the worst of the Depression was over, twice as many institutional members as the year before sent representatives.[1]

As part of the capital's establishment, the ACE held its formal sessions in the lecture room of the National Academy of Sciences, its luncheon at the Cosmos Club, and its banquet at the Mayflower Hotel. President Roosevelt sent a letter. No mere greeting, it called for consolidated school districts, better-trained teachers, and more modern equipment. Mrs. Roosevelt arrived at the opening session to commend the ACE for its new Youth Commission and to urge giving young people a voice in planning.

The formal address of the opening session signaled the ACE's expanding domain. New York's superintendent of schools evoked the problems of urban youth, taking examples largely from his own city. Youth seeking to escape "the narrowness of life in the tenement districts" found avenues that encouraged delinquency: "games of chance, undesirable movies, gang influences and poolrooms." He saw some hope in New Deal programs and local initiatives but admitted that "the city sometimes gets the better of us."

The second paper, by the sociologist William F. Ogburn, sharply challenged the shibboleths of character education which had been heavily emphasized at the previous annual meeting. He contrasted "character" with "personality," declaring that, as values lost their fixity, attention was shifting to the latter. As legatee institutions, colleges and high schools could not limit themselves to intellectual concerns, but trying to "build character" was inappropriate. To meet their new responsibilities for "personality," schools should set up psychiatric services, expand extracurricular activities, and add courses in art and social science. In floor discussion, a dubious President Rufus von Kleinsmid of the University of Southern California associated "personality" with the promotion of stars he witnessed in the movie capital, but President Raymond M. Hughes of Iowa State declared that the colleges had an obligation to improve students' personalities to help them get jobs.

The defensive tone of the next invited speaker, U.S. Commissioner of Education John W. Studebaker, may have reflected the fact that George F. Zook, the new head of the ACE, had recently left the commissionership for this "better position." Studebaker declared himself "at the educational vortex." Since millions of young people were out of work, he expressed some skepticism about the ACE's new American Youth Commission with its big budget and research orientation. He boasted of the USOE's weekly radio broadcasts and praised federal programs for adult education, nursery schools, and student aid, without carefully distinguishing those controlled by other federal agencies. In fact, Roosevelt had already displayed his penchant for bypassing the USOE, and the commissioner grumbled that its personnel were underappreciated. Though rambling, the address carried a strong implication that the USOE was better situated than the ACE to give the American public school system a badly needed jolt.

In the absence of the ACE's chairman, its first vice-chairman, Sidney B. Hall, Virginia's state superintendent of public instruction, addressed the group. An extract from a curriculum study, his remarks were short on inspiration. There was apt symbolism, however, in having a representative of the lower schools give this official annual address before an organization striving to widen its field.

Movies were frequently mentioned at the meeting. They were the central theme for Ohio State's W. W. Charters, who saw them as a teaching tool of unimagined possibilities. He named makers of educational films and praised the work of amateurs using 16-millimeter stock, some of whom were teachers. In keeping with the goals of the ACE, he declared the need for a central agency that could locate and classify films.

The next speaker, Clarence S. Marsh, had recently become associate director of the ACE "in the field of higher education," an appointment intended as a message to college and university administrators that the ACE remained relevant to their needs. Little such reassurance emerged from his remarks, however. They simply described his recent experiences as educational director of the Civilian Conservation Corps.

Like Studebaker's and Marsh's addresses, that of Goodwin Watson of Columbia University showed the deepening influence of the New Deal. His prescription for developing human resources was in fact a preliminary version of a report requested from the ACE by the newly appointed National Resources Board. Citing the costs of illiteracy, accidents, and mental illness, Watson called for social planning. National, regional, state, and local boards should push far beyond formal schooling and treat such matters as human genetics, vocational guidance, and consumer education. Although the remarks had come from a committee, they were an exciting evocation of social possibilities, a "World of Tomorrow" like that soon to be conjured up by the planners of the New York World's Fair.

A banquet Friday evening honored Charles Riborg Mann, who had recently left the ACE directorship to take emeritus status. Relief at his departure had generally blended with an abiding respect and affection. At the banquet ceremonies his successor George Zook and his predecessor Samuel Capen said more about the ACE than about Mann himself, but the toastmaster, President Frederick B. Robinson of City College of New York, dwelt on Mann's sweetness of disposition and his tolerant way of planting ideas. The longest encomium came from General Robert I. Rees, who had worked with Mann in setting up the Students' Army Training Corps during World War I and later in building the army's educational and recreational program. After jesting about Mann's efforts as head of the ACE to purge his language of military terminology, Rees declared that the honoree shared John Dewey's educational philosophy but had made it more human by simplifying its expression.

Appearing very much at ease, Mann spoke at length, describing his ancestry and declaring his debt to A. A. Michelson, whom he had assisted in research at the University of Chicago. Less flattering was his praise of Chicago's President Harper for having changed from "a man intent on ostentation of academic respectability to the creator of an institution that would really teach its students to be men and women." Mann took some credit for that change through his own work on a curriculum committee at Chicago which had pared down admission requirements and freed baccalaureate candidates from having to take Latin. True to his reputation as a philosophizer, he ended with a plea for a big idea in education, one as significant as energy in physics or evolution in biology.

The next morning it was Zook's turn. He led off the session with his first annual report, avoiding sweeping proposals and selecting only some of the current activities for discussion. In what was less an inaugural address than a progress report from a leader already hard at work, he tried to reassure skeptics that the organization's broadened focus did not mean neglect of higher education, citing relevant projects such as a financial advisory service. Besides praising the loyalty of institutional members, he announced the executive committee's decision to reduce their $100 dues by half.

In developments closely linked to his taking office, Zook announced grants received from six different foundations, the largest the GEB's grant for the American Youth Commission. Two other parts of the ACE that Zook selected for praise rested on foundation support, the Problems and Plans Committee, established five years earlier with support from the Rosenwald Fund, and the Cooperative Test Service, now halfway through its ten-year grant from the GEB. Zook obviously hoped for foundation assistance to the proposed National Educational Film Institute, for which he judged neither government nor industry appropriate sources of funding. Echoing Charters's Friday address, Zook promoted the institute, warning that unless schools adopted modern devices, they would "surrender their influence to the county agricultural agent, the motion picture theater, and the radio."

Among the new committees, Zook showed particular interest in the one on international relations, which involved the ACE in a quasi-governmental function. He noted that the reason for the absence of the ACE's chairman, Dean William F. Russell, was his attendance at a conference of educational directors in Paris sponsored by the International Bureau of Education. Until the United States government chose to join that body, Zook said, the ACE had an obligation to represent the country. Standing in for the government in this case, in others the ACE was offering the government information and counsel. Soon after Zook had taken office, the ACE and the USOE had met to discuss desirable changes in federal student aid. In an adroit compliment to the college and university administrators present, Zook called this the best handled of all federal relief programs, largely because of the free hand given the individual institutions.

The report moved deftly among possibilities for both government and private support. Zook hoped that some funds from the giant appropriation bill pending in Congress would be used for research through the National Resources Board and its ACE-appointed advisory committee. But his highest expectations attached to the ACE's foundation-supported American Youth Commission. Unemployed young people were flocking into secondary schools or walking the streets. In response to "the youth problem," schools must provide educative work experience, practical contact with government, and of course "wholesome recreation activities." The commission's inquiry, planned to run at least five years, would reach far beyond traditional schooling.

Lingering resentment over the changes of 1934 surfaced during discussion. James H. Dunham of Temple University, identifying himself as "nothing but a dean," complained about how little of the meeting's program bore on higher education and belligerently recalled that colleges and universities had paid $21,000 in dues the previous year. In response Zook declared himself devoted to higher education, but Dunham was not much mollified, citing again the $21,000 figure. Robert L. Kelly, executive secretary of the AAC, then spoke, seeking to dispel rumors that his association was alienated from the ACE but also making the slightly barbed suggestion that it would be wise "to consult with us and possibly to assign us definite tasks." During floor discussions, running banter about regional speech variations suggested tensions seeking release.

In the opening committee report, Cloyd H. Marvin, president of George Washington University, revealed that in him the ACE had a newly active lobbyist. He told how his "NRA committee" obtained exemptions for colleges and universities from certain National Recovery Administration provisions. But with the NRA on its last legs, there was more significance in his summary of the pending Social Security Act. Eager for the ACE to speak with one voice, Marvin sought to keep Congress from distinguishing between public and private institutions. Both were part of "the integrated public educational system."

For the Standards Committee, George A. Works of the University of Chicago reported the deep changes made by the North Central Association. Its new Statement of Policy moved away from quantitative standards and allowed for institutional individuality that broke the dominance of "the liberal arts type" and opened the way for experiments. Later, in the business session, the ACE voted to drop its own publication of accrediting standards to demonstrate sympathy for the North Central's new direction. Zook's report had urged this step, suggesting that it rendered possible new secondary school practices likely to be suggested by the Youth Commission.

After committee reports, the meeting moved rapidly to its business session, promptly adopting recommendations from the executive committee. Marking the emergence of new leadership, Zook's title was changed by constitutional amendment from "director" to "president." To an inquirer about the origins of the change, Capen explained that Dean Russell, chairman of the ACE, had wanted to give the post more dignity while freeing the title "director" for those heading major projects. Mann displayed his simpler tastes by mildly protesting his simultaneous elevation to "president emeritus." New members were elected to the elite Problems and Plans Committee: President James B. Conant of Harvard, Professor Mark A. May of Yale, and Paul

C. Stetson, the Indianapolis superintendent of schools. If the new members of the Problems and Plans Committee seemed tilted toward the Ivy League, there was reassurance in the full slate of officers, which included the presidents of a technological institute, a women's college, and a state university, as well as the head of the National Catholic Educational Association.

As if for reassurance amid the many changes, a former chairman of the ACE returned to that office: Lotus D. Coffman of the University of Minnesota. After lightly satirizing those who greet their election with protests of surprise and unworthiness, he recalled the founding of the ACE and its wartime services to the government. But new issues were every bit as important as those faced in the war. He hailed the association's voluntarism as its "glory and strength," befitting the unregimented character of American education.

CHAPTER 6

When Is a Lobby Not a Lobby?

FEW educators wanted to admit that the world of teaching and learning constituted a "special interest." They saw that world as an unquestionable good for the entire society. Even when the associations sought influence by means resembling those of a textile manufacturers' alliance or a labor union, they expected politicians and public administrators to grant the indubitability of education's social benefit. The altruistic stance was easier to take for an institutional association than for an association of individual members. Whereas the NEA or the AAUP might be suspected of narrowly seeking to improve members' salaries and perquisites, the institutional associations could claim to speak for higher education as a whole, or at least a substantial sector of it.

As with the professions, emphasis on service, standards, and ethics helped higher education associations deny what later critical analysis makes plain: their goals did not necessarily benefit the entire society, and other "interests" could legitimately oppose them. Understandably, however, representatives of the associations did not like to be called "lobbyists," a name that long retained its connotations of corrupt influence. After 1946 the requirements for registration and after 1954 the Internal Revenue Service's restrictions on tax-deductible dues and gifts made it highly desirable to be able to deny involvement in lobbying. Nevertheless, influencing legislation had been an important function of such associations from 1887 on.[1]

As interlocking interests have increasingly come to unite associational representatives, congressional committees, and sections of government bureaucracy, such collaborations have been variously identified as *triocracy, subgovernments,* or, more journalistically, *iron triangles.* Successful resistance to most of the student-aid cuts proposed by the Reagan administration was a sharp reminder of such effective cooperation in the 1980s. Although association officers sometimes saw themselves in conflict with their political or bureaucratic counterparts, relations over the years tended toward accommodation and mutual respect, with gradual institutionalization of government programs that had been originally suggested by the associations.[2]

The Associations and the Lawmakers

In congressional relations before World War II, the associations differed considerably, all the way from steady involvement aimed toward specific legislation on the part of the land-grant group to the disengaged self-sufficiency of the AAU. The ACE—youngest of the five, the most inclusive, and marked by its unique wartime creation—long remained the only one with a Washington office. Although proud of its broad membership and counting government relations among its chief reasons for being, the ACE still leaned toward the interests of private institutions and displayed much of their suspicion of government intervention. In wartime, of course, accustomed behavior could change radically. The records are varied enough to justify examining each association in turn.

For many years the land-grant association stood out for its boldness in trying to influence legislation. The group had been formed amid jubilation over the success of coordinated efforts to pass the Hatch Act, soon reinforced by a similar achievement, the second Morrill Act. Indeed, the activism of the college presidents in 1890 was so intense that one congressman felt obliged to indicate during floor debate the difference between them and railroad company lobbyists. After urging by the association, Congress voted in 1900 that, if sale of public lands should prove insufficient, the annual appropriation to the Morrill colleges would come from general Treasury funds. Understandably, there was little resistance the next year to an increase in AAACES dues, presented as necessary to support trips to Washington by executive committee members.[3]

In 1905, after legislative defeats were blamed on scattering of effort, the association decided that the executive committee should emphasize one piece of legislation at each congressional session. Each of the next two years saw a major legislative victory. The Adams Act of 1906 doubled funds for experiment stations, with new provisions for "original investigation." The Nelson Amendment of 1907 provided for annual increases in the grants that had begun in 1890.[4]

In two other cases, persistent lobbying by the land-grant association came to nothing, partly because it tried to monopolize federal grants for Morrill institutions. The Mining School Bill, it will be recalled, stirred the NASU to action when a version that barred non-land-grant universities from participation seemed about to become law. Efforts to win federal support for engineering experiment stations on the model of the Hatch Act lasted for decades. The proposal ran afoul first of pressure to include non-land-grant state universities and then of the "best science" elitism of scientists who, with a new base of federal influence in the National Research Council, resisted spreading funds equally among the states.[5]

Although there were disappointments, the land-grant association had a stunning victory when its support helped put through the Smith-Lever Act in 1914, establishing federal funding for extension programs in agriculture and home economics. In fact, two of its committees helped draft the bill. In a further demonstration of strength, the association, by its reluctance to have the federal government begin supporting secondary education, managed to postpone the passage of aid for high school vocational training till 1917. The Smith-Lever Act initiated the device of matching grants in federal funding, a pattern with future influence well beyond the field of education. The act also began the requirement of preliminary approval by a federal agency for federally funded state programs. Such increases in federal control did not bother most members of the land-grant association. It was enough for them that the new act ratified and helped fund their extension programs, important avenues to popular approval. Moreover, the new funds meant the release of researchers from "the routine of lecture platform and institute meeting."[6]

As state appropriations and private giving rose, the Morrill colleges became less conspicuously federal charges. Whereas a third of their total income came from federal sources in 1909, the proportion dropped to a tenth by 1930. Even so, institutional leaders had no wish to sacrifice the special "land-grant" status. Overall they had experienced a fruitful cooperation with the Department of Agriculture, especially its Offices of Experiment Stations and of Extension Work.[7]

During the Great Depression, the uniqueness of these colleges' relation to the federal government diminished as other public institutions came to share in building grants and even private institutions benefited from programs for student aid. Yet the ALGCU persisted in presenting the special claims of its members. In 1933 the chair of its executive committee moved vigorously to counteract a presidential order cutting federal funds to land-grant institutions by 25 percent, and the funds were restored by a later order.[8]

The scare of 1933 aside, the land-grant association found leading New Dealers highly congenial. Henry A. Wallace and Harry Hopkins received heroes' welcomes at its conventions. Members considered their institutions well prepared to contribute to new federal programs such as the Agricultural Adjustment Administration (AAA) and the Tennessee Valley Authority (TVA). In Congress, the association helped shape and assure passage of the Bankhead-Jones Act of 1935, which instituted gradually increasing federal support for research, teaching, and extension in land-grant institutions. The association conveyed fears of overcentralization in soil conservation and other new programs to the Department of Agriculture, and compromises were worked out.[9]

The legislative record of the NASU, by contrast, was modest. It had failed in the late 1890s to win federal aid for state universities founded with the aid of pre–Morrill Act grants of townships. Part of the trouble was variation among its members. An older state university, such as Virginia, would not have been eligible under such a formula. Members that were both state universities and Morrill-grant institutions had their federal interests effectively represented through the AAACES.[10]

Fearing that their interests would always be overshadowed within the NASU, a group of non-land-grant state universities held meetings in the 1920s that evolved into the Association of Separated State Universities, with the name changed in 1930 to the State Universities Association (SUA). The new twenty-one-member association got a hearing from Secretary of the Interior Wilbur, arguing that current federal support policies for higher education threatened "the efficiency and development of the whole system." These complaints may well have played a role in Wilbur's appointment of the National Advisory Committee on Education. The new association wanted to assure that the Morrill-grant institutions would not monopolize federal aid to social science or engineering research and in 1937 pressed for aid to its members' schools of business. Land-grant leaders considered the SUA something of a menace.[11]

No institution withdrew from the NASU upon joining the SUA, but this new proof of differences among state universities weakened the older association. Although it sometimes cooperated with the land-grant association in seeking federal aid, the NASU lacked its vigor in lobbying. The absence of a center of support among government bureaus explains some of the NASU's ineffectuality.[12]

Deeply interested in state government, both the land-grant association and the NASU sponsored studies comparing practices among the states in public higher education. Annual meetings often saw a sharing of information and mutual counsel on the ways of governors, legislators, and state boards of control. Sometimes the standards embraced by a national association or evidence about what other states were doing could be used to stimulate increased state appropriations, but the associations had to proceed carefully in individual state matters, facing always the onus of being outsiders.

From its beginning the AAU included both public and private institutions, but the private wing dominated even after quantitative membership parity was achieved in 1909. As a result, in the years before World War II, the AAU tended to suspect any federal aid to higher education. In 1937 Conant wanted the annual conference to discuss the danger of federal control, which he feared could entail a gradual drying up of private funds for universities. At the 1939 meeting, Princeton's Harold W. Dodds argued that comprehensive federal aid would bring dangerous political influence and administrative control. The next year Cal Tech's Robert A. Millikan warned even more strongly against "the ever increasing pressures toward getting our educational feet farther and farther into the federal trough."[13]

Although they did not set the dominant tone for the AAU, presidents of member state universities defended alternative views. Minnesota's Guy Stanton Ford offered "to match case for case the influence of low politics upon endowed institutions with every case that can be cited on [sic] the public institution," and North Carolina's Frank Graham claimed that the federal government had leaned over backward to avoid controlling land-grant institutions. While joining colleagues in criticism of the New Deal, MIT's Karl Compton explored possibilities for federal aid more sanguinely than most and with a keener eye for the future. He saw benefits in dispersing general federal support of education by region but insisted that demonstrated quality should be the basis of additional allocations for specific objectives. There could be no question, in his view, of the legitimacy of such contract grants by government bureaus as those for cancer research, weather-forecast improvement, and airplane deicing. He assured other university presidents that he was not influenced by MIT's current federal funding: it was "just about enough to pay the clerical expense of filling out questionnaires."[14]

With its mission enlarged in 1918, the AAC established a Committee on Legislation the next year, seeking to keep member institutions informed (the implication being that they might then choose to give Congress their views individually). During the Great Depression the association moved more directly into legislative activity, originally because of fears that tax revisions would discourage gifts to private colleges. Its witnesses before congressional committees vigorously opposed the idea of taxing income from revocable trusts.[15]

In 1933, at the same time that Executive Secretary Robert L. Kelly was warning member institutions against "extravagant and unnecessary expenditures and apparent prosperity based on borrowed money which eventually must be paid or repudiated," he was describing in tempting language recent examples of college construction he had seen in the South. "A building was being entirely reorganized as to its interior for dormitory purposes with practically no cost to the college. . . . The common laborers are receiving 80 cents per day, 8 cents an hour for 10 hours, and are glad to have the work. The plasterers in this building are receiving $1.25 per day and their wages are paid out of unemployment funds." Kelly appears to have played a role in the formulation of the National Industrial Recovery Act (1933) with his argument that "so-called private colleges are really public institutions carried on as nonprofit corporations operated for public benefit."[16]

Although the AAC was interested in having students in private institutions declared eligible for new federal grants under the Federal Emergency Relief Administration and the National Youth Administration, it sought exemption of these institutions from NRA wage and hour regulations and from the Social Security system. In its drive for legislative influence the AAC appointed President Daniel C. Marsh of Boston University a special emissary to Washington. Along with Kelly and others on a new Committee on Federal Legislation formed in 1934, Marsh spent much time in the capital, utilizing what he characterized as "strategically friendly access to Congress." The outcome in all of these cases suited the preference of the AAC, and it learned how to obtain desired results through rulings by administrative agencies. But it failed in efforts, which included a call on President Roosevelt, to have the Reconstruction Finance Corporation aid colleges through debt refinancing. In the sensitive new area of federal aid to private colleges, Marsh maintained, public officials should look for guidance "not to self-seeking politicians but to experts in educational administration."[17]

Others in the AAC remained wary. The executive committee allowed AAC officers to express appreciation for federal student aid only with an accompanying explanation that no endorsement of general New Deal policy was implied. Such caution may explain the surprising decision to suspend the Committee on Federal Legislation in November 1935. As the committee was dropped, the AAC created a much more sedate Special Tax Service, which informed members about federal and state tax laws and possible changes. In spite of a membership that included some tax-supported institutions, AAC legislative policy steadily took the position of the private sector. "The colleges," wrote Kelly, "have not asked that they become the wards of the state or nation. They have asked and are asking that their funds and properties shall not be exploited."[18]

An early student of group representation before Congress dubbed the ACE, somewhat excessively, "the respected spokesman of a powerful group." He had to concede, however, that its varied membership sometimes forced it to equivocate. That was in 1929. The chair of the ACE's Committee on Federal Legislation during the 1920s, President John H. MacCracken of Lafayette College, favored "the voluntary maintenance of representatives of all important interests in Washington" and did not consider the ACE to be above politics. Surveys of pending legislation in early issues of the *Educational Record* helped keep institutions informed, and there was some rallying of members to make themselves heard on Capitol Hill. One issue was the threat of import taxes on books and scientific equipment. The ACE's legislative committee dwindled away, however, as anticipations for influence shifted to Hoover's National Advisory Committee on Education, which Mann chaired. Vain hopes. As the Hoover administration lost support, chances evaporated that Mann and his committee could command congressional attention.[19]

"In all the recent welter of social legislation," Zook complained as he looked back on the New Deal record, "totally inadequate consideration has been given to the part which higher education plays in social progress and to the necessity of adequately supporting it from both public and private funds." Indeed, the New Deal's low priority for educational matters was early evident to Zook and his associate director, Clarence S. Marsh. Zook arrived at the ACE directly after his year as head of the USOE under Roosevelt, having watched its appropriation drop some 17 percent, and Marsh left the educational directorship of the Civilian Conservation Corps (CCC) after his proposals for program expansion had been rejected. Although the ACE-sponsored American Youth Commission developed experimental programs as models for both the CCC and the National Youth Administration (NYA), as well as issuing Newton Edwards's *Equal Educational Opportunity for Youth: A National Responsibility*, the commission had little effect on the New Deal. As vice-chairman of Roosevelt's Advisory Committee on Education, 1937–38, Zook took pride in its reliance on a number of the ACE's earlier research studies, but the Advisory Committee's proposal for federal grants to lessen inequalities in public schools never advanced beyond a congressional committee. Roosevelt himself was found to oppose the idea.[20]

In its 1930s legislative policy for higher education, the ACE sought more often to block government action than to increase federal aid. In 1933, eager to assure the exemption of educational institutions from NRA codes, the ACE set up a Committee on the National Recovery Act, renamed in 1935 the Committee on National Legislation. Headed by President Cloyd H. Marvin of George Washington University, who skillfully exploited his location in the nation's capital, and including representatives of the AAC, the NEA, and the National Catholic Educational Association, the committee flourished during 1935. It helped defeat provisions of revenue bills that would have discouraged gifts and bequests to educational institutions. Similarly, it helped assure exemption for educational institutions from the Social Security Act, the employers' tax provision being viewed as onerous. After lapsing into little more than a standby, the Marvin group revived in 1938, when it lobbied successfully against a donor-discouraging section of the pending revenue bill.[21]

Proposals for increasing federal aid were largely restricted to elementary and secondary education. During the shake-up of 1934, the ACE established a Committee on Education and Government (later the Committee on Government and Educational Finance) to continue Zook's recent efforts as commissioner of education to demonstrate the need for federal aid to schools. The committee highlighted the widely differing levels of support among the states, showing those with least resources to have most school-aged children. A prior ACE project, the Educational Finance Inquiry, had produced similar data in the early 1920s.[22]

Although it tended in congressional relations to support the position of private institutions, the ACE provided its tax-supported members with an elaborate research program on state government's role in education. The Committee on Government and Educational Organization, appointed in 1932, investigated the educational role of states and their subdivisions, publishing studies such as Alexander Brody's *Higher Education and the American State,* based on court decisions. As its concern for elementary and secondary education deepened, more and more of the council's publications dealt with state issues and, beginning in 1937, it issued the *Yearbook of School Law.* It also considered ways to bring educational associations closer to organizations of state and local officials, recently united in the Public Administration Clearing House in Chicago. Zook hoped at one time that educational associations might develop "secretariats" and locate them in the same Chicago building as the Public Administration Clearing House, suggesting his admiration for its effectiveness in influencing New Deal policy.[23]

In 1939 the ACE grappled directly with the issue of whether its mission should include efforts to influence legislation. The catalyst was a debate over whether or not to resist the inclusion of educational institutions under Social Security in pending revisions of the law (in the event, they were not included). As often before, the ACE had to consider its special situation as an association with other associations as members. Most of these constituents had a homogeneity that the ACE lacked. Accordingly, they seemed better suited to protect their institutional members' legislative interests, or so the ACE executive committee reasoned. There was opposition to this retreat, especially from Marvin. Only after spirited debate on the floor of the annual meeting did the disclaimer of lobbying become established ACE policy. The approved resolution reasserted the council's "fundamental nature as a research and general promotion organization in American education," which "should not take an active position for or against specific legislative measures." A loophole remained, however. It was deemed desirable to give legislative bodies "information bearing on specific proposals." Perhaps the approaching end of the five-year subvention from the General Education Board explains this renewed emphasis on apolitical functions. Its growing reputation as a lobbying group had tended to weaken the ACE's claims to be a source of objective research data. Skeptics had come to doubt that a lobby was not a lobby when it was an educational lobby.[24]

The Drive for a Department of Education

The Bureau of Education, founded in 1867, antedated the higher education associations. Although originally called "the Department of Education" it was not of cabinet status, and after two years Congress reduced it to a modestly funded section of the Department of the Interior. Since limits on the federal government's role in education helped justify establishment of the higher education associations, they might have been expected to oppose USBE expansion, but these groups did the opposite. The case invites close inquiry.

The associations promised cooperation to Kendric C. Babcock, who had left the presidency of the University of Arizona in 1910 to take a new post at the USBE as Specialist in Higher Education. He forecast for his office the roles of inspector, critic, and standardizer. Such activist plans were discouraged when Presidents Taft and Wilson blocked the bureau's first accredited list. Still, during the 1910s and 1920s, the head of the USBE Division of Higher Education not only attended association meetings, sometimes as a voting member, but often visited institutions and conducted invited surveys of higher education in various states.[25]

For some time the bureau was responsible for oversight of the land-grant colleges in conjunction with distributing federal funds to them. They were generally satisfied with these activities, even though one educator imagined the bureau conspiring with foundation leaders to gain control of state university policies. Such suspicions were atypical. In 1926, hoping apparently to put pressure on laggard members and penurious state governments, the ALGCU asked that the USBE conduct a detailed survey of land-grant institutions. Congress voted special funding, and the study, with recommendations for every phase of institutional development, appeared in 1930 after preliminary sharing of findings with the ALGCU.[26]

A survey in 1939 of the activities of the Division of Higher Education in the USOE included virtually nothing that some association was not also doing. The overlap in functions between government agency and third-sector associations suggested the willingness of those in charge to live with organizational ambiguity. Often the availability of funds seemed to determine whether the USOE or an association performed a function. In fiscal 1935, when expenditures for the USOE were $588,000, those for the ACE were $209,000. The increase in the number of professionals in the USOE's Division of Higher Education from four in 1930 to eight in 1940 kept it only moderately larger than the ACE central office.[27]

In dealing with the federal education agency, association leaders revealed no sense of encountering an overwhelming bureaucracy or sharply different functions from their own. Indeed, those who held the directorship of the ACE, when they did not count themselves leading candidates for chief federal educational officer, felt at least entitled to a role in determining the appointment. The commissionership in 1921 went to John James Tigert IV, a professor at the University of Kentucky whose Chautauqua lectures had attracted the support of the American Legion. From his office at the ACE, Capen sought to organize a protest, branding Tigert a "person practically unknown to educational leaders." Capen felt that the post belonged, if not to him, at least to someone among the elite who had recently struggled with issues of educational centralization and wartime service. Critics of the "Educational Trust," however, could see Tigert's appointment as a triumph for grass-roots democracy.[28]

Forecast of the associations' backing for a Department of Education can be found in the support the AAACES gave the elevation of the commissioner of agriculture to cabinet rank in the 1880s. Those pursuing their interests through government expected to benefit from prestige in the responsible governmental agency. As the theory of triocracy suggests, voluntary groups that perform quasi-governmental functions may well seek to strengthen a related government agency and vice versa. Although their ideology decreed limits and caused ambivalence, the association leaders were not opponents of governmental expansion. To further their interests, they were willing to use various means, including government.[29]

A sustained drive for a Department of Education began during World War I. Early in 1918, the joint meeting of association executive committees that set up a constitution-drafting committee for the new ECE appointed another committee to draw up recommendations for a Department of Education. A single brochure announced the proposals of both committees. Besides coordinating the many wartime educational initiatives, the case maintained, a department could better treat international educational problems. It was seen not as a disburser of funds, but as an agency to "unify, direct, and stimulate effort, and . . . give just recognition to the dignity and practical importance of education in the national life." The AAC had backed such an initiative at its annual meeting in January 1918 and reaffirmed its support a year later. An ECE committee calling on President Wilson found him unwilling to support the change during wartime, but the campaign continued. It remained the particular concern of Lafayette's Mac-Cracken and the ACE's Committee on National Legislation.[30]

About the same time, the NEA also began pressing the matter. With Professor George D. Strayer of Teachers College using the NEA's Emergency Commission as a vehicle, that association became the nation's most active proponent of a federal Department of Education. The NEA group favored an omnibus bill that included generous disbursement of funds to states, a version expected to benefit public school teachers and win more congressional votes. ACE members were far more cautious about federal financial aid. Proposals from both the ACE and the NEA were submitted to Senator Hoke Smith of Georgia, who favored the NEA version but modified it to bring it closer to the matching-grant approach developed for his earlier legislative triumph, the Smith-Lever Act of 1914. He saw no point in a department that did not have plenty of money to spend. The ACE committee, having decided that it could neither support nor oppose the bill that resulted, was upset when Robert L. Kelly testified in the fall that the ACE favored it. Smith's bill and later variants became a major issue for the young ACE.[31]

When chosen to head the ACE, Capen was already identified with support for elevating the USBE to department rank. Like many others who had experienced the organizational drive of World War I, he believed in assigning government leadership posts to representatives of private institutions. For Capen, it was not federal financing that seemed important, but rather the recognition of specialized intelligence through official status in the federal government. He considered the use of matching grants inferior to "the exercise of genuine intellectual leadership." According to him, the proposed department should be primarily "a coordinating, planning and investigating body." After the NEA's aggressive widening of the project and Kelly's indiscreet announcement of ACE support for the omnibus bill, Capen moved cautiously.[32]

The issue of the federal role in education dominated the ACE's annual meeting of May 1920, giving early evidence of the strains inherent in an umbrella organization. Charles H. Judd, head of the School of Education at the University of Chicago and guiding spirit of the elite network of educational experts that met privately as the "Cleveland Conference," minced no words. He condemned the Smith-Towner bill as "a strong states rights measure" that ignored the possibilities of central professional leadership and treated the federal government "as a kind of unintelligent reservoir." In line with his cautions, the meeting voted to support only further study of the issue. This decision came in the face of strong protests from an NEA representative that the Smith-Towner bill was already widely understood and supported by groups often at odds on other issues (among them, the American Legion, the American Federation of Labor, the Daughters of the American Revolution, and the League of Women Voters). With the two organizations at cross purposes, the NEA withdrew from membership in the ACE, returning only in 1923.[33]

It was easier for the ACE annual meeting to withhold support of the proposed legislation because the executive committee had already scheduled a referendum among members. Faculties and executive committees of constituent associations found themselves addressing the matter in the fall of 1920, and the *Educational Record* reported in April 1921 the results from seventy-seven responses (about a 50 percent return). Diverse modes of responding made it impossible to derive an exact count. Although an "overwhelming majority" favored a Department of Education, an almost equal number objected to the Smith-Towner bill as it stood. Nor did the poll endorse the Kenyon bill to establish a Department of Public Welfare that would include educational functions (a position favored by President Harding). Since nine questions had been submitted, results had a miscellaneous quality that made an ACE endorsement of any particular bill unlikely. But Capen hoped that this problem would not prevent the group's advising Congress on "the views of educational officers."[34]

Results from constituent members suggested troublesome variation among associations within the ACE. An AAU poll in 1918 had shown that, of its twenty-four members, fourteen (including almost all state university members) favored a federal department. In 1920, perhaps because it recognized a divisive issue between public and private universities, the AAU executive committee decided against participating in the ACE's referendum. The land-grant association's response showed its unique position in having established strong bonds to a federal agency. Although approving the general purposes of the Smith-Towner bill, the group asked for guaranteed continuation of its members' connections with the Department of Agriculture, especially in research and extension.[35]

At its 1921 meeting, the ACE formally recognized that its referendum results favored a Department of Education but noted that this was not equivalent to endorsing "any measure now before Congress." The gathered delegates listened skeptically as a representative of President Harding plumped for a Department of Public Welfare. Shortly thereafter, ACE representatives joined in congressional testimony urging that education be dropped from the proposed department, which they predicted would be preoccupied with veterans' problems. Concern for status weighed importantly in associational leaders' appraisals. "Indeed, the prestige of education is damaged rather than enhanced by replacing the Commissioner of Education by an Assistant Secretary of Public Welfare."[36]

Having helped forestall the creation of a Department of Public Welfare, the ACE returned to advocacy of a separate Department of Education, and in 1923 Capen joined in petitioning the president on behalf of that cause. MacCracken, speaking for the ACE's legislative committee, attacked the U.S. Chamber of Commerce for its opposition, scoffing at its contention that a Department of Education would lead to federal domination. With the American Federation of Labor supporting the pending bill for a department, he predicted a successful coalition of labor and educational interests. Later, he warned "the educational spokesmen of capitalism" against resisting "the natural and justifiable ambition of the educational forces of the country to be represented in the national councils." It was a surprisingly blunt claim to political power. As in earlier pronouncements on the issue of a department, concern for professional status added an edge of passion.[37]

The proposed financial aid to states continued to alienate some leaders of private higher education; nevertheless, at its January 1924 meeting the AAC tabled a motion to oppose the current omnibus bill for a Department of Education. A year later, as already related, the AAC sponsored a debate between Strayer and Judd on the bill's merits. In fact, repeated failures to win a Department of Education linked to matching grants had discouraged that strategy's proponents, and hopes were shortly to shift to a new drive for a more limited department. The resulting Curtis-Reed bill, which omitted any provision for subsidies, resembled the plan originally proposed by the Emergency Council on Education in 1918. The new approach, signaled in the 1925 annual report of the ACE's director, was soon embraced by Strayer, then influential in both the NEA and the ACE. He urged the two groups to cooperate in support of a new bill free from the omnibus features that had divided leaders of higher education.[38]

Appraising the situation in 1925, Mann expressed irritation that agriculture, commerce, and labor were accorded a rank in the federal government denied to education. After all, education was becoming a science, and it embraced far more than formal schooling. He spelled out the associationalist ideal for a department even more fully than Capen had. It should be dedicated, not to distributing funds, but to "intelligent collection, classification and dissemination of facts," including results of educational experiments. A proper agency should be "manned" by experts, whose competence would allow them "to use discretion in the selection of facts." This design for a department, unlike a program of grants, would offer guarantees against unwarranted centralized power: "a properly constituted fact-finding Federal office could not if it would either drag education under political control or impair the powers of the indestructible states." Associationalism would retain its importance. "The various voluntary professional organizations of teachers, of educational institutions and of religious denominations" were also fact finders and could counteract any slanted presentations. Those who had blamed the link to federal grants for blocking earlier efforts for a department learned to their distress that a stripped-down plan also lacked adequate political appeal. The Curtis-Reed bill, introduced into both the Sixty-ninth and Seventieth Congresses, never came close to passage.[39]

In 1929, educators' attention was diverted from the issue of a new department by President Hoover's appointment (through Secretary of the Interior Wilbur) of the National Advisory Committee on Education. Wilbur, who saw centralization as a menace, had elevated the Bureau of Education to an "Office" in 1929, probably hoping to derail the drive for a new department. As director of the ACE, a Republican, and a critic of federal grants to public education, Mann was named chairman of the Advisory Committee in spite of his recent support for a department. That the NACE brought in the surprising recommendation for a cabinet-level department owed less to Mann's predilections than to the breadth of the NACE's membership and its unusual procedure in releasing a preliminary report for criticism and commentary. Wilbur, pleased at the general decentralist tone of the report, indicated that its recommendation for a department should have further study. By the time the report appeared, the Depression overshadowed any interest in such administrative reorganization. The bill for a research-oriented department of the type the NACE favored was stillborn.[40]

To New Dealers, with their bold creating and regrouping of agencies, mere cabinet restructuring seemed a very old-fashioned idea. The drive for a Department of Education, in which association leaders had been involved since 1918, sometimes intensely, faded from their attention and even their memory.

CHAPTER 7

Minerva and Mars

UNLIKE the USOE, which was a steady but weak ally for the educational associations, the War Department could shift dramatically in its relations with academia, and its power was sometimes immense. As creatures of the twentieth century, it was the fate of the institutional associations to devote much of their effort to their members' involvement in war, preparations for war, and war's aftermath. With their links to world power politics, these endeavors severely tested the associational ideology, especially its resistance to expanded government power and its claim both to meet members' institutional needs and to serve a wider national interest.

THROUGH WORLD WAR I

Even among land-grant colleges, which were obliged by terms of the Morrill Act to teach "military tactics," interest in things military varied widely during the late nineteenth century. Inactive institutions tended to blame lack of support from the War Department, while others made do and claimed to find great moral, mental, and physical benefits for students in compulsory military drill. In 1889 the AAACES initiated negotiations with the department which regularized the providing of Army officers as instructors and clarified course content. These changes improved training enough to let one association stalwart boast that in the Spanish-American War many land-grant college alumni had proved "quite as well educated and quite as capable as graduates of West Point."[1]

After association protest, the War Department eased both the directive that had limited officers' academic terms to two years and the stringent specifications of proper military instruction. At the time of this settlement in 1904, the AAACES displayed its solidarity through a resolution declaring it "unwise to require military drill from each student more than two times per week during two years." But the War Department could still be coercive. Although the Morrill Act did not provide that military training must be required of male students, the department refused to detail officers to land-grant institutions unless they made that their policy. The closest student of these early encounters with the military has concluded that the land-grant colleges won their struggle for curricular autonomy but lost in efforts to get support for equipment.[2]

Offended by the haphazard quality of military training in colleges, especially in the land-grant institutions, Chief of Staff Leonard Wood began planning summer military training camps for college students. First held in 1913, these camps were the germ of the "Plattsburg system." Besides attracting business and professional men to become trainees, the Plattsburg program served as a vehicle for advocates of universal military training. Particularly in certain private eastern colleges, presidents encouraged their students to qualify as reserve officers, partly out of concern that these young men lacked discipline and partly to gain for those institutions some of the reputation for social service that increasingly attached to midwestern state universities. The movement's Advisory Committee of University Presidents consisted exclusively of heads of non-land-grant institutions, including Harvard, Yale, Princeton, and the Universities of Alabama and Michigan.[3]

Opinions differed on military training for collegians. President Schurman of Cornell hailed gains in national preparedness and student discipline, whereas President Strong of Kansas feared that universities would "forfeit their claims to spiritual leadership." But there was virtually no resistance when the associations tried to help member institutions learn about military training and the ways of the War Department. Addresses from Army representatives became standard fare at annual meetings, and the executive committees of the NASU and the AAACES met jointly in 1915 to consider increasing the amount of compulsory military training in member institutions. Representative presidents launched a lobbying drive on behalf of various bills to support military training at colleges and universities. Satisfaction came with the inclusion in the National Defense Act of June 1916 of provisions for reserve officer training, for which any college that could muster one hundred able-bodied male students might apply. The plan was a careful piece of work whose essential provisions have controlled the Reserve Officer Training Corps (ROTC) program ever since.[4]

Operating under the newly passed bill, the War Department proceeded with plans to extend military training programs in colleges to four years, thus fitting graduates for officers' commissions. In some cases, the department even sent officers and equipment without waiting for institutional applications. When the proposal was debated at the AAU meeting of November 1916, President Arthur Twining Hadley of Yale called for cooperation, declaring that recently exposed inadequacies of the militia created both a duty and an opportunity for colleges. Yale, in fact, was already building an armory for its extracurricular program to train reserve artillery officers, a program Hadley was eager to have included in the regular curriculum. But Dean David Kinley of Illinois, whose institution had long included military training, mentioned past War Department high-handedness and suggested that, "when the federal government once gets its fingers in a university pie . . . , it is likely by administrative [decree] . . . to get its whole hand in." The universities, he feared, could be left with a curricular white elephant.[5]

Doubts about federal interference were laid aside when the United States entered World War I, and the academic community embraced the national cause unreservedly. Extravagant promises of support for the president and the armed forces were issued by academic chieftains, made on behalf of what one of them called "our great army of students and teachers." Within a week of the declaration of war, the AAC held an emergency meeting in Chicago, and both the AAC and the NASU held special meetings in Washington in conjunction with a conference of academic administrators the next month. The conference had been initiated by Hollis Godfrey, president of Drexel Institute and "a somewhat erratic egomaniac." Godfrey's unrelenting promotion of preparedness had made him the representative of engineering on the Advisory Commission to the Council of National Defense (CND— made up of six cabinet members and itself a presidentially appointed advisory group). With no member of the Advisory Commission assigned to education, he moved into that area.[6]

Godfrey was in the chair when representatives of the four institutional associations, the Society for the Promotion of Engineering Education, and about 180 institutions of higher education met in the "joint conference" of May 5, 1917. The gathering established a new committee of twenty-four, including representatives of the institutional associations. Although colleges and universities were assured that this link would keep them informed of their role in the war effort, the committee proved highly ineffective at providing liaison. Neither Godfrey's branch of the CND's Advisory Commission nor the USBE did much better. Confusion mounted among colleges and universities trying to adapt to wartime conditions.[7]

Without dissent the conference had resolved, "In the supreme crisis that confronts the nation, the colleges and universities of America have the single-minded thought and passion to summon to the country's service every resource at their command." But wartime patriotism did not in fact render academic leaders single-minded. The invitations to the joint conference noted as among its purposes "to secure conservation of our colleges and universities by concerted cooperation with Government." Part of the presidents' eagerness for military training programs sprang from their worries about the war's encroachments on faculty, administrators, students, and income.[8]

In wartime the military and higher education found themselves entangled, especially through their mutual interest in the recruitment of young men. Without male students, most colleges faced a financial threat from fixed costs. Wartime departures of faculty and administrators could also cripple an institution. While pledging support of the war, the joint conference recommended steps to prevent depopulation of academic institutions. It wanted college students under draft age to remain in school, with those in technical courses deferred and the number of ROTC units increased. In fact, the conference's preoccupation with institutional preservation so offended President Alexander Meiklejohn of Amherst College that he countered:

> If our boys are to go out to the front and risk their lives
> for the services [*sic*] of their country, willing to take death
> if it comes, I should say our institutions ought to go in the
> same mood; and I for one am willing to say I do not care
> whether or not, in that sense, Amherst College goes down—
> I am determined that she shall do what she can in the service
> of the country.

Other presidents were less self-sacrificial, even rhetorically.[9]

Although medical and dental students were given deferments under the Selective Service Act, which became law on May 18, 1917, there had been no attempt to defer other student categories. The draft at first affected only students over twenty-one, but the colleges suffered wide losses from enlistments, which academic leaders could not easily discourage without seeming unpatriotic. The spring and summer of 1917 saw a flood of efforts to get ROTC programs but with a war on, the Army had more pressing uses for officers and equipment. The land-grant colleges were the group best provided with military-training resources, yet they too were dissatisfied with War Department response. Small colleges belonging to the AAC pled for permission to merge their contingents of male students to get the minimum one hundred trainees and for summer officer training of faculty members who could then return to campus to give military instruction. The War Department rejected both plans.[10]

An angry letter from the head of the AAACES executive committee to presidents of land-grant colleges assailed the failure of the War Department to meet the provisions for ROTC programs in the National Defense Act.

> This would not seem to be a time for indifference toward the most permanent and most important resource the nation has. These colleges have been operating under the law and with the approval of the War Department ever since their founding. The Government should be brought to feel its obligation and no technical objection or military necessity should defeat the law.

A USBE study found that between the fall of 1916 and the fall of 1917 there had been a drop of one-third in the male enrollment at 38 agricultural colleges and one-fifth at 313 liberal arts colleges. There was only slight exaggeration in the recollection that "by the opening of the fall term [in 1917] the provision of military training was recognized as the sine qua non of a college's existence."[11]

When the AAU met in November 1917, the gathered administrators heard from President Marion Burton of Minnesota that, even if others might take it for granted that the AAU was behind the government, he had experience of "some rather strong undercurrents of disloyalty, if not sedition and treason." He prevailed upon his colleagues to express to President Wilson the association's "unswerving allegiance to the government of the United States and unwavering determination to fight the war through to a successful conclusion." In addition, however, the AAU wrote Secretary of War Newton D. Baker, telling him of the message to Wilson and—"prompted by the same loyalty and devotion"—urging that professional students be placed in a reserve corps until they finished their studies (the plan already in effect for medical and dental students). A similar blend of patriotism and institutional concern characterized much of wartime associational activity.[12]

In spite of the bandwagon effect and the tendency of institutions to vie with each other in demonstration of national loyalty, other values impinged on the associations as they pledged support of the war. Even in the euphoria of the May 5 joint conference, the president of the AAC had warned against "unreasoning devotion and response," citing as negative examples the Manifesto of the German Intellectuals and the indiscriminate enlistment of men from the British universities. At the NASU emergency meeting, one president warned against the creation of centralizing machinery that might threaten postwar institutional autonomy. Then, after a debate that impugned the Army's past permissiveness toward prostitution, the group passed a resolution calling for preventive steps, as well as wartime liquor prohibition. The AAC passed similar resolutions the next day, and its regular meeting the following January instructed the executive committee to take, besides measures for applying college resources to war service, other steps directed toward "making effective in the councils of the nation the collective public opinion of American higher education."[13]

Uncertainties about government policy increased as the academic year 1917–18 advanced. The inaccessibility of the War Department and its minimal attention to the dilemmas of higher education encouraged the elevation of academic leaders who thought of higher education nationally and wanted to influence government agencies. These men—among them Samuel P. Capen, Robert L. Kelly, Charles Riborg Mann, and William O. Thompson—would remain dominant as association officers after the war. Faced with the inadequacy of the coordinating apparatus under the CND, the colleges and universities again turned to an associational response, creating the Emergency Council on Education as a federation of federations. The founders hoped for improved coordination, greater visibility, and more influence with government, especially the military.[14]

The War Department meanwhile was designing its own program for educational centralization. Its new Committee on Education and Special Training (CEST) consisted of three officers who worked in conjunction with a Civilian Advisory Board, headed by Mann (identified in 1918 as "Expert in Engineering Education for the Carnegie Foundation"). Both the ECE and the CEST were formed early in 1918, and the ECE was consulted on the structure of the Advisory Board. Strongly skewed toward technical education, the board did, however, include as a representative of "universities and colleges" James Rowland Angell, Dean of Faculties at the University of Chicago, and as a representative of "agriculture" a pillar of the AAACES, President Raymond A. Pearson of Iowa State College.[15]

Although short-term training of technicians was given priority, the CEST concerned itself from the beginning with the need for more advanced technically trained men ("professionals") and officers. In May, the eagerly waiting colleges learned of a new Students' Army Training Corps (SATC) for eighteen-to-twenty-one-year-olds, whose status would be that of enlisted men furloughed for schooling. Meanwhile, the ECE agreed that its publicity drive to keep students in college and attract more would stress the merits of the SATC. From his perspective on the CEST Advisory Board, Capen judged the ECE a very docile organization.[16]

The original prospect for colleges was cheering. With minimal disruption, they could both attract students and serve the war effort. A drastic change in plans for the SATC came, however, in late summer, 1918, with the lowering of the draft age from twenty-one to eighteen. This meant that some students in the SATC would be trained for only three months with no time for academic courses, and all students in the program would be considered on active service, living on campus under full military discipline. The future alternatives for the students were regular service as enlisted men as soon as needed (the most likely), officer or noncommissioned officer training camps, or continued study in a technical profession. Contrary to newspaper accounts, Capen predicted, the War Department's prescriptions would be limited and humane; besides, the new arrangements would let poor men's sons get into college. From the Army's point of view the plan kept men mobilized at a cost somewhat less than that on military bases, but this attitude bred uncertainties that undercut educational goals, even highly instrumental ones.[17]

Back in 1903 Penn State's George W. Atherton had complained that some officers arrived "with an impression that they have been sent to take command of the institution." Now there was even more likelihood of such an offense. Cadets were kept from classes and laboratory sections by guard duty, drill, or kitchen police and were abruptly called out of classrooms. There was, as one of the more sympathetic accounts put it, "an unfortunate dualism of authority." Academic presidents, many of whom had earlier begged for military training in their institutions, now felt their control challenged by officers in charge of the program. Faculty, feeling the sanctity of the classroom violated, were even readier to protest. Perhaps worst of all, they found academic work denigrated by officers in charge and academic standards deteriorating. Some who had at first been proud to have colleges recognized as an essential industry decided that the new program was close to a disaster.[18]

The influenza epidemic increased the difficulties of the program and further associated it with danger to academic communities. The NASU annual meeting, which took place on the day the armistice was signed, found the presidents vying with each other to tell of Army mismanagement and arrogance, complaints not silenced by conciliatory addresses from Mann and General Robert I. Rees, head of the CEST. Although some within the CEST hoped to maintain the SATC "as an educational experiment and as an organization for training discharged soldiers for higher usefulness in civil life," influential congressmen quashed the idea. By late December 1918, the last of the SATC members were mustered out.[19]

Bitter memories of the SATC period lingered. It did not help when the program's final report insisted that former college loafers had become enthusiastic learners in Army programs and claimed despite contrary evidence to find "a universally expressed desire that the remarkable spirit and snap of the war training be maintained and made permanent in all education." The CEST review ended with plugs for ROTC and a "universal service law" modeled on Selective Service. The associations provided a setting where representatives of the CEST and its Advisory Board could try to patch things up. Appearing before the institutional associations and elsewhere, these men admitted the SATC's great unpopularity with faculty and administrators. They pled that its six weeks in use had been long enough to expose its weaknesses, but not long enough to reform the system. The War Department, faced with a sudden loss of authority in higher education, promptly bent its efforts toward resurrecting ROTC programs. Despite the sour aftertaste of the SATC, many institutions proved eager to cooperate, and association meetings featured sessions on how to apply for an ROTC program and what to expect from military authorities in Washington.[20]

DURING WORLD WAR II

In retrospect, the most telling change for higher education during World War II was the movement of its scientists and engineers into weapons development. The new government policy of contracting with professors who continued to work in their university laboratories set a pattern of government contract research that was to remake postwar institutional budgets. Spectacular successes under the Office of Scientific Research and Development, notably its initiation of atomic weapons research, ultimately overshadowed the problems of "manpower" and training that bedeviled institutional administrators and tested the associational tradition. Still, it was those problems that chiefly disturbed educators, beginning in 1939.[21]

With participants in World War I military training still on the scene and with a matured ROTC program, there was reason to believe that higher education and the military understood each other's methods and values better than they had in 1917. The greatest difference for educational associations from the situation at the outbreak of World War I was, of course, the existence of a national umbrella organization. Much of the hope for improved relations between higher education and government during the new war rested with the ACE, particularly its central office in Washington.

The ACE took very seriously its duty to plan ahead. In November 1939, it employed Francis J. Brown, a sociology professor from NYU, to interview government officials about defense measures and hold planning conferences. He developed close relations with representatives of the National Resources Planning Board and the War and Navy Departments. Statements on ACE goals, which had recently stressed equal educational opportunity, began shifting to themes of military preparedness. In August 1940, under ACE auspices, the first issue of an information bulletin, *Higher Education and National Defense*, appeared and an ACE committee redesigned teacher qualification examinations to make them usable by the military in officer selection, yet protection of member institutions remained the major associational objective. The ACE's new Committee on Education and National Defense took pains to ask that efforts to mobilize be weighed against the need for "conservation of educational values, resources, and personnel."[22]

Facing the pressure of pending selective service legislation in the summer of 1940, the ACE and the NEA jointly established a National Committee on Education and Defense, superseding the ACE's defense committee. The drive for a peacetime draft came most importantly from the Military Training Camps Association, an influential group created out of the Plattsburg movement. Although this organization dominated the design of the bill, most of the educational associations offered testimony, generally favorable, before congressional committees. Since no one under twenty-one was to be drafted, there was little immediate threat to undergraduate enrollments. Still, the potential impact on graduate enrollments and a possible future drop in the eligibility age caused uneasiness among institutions whose financial condition had already been weakened by a decade of depression. The educators arranged for the act to postpone induction of a drafted student till the end of the spring semester, but in their wish to defer students in designated essential fields they had to settle for language citing "endeavors . . . necessary to the maintenance of the national health, safety, or interest," rather than an explicit reference to students. As the Selective Service regulations on deferment emerged, however, they proved largely to the educators' liking.[23]

National defense set the tone of the associations' 1941 conventions. The AAU heard addresses by the Director of Selective Service and Admiral Chester W. Nimitz. The meeting dwelt on the draft's effect on students and the loss of staff to defense activities. A stiff upper lip muted complaining, but there was much insistence that, even in a war emergency, higher education must not forget its long-range duty to humanistic values. The land-grant association joined in the AAU's earlier resolution deploring the drain of defense projects on university personnel, asked for more ROTC buildings, and heard an optimistic answer from the chancellor of Oregon State College to his question, "Can America Develop an Antidote for the Doctrines of Hitlerism?" Small colleges once again turned to the AAC with their fears of being bypassed in military training plans and perhaps having to close for lack of students. That association requested an amendment to the draft law that "would put all institutions of higher learning upon the same basis" and resolved that citizenship education was as important as military science for the perpetuation of democracy.[24]

In the wake of Pearl Harbor, early in January 1942, at a meeting jointly sponsored by the USOE and the ACE-NEA National Committee on Education and Defense, one thousand college and university presidents pledged their institutions' "total strength" to the war effort, promising to accelerate programs and improve student health. After hearing Capen recount the history of academic-military relations in World War I and draw hopeful contrasts with the present, the gathering requested surveys of trained personnel requirements for war and peace as well as an explicit national policy to assure continued effective instruction. Selective service—with proper deferments—was endorsed as the most rational means for matching individual capabilities with national wartime needs.[25]

During the next few months, however, educators' frustrations with government mounted. "The Washington jungle grew more tangled and dense as the months of 1942 went by," one university president recalled. Various committees, most of them linked to the institutional associations, sought to influence training policies of the Army, the Navy, and (after its creation in April 1942) the War Manpower Commission. The existing programs (the Army's Enlisted Reserve Corps and the Navy's V-1, V-5, and V-7), created from men already enrolled in college, seemed unfair and confusing, with little reassurance that they would in a long war sustain college enrollments.[26]

Well aware that the draft age could soon be lowered to eighteen and fearing a public reaction if students who were training for "necessary" fields continued to be deferred, the ACE convened a conference of about one hundred academic presidents in July. Deploring a lack of coordinated planning for wartime training and current underutilization of higher education, the conference proposed to make colleges and universities the source of "a continuous flow of highly trained manpower." Since it would also mean a continuous flow of students into academic institutions, the plan was transparently self-protective. It included not only future military and naval personnel, but also technical specialists for essential civilian posts, many of whom would be women and men physically unqualified for the armed forces. "Economic status, race or creed" ought not to be permitted to restrict entrance into the program. To show that smaller institutions could be involved, the plan stressed qualities of understanding, stamina, and leadership as essentials for good officers. The ACE, it was suggested, should become the nongovernmental agency to implement the proposals and facilitate government-institutional cooperation.[27]

In response to this initiative, the War Manpower Commission began intensive consultation and study. The outcome was an August ruling that all able-bodied male students were destined for the armed forces and that "responsibility for determining the specific training for such students" rested with the Army and the Navy. Although greatly disappointed to have military training disjoined from civilian, the ACE prepared to cooperate in designing new programs. Edmund E. Day, president of Cornell, a former foundation officer who had recently emerged as an important leader in the ACE, headed its new Committee on the Relationships of Higher Education to the Federal Government. "The Day Committee," carefully representing various categories of higher education and with an executive committee of its own, became the chief educational liaison with military and naval planners.[28]

The Army showed little inclination to negotiate with educators, some of whom feared undue curricular narrowing. A special assistant to the secretary of war told the Day Committee that, since increasing military effectiveness was the only acceptable ground for assigning men to academic institutions, it was "the responsibility of the Army to determine the kind and speed of such training." Word of the Army's obduracy reached the White House from various sources, and, after a plea by Guy Snavely of the AAC, Roosevelt asked the secretaries of war and the Navy to launch a new study. It should seek "the highest utilization of the American colleges," bearing in mind the likelihood of a draft age lowered to eighteen.[29]

Unhappy with preliminary proposals for Army-Navy use of colleges and universities, the Day Committee recommended a single Enlisted Training Corps for both armed services with oversight by a joint Army-Navy-civilian board. The plan had many advantages from the institutions' perspective. It would include junior colleges and smaller liberal arts colleges, the institutions would have considerable control over admission of trainees, and entry would operate "democratically" through competitive standards supposedly independent of economic status. Conveniently timed annual meetings of the NASU and the AAC endorsed the plan, which, not surprisingly, won wide approval when submitted to the institutions.[30]

Although the Navy established its V-12 program close to the suggested pattern, the Day Committee proposal failed to evoke the desired coordination between the two armed services (their main programs even had different term lengths). The Army Specialized Training Program (ASTP) emerged little changed from the plan the War Department had shown the committee in September 1942. All enrollees would undergo basic training before moving to a college, an arrangement that would allow them to be quickly called as emergency replacements. All assignments to specific institutions would be made unilaterally by the Army. Although ACE-nominated educators did participate in ASTP curriculum design, the training allowed very little general education. Still, the programs added approximately 200,000 enrollments in the fall of 1943, bringing the number of male students to about four-fifths of the prewar figure.[31]

ACE-sponsored plans had called for more. Zook continued to criticize the armed services and the War Manpower Commission for their failure fully to utilize academic capacity. He complained in January 1944 of the small number of contracts compared to the number during World War I. With the perspective of a national coordinating association, he cited categories of institutions that were underutilized: "teachers colleges, colleges for women, small liberal arts colleges, colleges for Negroes, and junior colleges."[32]

The ASTP and the V-12 placed enrollees under military discipline and gave them the base pay of enlisted men. The associations approved the arrangement, seeing in it protection against charges that student trainees were slackers. Entry from among men already in the Army was based largely on results of the Army General Classification Test. Another avenue let high school students establish eligibility through preinduction tests. In short, the program allowed some men who otherwise would not have attended college to do so, a step welcomed by academic administrators who feared accusations of class-based favoritism. Such fears had been part of the motivation of the associations when in 1942 they helped secure passage of a federal loan program for students pursuing "necessary" programs with accelerated schedules that prevented their taking summer jobs. Most academic leaders were genuinely eager to make higher education more accessible, but they were also attentive to public relations considerations.[33]

Although academic and military authority necessarily overlapped, the ASTP kept the distinction much clearer than had its World War I predecessor. Some faculty and administrators admired the ASTP's precision of aims, concentration of effort, and meritocratic standards. But others complained. Classes and study time were interrupted by routine military obligations, such as inspections. The demanding pace raised doubts about whether lessons could be assimilated. One disgruntled academic president charged that the special programs had brought "curtailment of health service to civilian students because of a depleted medical staff" and "additional loads of clerical work in administrative offices with depleted clerical personnel." Such misgivings, however, were not the main source of bitter recollections left by the ASTP.[34]

Overtones of failure and tragedy arose from the program's virtual termination in February 1944. Already in a replacement crisis and facing urgent need of troops for the invasion of France, the War Department at that time transferred most ASTP students directly to infantry units as privates. For all their earlier rhetoric about wartime sacrifice, academic leaders felt betrayed, concluding that their institutions had served as stockpiles of replacements rather than part of a reasoned, coordinated training policy that fit abilities to national security needs. The academic year 1944–45 was the leanest of the war period. Army and Navy contracts with colleges and universities amounted to only 37 percent of those of the previous year, and civilian male enrollment to only 27 percent of the 1939–40 figure. There was little the associations could do, although some propagandized on behalf of more higher education for women and the acceptability as college students of seventeen-year-old males.[35]

The ACE came into its own in mid-1942, the historian William M. Tuttle, Jr., has concluded, when it called the special July meeting to press the government for a coordinated training program. Although the proposed training corps to include civilians and members of both armed services was not achieved, the Navy's V-12 program emerged largely within the Day Committee's guidelines. Perhaps the strongest evidence that colleges and universities had clout in Washington was the complaining within the War Department about the creation of the ASTP. Undersecretary of War Robert P. Patterson declared the program a boondoggle, its creation representing capitulation to "heavy pressure from college presidents" who wanted a large program that would "take care of their colleges." Although the ASTP was established, however, it bore only slight resemblance to the proposals from academic leaders and collapsed when the Army needed its enrollees elsewhere. A group of presidents tried fruitlessly to save the ASTP through a plan to bring in seventeen-year-olds.[36]

On balance, the ACE and its constituent associations increased their stature with the federal government during World War II and improved their interest-group skills. They learned to bypass the USOE and go directly to more powerful parts of the administration. Profiting from its greater wartime visibility, the ACE established its position as the best-situated nongovernmental body to coordinate higher education. Its interests in the lower schools dwindled as it developed this new identity.[37]

Taking on quasi-official authority and sometimes bringing about policy changes, the ACE worked closely with the War Manpower Commission and the War and Navy Departments. In the crunch, however, the ACE remained an outside voluntary agency, a "pressure group" that could be stopped short by conflicting governmental purposes. Its leverage did not, for example, match that of the establishment lawyers in the Military Training Camps Association who had sought a peacetime draft of 1940. No balanced appraisal could maintain that the associations should have gotten all they asked for. One careful student of the period has granted that tangled lines of federal authority led to delay and confusion which virtually required academic leaders to frame coordinating plans of their own but has concluded that many of their proposals "had an air of impracticality and an unseemly concern with the problems of the institutions."[38]

Postwar Planning

Attention by the associations to postwar planning drew on memories of the disorderly aftermath of the 1918 armistice. Sometimes the issue was "standards." Believing that colleges had too casually given academic credit for World War I military experience, the ACE urged appraisal in the future by means of tests. It won the concurrence of the Joint Army-Navy Committee on Welfare and Recreation and in 1943 published *Sound Educational Credit for Military Experience*. The ACE also helped establish the United States Armed Forces Institute, widely known as USAFI, and appointed its advisory committee. USAFI, which outlasted the war, provided independent study for military personnel with possibilities for college credit.[39]

Even before the United States entered the war, the AAC established a commission on postwar problems. In mid-1942, the ACE set up a study group on education for veterans. Then, in November 1942, when Roosevelt signed the act lowering draft eligibility to age eighteen, he sweetened the occasion by pledging federal aid to veterans whose education had been interrupted by the war. The resulting Armed Forces Committee on Post-War Educational Opportunities for Service Personnel (the Osborn Committee) worked closely with advisors from the ACE (chiefly subgroups of the Day Committee).[40]

Although it had representatives on the Osborn Committee, the ACE also acted independently, sending information on its members' views about veterans' education to every member of Congress and forwarding its own plan to the White House in October 1943. Still preoccupied with deferment categories, the ACE, like the Osborn Committee in its plan, recommended limiting educational aid of more than one year to veterans selected on the basis of intellectual and educational qualifications. This limitation appeared in the original bill introduced for the administration in November 1943 by Senator Elbert D. Thomas. The mood of Congress proved generous, however, and expectations rose. Wider educational opportunities for veterans appealed to colleges recently suffering from war-diminished enrollment. An ACE-sponsored conference of associations in January 1944 endorsed support of virtually all veterans for four years of schooling. Meanwhile, Zook testified against two restrictions in the Thomas bill: one establishing state quotas on the number of veterans to be given educational support and another linking support to specific employment openings predicted in the economy.[41]

Addressing the bill's provisions for administrative control, the associations favored their longtime partner, the USOE, over the Veterans Administration. But conservative congressmen associated the USOE with New Deal radicalism, and the American Legion feared a bureaucratic run-around if veterans' programs were spread among different agencies. The associations had to surrender their hopes for USOE control, although they did manage to block a proposal for Veterans Administration accreditation of educational institutions. An unprecedented meeting of the ACE's constituent (organizational) members in May 1944 may well have been scheduled to influence congressional action. The assemblage accepted the general purposes of pending legislation for veterans' educational aid but strongly hedged its support with resolutions urging that most oversight of the program be assigned to the states to avoid "federal bureaucratic control."[42]

Showing itself politically more adept than the educational associations, the American Legion drafted a far bolder measure than the Thomas bill, dubbed it "the G.I. Bill of Rights," and had it introduced in both houses of Congress. As finally adopted, the Servicemen's Readjustment Act (Public Law 346, Seventy-eighth Congress) was much closer to the legion version than to various proposals from the institutional associations. Although remembered largely for its educational provisions, the act was an inclusive veterans' support measure, an omnibus bill that no member of Congress cared to vote against. By aid in early planning and timely acquiescence in changes suggested by others, the educational associations managed to share credit for the act. No more than other advocates, however, did they foresee its revolutionary implications. After the GI Bill became law in June 1944, the associations listened to accounts of its educational provisions from

government officials and complained about the inadequacy of payments to institutions. Only an occasional comment hinted that the
results might have a major influence on enrollment.[43]

It was all very well to support a federal law that would turn veterans
into students, but proposed legislation for universal military training,
which would delay entry into college by high school graduates, was
quite another matter. The entanglement of the associations in the
issue of postwar universal military training would have come in any
case, but it had an early and directly presidential origin. In February
1944, three representatives of the ACE's Problems and Plans Committee called on Roosevelt to urge that seventeen-year-olds be admitted to the ASTP. Characteristically, the president diverted the
conversation to something else. He asked the visitors' opinion on a
compulsory national service system, himself putting the case for it
quite strongly. "There wouldn't be only military training; there would
be all sorts of educational aspects, and these boys would be in the
camps which are now largely empty." Expressing some misgivings, the
delegation suggested that the president might like a memorandum
on the subject from the Problems and Plans Committee. He said he
would.

This initiative stirred the committee into action. Its members, who
already had a study of the menace of federal control under way, greatly
disliked the president's scheme. They framed a statement relating the
proposed training to "Invasion of Education by the Federal Government," "The Probability of Military Control," and "Possible Totalitar-
ian Hazards." Later a joint meeting with the Educational Policies Commission (the comparable elite group based in the NEA and the AASA)
moderated the statement. The version sent to the president relied
chiefly on an argument for delay, given the profound abnormality of
wartime conditions. He failed to acknowledge the communication.[44]

When sent to all members of the ACE for a mailed ballot response,
the statement against universal military training received their endorsement ten to one. As in other cases, some presidents chose to
address the issue through ad hoc groups rather than the established
associations. Conant and eleven other university presidents published
an open letter to Roosevelt objecting to his advocacy of the national
service plan in the 1945 State of the Union address. Most but not all
of the twelve presidents headed institutions belonging to the AAU.
Shortly, fourteen other presidents of comparably prestigious institutions issued a letter favoring a prompt decision and warning of a
false sense of security once the war ended. "The fraternity of college
presidents," Conant recalled, "was split wide open."[45]

Lessons from wartime regarding government relations proved

sharply diverse. The vast potential of federal funding was dramatically demonstrated. In 1943–44 it provided both public and private institutions approximately 36 percent of their income, compared to about 5 percent in 1939–40. Wartime experience left academic leaders unsure of the desirability of continuing such support. Contract research and training programs had helped preserve the institutions during an emergency period, but negotiations and accounting had proved burdensome. More ominous was the perceived threat to institutional autonomy. In 1943 an AAC commission, while advocating educational aid to veterans, cautioned against direct federal grants to institutions.[46]

One worried member of the ACE Problems and Policies Committee (as it was now called) warned that "the overwhelming verdict of history is that control follows aid." Although a report by that committee, issued in January 1945, dealt with the lower schools, its animadversions on federal control had important implications for higher education. Meanwhile, however, the ACE's Francis J. Brown, as head of the staff for a House Education Committee report, helped make the case for federal aid. Many institutions during the war had "maintained themselves much as an animal lives off its own fat" and were now in "a state of low vitality." Softening the public-private distinction by referring to "privately administered" and "publicly administered" institutions, the report called for general tax-based aid.[47]

The interwar decades had done little to divorce educational opportunity from social class. The growth of urban universities had increased accessibility and New Deal student aid had made some difference, but in 1939–40 only 15.7 percent of Americans eighteen to twenty-one years old were in college. During the 1930s, Zook had used his platform at the ACE to urge equality of educational opportunity, but he usually tied this ideal to the lower schools and their need for federal aid.[48]

War accelerated change. The ACE-sponsored conference of July 1942 urged liberating wartime training from class, race, and religious distinctions. The Day Committee's plan for an Enlisted Training Corps for both military and civilian occupations would have admitted students competitively to a program financed by the government. Entry into the ASTP by soldiers who had scored well on the Army General Classification Test, as well as entry into the ASTP and V-12 through the preinduction Army-Navy College Qualifying Examination, brought colleges students with backgrounds unlike those of the regular academic clienteles. The results were usually interpreted positively, as an argument for greater academic openness. During the development of the GI Bill, the ACE came to support the most inclusive version.

Equal educational opportunity fit the democratic idealism of the war. For the institutional-minded, appeals for greater educational fairness suited concern about low enrollments and offered a promising rationale for federal funding. The role given examinations made greater inclusiveness appear safely meritocratic. Only the passage of the GI Bill, however, gave any hint that something revolutionary was at hand, and few caught the hint.

Seeking to identify positive aspects of the increased federal involvement in higher education, the ACE in 1945 created a foundation-funded Commission on Implications of Armed Services Educational Programs. In its monographs and summary report, particular praise went to wartime curricular innovations in interdepartmental courses, area studies, and "total immersion" language instruction, as well as "techniques for the democratic selection of high caliber students on the basis of native ability rather than economic status." Although concluding that government support of research raised issues of political control, overemphasis on applied inquiry, and diversion of talented teachers, the report endorsed plans for a National Science Foundation. There could be no denying "the need for a unified plan for the selection, training, conservation, and utilization of those possessing the potential abilities essential for the maintenance of America's leadership in scientific pursuits."[49]

Although many of their complaints about underutilization and calls for democratic fairness represented the narrower interests of their own members, the institutional associations had legitimately urged the social benefits of better coordination of wartime "manpower" policies. The associations did not have much success in that attempt or in their pursuit of timely information about the armed forces' intended use of higher education. Still, the associations played a creative role in shaping the GI Bill and debating universal military training. The ACE and the AAC, particularly, had insisted that victory in the war was not an adequate controlling goal for the nation or for organized education, although the perils of war and the elation of victory had muted criticisms of government wartime policy.

The associations entered the postwar years still ambivalent about their connections to government. Reinstitution of the ROTC was eagerly sought, but some leaders hoped the associations could revert to their earlier range of functions, with government relations dropping in importance. There was no such return, however. Relations with the federal government would dominate the agendas of the associations in the years to come.

The NASU Assembles in Wartime, 1945

•

SOME associations omitted an annual meeting during World War II. Not so the NASU. On April 27–28, 1945, it held its fourth wartime meeting, gathering in the luxury of Chicago's Edgewater Beach Hotel. Franklin D. Roosevelt had died two weeks before. Although Berlin had not yet fallen, V-E Day was clearly at hand. In the Pacific, however, the battle for Okinawa raged at terrible cost, and the expected invasion of the Japanese home islands portended long casualty lists.

The government still urged restraints on travel. No one from the West Coast attended the meeting, but thirty-two member institutions were represented, twenty-seven by their chief executives. The NASU cast had changed totally since 1905. The script, while revealing the same assertive institutional self-interest and the same uncritical nationalism, contained evidence of new concern about Washington's educational policies.

Although entitled "The State University and Its Neighbors," the presidential address by John C. West, head of the University of North Dakota, struck a tone less of neighborliness than of competition. He drew a disturbing analogy to what paleontologists had discovered in California tar pits. There, buried together, lay bones of both the extinct saber-toothed tiger and the adaptive and persisting coyote. In a world of struggle some educational institutions would survive. Others would not.

Apprehensively, West observed that, when state universities and other institutions were controlled by the same statewide board, there was a tendency to treat them all alike. Influenced by localist pressures, legislators showed a similar propensity. Aside from the issue of private-public competition, West was most worried that other public institutions would begin to share the reputation and financial support built by state universities during the last half-century. His institutionally protective attitude foreshadowed later efforts to assure "flagship" status to one part of a multiunit state higher education system. Even as he forecast danger from "neighbors," West assured his colleagues that the

NASU instilled "a feeling of deep respect and even of fear" in other groups, that Congress saw its power as potential but real, and that this "sleeping giant" had the capacity to "give public education a voice."

After the secretary-treasurer's report, Fred J. Kelly, head of the higher education division of the USOE, told about educational legislation recently introduced in Congress. His description of a bill to create a federal board for character education produced smiles, but he urged the assembled administrators to take the matter seriously. Other proposals were more likely to go through, such as school support under a federally funded equalization formula. One such plan allowed inclusion of private institutions, and another extended through the junior college level. In a second address that afternoon (substituting for "unavoidably detained" Commissioner of Education John W. Studebaker), Kelly linked this jumble of new calls for federal activity in education with plans to expand his own home agency. He put the case for the USOE with a conservatism intended to appeal to the NASU. The agency would encourage schools to do things voluntarily, without federal money, and would resist tendencies toward any system of federally controlled schools. Asking for no authority, the USOE would follow "normal processes of influence." Later the association voted to inform Congress that it supported USOE expansion.

Of more immediate interest to the presidents was the report from the "Special Committee on Perpetuation of the ROTC." At various conferences called by the War Department, members of the committee had urged that the military-academic alliance continue in peacetime, not only through expansion of the ROTC but in scientific and technological research, as well as defense industry development. Plans to enlarge the ROTC included making military science an undergraduate major and offering graduate training. Two Army officers next addressed the group, off the record, but doubtless supporting the earlier claim that "the contributions of the colleges to the training of officers are fully understood and highly appreciated" in the War Department.

In the afternoon, after Kelly's second address, the Special Committee to Study Postwar Educational Problems offered accounts of curricular reform. Dean Harry K. Newburn detailed the new liberal arts curriculum at Iowa. After two years of debate, some of it heated and including "interesting personal sidelights," which he assumed the presidents could recreate out of their own experiences, the faculty had adopted a new curriculum. The process reflected the difficulties of putting into curricular practice the widespread desire to promote general education. A foremost national advocate of general education, Norman Foerster, had resigned from the Iowa faculty in protest over inadequacies of the new program. Under the plan adopted, about one-fourth of a student's work must be in "core courses" divided among four divisions. These, Newburn insisted, were neither surveys nor lecture courses, provision being made in all cases for student participation in small sections. Following his dean, Iowa's President Virgil M. Hancher summarized his recent survey of member institutions' curricular activities. He had spotted trends toward competency examinations (a feature of Iowa's new plan), intensive foreign language training, fewer broad divisional survey courses, and majors that would be less strictly departmental, as in the case of area studies.

The principal "invited" address came from the recently retired dean of Harvard's Graduate School of Business Administration, Wallace B. Donham. Claiming that his deanly experience with graduates of five hundred colleges let him speak with authority, Donham pulled no punches. Products of engineering programs, he declared, emerged "in blinders" and helped cause "shocking failures in American industry." Liberal arts graduates did not escape denigration: mostly they were aimless victims of the elective system and of poor teaching by the overspecialized products of graduate schools. As to accrediting agencies, they were pushing education toward mediocrity through their literalness and rigidity. He quoted Alfred North Whitehead's observation that "knowledge does not keep any better than fish." Old knowledge must reach the students as if "just drawn out of the sea and with the freshness of its immediate importance." Donham joined the call for general education—"a core of habits and skills, capacity of cooperation, trained imagination, which can pull this country together again."

At the evening banquet, where participants no longer presented the "array of 'boiled shirts' and dinner jackets" which, a member recalled, had marked the event ten years before, the delegates heard briefly from a representative of the National Conference of Canadian Universities. The star of the evening was recently elected Senator J. William Fulbright. As a former state university president, he provided a special source of pride for NASU members. His verbal tour "Behind the Scenes with a Senator" was an intimate affair not destined for the printed page.

A late arrival at the next morning's session would have missed two humdrum commentaries from the Committee on Group Life of Students. President A. C. Willard of Illinois told about the benefits of his university's new union building. President Arthur A. Hauck of Maine pondered relations between returning veterans and civilian students. In discussion Colorado's Acting President Reuben G. Gustavson explained that on his campus the veterans' own organizations had helped administrators identify problems, notably the housing needs of married veterans.

The meeting turned its attention increasingly to the question of student veterans. References to tensions between the universities and General Frank T. Hines, head of the Veterans Administration (VA), had emerged the day before. At a conference sponsored by the ACE, West and Secretary-Treasurer Deane Malott had found the VA representatives avoiding hard questions. Hines, who had held his office since the exposure of the Harding scandals, had been scheduled to appear but sent one of the VA's regional officers to give the expected address. Said to be written by Hines, this compendium of statistics was linked to vague advice for colleges to get busy and plan. A significant warning, however, was implicit in data showing that three-fourths of those already using GI Bill educational provisions had opted for universities and colleges rather than trade and industrial training.

Called to the telephone, the speaker was not recorded as participating in the ensuing debate, which soon grew caustic. The chief irritant was a month-old VA revocation of an understanding that public universities could bill the government for state-resident student veterans at nonresident tuition rates. States would now have to pay most of the cost for this influx of students, President Alfred Atkinson of Arizona warned, and some deserving applicants would be turned away. President John Mosely of Nevada proudly announced that his state's Senator Patrick McCarran had just introduced a bill to allow universities to charge the government "actual cost," not to exceed $500 a year. Although pleased at this evidence of their influence in Congress, the group preferred the term "fair and reasonable cost" and wording to make the legislation clearly mandatory for the VA.

Drawing of his many recent contacts in Washington, Kentucky's Herman Donovan offered assurances that the pending plan was intended to force the VA to rescind its recent ruling and pay full costs for student veterans—"just the same," he explained in a startling parallel, "as when a man comes back and has to be sent to a mental hospital." The VA had been resisting the proposal, he reported. Since the route to rectification led through Congress, he found encouragement in Senator Fulbright's presence at the session. Before the meeting concluded, the NASU adopted appropriate resolutions.

Even more inside knowledge of Washington came from the next speaker, ACE staff associate Francis J. Brown. This former sociology professor (Dr. Brown, the chairman called him) had shown particular skill in liaison between the educational sector and the government. He began with the persisting wartime tensions over "manpower," analyzing continued pressure from monthly induction quotas, which had risen again after the Battle of the Bulge. Students as well as faculty under thirty were now more likely to be called. Officials at medical and engineering schools judged recent enrollment drops critical. Amelioration was most likely to come from Congress, where "an organization such as [the NASU] can have a tremendous weight."

Brown sought to dampen administrators' hopes for early release of faculty members from the armed forces. Military authorities, he said, planned to set up educational institutions in theaters of war that became inactive and wanted instructors and administrators to be in uniform. Since service personnel would remain overseas "not weeks, but months, and possibly years," various levels of education would be made available, perhaps even graduate study at centers linked to European universities. In addition, the military had placed vast orders for self-teaching textbooks. The reaction of the gathered state university leaders is not difficult to imagine. The menace equaled any that West had suggested in his address. After a series of wartime conflicts with the military, which seemed only perpetuated by relations with the VA, here was a proposal for a vast incursion into the educational realm that would deprive existing institutions of faculty, students, and no doubt funds. The soon-to-emerge slogan "Bring the Boys Home" may have been gestating in the minds of academic leaders at the Edgewater Beach.

Nine amendments to the GI Bill had just been proposed in Congress, and Brown discussed them in detail. The joint ACE-NEA National Committee on the Relationship of Higher Education to the Federal Government (on which he served) had already taken a position on most of these, positions not over-generous toward returning veterans. The committee had come out against dropping requirements in the original bill that made eligibility for educational benefits difficult for anyone who had already reached age twenty-five at the time of induction. The ACE-NEA group had rather short-sightedly concluded that, without this limitation, colleges and universities might be forced to accept "many individuals who are there not for education, but for the security that would be provided."

Fearing competition and eroded standards, the National Committee also opposed an amendment to allow the use of GI Bill funds for correspondence courses from institutions with no residence requirements. On this and other matters, the National Committee had found itself in conflict with the American Legion. Brown hoped the NASU would take stands to help counteract this and certain other legion positions. (It did so in resolutions passed at the final session.)

Altering the agenda, President West called for the nominating committee's report before the morning session adjourned, declaring it would thus be possible during the noon hour for delegates to "rib and razz the new officers." Promptly adopted, the slate suggested no dissatisfaction with the role of NASU stalwarts: Illinois's A. C. Willard, president; Iowa's Vigil Hancher, vice-president; Kansas's Deane Malott, continuing secretary-treasurer; and Kentucky's Herman Donovan, new member of the executive committee.

The luncheon session, which ended the convention, included various reports, notably that of the Committee on Accrediting Agencies, now largely subsumed under the interassociational Joint Committee on Accrediting. Recent negotiations with accreditation bodies for social work, architecture, and journalism had aimed at settling on only one accrediting agency for each field, but the JCA had had to accept two in social work. The report of the Special Committee on Vocational Education showed the NASU working closely with a group from the land-grant association. Proposed national legislation for federal support of vocational schooling was seen by West and others as potentially encroaching on higher education, and university representatives had met in conference with counterparts from the American Vocational Association. The AVA had agreed to a revised bill that clearly limited any new federal support to "education of less than college grade."

For the Committee on Radio Broadcasting, Howard Bevis of Ohio State told of his appearance (representing both the NASU and the land-grant association) before the Federal Communications Commission. That agency had been generous in its allocation of FM channels for educational use. Accordingly, a diligent state university could now "reach its total state-wide constituency by FM radio." The next report indicated that NASU members foresaw a constituency that was worldwide. The Committee on Relations with Foreign Students and Universities, headed by Michigan's Alexander G. Ruthven, had important suggestions. Some central agency, perhaps the Institute of International Education, should operate to assist applicants from abroad. It should also manage orientation centers and channel students to institutions best suited to their needs. No foreign student's program, the committee maintained, should be limited to technical or professional studies. All should include courses that brought "critical understanding and appreciation of our way of life."

Besides those from the Committee on Resolutions, additional motions were offered from the floor. Eleven passed in all, over half bearing on veterans' education and drawing on earlier expressions of discontent with the GI Bill as it stood and with some of the proposed amendments. U.S. Representative Fritz Lanham, who had made housing his special wartime interest, was to be directly contacted in regard to the crisis in housing families of married veterans. Great urgency was attached to having the executive committee prevent material needed for ROTC units from being declared surplus property by the Army or Navy.

There was a whiff of yearning for normalcy in the resolution that called for abandoning accelerated programs as soon as possible. They were declared financially costly, burdensome to academic staffs, and restrictive of the educational process.

The University of Texas had been unrepresented at the convention. The previous November, after battles over the dismissal of allegedly radical professors and the removal from course reading lists of such "offensive" books as John Dos Passos's *U.S.A.*, the Board of Regents had fired liberal President Homer P. Rainey. His NASU colleagues rallied, expressing their corporate concern over reported violations of "the principles of intellectual freedom" at the university and authorizing the executive committee to make this position "unmistakably clear."

A delegate might well have returned home from the 1945 NASU meeting with heightened awareness of rising competition for the state university in his charge. Laboriously achieved support seemed threatened by an assortment of other educational institutions. These included wealthy endowed institutions, of course, but also others long thought of as inferiors, like teachers colleges and junior colleges, besides upstarts like federally funded vocational schools and Army-sponsored schools for service personnel.

Other unpleasant external realities had been vividly portrayed. The American Legion did not hesitate to tread on academic toes. The Veterans Administration had issued regulations that were educationally unperceptive and financially costly to affected institutions. Accrediting agencies insisted on telling universities what to do—and charging them for the service.

Yet the meeting had also instilled a feeling of confidence that state universities, especially when they displayed solidarity, had allies in Washington. Modest though its powers were, the USOE seemed committed to university interests. The Federal Communications Commission had proved cooperative. More important, influential congressmen were responding positively to recommendations from academic leaders. The presence of Senator Fulbright and his continuing solicitude for academic life had been reassuring. With advocates like Francis Brown helping to map strategy, the imminent peacetime readjustments might bring state universities much of what they wanted from the federal government.

CHAPTER 8

Into the Postwar World

"WE didn't seek world leadership, it was thrust upon us." In the aftermath of World War II, that platitude soon lent itself to satire. Leaving questions of agency aside, however, there was no denying new American power. In a series of undertakings that sometimes bewildered the American public, the government sought to reform the conquered nations, restore war-ravaged areas, establish the United Nations, find alternatives to a dying European colonialism, and build a new system of collective security. Often with government encouragement, private groups joined in these international undertakings. In this new world activism, organized American education found an exhilarating role.

Educational leaders became world travelers—consulting, conferring, even directing. They had little doubt that the United States had educational models worth sharing. Not that differences were to be disallowed. A nation of many peoples should be able to help build a peaceful world of many peoples. How better than through education could humanity achieve the mutual understanding that was the only sound basis of peace? Accordingly, leaders of educational organizations, who had been pluralistic systematizers before the war, now found themselves trying to bring unity amid difference to education all over the world.

Articles in the March 1946 *AAC Bulletin* suggested a mixture of buoyancy and uneasiness. The "Contribution of the Academic World to the War Effort" offered some assurance of public gratitude and confidence. Still, members had to worry about being ready for "The New Veterans," as well as another expected influx, "The Foreign Students as Present Problem and Challenge." That challenge was only part of the task of "Getting America Understood Abroad." Finding the relationship between "Education and World Order" had new urgency, given the spectre of "The Atomic Bomb *versus* Civilization."

Could the institutional associations move importantly in this revolutionized situation? Did their leaders realize how much the world had changed?

Domestically, the years 1945–50 are lost to general historical memory. The forties has no such easy tag as Depression Decade or Age of Affluence. After sixteen years of depression and war, Americans turned enthusiastically to the material betterment of everyday life. The Republican congressional victory of 1946 promised lessened domestic governmental activism, but the Democrats' surprise victory in 1948 stirred expectations for a significant Fair Deal program. Ethnic inclusiveness, long found in electoral slates and more recently in wartime battle movies, gained fresh urgency. Jews, Catholics, and Afro-Americans raised new protests against long-suffered discrimination and demanded that democratic society live up to its promises of fairness. How was the educational establishment to find a way through this tangle? How could a tradition of voluntarism fit such times?

THE GI BILL, UNIVERSAL MILITARY TRAINING, AND SELECTIVE SERVICE

Although suggesting how tired of war Americans were, rapid demobilization served to extend war-related educational obligations, since schools had to deal with the influx of returning veterans. At Kansas State College in 1946, the weekly teaching load reached eighteen hours, the student-faculty ratio 20–1. The legislature had refused to raise salaries during the war, and though the inflation rate in 1946 was 20 percent, the legislators would not convene till the next year. Warned that mutiny threatened, President Milton S. Eisenhower told the faculty that until the legislature met, the only way to raise salaries would be to cut enrollment and faculty size, steps that would reduce admission of returning veterans. This appeal to public duty (and colleagueship) put matters in a different light. The faculty agreed to be patient. Across the country, administrators, faculty, and nonveteran students accommodated themselves to an unprecedented rise in enrollment.[1]

Like the educational results of the Morrill Act of 1862, those of the GI Bill of Rights are not easily fathomed. It bred new campuses, accustomed institutions to radically increased numbers of students, created new awareness of academic possibilities among members of social classes that did not usually send their offspring to college, and promoted acceptance of married and older students. Further, the GI Bill encouraged colleges to continue their wartime stance of service to national goals and justified acceptance of federal support by private institutions. Some of this support was direct, but these institutions learned that they also benefited from federal aid channeled through students. The bill elevated the role of the institutional associations as intermediaries between their membership and government, and they participated in both amending the original law and modifying VA administrative rulings.[2]

As inflation ate away at subsistence allowances to student veterans, Congress passed one increase in December 1945 and contemplated another early in 1948. Although the veterans' overall record was excellent, suspicion that they were in college primarily to collect their allowances lurked among educational leaders. Some fly-by-night schools were indeed making a killing with undemanding courses, and some veterans exchanged government-purchased textbooks and slide rules for watches and jewelry. In committee hearings on subsistence, the ACE drew on its recent nationwide study to recommend limitation of any increase to $10 a month for the first child and $7.50 for each additional child. When Senator Claude Pepper insisted that the law had been intended to allow recipients a decent living standard, the ACE's Francis J. Brown begged to differ. He had sat through all of the hearings on the GI bill and averred that the act was never intended to give full support to veterans pursuing further education. The increase finally adopted considerably exceeded the ACE recommendation, raising monthly subsistence grants from $90 to $105 for married veterans and to $120 for those with more than one dependent, with a comparable rise for single veterans. Still, the larger allowances fell short of the "minimum comfort" level. Many veterans (and their spouses) took jobs and borrowed to meet expenses. Clearly the ACE was not their organization.[3]

The associations took a livelier interest in matters that directly affected institutional income, particularly limits on tuition payments for veterans. It was less the cap of $500 (on tuition, fees, books, and supplies) that raised problems than the question of whether the formula penalized public institutions with low tuition. Such institutions were allowed to base veterans' tuition charges on "fair and reasonable compensation" for "estimated cost of instruction." Putting dollar values on such phrases was not easy, and, even with an advisory committee of educators, the VA stirred the ire of some institutional administrators. A joint committee of the NASU and the ALGCU, charging that VA rulings discriminated against publicly supported institutions, sent representatives to meet with VA head Omar Bradley. Although only about one percent of the two billion dollars paid for tuition under the bill came into controversy, for an individual institution the amount involved could be highly significant.[4]

To the consternation of land-grant institutions, the VA set a new formula for "fair and reasonable compensation," requiring that the grants which set this group apart—those based on the Morrill, Nelson, and Bankhead-Jones Acts—must be subtracted from the amount the government owed the institution for GI Bill instruction. Conferences on this issue with VA officials, in which the ALGCU stressed the integrity of land-grant funds as meant for endowment, brought no success, and leaders alerted members at the 1949 meeting to "an opportune time for every institution to contact the Congressmen and Senators of its state." Meanwhile the group's executive secretary gathered historical evidence and legal opinions to convince the lawmakers. During strenuous lobbying, President Frank Poole of Clemson Agricultural College told John Rankin of Mississippi, chairman of the House Veterans Committee, "Those Yankees over in the Veterans Administration are trying to steal our land-grant teaching money that Congress appropriates every year." A new law, passed in June 1950, not only forbade the deduction, but also made the decision retroactive. Although chiefly designed to protect Morrill-grant institutions, the statute (Public Law 571, Eighty-first Congress) also preemptively protected other nonprofit educational institutions from any reduction based on receipt of nonfederal public funds or private gifts. Both the Veterans Administration and the Bureau of the Budget had opposed the action, but the ALGCU, with member institutions in every state, was well situated to convince congressmen of the justice of protecting these "sacred funds." The association even claimed to have prevented a presidential veto by timely intervention.[5]

As the question of how to treat land-grant funds indicated, seeking to change VA regulations sometimes proved more difficult than changing the statutes. One rule against supporting college training that was recreational or vocational threatened for a time to become a curricular straitjacket. An official at the University of Buffalo wrote the ACE asking for ways to take collective action against the VA's tendency toward "vague terminologies, retroactive policy changes, and over-rigid accounting procedures," since "attempts by the individual institution to deal directly with the Washington source of a questionable matter usually result in a polite but fruitless exchange of letters." Associational links to VA administrators and the work of various advisory committees sometimes ironed things out, and on occasion the institutional associations joined with major veterans organizations to seek program liberalization. The ACE took credit for modification of an order that class attendance records be kept for those studying with GI Bill assistance. In mid-1950, however, the ACE's Brown held out little hope of changing attitudes within the VA. Encounters with its bureaucracy often proved frustrating, and probably the government never fully covered the increased administrative costs that the GI Bill imposed on institutions. But all in all, the demonstration of federal capacities in regard to veterans' education awakened a new appetite among the colleges and universities for good things from Washington.[6]

A proposed government program that attracted educators far less than did the GI Bill—universal military training (UMT)—was being pushed hard during the peak years of veteran attendance. Colleges complaining about overcrowding simultaneously expressed fears that UMT would dangerously reduce enrollments in the future. The nervousness with which educators had greeted Roosevelt's suggestion of compulsory national service continued as the idea merged with older proposals. In testimony before a House committee, Zook presented an array of alternatives to UMT. With the ACE in the lead, associations insisted that national security planning was too important to be left to the military and called for a presidential commission to study defense needs broadly considered. A better-educated citizenry with careful development of individual talents, so the argument went, should be central in national security strategy.[7]

Although strongly pro-UMT himself, Truman agreed to appoint a President's Advisory Commission on Universal Training, headed by MIT's Karl Compton. When it declared for UMT in 1947, disappointed educators tried to find solace in its having listed first among national security essentials "a strong, healthy, educated population." Conant, a former opponent, now joined in urging UMT legislation, but other college administrators hoped to delay and ultimately defeat the plan.[8]

More interested in getting help with its members' ROTC programs, the land-grant association had resisted taking a position on UMT. An address by Daniel A. Poling, a member of the Compton Commission and editor of the *Christian Herald,* offered assurances that UMT was not unchristian and that its training would save lives, but the association waffled. Its senate at first supported the Compton recommendations, then rescinded its vote and referred the matter to a committee.[9]

The smaller the college the greater the injury if UMT deflected young men from attending; accordingly, many members of the AAC feared the plan. In a show of open-mindedness, the association at its 1948 meeting heard President Harold W. Dodds of Princeton in favor of UMT and President Alexander Guerry of the University of the South against. Intensely concerned, at least eleven other presidents participated in floor debate before the delegates voted 219–69 to go on record against the proposal. Snavely, who had been criticizing UMT regularly since 1945, presumably felt vindicated.[10]

Early in 1948, on the basis of a questionnaire showing roughly three-fourths of educators rejecting the view that UMT was essential to national security, representatives of the ACE's constituent members voted to oppose a UMT law and Zook testified accordingly before congressional committees. Educators' reluctance contributed to congressional delay, and the UMT initiative hung fire. Paradoxically, its conclusive defeat came only with the outbreak of the Korean War and the need for immediate inductions into the regular armed forces.[11]

Debate over Selective Service, which continued in force as UMT was being debated, had not been ignored by the associations. Although they failed in their effort to have deferment policy controlled by the National Security Resources Board, they did help shape advisory boards that worked out deferment regulations protective of college students. The policy adopted hewed fairly close to one recommended by the ACE, postponing induction for full-time students whatever their field of study as long as they were making satisfactory progress.[12]

THE PRESIDENT'S COMMISSION ON HIGHER EDUCATION

In establishing the President's Commission on Higher Education (PCHE) in July 1946, Truman used current experience with student veterans as his point of departure. He asked, however, for a broad reexamination of the social role of "our system of higher education" and listed first among particular issues "ways and means of expanding educational opportunities for all able young people." The twenty-eight members of the PCHE represented ethnic, gender, and institutional variety, but it was later charged that private institutions, particularly prestigious ones in the northeast, had been slighted. With his wartime efforts widely acknowledged, Zook was the not-surprising choice to chair the commission, and his trusted ACE associate Francis J. Brown became its executive secretary. It was probably no coincidence that the commission's appointment came just in time to be endorsed by the ACE-sponsored Conference on Emergency Problems in Higher Education. Other presidential commissions had studied education in general, but this was the first charged to treat higher education specifically.[13]

In its first publication, the PCHE struck an audacious note: "American colleges and universities . . . can no longer consider themselves merely the instrument for producing an intellectual elite; they must become the means by which every citizen, youth and adult, is enabled and encouraged to carry his education, formal and informal, as far as his native capacities permit." Moreover, native capacities were declared higher than generally assumed: 49 percent of the population was intellectually competent to pursue education beyond high school. Various factors, however, greatly reduced the number who did so— notably "economic handicaps," "racial, religious, and geographical barriers," as well as a restricted curriculum. Declaring such roadblocks removable, the PCHE proposed virtually doubling college and university enrollment by 1960 (table 4). Such an expansion would intensify the need for balancing specialized training with general education, which the PCHE described as "not sharply distinguished from liberal education" although shifting "from its original aristocratic intent."[14]

As five more small volumes rapidly followed the first, the PCHE carefully spelled out the means to reach its goals. The federal government should fund undergraduate scholarships and graduate fellowships, based on need and ability, not the country's requirements for certain sorts of training. Besides such direct aid to students, new federal grants should support both operating expenditure and capital outlay in publicly controlled colleges and universities. Such grants should go to states, based on an equalization principle that took into account taxable wealth and college-age population. Adopting a term first given wide currency in this report, the PCHE called for creation of "community colleges." Equivalent to the thirteenth and fourteenth grades, these institutions should be part of public school systems, tuition-free and widely dispersed. To provide other ways to ease access, public institutions should roll back student fees at least to prewar levels, and states should pass laws barring racial or religious discrimination by educational institutions. These were daring proposals, only partly explained by the exuberance of victory in war and educators' conviction that their institutions had contributed importantly to the struggle.[15]

General scholarly neglect of the commission's work belies its importance. Its report raised academic leaders' sights above immediate postwar adjustment to a vision of higher education expanding in the name of democracy and doing so with major federal financing. In a test of likely reception, the ACE polled both organizational and institutional members, finding that 89 percent considered federal aid to education both necessary and desirable (without federal control of administration or instruction, of course). The question of whether private elementary and secondary schools should share in such aid found respondents nearly evenly divided. On the possibility of federal scholarships available to students in both private and public higher

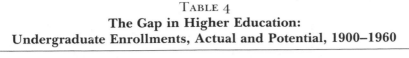

TABLE 4
The Gap in Higher Education:
Undergraduate Enrollments, Actual and Potential, 1900–1960

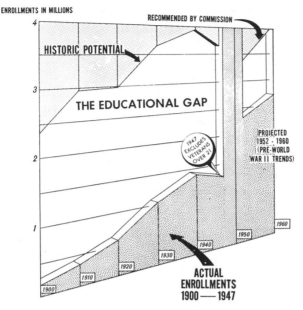

The Educational Gap: 1900–1960—Resident enrollments in thirteenth to sixteenth grades in institutions of higher education in the continental United States and the number who might have enrolled under recommendations of the President's Commission on Higher Education

Year	Enrollment in 13th–16th Grades	Lost Leadership	Number recommended by President's Commission on Higher Education
1900	146,000	2,226,000	2,372,000
1910	345,000	2,630,000	2,975,000
1920	582,000	2,404,000	2,986,000
1930	1,053,000	2,616,000	3,669,000
1936	1,130,000	2,625,000	3,755,000
1940	1,388,000	2,586,000	3,974,000
1947	1,286,000	2,383,000	3,669,000
	Prewar Trend Prediction	*Added Number Recommended*	
1952	2,305,000	1,080,000	3,385,000
1960	2,704,000	1,296,000	4,000,000

Source: *Higher Education for American Democracy: A Report of the President's Commission on Higher Education* (six vols. in one, New York [1947]), 1:45; 6:20. Based on resident enrollments and projections of pre–World War II trends from U.S. Office of Education.

education, however, the favorable response was 87 percent.[16]

Higher Education for American Democracy, as the report was named when reissued in a single volume, dominated discussions of higher education in 1948 and 1949. The January 1948 meeting of the ACE's constituent members heard a great deal about the report and at the annual meeting in May, Zook gave an optimistic appraisal of early reaction. He stressed steps that the individual institutions in his audience could take without waiting for government measures, particularly improved recruitment and preparation of college teachers, the theme of the PCHE's fourth volume. Citing negative effects of specialization and graduate concentration on research, he called for colleges to launch their own experiments and promised that the ACE would help in sharing results. A special meeting of the Problems and Policies Committee in June, "deeply impressed" by the need for expanding higher education, declared support for both community colleges and a national scholarship program.[17]

Zook and Brown's roles in the PCHE did not prevent their encouraging genuine debate on the issues posed. The April 1948 number of the ACE's *Educational Record* opened with Robert Hutchins's biting review, which branded the report antihumanistic and anti-intellectual: "It is confident that vices can be turned into virtues by making them larger. Its heart is in the right place; its head does not work very well." A more sympathetic account came in a later issue from William P. Tolley, chancellor of Syracuse University, who praised especially the commission's willingness to call for federal aid beyond piecemeal emergency funding.[18]

The land-grant association displayed less inclination than the ACE to foster even-handed treatment of the report. Given the Morrill mystique of serving "the industrial classes," the association was eager to applaud greater educational opportunity. Federal support of higher education had, after all, been the stimulus that had launched the association. The PCHE report was declared the theme of the 1948 ALGCU convention. In his presidential address to the association, Minnesota's aptly named James Lewis Morrill proclaimed the land-grant institutions to be the seed of the PCHE recommendations. Only on the issue of general education did the land-grant colleges fail as examplars, he said, and even here Minnesota and Michigan State had initiated commendable programs.[19]

In a major address at the same meeting, one of the four land-grant college officials on the PCHE, President Lewis W. Jones of the University of Arkansas, responded to recent criticisms. Deriding Hutchins's claim that the report favored quantity over quality, Jones suggested that "knowledge unlike peanut butter, does *not* diminish by being shared. It is more likely to increase." He belittled warnings of "a dangerous class" of the educated unemployed, warnings that drew analogies with the rise of nazism. In fact, he said, the Germans had been undereducated. The PCHE recommendations would require a revolution in educational financing, he admitted, and finding enough trained teachers posed a problem. But the country needed to rouse itself from the habit of providing education in response to economic demand rather than social need.[20]

At the next annual meeting, Michigan State's John A. Hannah, the new association president, relied on PCHE statistics to support his warning that "every year our high schools graduate thousands upon thousands of talented and capable young men and women for whom a college education is out of the question simply because it is too costly for them." He went to the same source for evidence that student fees were creeping upward, a tendency contrary to democratic land-grant ideals. As in 1948, a member of the PCHE addressed a plenary session. This time it was Commissioner of Education Earl J. McGrath, who pressed the case for community colleges and described an Office of Education proposal that followed PCHE recommendations for direct federal grants to students. He dubbed it "a civilian bill of rights." Meanwhile the executive committees of the ALGCU and the NASU had been working jointly on desiderata for any federal student-aid program. (Predictably, they called for specific language to ban any deduction of Morrill funds in computing instruction costs.)[21]

A chillier response met the PCHE report in gatherings of the AAC. There private college representatives dominated, and skepticism about federal aid set the tone. The commission's first volume, *Establishing the Goals,* had appeared in December 1946, with its trenchant indictment of inadequate student access to higher education. Within a month, the AAC had responded through its Commission on Liberal Education, chaired by Gordon Keith Chalmers, president of Kenyon College and an outspoken conservative. He had earlier poured scorn on attempts to make liberal education utilitarian, praised Irving Babbitt's humanism, and scoffed at having students read poetry in translation. Resolutions from his commission cited danger to standards from advocates of equality of access, and one of its reports declared that "the study of Greek offers the finest discipline that may be had in literature."[22]

It was hardly surprising when Chalmers and his associates rejected what they interpreted as implications that liberal education and selection of students were undemocratic. Further, the Chalmers group doubted that large numbers were capable of completing two years' work in an expanded network of community colleges, as urged by the

PCHE. Two members of the AAC's commission refused to go along with its majority. Thomas Raymond McConnell, dean of arts and sciences at the University of Minnesota and a member of the PCHE, dissented from the entire response, and Mordecai W. Johnson, president of Howard University, presented a partial demurrer.[23]

A year later, after the Presidential Commission's full report had appeared and when Truman's re-election suggested that action might follow, acrimonious debate broke out at the AAC's annual meeting. Many in the association felt menaced by the PCHE's recommendations for dramatic increases in the number of students completing fourteen years of education, broad federal aid to public institutions, and proliferation of two-year colleges. Here were some of the same threats that had helped inspire the formation of the association in 1915: mounting competition from public institutions, including high schools reaching beyond the twelfth grade. Yet the AAC was inclusive enough that challenges to its traditional posture now arose from within. The new voices included black college presidents, who had direct experience with injustices in institutionalized education, and Dean McConnell, who had shared in the University of Minnesota's programs to widen undergraduate admissions. Confrontation tested the meaning of the association and its definition of liberal education.

For the second year in a row the AAC's Commission on Liberal Education concentrated on the PCHE's report. Chalmers and his commission defended the colleges' insistence on "intellectual interests and verbal skills," declaring that "all the achievements of civilization are made possible by communication of the kind peculiar to universities." Liberal education was not only civilizing, the Chalmers commission insisted, but also democratic.

> Educational standards are of first importance to democracy, for citizenship depends as well upon the hard intellectual task of understanding human experience as upon the ability and will to take part in the community. Federal scholarships should, therefore, be available only to those who meet firm personal and intellectual standards. Like all opportunities for higher education they should be earned by the beneficiary; should not be regarded as a natural right.

Although approving the calls for more facilities for minorities and federal scholarships for the highly qualified, the Chalmers group proposed a series of motions that strongly resisted the egalitarian thrust of the PCHE's report. The motions cited danger in any sudden increase in the number of college students and deplored the implication that liberal education was aristocratic. Additionally, plans for federal scholarships and fellowships were to be approved only with assurances that educational standards would be maintained. With McConnell maneuvering vainly to table the motions, the AAC waded into one of its most impassioned debates. When it came time to vote, all of the Chalmers motions were passed, and an effort by McConnell to distance the association from the condescending language of the Chalmers preamble was reduced to an agreement that the entire report be "received and filed."[24]

Some arguments against the PCHE's position rested on grounds other than the need to protect standards. When the USOE proposed a program of scholarships to carry out some of the commission's proposals, Snavely warned of a possible oversupply of college graduates and objected that the grants could give young people "the notion that we must have a real 'welfare state' where the government will not only guarantee a college education but furnish suitable and good paying positions thereafter." He included in the *AAC Bulletin* a passage from the annual report of President Carter Davidson of Union College challenging the assumption of the PCHE that, if those with adequate mental capacity to pursue higher education were given federal support, enrollment would double by 1960. Ability did not necessarily mean interest, Davidson maintained, since rather than going to college many young people preferred early entry into the workplace and many women preferred early marriage.[25]

A quarter-century after it appeared, the PCHE report could be read as a prescription for American higher education that had been largely followed. The federal government had dramatically increased aid to higher education through both capital improvement grants and direct payments to students. Racial and religious discrimination were outlawed. By 1970, the 634 public two-year colleges marked a 162 percent increase over 1948. The number of students enrolling for the first time for higher education degree credit had risen in 1968 to 46.8 percent of the number of eighteen-year-olds, having been 26.0 percent in 1947. But the early reaction had been discouraging. Except for the USOE's failed scholarship plan and Truman's hint in 1950 that the government might aid development of community colleges, there was little implementation from the administration that had appointed the commission. The Housing Act of 1950 authorized $300 million in loans for student and faculty housing, but generally congressmen feared that efforts to aid higher education would encounter the same disputes over aid to denominational and racially segregated institutions that had recently scuttled bills for federal aid to lower schools.[26]

As its mauling in the AAC indicated, the report was "not a striking success," to use the words of an investigator indirectly sponsored by the AAU. In explaining the lack of acceptance, he cited the PCHE's projection of "an expansion of enrollment that many believed to be incompatible with high standards of education. In addition, it was felt that the commission unduly favored public higher education, or at any rate did not take the problems of private education fully into account." By its stress on widened access and federal funding, the PCHE had highlighted the public-private distinction within and among the associations and had exacerbated related tensions.[27]

THE FEDERAL EMBRACE

Probably no one wanted federal involvement in higher education to continue with its wartime intensity, but leaders of the ACE were not displeased that their capacities for federal liaison remained important. Far more than after World War I, higher education needed a center of information and influence in Washington. In an apt phrase, Zook spoke of the almost innumerable agencies with which the ACE's staff and committees "alternately have to wrestle and cooperate." Some of the wartime urgency carried over into an emergency conference of educators and government representatives called by the ACE in July 1946, an encounter that showed there was still plenty of chance for confusion and cross-purposes.[28]

Notably different from the aftermath of World War I was the continued flow of federal money to colleges and universities. A survey made in 1948 concluded that "institutions which only a few years ago were concerned that any federal moneys coming to them, or even to their students as in NYA, would eventually lead to federal control are now receiving relatively large sums of federal money for a variety of specialized activities—and like it." By 1949, research grants from the Department of Agriculture, at one time the most important form of such support to higher education, were at $19 million, relatively modest compared to grants from the Department of Defense ($53 million) and the Atomic Energy Commission ($81 million). Federal funds for training in special fields now came from not only the Agricultural Extension Service, but also the Public Health Service and the Atomic Energy Commission, all rising in the late 1940s. Expenditures for higher education under the new veterans' programs, peaking in 1948 and 1949, reached five and a half billion dollars, and although this included subsistence, about one-fourth of the total went directly to institutions. Laws of 1945 and 1946 granting access to government surplus supplies, first for housing and then for other educational facilities, were justified by the need to educate thousands of veterans. This rationale muted any complaints of illegitimate federal involvement with education, and the new income brought a heady sense of prosperity to replace prewar academic parsimony.[29]

In the context of rising federal aid, the land-grant association could credibly present itself as a model for latecomers to federal subvention and assert on the basis of its long experience that federal aid did not necessarily entail political control. Nor did it matter much which party was in power. "Our important federal relationships over the decades," Minnesota's J. L. Morrill boasted in his presidential address to the association, "have been serenely superior to political shifts at either end of the Avenue." Representing the ALGCU and the NASU jointly, a committee of business officers had by 1950 worked out an agreement whereby most federal agencies adopted a uniform policy of full re-imbursement for indirect as well as direct costs of sponsored research. Some institutions had carelessly ignored overhead costs when entering contracts and others had been only partially reimbursed. The new arrangement brought direct financial benefits conspicuously achieved through national organization.[30]

Variations among the associations appeared when they joined with scientific groups in pressing for creation of a National Science Foundation (NSF). Vannevar Bush's report to the president, *Science, the Endless Frontier* (1945), building on the success of the wartime Office of Scientific Research and Development, had called for federal aid to basic research, and the Office of Naval Research, founded in 1946, provided a promising model. Cornell's Edmund E. Day, reporting on efforts to shape the legislation, urged the ALGCU to prove its "vision and breadth of understanding" by working as hard on a bill for basic research as it had earlier on those for agricultural research.[31]

When two competing plans emerged in Congress, the associations divided in their preferences. The AAU tended toward the Magnuson Bill, which left most power with a board of scientists, presumably well-established figures connected with AAU institutions. Also favoring the Magnuson plan, the AAC particularly dreaded imbalance toward natural science and resolved that any subsidy should include social science and humanities. The land-grant and state university associations preferred the Kilgore Bill, which by giving a greater role to a presidentially appointed head, foretold wider distribution of grants. Some early versions of the bill, at these two associations' behest, would have required partial distribution of NSF funds to tax-supported universities on a geographically proportioned basis.[32]

As so often, the ACE tried to be even-handed, and in fact most association leaders were inclined toward compromise. They kept at it as Congresses came and went. Only after repeated congressional testimony and one veto (by which Truman insisted on presidential appointment of the advisory board) did the NSF emerge in 1950. Fifteen years after its founding, the NSF provided only 8 percent of federal funds for basic research; since its grants tended to go to academics and since science education was among NSF responsibilities, however, members of the institutional associations judged the years of lobbying well justified.[33]

Robert A. Taft, a presidential aspirant who found the ACE annual meeting an attractive audience for his version of federal aid, assured members that, though the compromise on the NSF forced by Truman's veto was unfortunate, the agency soon to appear would still give very real power to scientists on its board. In addition to recipients of NSF grants, medical schools with their heavy expenses seemed to him in 1949 reasonable candidates for federal support. But Taft's principal interest was his plan, which the Senate had just adopted, for aid to primary and secondary education through an equalization fund. The bill left it up to the states to decide whether to use some of the money for Constitutionally permitted aid to church-related schools. Under such a program he foresaw a role for the ACE in helping educators to spend the money wisely. But if Taft had expected a unified audience, he was soon disabused. During the discussion period, Catholic educators exposed differences within the ACE by repeatedly challenging his plan's failure to guarantee benefits to parochial schools.[34]

As good pluralists, some association officials cautioned against overdependence on any single source of funds. Having in 1946 announced its view that tax deductions to encourage charitable contributions were "far more desirable than increased tax revenue which would then be diverted to research purposes," the AAC petitioned private foundations a year later to correct the disproportionate support of science and technology by helping "the studies which assist morality, and an understanding of man and his society." Eager, like the AAC, to keep private funds flowing, the AAU in 1949 became the conduit for Rockefeller and Carnegie funds to a new Commission on Financing Higher Education. With its board dominated by private university leaders and John D. Millett, associate professor of public administration at Columbia, as its director, the commission began a series of studies which generally rejected the policies advocated by the PCHE. The studies warned that federal aid would be both inadequate and subtly coercive. Business corporations and alumni groups were presented as promising alternative sources.[35]

When in 1948 a proposed limit on federal income tax deductions threatened private gifts to education, the AAC responded with an impassioned resolution. Its preamble, generously sprinkled with evocations of founding fathers and frontier days, constituted a vigorous statement of associational ideology. There must be no confusing colleges and universities with private business, the AAC maintained, since these institutions' entire income was "already devoted to the purely public and wholly essential purpose of education." For good measure the group assailed the government's low interest rate policies, said to reduce endowment income. Members vowed to make urgent appeals to Congress. Similar protests marked the ACE convention the next year.[36]

But was it indisputable that educational institutions were not businesses? The Washington stage was a wide one, where other interests besides the educational coalesced to gain influence. An example hard for educators to ignore was the American Council of Commercial Laboratories, which charged in 1947 before the House Ways and Means Committee that land-grant universities unfairly engaged in remunerative ventures on which they paid no taxes. The land-grant association reacted sharply, and with its cooperation a new ACE committee began to correct "misinformation," declaring that only about 150 institutions had "non-educational" commercial involvement. The question was settled for a time with a modest requirement of taxes on some real estate but full exemption for such enterprises as college bookstores.[37]

The election of 1948 heartened advocates of greater governmental endeavor in education. By May 1949, some three hundred bills with direct educational connections had been introduced in the new session of Congress. Most of these bills failed, but three measures that educational associations had been advocating since the war's end became law: establishment of the NSF, provision for academic housing loans, and a change in Social Security eligibility. In a marked reversal of their policy in the 1930s, the ACE, the AAC, and the AAU had come to support inclusion of member institutions' employees under Social Security. The legislative victory that permitted such coverage was only partial, however; in spite of lobbying by the ACE, along with the NASU and the land-grant association, publicly supported institutions were not included if they already had retirement programs, even inadequate ones.[38]

For a time, federal aid to medical education seemed likely. Assuming a shortage of doctors, the Senate considered a bill for a five-year program of "emergency" medical training aid, both grants to medical schools and scholarships to students. Jointly managed on the floor by Senators Pepper and Taft, the measure sailed through the upper house. At that juncture, eighteen associations, including the ACE and the AAU, supported the bill. During its consideration in House committees, however, the American Medical Association, which had given tentative approval, began to see hidden threats in the measure. Although the Association of American Medical Colleges and other groups continued their support, the companion version of the bill never reached the House floor. The outbreak of war in June 1950, although it presumably exacerbated shortages of health personnel, was used as a justification for economy in domestic programs. Senator Taft dropped his support. For all the talk of "iron triangles," there were frustrating limits to what educational advocates and their allies in government could accomplish.[39]

The tension between urging federal aid and blocking federal control persisted. The fellowships of the Atomic Energy Commission required troubling oaths about past associations, and various federal research programs required secrecy, something that contravened the academic ethos of free and shared inquiry. In November 1949, a warning to the ACE's Problems and Policies Committee about the federal government's apparently growing tendency "to limit in various ways freedom to teach and freedom to learn" came from Aaron John Brumbaugh, who had left a University of Chicago deanship for the vice-presidency of the ACE in 1944. In his last annual report, Zook declared that constant alertness and determination had succeeded in protecting institutional freedom from governmental interference. The House Un-American Activities Committee (HUAC) provided him a convenient parable of his organization's guardianship. The committee had requested from about one hundred institutions lists of "approved textbooks and supplementary reading material." A prompt telegram from the ACE warned the institutions of "grave issues" involved and promised to obtain legal counsel. After conversations with the HUAC chairman, who expressed surprise at the negative reaction, the ACE telegraphed again urging delay and reporting that no use of subpoena power was planned. The HUAC request was shortly withdrawn.[40]

Although other organizational purposes continued, the associations found in the postwar years that federal relations increasingly demanded attention, on matters discussed here and others as well, such as postal rates, channels for educational television, and a proposed labor extension service. Anyone who had expected higher education's involvement with Washington to recede after a period of postwar adjustment, Zook commented in 1948, should now be disabused. Bigger committees on federal relations, headed by some of the ablest institutional presidents, kept busy throughout the year, and their reports were highlights of annual meetings. As chair of the land-grant association's Special Committee on Federal Legislation, John A. Hannah of Michigan State, "an administrative genius, with a remarkable capacity for inspiring the cooperation of others, . . . and tremendous energy," met regularly with the executive committee. For both the redoubtable Hannah and his successor, Arthur S. Adams, president of the University of New Hampshire, the position proved a steppingstone to the association presidency. In the fall of 1949, Adams told of 110 pieces of legislation reviewed by his committee in the past year, assignment of individual members to track specified bills, and files a foot thick.[41]

The ACE's federal relations committee met as often as eleven times a year, special committees on taxation and on social security were active, and the Washington staff kept in daily contact with various federal agencies. Sometimes staff members dealt with former colleagues. In a growing market for bureaucrats, individuals moved readily between government jobs and those in associational headquarters. The distinction between voluntary organizations and formal government sometimes blurred. The former tended to have information and grass-roots communication, whereas the latter had public money and the authority of law. A complex process of policy formation was emerging, a mode that drew on traditions of lobbying, professional consultantship, and opinion polling. The amalgam sometimes led only to general frustration, but on occasion compromise proved mutually convenient.[42]

DISCRIMINATION UNDER FIRE

World War II's exposure of the ghastly workings of applied bigotry obliged higher education, like other American institutions, to square its claims of democracy and enlightenment with the treatment accorded minorities. Moreover, the wartime rise in tensions between racial and religious groups, sharply contrasting with the democratic goals attributed to the war, shocked many educators. They hoped to purge their institutions of hypocrisy or, better yet, take the lead in a broad liberalization of attitudes toward minorities. In New York, documented evidence of private education's discrimination against Afro-Americans, Catholics, and Jews helped make the case for founding the State University of New York. At the federal level, decisions of the Supreme Court began broadening applications of the Fourteenth Amendment in ways bound to affect higher education. The national associations, however, found themselves constrained by their inclusiveness and their voluntary traditions. As one committee on intergroup relations phrased it, institutions were "fully autonomous, and with different situational pressures." Partly because of its wide membership, partly because of its long-standing apprehensions about governmental intervention, the AAC held particularly intense discussions of racial and religious discrimination. Barriers at some member institutions raised both moral and legal questions.[43]

Although reasserting its dedication to religion in education, the AAC moderated its Protestant emphasis. As president of the association, Denison's Kenneth I. Brown in 1949 assailed the country's secularized nationalism. Praising Newman and Wesley clubs and Hillel, he called for courses on religion that would instruct without proselytizing. Another sign of the AAC's growing ecumenism was the election as Brown's successor of the Rt. Rev. Vincent J. Flynn of the College of St. Thomas, who expressed effusive thanks for the honor that a predominantly Protestant organization had thus bestowed on the Roman Catholic Church. Of Judaism there was only occasional passing mention in AAC rhetoric. Newly opened Brandeis University seemed in no hurry to become a member, although the older Yeshiva University belonged. The AAC's Commission on Christian Education had long had its own executive secretary, a position made full-time in 1948, and the AAC continued to coordinate its meetings with those of church educational bodies.[44]

For some academic leaders religious values doubtless helped strengthen opposition to racial discrimination. At least three historically black colleges had been members from the AAC's founding, but the association had rarely discussed education's racial barriers. In 1948, however, sharp debate greeted a proposed resolution from the Board of Directors opposing any curtailment of federal tax exemptions for educational institutions, a resolution reacting against recent testimony before the House Ways and Means Committee urging restriction or even elimination of such exemptions. Two black college presidents, Howard's Mordecai Johnson and Morehouse's Benjamin E. Mays, believed there were cases in which the government should use its taxing power for intervention in education. They sought an amendment favoring withdrawal of exemption from institutions excluding citizens "on account of race, color, religion or national origin." The amendment failed, but this initiative marked an end to the AAC's long indifference to racial exclusion in education.[45]

Others broke silence. Wellesley's Mildred McAfee Horton, with her special patriotic aura as wartime organizer of the WAVES, used her AAC presidential address to criticize liberal arts colleges for their slowness in recognizing race prejudice as a threat. A second chance for the black spokesmen came when a special committee on "Minority Groups in Higher Education" issued its report, expressing "deep concern, shame and humility" about "the ugly side of American higher education." The report implied, however, that the problem was regional and included exculpatory language for southern colleges that barred Negroes and eastern colleges that discriminated against Jews.[46]

In the resulting floor debate, black college presidents again emerged as advocates of federal intervention. Warning of doubts abroad about American democracy, Johnson tried to get language passed that would approve government intervention through ending tax exemption and cutting off appropriations for institutions that discriminated. The association voted instead that problems of ethnic admission barriers "should be solved by education and voluntary actions and not by coercive legislation." The resolution did, however, call for "repeal of legislation restricting the right of any institution to admit qualified students without regard to race, color, or creed." A gesture toward alleviating academic discrimination came when, by a vote of 261 to 40, the delegates replaced the temporary committee with a "Commission on Minority Groups in Higher Education." Designed to provide academic self-policing through fact-finding and publicity, the commission apparently aimed at forestalling legislation and reaffirming the AAC's confidence in voluntarism.[47]

The more determined members of the new commission wanted it to have its own budget and executive secretary, but replies to a questionnaire showed majority opposition within the AAC to either measure. Although various institutions had new interracial councils or were emphasizing Brotherhood Week, some administrators responding to the questionnaire warned that "more harm than good can be done by attempts to force issues too rapidly." As to discrimination by fraternities, the survey indicated little active opposition from college officials. The commission had originally offered to investigate cases of alleged discrimination, but none was brought before it. In a weak attempt at exoneration for its inactivity, the commission referred to the ACE, asserting that its wider scope gave greater opportunities for constructive results.[48]

There had indeed been some stirrings within the ACE on the antidiscrimination front, recalling earlier work of its American Youth Commission. Just as the war ended, the *Educational Record* presented a study of black colleges that found them "typically small and characteristically poor," facing severe problems that made them, in spite of their resemblance to other colleges, "almost different in kind." Implications about barriers that excluded black students from other colleges were not spelled out.[49]

In September 1945, with a grant from the National Conference of Christians and Jews, the ACE began assisting projects in intergroup relations in certain public school systems, concentrating on developing instructional material and training teachers. A parallel College Study in Intergroup Relations, headquartered at Wayne University, emphasized "current social problems involving race, creed, immigrant cultures, and socio-economic class levels." Later, the range was widened to include cases where age, gender, or rural-urban background were the basis of potential conflict. Curricular projects at teacher-training institutions dominated the program, but there were also statewide conferences and workshops. A sense of educational limits emerged during the study, picked up in Zook's annual report: "It is not . . . what a community says, but its discriminatory practices that teach its children their undemocratic behaviors." Discouragingly, the study dropped from twenty-one to ten participating institutions between 1946 and 1947, and testing showed that "whatever the method used, it has been extremely difficult to secure attitudinal changes in college students." But the final report included some bright spots, and the project joined with the Southern Regional Council and other groups in sponsoring a conference that took as its point of departure *To Secure These Rights,* the report of Truman's Committee on Civil Rights. Held at Atlanta University, the racially integrated conference attracted fifteen hundred participants, almost all from the South.[50]

Continuing the attention to college admission inequities that had been highlighted by the President's Commission on Higher Education, the ACE employed the Elmo Roper organization to interview a cross section of high school seniors. For "purely methodological" reasons, this study of the class of 1947 excluded black students, with this revealing explanation: "The number of Negro seniors applying for admission to college is so small even in the North that a huge sample of high school seniors would be necessary in order to get enough Negro applicants for purposes of analysis." The investigation, funded by B'nai B'rith, concluded that religious background was not a bar to getting into *some* college, though less often the preferred one for Jewish applicants than for others. The study named economic factors as the chief deterrent to college application.[51]

A major conference on admission discrimination (November 4–5, 1949) urged academic institutions to take the lead in fulfilling "the American principle of equality of educational opportunity," which was "fully applicable to higher education." As to the federal government, it should deny appropriations to graduate and professional programs with restrictive admission policies and combat economic barriers through grants-in-aid to students. Cosponsored by the ACE and B'nai B'rith, this Chicago meeting provided a transition between the ACE's research and further activity. A new office in ACE headquarters served as an information clearing house and planner of further conferences, and, in a series of regional gatherings, institutional presidents and admission officers recommended reformed procedures. Admission discrimination (especially of the anti-Semitic variety) was fast becoming disreputable, and leaders of neighboring institutions supported each other in ending once taken-for-granted admission biases. Gradually the guiding ACE committee expanded its attention beyond admission to equalization of opportunities within institutions. In March 1951, the ACE took the lead in arranging a conference of student leaders on "human relations in higher education." Held at Earlham College with the NAACP among its sponsors, the meeting addressed issues that had earlier been passed over, such as discrimination in athletics, student organizations, and roommate assignment.[52]

Only one of the major institutional associations appeared to be explicitly segregated. The land-grant group had taken for granted the propriety of a separate association comprising the seventeen Morrill-grant institutions "for Negroes." In the 1890s, representatives of these colleges had sometimes attended annual meetings of the land-grant association. After the Conference of Presidents of Negro Land-Grant Colleges was formed in 1923, its members tried to stay in touch by holding their meetings at the same time and in the same city as the larger association, but the practice fell into abeyance.

In the postwar reexamination of discrimination and segregation, Cornell's Day and a few other land-grant leaders began moving delicately toward inclusion. Their efforts were aided by the portent in Supreme Court decisions against existing segregated public professional schools. The larger association's long-inactive committee to cooperate with the black presidents' conference reported its opinion that the existing constitution already made the black colleges eligible for membership, and in 1954 the senate voted without dissent to extend formal invitations. All of the previously excluded institutions joined, and their presidents dissolved their own association in 1955. That year one African-American college president, Edward Bertram Evans of Prairie View A&M, became a member of the executive committee of the merged association, and in 1974–75 another, Lewis C. Dowdy of North Carolina A&T, served as its president. Some white administrators may have accepted the change in hopes of preserving racially separate higher education in their home states by raising the status of black land-grant colleges, but at least one discriminatory barrier had been removed.[53]

BEYOND NATIONAL BORDERS

Given the nation's lack of a Ministry of Education, certain associations, notably the AAU and the ACE, had long seen academic foreign relations as an important part of their responsibility. If early in the Great Depression the ACE, like much of the rest of the nation, had proved inward looking, in 1937 Zook had turned actively to world cultural affairs, attending several conferences in Paris, including one sponsored by the International Committee on Intellectual Cooperation, an affiliate of the League of Nations. The frustrating lack of unity in international educational programs, he maintained, traced to "the mad struggle between political systems, with the accompanying armament races." Meanwhile, he pressed unavailingly for the United States to join the International Bureau of Education in Geneva.[54]

World War II foretold better times for international educational relations, as did the interest taken by the president of Indiana University, rolypoly (to borrow from *Timese*) Herman B Wells. "A jolly, convivial gourmet, and a Rabelaisian storyteller" who insisted that the "B" took no period since it stood for nothing, Wells spent part of each week in Washington, helping out the State Department. In 1944, he applied some of his boundless energy to chairing the ACE's new Committee on International Education and Cultural Relations, which undertook projects to aid foreign students in the United States and to encourage an international office of education. The same year, a statement by several voluntary organizations urged the State Department to place maximum reliance on their groups, since they were nationally organized and widely recognized. They also noted their experience in operating with government funds and suggested that it accorded with "American tradition" for voluntary agencies to administer international educational programs. The ACE handled several new Latin American projects for the State Department and with the war's end declared itself ready for new assignments.[55]

In a commonly expressed rationale, the educational part of America's new international responsibilities was ultimately the most important. Peace was the goal. It could be achieved only through mutual understanding among peoples. Understanding was the result of education. No one stated this case more persistently than George F. Zook. The challenges were multifold: restoring education in devastated regions, democratizing education in the defeated nations, building up schools and universities in what were still called "backward areas." Besides being good educational missionaries, the associational leaders devoted themselves to building a new international structure of organizations. Having lived by the associational ideology in their own country, they not surprisingly saw voluntaristic yet bureaucratized organizations as a desideratum for the educational pursuit of world peace.

The vastness of American power at the end of World War II gave new impetus to academic foreign relations. As federal agencies became more active educationally, they left plenty of room for third-sector participation, and associations sometimes exercised considerable influence. When in 1946 the State Department sent a committee to provide expert advice for the troubled educational program in the American Zone of Germany, Zook headed the mission, despite Secretary of War Patterson's opinion that he was "a high-pressure salesman and not an educator," an afterglow perhaps of wartime struggles over training programs. After a month-long inspection tour, the committee suggested more vigorous intervention, especially the replacement of the traditional German multitrack system. Results of subsequent efforts to force "democratization" varied among the German *Laender* under American occupation, and American educational officers on the scene had little success in overturning local traditions. The shrewd appointment of Herman Wells as cultural adviser to the military government in the American Zone marked a new approach. At his instigation, the ACE convened a conference of organizations to help with his redesign of the faltering academic exchange program. Later, with Wells as chair and funding from the Rockefeller Foundation, the ACE established a Commission on the Occupied Areas, important as a pioneer agency in German-American cultural exchange.[56]

The Fulbright Act of 1946 assigned its program to the State Department, but candidates were sifted by the Committee on the International Exchange of Persons, a subsidiary of the Conference Board of Associated Research Councils. This board had originally included only the ACLS, the NRC, and the SSRC. The decision to include the ACE was a distinctly relished boon to the educators' prestige. ACE leaders had long tried to equate their council with these others, without in fact matching their status. The choice of the ACE vice-president to chair the new committee was something of an associational coup.[57]

Although Zook was the central figure in building the postwar exchange establishment, Snavely had a knack for getting included on various advisory boards. The more inclusive Association of American Colleges, but not—to its chagrin—the AAU, had been invited to join a commission advising the State Department on the formation of UNESCO. Twice Snavely joined world tours of the Town Meeting of the Air as a spokesman for higher education. Whereas Zook praised attitudes in the State Department and foresaw the emergence in international cultural affairs of an ideal blend of government and voluntary organizations, Snavely and the AAC remained cautious. Ever alert to encroachments from federal power, the AAC reminded Congress in a formal resolution of the vital importance in international exchanges of hewing to the American traditions of localism and voluntarism. Later, through resolutions and lobbying, the AAC sought to have the Department of State's information services distinctly separated from educational exchange. There was some self-interest here, since appropriations and visibility for education would be lessened in a merged program, but the AAC's warnings about other nation's fears of "cultural imperialism" were timely. Largely because Snavely and others lobbied on the issue, the Smith-Mundt Act of 1948 provided structural divisions between the two programs and separate advisory commissions.[58]

Some international programs had little governmental connection. A jointly sponsored Commission on International Educational Reconstruction, headquartered with the ACE and supported by the Carnegie Corporation, helped channel aid from many voluntary organizations. The work was an important supplement to government programs, besides having the advantage through its private sponsorship of minimizing, as Zook phrased it, "misunderstanding of American motives abroad."[59]

At least in prospect, UNESCO offered a similar distancing of educational activities from raw pursuit of United States interests. Steps to develop UNESCO exemplified the process. At the founding of the United Nations in San Francisco in 1945, Zook and Wells were among the consultants who pressed the United States delegation to overcome its reluctance to recognize education as a specific concern of the new organization. (The rubric "cultural" had seemed vaguer and safer.) After UNESCO was formed in November 1945 and its main office established in Paris, two ACE committees gathered to plan ways "to acquaint individuals in American education and citizens generally with its organization and provisions." As a first step, the ACE distributed over five thousand copies of the new UNESCO constitution. With its stirring preamble and relative brevity the document was expected to appeal to a constitution-oriented nation. In London an ACE staff member served as deputy secretary of the UNESCO preparatory commission, and the land-grant association meeting of 1946 heard an enthusiastic appraisal from Milton Eisenhower, who had just flown back from Paris, inspired by the first UNESCO general conference.[60]

Eisenhower's account of UNESCO had grown somber by the time he addressed his colleagues in 1949. Many member nations failed to pay their dues or answer their mail, he noted, and no other national commission was as active as the American (which he headed). Still, he hoped that UNESCO, having weathered initial flippant criticism, could help add rationality to the pursuit of national interests. Zook too saw many limitations. "I cannot honestly say that UNESCO has made a brilliant start," he commented in 1947, citing its glacial pace and limited membership, which still did not include the Soviet Union. As for the United States National Commission for UNESCO, Zook judged it a fifth wheel, all too similar to faculty meetings in its tedious discussions about which additional organizations should be admitted. Recognizing that little direction or financial support was likely to come from either Washington or Paris, Zook urged American voluntary organizations to find ways to implement UNESCO programs in the United States. He called for student international clubs, a drive against illiteracy, and study of the images of other nations projected in American textbooks. Zook tried not to grow discouraged. Like most educational groups, he said, UNESCO would never be a headline grabber, facing instead "the age-old, steady, unspectacular, long pull of spreading education to the people of the world in order that through mutual understanding of one another's ways of life they may choose peace."[61]

UNESCO served as sponsor for a 1948 international gathering of universities in Utrecht, an event that harked back to the 1937 conference under the International Committee on Intellectual Cooperation and to previous hopes for creating a permanent organization of universities. The ACE was in the thick of the preliminaries, with Brown given leave for six months to plan the meeting. The conference found plenty to disagree about: degree equivalence, academic freedom, admissions methods, and state controls. Disappointingly for the Americans, the question of a new organization was postponed, but Zook helped establish an interim committee that would arrange for a second conference as well as supervising a new UNESCO bureau of information on universities. Leaving the conference in high spirits, Zook inadvertently suggested the lameness of vast institutional confederations when he commented (concerning the dispute over academic freedom), "In such debates there is never so much actual difference of opinion as apparently there is. It is largely a matter of finding the proper words and accents to make up the formula."[62]

In 1949 Zook's predictions, like Eisenhower's, were less encouraging. UNESCO's Paris staff could do little more than study, stimulate, and coordinate. It would be folly to rely on it as a guarantor of peace in a world divided between democracy and totalitarianism. But this sober view only strengthened Zook's push for American activism. Supported by the Carnegie Endowment for International Peace, the ACE sponsored a conference on international education at Estes Park in June 1949, seeking to encourage more internationally oriented activities and courses within colleges. As planned, the conference also voted in favor of the proposed International Association of Universities. The conference ended with an almost formulaic call for the

ACE to set up a national coordinating commission, and Carnegie Endowment support continued.[63]

The pretensions of the ACE to international representation of American higher education suffered the limitations of an association of associations. The land-grant group had reason to be independently active, its members seeing their extensive experience with applied science and outreach to farmers as giving them a special international role. Reports on projects abroad, such as "A Mission to China," and expansive forecasts, such as "The Stake of the Land-Grant College in the Arab World," became staples of ALGCU meetings. Alliance with the Department of Agriculture was easily expanded. The executive committee announced that the association's offer of participation had helped secure passage of the Administration's Point Four program for economic assistance to developing nations, and a compact between the association and the government arranged for agricultural exchange programs to be coordinated through a single officer in the USDA, with comparable centralization on each campus.[64]

The AAU proved even more independent, taking steps to assure that membership criteria for the International Association of Universities (IAU), established in 1950, were kept close to those of the AAU. Member presidents traveled abroad not only to attend IAU gatherings, but to meet with associations even closer to the pattern of the AAU, such as the Conference of Vice-Chancellors and Principals in Britain. Continuing its concern for academic foreign relations, the AAU opposed any American organization that might insert bureaucratic layers between AAU members and their foreign counterparts. One association's helpful coordination was another's undue interference.[65]

International programs of consultation, assistance, and exchange attained a salience in associational activities between 1945 and 1950 that was not matched by their movement toward ethnic inclusiveness. Still, both the increased internationalism and the criticisms of discrimination traced to an undermining of parochialism by the experiences of World War II. Having sought from their beginnings to lessen institutional isolation and localism, the associations now bestirred themselves to help counteract nationalist and ethnic prejudice.

The associationalist perception of the federal government had also changed. The land-grant group had always treated the government as a source of support. Now, not only other public institutions but private ones as well had begun to draw from government coffers. Indirect aid to institutions through federal grants to students seemed, after the successes of the GI Bill, a promising way to increase accessibility for members of poor families. Direct grants for facilities, justified by the impact of enrolled veterans, appeared likely to continue through housing and defense policies. Research funds from various federal agencies, particularly those related to defense, had already become a main source of sustenance for academic science before the NSF emerged in 1950.

All of the associations' agendas partook heavily of the nation's dominant Cold War liberalism. But the cool reception given the PCHE's proposals at the AAC and the AAU, where private institutions generally dominated, revealed disagreements within higher education about its role in a democracy. Tensions mounted over the proper balance between "equality" and "excellence," though the matter was rarely expressed in those terms. The nation's return to a wartime footing in 1950, however, masked other issues by reviving common solicitude about preserving institutional health while supporting an embattled nation. Decades of striving to give higher education a national center had prepared the ground for yet another demonstration of hanging together.

CHAPTER 9

Reconfigurations

WHATEVER dreams of supremacy its designers might have had, the ACE had turned out to be a somewhat untidy congeries of academic functions and not a rationalizer of American higher education. The council helped other associations work out their interrelationships, but competition and organizational redundancy continued. There was a growing recognition, however, that the associations should agree on their division of responsibilities while reaching shared positions to present to federal authorities. Finding their representatives ever more frequently in Washington, other associations began to consider the need for central offices placed, like that of the ACE, at the seat of government. Meanwhile, some associations restructured themselves in ways that clarified their missions and promised to bring greater influence with Congress and executive agencies. For the land-grant association and the AAU these reforms were epoch-making.

STREAMLINING THE LAND-GRANT ASSOCIATION

Besides expressing recurrent dissatisfaction with its name, the land-grant association had a tendency to tinker with its governing structure. But the redesign that began during World War II went beyond patchwork to establish a new constitution. One motive was the mounting belief that, as an organization including many complex universities, the ALGCU remained inappropriately skewed toward agricultural interests. This revision surpassed all earlier efforts in thoroughness of reform, careful implementation, and success in practice. It lived up to the claim of one of its advocates by providing "both form and flexibility." By 1948 insiders judged the new arrangements essential in the palpable reinvigoration of the association.[1]

Central to the emergence of the new constitution had been the leadership of James Lewis Morrill, president of the University of

Wyoming when he became chair of the special committee on organization but president of the University of Minnesota by the time the new constitution was adopted in 1945. Recognition of his work soon placed him in the top offices of the association. (The coincidence of bearing the family name of the father of the land-grant acts may have contributed a small measure to J. L. Morrill's career, but in fact the two were not closely related.) He had practiced journalism for a time before returning to his alma mater, Ohio State, where in two decades he rose from alumni secretary to vice-president. Meanwhile, he became a shaper of national organizations concerned with alumni affairs. A joiner and a booster, Morrill did not hesitate in his ALGCU presidential address to make invidious comparisons with other associations, even some to which his institution belonged. With its unmatched sense of a common cause and its capacity to renew leaders' energies, he declared, the ALGCU compared favorably to both the ACE (too heterogeneous) and the NASU (too loquacious).[2]

The constitution itself was only two pages long, many matters being left to a set of more easily amended bylaws. Except for an added reference to "mutual cooperation," the vague original constitutional statement of the association's object had remained unchanged since 1887. Now the object was declared to be constant improvement of members in "resident teaching, research and extension." The means included, of course, cooperation among members and also "proper and legal relationships" with the federal government and other organizations. At last the constitution directly stated the association's intention to take "appropriate action on proposed or actual Federal legislation."

Since its founding, the land-grant association had been more than a "presidential association." The activism of experiment station heads at the early meetings began a process by which other administrators within the land-grant colleges came to look on the annual convention as a time to confer and take action. The practice of meeting in subgroups was well established by 1895. Divisions continued under the new constitution, and in 1949 Morrill declared each of them "almost a professional association in itself."[3]

The monopoly of legislative power given the presidents through an "executive body" created in 1919 had finally stirred something of a revolt. Mere representation in divisions and attendance at powerless plenary sessions left other convention delegates dissatisfied. To replace the executive body, the new constitution created a senate as "the principal deliberative, policy-making, and legislative body." Like the executive body, the senate gave seats to the chief executives of all member institutions, but it also included three representations from each division. Comprising in 1947 agriculture, home economics, engineering, and arts and sciences, the divisions met separately at ALGCU conventions and had their own officers and committees (and sometimes sections and subsections). Within this structure of senate and divisions, an elaborate array of committees had by 1950 increased to approximately sixty-five.[4]

Granted much less power than the divisions, "councils" were permitted by the constitution but not mandated. These were to represent "institution-wide functions such as Graduate Work, Research, Extension, etc." As might have been foreseen, the first council to emerge, that on graduate work, agitated almost at once to be upgraded to a division.[5]

Amid these changes, an executive committee continued, functioning as a "nerve-center" at annual meetings and given wide authority to act during the year. Modifications in the executive committee, however, suggested greater recognition for specialized parts of the universities and some wish to encourage circulation of elites. Previously the executive committee had been virtually limited to institutional presidents; now it had nearly the same number of division representatives. Under the new bylaws, executive committee terms were reduced from four to three years, with no reelection allowed for one year after termination of service.[6]

In keeping with the original voluntaristic pattern, Thomas P. Cooper had been for sixteen years the association's secretary-treasurer, serving without salary and amid his duties as dean of agriculture and director of the experiment station at the University of Kentucky. Now the era of casual record keeping was ended. The new bylaws brought the land-grant association abreast of the AAC and the ACE by creating a full-time paid officer, designated "executive secretary-treasurer." Moreover, this new official would "conduct the national headquarters of the Association which shall be in Washington, D.C."—a distinct upgrading of the ALGCU office, headed by an "assistant secretary," established in the nation's capital in 1939. Partly to support "more adequate representation in Washington," the association agreed to double its dues.[7]

A new generation of land-grant college presidents had emerged during World War II. Among them was Milton S. Eisenhower, who had not needed a famous older brother to establish himself as a major presence in higher education. Influential in his own right through rich experience in the federal bureaucracy, he had returned to his home state in 1943 and initiated new ventures in general education as president of what was then called Kansas State College of Agriculture and Applied Science. As both a former Department of Agriculture officer and the head of a land-grant college, he was intensely aware of the need to keep communications open. When the ALGCU's small Washington information office ran into trouble, he assigned some of his own staff to keep it going.[8]

In a signal service to the association and at considerable sacrifice to his own staff, Eisenhower backed his dean of administration, Russell I. Thackrey, for the new executive secretary-treasurership. A rough-hewn extrovert, Thackrey had been a newspaperman and a teacher of journalism. He thrived on amassing accurate, readily available information and developing channels of communication, precisely the duties spelled out for the new position. As at Kansas State, he did not seek the limelight but gained respect through his abounding capacity for hard work and his incisive contributions at committee meetings. Demonstrating a resourceful awareness of institutional administrators' needs, his information bulletins led various presidents to declare themselves truly in touch with the association's activities for the first time.[9]

The central office, which he managed till 1950 with a single secretary and temporary clerical help, turned out to be even more effective than anticipated, playing a key role in the victory over the VA on the question of subtracting Morrill grants from federal payments for veterans' instruction costs. Praise for Thackrey from association officers mounted year by year, and his initial salary of $10,000 a year was raised in 1949 and 1950. Hannah, chairing the executive committee in 1950, observed that "the total program of the Association is pretty largely wrapped up in the efficiency of our Executive Secretary." Thackrey shrewdly defended an expansion of his office as based on the voluntaristic nature of the association. Given its dependence on actions by individuals within member institutions, he explained, members must have prompt access to dependable information.[10]

The new constitutional apparatus functioned almost too smoothly. At the annual meeting in the fall of 1947, the senate grew nervous after voting resolutions on the merits of proposed federal policies such as establishment of a Department of Health, Education and Security. Although the procedures were constitutional, some members discerned overcentralization and peremptory action. Rescinding several votes, the senate referred matters to a new committee, meanwhile asking the executive committee to find "reasonable safeguards against committing the Association to a position which will not be in accord generally with that of its individual members." With similar concerns, the executive committee declared explicitly that Thackrey did not represent the association to the federal government, that function resting entirely with "duly designated and authorized committees

. . . and individual institutions." But grass-roots communication with individual legislators was often orchestrated from the center. The association, whose links to the federal government had always encouraged an elite leadership active in Washington, had moved decisively toward bureaucratic centralization and was gaining strength in a discernible Washington higher education establishment. Two knowledgeable observers called it, in 1962, "probably, pound for pound, the most effective educational association on the national scene."[11]

THE NASU AS A MERGER PROSPECT

The NASU had not kept up with the increasing salience of state universities, having left policy formation "to individual institutions or to other associations." So declared President Herman B Wells of Indiana University in a blunt appraisal of 1943. Immense problems would follow the war, involving relations with the federal government and demands for new sorts of education. It was high time, he maintained, for the NASU to reassess its purpose and get new organizational machinery. Not much change followed. The NASU's new committee to study postwar educational problems reported in 1944 that they would "be essentially the unsolved problems of prewar days," and the chairman ducked making a report the next year. Convivial and slow-paced, the association at the end of World War II still included as special members individuals who formerly headed state universities, and the necrology committee still pronounced eulogies.[12]

Public higher education, however, was undergoing changes that the NASU could hardly ignore. Some once-modest public institutions were expanding and taking on more complex academic missions, blurring older categories and complicating the grounds for NASU membership. When the former Florida State College for Women transformed itself into coeducational Florida State University and (fruitlessly) sought NASU membership, some of the presidents were appalled. Would teachers colleges by applying next? The NASU voted in 1949 that it properly included only universities "of complex type with numerous professional schools" and that it should thenceforth admit only one university per state. (It already included three from Ohio and promptly violated its new rule by admitting the newly formed State University of New York, even though Cornell was already a member.)[13]

At the 1950 NASU meeting, one-third of member universities were unrepresented. Although the change might have increased attendance, members declined to meet at the same time as the land-grant group, seeking to avoid the long stint for the many presidents who were in both associations. But the NASU tended to rely on its more vigorous counterpart, receiving a 1949 report on new federal legislation which again and again cited some decision by the land-grant association's executive committee. On at least one proposal the NASU voted language identical to that recently adopted by the older association.[14]

Contending that the two organizations needed a common voice, especially "on the Washington front," President Frederick A. Middlebush of Missouri convinced the NASU that the two executive committees should hold some joint meetings each year. The collaborative idea was nothing new. Proposals for improved cooperation between the NASU and the land-grant association had surfaced about every ten years, including a call for full union by Purdue's Edward C. Elliott in 1926. Backers of this latest effort persisted when the plan for executive-committee collaboration proved unworkable. They obtained authorization for a joint committee with a long name, chaired by Middlebush and including Michigan State's Hannah.[15]

Even though its mandate suggested merely "the possibility of closer relationships between the two associations at the presidential level," the committee in late 1949 reported unanimously in favor of full merger. As to procedure, the committee suggested admitting the twenty-one "separate" state universities into the land-grant organization and adding "State Universities" to its title. The ALGCU's recent reorganization made it a flexible recipient for new members, and its executive secretary and central office had already proved effective in government relations and in keeping a widespread membership informed.[16]

A majority in each association belonged to the other (thirty-one of fifty-two NASU members and fifty-eight ALGCU members), and these institutions seemed likely to favor consolidation. Prospects were less clear for "separate" state universities and "separate" land-grant institutions. Showing careful respect for collegial variety, promoters of union adopted the standard of concurrent majorities. Merger, it was repeatedly affirmed during the discussions, should not occur unless strong majorities in both of the "separate" groups favored it. "A shotgun wedding," Hannah suggested, ". . . might be unhappy in the long run." The NASU voted at its 1950 meeting to approve the idea of a merger in principle, and some thought the event might occur as early as 1951.[17]

Recalling many earlier arguments for fusion, the committee gave primary emphasis to the need for a single voice to represent public higher education, especially on national issues. Rising involvement of the federal government in higher education spoke strongly for the change. With a merger, J. L. Morrill declared, "public-supported higher education, at the highest level, could speak with one voice in matters of Congressional action and relationships with the federal government." The decision to send Thackrey's newsletters on national issues to all "separate" state universities (after some had requested copies) strengthened the acknowledgment of common interests. Beyond shared representation in Washington, reasoned President Harry K. Newburn of the University of Oregon, a united organization would reach the whole citizenry with a shared vision of public higher education. Growing similarity among large public universities formed part of the rationale for merger. Sources of funding set "land-grant colleges" apart from "state universities" only marginally. Both accepted federal support, both relied more heavily on state funding. There had, in fact, rarely been a more convincing case for increased state support than that made before the ALGCU by Michigan State's Hannah.[18]

Opponents of merger also had a plausible case. With the ethos of each association so distinctive, was something valuable not jeopardized by merger? Some presidents in the NASU, the most clubbish of the major institutional associations, forecast loss of intimacy and frankness in a larger organization. It was a question not only of size, but of confidentiality. President Ruthven of the University of Michigan welcomed the plan for an off-the-record roundtable at the 1949 NASU meeting, to be led by President Allen of the University of Washington, already embroiled in an effort to purge Communists from the faculty. The land-grant association had as delegates not just presidents but other university administrators, including some of those whom a president might enjoy complaining about to other presidents in a confidential gathering. Furthermore, if presidents represented competing public institutions from the same state, they might experience some unwelcome constraint in each other's presence. Another characteristic raised suspicions about the land-grant association. It verged on being an agency of the federal government in such matters as extension programs and other interlocking arrangements with the Department of Agriculture. Perhaps most tellingly, the proposed mode of unification showed little sensitivity to organizational pride. Even Middlebush, a supporter of the change, admitted that the plan looked more like absorption than merger.[19]

Then there was the prospect of power dilution. Not only would each vote be cast in a larger group but, under the new constitution of the ALGCU, which was expected to serve the merged organization, legislative authority was shared with representatives from the divisions, who were mostly deans and directors from member universities.

Was this not a violation of academic hierarchy and an incursion into presidential prerogative?

Some negative arguments appealed only to the separate state universities, which belonged not only to the NASU but to a modest organization of their own, now called the State Universities Association. Although recently muted, recollections lingered of antagonisms over which institution in a state would receive federal money for specific programs. Such controversies had derailed bills on mining schools and engineering experiment stations. When in 1949 the president of Rhode Island State College urged that funds for a proposed federal labor extension service be channeled through land-grant institutions, the head of the SUA, President John C. West of the University of North Dakota, called for resistance and got support from Iowa's Hancher. At the state level, competition for funding had been a perennial cause of disputes, leaving a long record of bitterness in the state of Washington and elsewhere. Quite aside from financial questions, some separate universities had taken pride in being "real universities," unlike the state's "cow college," and some of their leaders perceived comparably greater prestige in the NASU. West used the ideal of distinctive missions to oppose the proposed merger of associations. Such a unification, he believed, "might well be interpreted as a recognition that the separated land-grant college has reached the estate of a university. In legislative circles it might well be interpreted as an acceptance of the multiple university system on a state-wide level." The threat to institutional autonomy was yet another reason to preserve separate associations. As University of Alabama President George H. Denny read the record, the Morrill-grant programs had been "a cruel invasion of the work of the State University," evidence of encroaching federal power aimed at superseding "the historic state universities established by the several states themselves."[20]

There had once been a special rationale for a state university as the capstone of education in the state, a source of unity for the entire system. This ideal dwindled as state universities lost their singularity and lower public schools developed nonacademic missions and greater independence. Still, the NASU sought to revive the older ethos through a symposium on "The University's Responsibility in Elementary and Secondary Education" and a new Committee on the Study of the Role of the State University.[21]

Oregon State's President August Leroy Strand, a member of the 1949 joint committee, did not get around to his assigned task of polling the presidents of separate land-grant institutions. He sent word to the chairman that, though he considered merger inevitable, "there will be some crabbing about it afterward." Even more than the state universities, the land-grant institutions had a mystique, and it was renewed annually at gatherings of the association that used Morrill status as the determiner of membership. The traditional claim on the federal government was also something that might be threatened by the merger. Without specifying the means, the ALGCU executive committee promised to safeguard traditional land-grant identity and influence in any associational union.[22]

Beginning a series of steps to render itself more appealing to its counterpart, the ALGCU in 1950 formed a Council of Presidents. This alternative setting for good-fellowship and unfettered discussion would presumably appeal to those presidents who had valued the NASU for such benefits. Besides an earlier constitutional amendment that allowed any member of the NASU to join the ALGCU, the group in 1955 changed its name to the American Association of Land-Grant Colleges and State Universities.[23]

After the Middlebush committee report was debated by both organizations in 1950 and 1951, another committee on union reported in 1952. Although some of the separate land-grant institutions dragged their heels, the stronger resistance came within the NASU. As a countermeasure, the group invited the separate land-grant colleges to attend the NASU convention in 1951 and perhaps join it. There was probably no thought of absorbing the ALGCU, but the plan might let the NASU survive as a separate organization with a strong presidential identity. The advocates of merger had underestimated the value some NASU members still placed on their "presidents' club."[24]

Fusionists believed that the Korean conflict, by intensifying federal academic involvement, strengthened their case. In fact, merger did not occur until 1963. The chief cause of delay, Thackrey recalled, was the reluctance of certain separate state university presidents and the unwillingness of other presidents to act coercively. Having resisted merger, the separate state universities strengthened their organization, the SUA. In 1950 it established dues high enough to support a representative in Washington, soon thereafter adopting its first constitution. By 1954 a former alumni officer at William and Mary, Charles P. McCurdy, Jr., was the SUA's half-time executive secretary, and he shortly expanded his duties with an identical post in the NASU.[25]

Demonstrating that associational separatism was in decline, McCurdy chose an office next door to Thackrey's, whose cooperative spirit even the diehards of the SUA recognized. In 1958 the land-grant association and the SUA established a Joint Office of Institutional Research. To direct it they brought in, from the University of Wisconsin communications office, Allan W. Ostar, later the influential head of the American Association of State Colleges and Universities (AASCU), founded in 1961 by former teachers colleges and other multipurpose public institutions. Meanwhile, the executive committees of the SUA and ALGCU held regular joint meetings, with the NASU settling into a discussion forum that rarely took positions. After lengthy maneuvers, in 1963 both the NASU and the SUA merged into the land-grant association, which adopted yet another name, one more durable than all of its predecessors: National Association of State Universities and Land-Grant Colleges. Skeptics found that NASULGC was pronounceable after all.[26]

REVOLUTION FROM ABOVE AT THE AAU

Among the associations, the AAU underwent the greatest transformation in the wake of World War II. It had become little more than a comradely annual meeting of graduate deans. They carped about the rarity of presidential attendance, but some deans were not really displeased to be running the show. In 1946, when at least five committees reported no action, the Committee on Federal Programs of Education in the Postwar Period succeeded in having itself abolished. The AAU's most visible activity in the world of learning was issuance of its Approved List of institutions whose graduates presumably were good bets for admission to AAU members' graduate schools. This passivity was sharply challenged in the late 1940s, largely because a few presidents of member institutions discerned in postwar developments the need for a national rostrum.[27]

Certain of the AAU presidents, notably James B. Conant of Harvard, concluded that the ACE, for all its claims as a peak association, was inadequate for the new challenges. Its wide membership diffused its energies and often blurred its policy positions, and George F. Zook, despite his bureaucratic skill, lacked incisiveness as a public spokesman. As chairman of the President's Commission on Higher Education, Zook was associated with making the case for federal grants only to public institutions, a position that deeply offended various private university heads. The ALGCU and the NASU threatened to establish themselves in Washington as the voice of advanced education, to the detriment of private universities. Other associations also caused nervousness about the prestige of the AAU. The Association of American Colleges, but not the AAU, had been invited to join a new commission advising the State Department on the formation of UNESCO.[28]

Significantly, most of the presidents who took the lead in the AAU's transformation were from the private institutions. Invoking the spirit of noblesse oblige, the University of Rochester's Alan Valentine observed that business and political leaders were asking greater clarity and visibility from their counterparts in higher education. Donald B. Tresidder, who attended every AAU meeting after he assumed the Stanford presidency in 1943, expressed his discontent first in 1945 and then, by invitation of the executive committee, in a blunt address to the 1947 meeting. He cared less for federal aid, which he believed inevitably brought controls, than for a stronger voice to reach private sources of funds. Why Tresidder emerged so centrally invites reflection. He doubtless knew of the efforts of his predecessor Ray Lyman Wilbur to bestir the presidents to make use of "their" association. Distance from the seat of government in Washington and foundations in New York gave special reasons to embrace the national identity offered by the AAU, and, unlike its neighbor in Berkeley, Stanford could not rely on associations of public universities. Tresidder had been dean of Stanford's medical school. Probably it distressed him to see the AAU controlled by graduate school deans who might presume to speak for sections of universities where they lacked experience and authority. Besides, Stanford for many years had no graduate dean, and its presidents had one of the better AAU attendance records.[29]

James B. Conant's address at the University of North Carolina's sesquicentennial ceremonies marked the high point of the AAU's 1945 meeting. Delegates seemed awed by the Harvard president's closeness to power and his insider knowledge of atomic energy's recent development. Redesigning the AAU was simply one of many reconstructions of American institutions with which Conant busied himself. At the same time, for instance, he was negotiating the merger that created the Educational Testing Service. To Conant, who fathomed the ways of politicians and foundation executives, academic officials were even more familiar. Since becoming Harvard's president in 1933, he had attended their gatherings and helped set their policies, and he had formed an unflattering opinion of the AAU.[30]

Another leader in the reforms, Brown's Henry M. Wriston, offered a lively and witty counterpoint to Conant's austere determination. Wriston too was very much at home in the world of associations and foundations, but the AAU had a special claim on his attention. Somewhat overshadowed by Harvard and Yale, Brown University could gain in prestige through a revivified association of "leading" universities. Wriston took on the tasks of AAU president during the shift to the new pattern from 1948 to 1950.

Although dissatisfaction with the course of the organization was already evident, most AAU delegates were probably surprised by the sweep of Tresidder's criticism in his address at the 1947 meeting. The indictment was merciless. Unless the association changed course, he foresaw "innocuous desuetude." Published proceedings were slow to appear and largely unread. The deans might gain refreshment and new ideas from the gatherings, but not the presidents, whose separate evening session too often dissolved into desultory conversation. If the AAU was to live up to its name and be more than an association of graduate schools of arts and sciences, the presidents must begin active participation. "However dull-witted a president may be, he and he alone by virtue of his position is compelled to see the institution as a whole and the relationships of the integral parts to each other."[31]

Besides Tresidder's address, the 1947 opening session, planned by the executive committee to stimulate organizational self-examination, included a somewhat milder critique by Missouri's President Middlebush. This political scientist reasoned that the prestige of AAU members gave it national responsibilities that it was failing to meet. The situation was serious enough to call for revising the group's constitution. Some deans were defensive about the effectiveness of the status quo, but after separate informal conferences by presidents and deans, amid calls for "a fundamental overhauling," delegates agreed to put Tresidder, Middlebush, and Valentine on a strengthened Problems and Policies Committee.[32]

The annual meeting of 1948 at the University of Pennsylvania changed forever the direction of the AAU. With Harvard holding the presidency, Conant conducted the sessions. Impeccably fair, he obviously knew how to guide meetings, in this case toward reversal of what he had long regarded as the association's fecklessness. The Problems and Policies Committee had drawn up an elaborate resolution but, in addition and probably more significantly, an ad hod group of presidents had gathered in New York to discuss the association's future. Soon after attending this meeting, Tresidder had suddenly died, but other presidents advanced his ideas for reducing the prominence of graduate deans in the association.[33]

Having twice submitted draft plans to all members, the Problems and Policies Committee recommended that the AAU begin to treat "university policies as a whole" and seek to become "the nationally accepted and nationally representative medium and spokesman of American universities." This claim was to be aided by enlarging the membership with perhaps as many as ten more institutions. The number of standing committees would be reduced, and a strengthened executive committee would take stands on issues of higher education. The possibility of subsections for professional schools was left open, but in any case the committee recommended reserving a unique role within the association for the graduate deans. To heighten responsibility, offices would no longer be held by institutions, but by individuals. With an urgency that reflected changes brought on by the war, the report reasserted familiar arguments for banding together. A "unified front" was now essential.[34]

To the embarrassment of Dean Arthur R. Tebbutt of Northwestern, who presented the Problems and Policies Committee's proposals to the 1948 annual meeting, one president after another attacked them as inadequate. Chicago's Hutchins objected that the plan still skewed the AAU toward graduate education and research and gave too prominent a role to the deans. Although private university presidents took the lead, there was vigorous support for more radical restructuring from the heads of three midwestern state universities: Iowa's Virgil M. Hancher, Nebraska's Reuben G. Gustavson, and Kansas's Deane W. Malott. Supporting Hutchins, Malott cited urgent problems beyond the AAU's traditional concern for standards, such as the "encroachment" of the federal government and relations with the armed forces. Leaving the chair to join the debate, Conant declared, "As it stands in the report, the graduate deans have merely permitted the presidents to add university policy to their agenda."[35]

Having long pled for presidential participation, the deans now got a larger dose than requested. Some of them were perceptibly distressed, fearing the results would leave no organization to represent graduate work and the university's "highest function," research. Long a power in the association, Dean Fernandus Payne of Indiana called for two entirely distinct organizations. Withdrawing into a private conference, the attending presidents worked out a revised constitution. It called for an executive committee solely of presidents. Voting would be strictly by presidents, and they must be present for their votes to count. Policy statements, now declared an express purpose of the AAU, could be issued with a majority vote of the presidents, though without binding individual institutions. The constitutional revision left room within the AAU for other "constituent associations" (presumably of university professional schools), but only that of the graduate schools of arts and sciences was expressly named (and in the event no others emerged).[36]

Assuring the deans that they had been the backbone of the organization, the presidents granted them a generous portion of dues and the sop of deciding what to call their section of the organization. (They settled on "Association of Graduate Schools in the Association of American Universities," soon initialized simply as "AGS.") A more important victory for the deans was the definition of AAU membership, which required that an institution demonstrate distinction in graduate work, not merely in professional schools.[37]

Skillfully presented by Brown's Wriston, who relieved tension with jibes at presidential foibles, the modified constitution was approved without dissent in the final business session. Clearly, the presidents had seized power and intended to use it for extramural influence. There was even a touch of the grandiose when Conant likened the process to another meeting in Philadelphia—that of 1787. Ratification ("agreement in writing of twenty-five of the executive heads") brought the reformed AAU into being by January 1, 1949. "One of the greatest surgical operations in history . . . ," concluded Virginia's Dean James Southall Wilson, "when by a Caesarean operation, a parent organization was born of its daughter."[38]

As the first president under the new plan, Wriston rejected the idea of a paid executive secretary. He declined to go "the typical American organizational way" of overinflated structure, although he found himself extremely busy. Caught in a barrage of meetings and correspondence as the new format brought the AAU to life, he rather enjoyed the challenge. Plunging into their new role, the presidents gathered three times to face "pressing issues" even before their first regular annual meeting under the new plan. They abandoned to the deans the *Proceedings,* which would no longer record presidential debates. As befitted the presidents' hopes for national influence, only their carefully crafted pronouncements were published, and a law firm had been hired to help address the issue of military training.

The refurbished AAU had received three grants, the largest of which allowed it to sponsor the new Commission on Financing Higher Education (whose studies seemed designed to deflate the hyperdemocracy of the PCHE report). Threats to the tax-free status of businesses owned by universities called for testimony before Congress, as did proposed federal aid to medical education. Although Brown lacked a medical school, Wriston had occasionally acted as a spokesman on the issue "by scrupulously following the line as developed in our conferences." Repeatedly, the AAU set forth the case against giving federal aid only to public institutions, and it long favored aid to special programs over general aid to students.

Believing that the AAU had prestige beyond its current merits, Wriston planned to help it live up to its reputation. He hoped that the association could become less reactive and begin to influence legislation from established policy positions. It was embarrassing with these new ambitions to have certain strong universities still excluded from the organization. Plans for a major infusion were soon under way, but these simply ratified the AAU's elite status.

At the annual meeting of 1949, only the dinner session was a joint affair of presidents and deans, though Wriston did give the deans an informal report. They learned that the presidents had scrapped plans to celebrate the AAU's semicentennial in 1950. Such ceremonies probably seemed too backward looking, and they would necessarily have stressed the organization's long domination by graduate schools. The deans were also told that any policy statements they made should be forwarded to the presidents to make sure of a common public position. As if to cap these demonstrations of power, the presidents used far more than their agreed upon portion of the dues. The new arrangements brought some prestige gains to the dean, however. After all, one of them would always head the AGS, and they were no longer obliged to fume about the shameful absence of the presidents.[39]

THE AAC: FAMILIAR STRUCTURES IN A NEW LOCATION

In the world of institutional associations, the AAC was special because of its inclusiveness. Although not a peak association like the ACE, it comprised representatives of almost all types of colleges and universities with liberal arts programs—state universities and technological institutes, among others. Sometimes this breadth proved influential, giving credibility to the AAC's long negotiations with the AAUP, which eventuated in the 1940 Statement of Principles on Academic Freedom and Tenure. After the war, the AAC again worked jointly with the AAUP to set standards for retirement and pensions. Generally, however, the AAC spoke not for all institutions that included the liberal arts but for certain sectors within the world of higher education: the small, the church-related, and the "private." Except for the ACE, it was the only major institutional association that included historically black colleges.[40]

Even among liberal arts colleges, of course, there were disagreements. The cultural elitism of President Chalmers of Kenyon diverged sharply from the pragmatic worldliness of Williams's James Phinney Baxter III. In the first postwar presidential address to the AAC, Baxter, who had helped organize the government's Office of Strategic Services, contrasted the improved public image of the scholar to caricatures during the New Deal. Fears early in the war that raw vocationalism would sweep education had proved groundless, he declared, and liberal education, tested by crisis, had come out stronger than ever. Baxter stressed international relations as a rising new field and proposed student roundtables with faculty members who had had public administrative experience. From his perspective, the liberal arts were healthy largely because of the nation's recent cashing in on special skills among the liberally educated.[41]

With its leaders' repeated strictures on federal aid and their rec-ognition that some expansion of higher education was appropriate, the AAC had obliged itself to demonstrate that nongovernmental sources could provide support to member institutions. As before the war, expectations were directed to churches, alumni, business cor-porations, and foundations. These as well as individual nonalumni donors were the imagined audience for broadened promotion of lib-eral arts institutions.

Increasingly, church financial contributions were overshadowed by the possibilities of business support. In 1949, when the AAC set up a Commission on Colleges and Industry, the program of the annual meeting included one address by the president of Standard Oil of New Jersey and another boldly titled "Touching Corporations." After a slow start under the University of Pennsylvania's Harold E. Stassen, the commission gained influence during the chairmanship of Frank H. Sparks, president of Wabash College. A former businessman, Sparks practiced the philosophy of coordinated voluntarism by en-couraging the formation of state committees of colleges jointly to seek corporate gifts.[42]

From its earliest days under Robert L. Kelly, the AAC had una-bashedly pursued public relations. In 1946 its Commission on Public Relations joined with the American College Public Relations Associ-ation (ACPRA) to form a counseling service for member institutions. Under President Raymond Walters of the University of Cincinnati, the AAC's commission developed a broadened definition of public relations as more than publicity, as signifying instead "the friendliness practiced by all within the institution toward the community in respect to information, guidance and cooperation." Along with its call for teamwork, the commission recommended that each institution have a trained public relations director. With the help of a $9,000 grant from the AAC, the ACPRA in 1950 established a full-time executive secretary in a national headquarters, which was in fact a room in the offices of the AAC. Snavely saw this assistance as preempting a move by the NEA to gain power in ACPRA, but Thackrey and J. L. Morrill of the land-grant association feared that publicity officers might en-croach on policy formation and refused to lend support.[43]

The AAC offices were now located in Washington, on Lafayette Park in the Brookings Institution Building, near the ACE. Having moved from Chicago to New York to be near various foundation headquarters, the AAC shifted again, largely in recognition of deep-ening involvement with federal programs. Snavely had complained about how much time he had to spend commuting from New York, and he achieved the move in late 1947 over the objections of some directors. As a gesture of compromise, the AAC's Carnegie-funded arts program remained behind.[44]

The AAC's federal relations activities involved some risk, since they were particularly prone to bring out policy differences between its private and public member institutions. These conflicts, mounting but tolerable in the late 1940s, soon began to strain the coherence of the AAC. Questions intensified concerning the best means of federal funding for higher education. Should there be grants to institutions, or grants to students, or tax credits to parents? Private and public institutions also relied on differing strategies to attract nongovernmental support. Beginning in the 1960s the AAC provided a home for an organization dedicated to fund raising for private institutions, the Federation of State Associations of Independent Colleges and Universities, reorganized in 1971 as the National Council for Independent Colleges and Universities. After a troubled self-examination, in which a study funded by the Carnegie Corporation and the Danforth Foundation played an influential role, the AAC decided to abandon both lobbying and mapping of strategies for institutional fund raising and to concentrate on liberal education in public and private institutions. In 1976, with a slight name change, the National Association of Independent Colleges and Universities (soon well known as NAICU) became a separate organization.[45]

THE ZOOK ADMINISTRATION WINDS DOWN

In obvious ways the ACE of the late 1940s was a success. It courted new members and won them. When it raised dues, almost none dropped out. By 1950, when dues income made the central office self-sustaining, Carnegie and Rockefeller money had ceased dominating the program. Smaller foundations and other voluntary organizations sponsored ACE projects, and federal contracts multiplied. Aside from Zook and Brown's leadership in the President's Commission on Higher Education, they also played critical roles in the emergence of UNESCO and the International Association of Universities. Beneath the evident growth and public recognition, however, all was not well. Zook's successor and others complained in 1951 that the ACE had not kept its members well informed or involved them adequately in policy discussions. The ACE had become the available educational agency for so many interests that its programmatic heterogeneity revived old uncertainties about mission.[46]

Was the ACE concerned with higher education only or with all levels of education, as the constitutional revision of 1934 and the work of the American Youth Commission had indicated? During World War II the council's involvement with lower schools had diminished, and although superintendents of city schools regularly held conspicuous ACE offices, the scales remained heavily tilted toward higher education. The ACE sponsored a small conference of elementary school leaders in 1949 to reassure doubters, but there was no followup. Although Zook's pronouncements on the crucial international role of education included the schools, stressing the struggle against illiteracy, he was nevertheless pulled increasingly toward higher education as indicated by his leadership in the founding of the IAU. Uneasiness about the overlap in function between the ACE and the NEA intensified when the latter plunged into the field of higher education with a series of conferences in 1946. Partly in response, the ACE began to downplay lower schools and concentrate on postsecondary programs, though Zook could always cite projects that let him deny the shift. At the 1951 annual meeting, some delegates raised the possibility of explicitly restricting the ACE's field to higher education, and by 1957 an inquirer at the central office learned that "the ACE is primarily interested in higher education and has no committee which concerns itself with legislation applying to the public schools."[47]

The hectic early postwar years did not invite systematic rethinking of the associations' interrelationships, and their clustering in Washington was still at an early stage. Zook saw strength in the ACE's unique comprehensiveness, but he failed to include coordination when summing up the organization's major functions in 1946. Still, coordination was advanced by the funds and office space that the ACE provided the Council on Cooperation in Teacher Education, and each year the ACE sponsored a conference of the associations that were its constituent members. Although, as Zook admitted, it was "not easy to select topics for discussion which are of common interest," these meetings succeeded in issuing pronouncements on government policies and allowed some informal associational interchange. Similarly useful was the ACE's published guide to its organizational members, briefly identifying their particular goals. Its *Higher Education and National Affairs* served some of the functions of the later *Chronicle of Higher Education* in keeping educators abreast of developments.[48]

The deficiencies of such coordinating efforts helped create the interassociational "Luncheon Group" of the 1950s and, after that became unwieldy in the early 1960s, a "Secretariat," which included the chief executive officers of about twelve associations. The Secretariat continued, but in the 1980s the more informal and exclusive "Brethren" emerged, a regular gathering of heads of six leading institutional associations (all those treated in this volume except the

AAC—replaced by the NAICU—plus the AASCU). Under the "lead agency" strategy, initiatives were assigned on the basis of special capacities and interests among the associations. A study in 1980 found that, though they often wanted stronger coordination, most institutional presidents approved of the existing arrangement, with the ACE continuing as the only umbrella group but exercising little direct control over others.[49]

Inadequacies as a coordinating agency traced partly to the ACE's involvement with its own projects. It was increasingly an operational organization. Under contract, for instance, the ACE was helping plan programs for the Office of Naval Research's Manpower Branch. The National Conference of Christians and Jews supported three ACE projects on intergroup relations. The American Foundation for Pharmaceutical Education made the ACE the conduit for funding a four-year study. Starting up new projects, wrapping up old ones, and trying to get "implementation" lessened the chances for ACE leaders to do systemic thinking.[50]

When an ACE project developed into an independent entity or entered a new alliance, working out the terms required onerous negotiations. A particularly troublesome separation was the departure of the Cooperative Test Service (CTS), which in 1947 merged into the new Educational Testing Service. The ACE's testing program had begun with publication of Louis and Thelma Thurstone's "psychological examinations" in 1924. The CTS had begun six years later from the initiative of Dean Herbert Hawkes of Columbia University and a $500,000 grant from the GEB. Headquartered at Columbia under the directorship of Ben D. Wood, the CTS's tests had sold well, and Zook could hardly welcome the loss of this self-supporting, even profitable, program. He also feared that an independent testing bureau might come to dominate the curriculum through its standardized tests. In 1946 ACE leaders stormily resisted efforts by the Carnegie Corporation to sweep the CTS into a merger of major national testing programs. There followed a mollifying report from a Carnegie commission, which recommended affiliation with the ACE for the new agency, but this plan met strong opposition. After complex maneuvering, the ACE had to settle for mere participation on the board of the Educational Testing Service and a Carnegie grant that supported continuing exploratory and evaluative work by a new ACE Committee on Measurement and Evaluation. The episode weakened the ACE's claims as an ideal national coordinator.[51]

The ACE's oddly assorted private donors included, besides B'nai B'rith for the survey of college admissions discussed in the previous chapter, the National Council of Soviet-American Friendship for an analysis of data on the Soviet Union in textbooks, General Motors (one of several supporting corporations) for a study of college placement services, and the Grant Foundation for a study of personal qualities of successful teachers. The State of Maryland supported a survey of its institutions of higher education. From federal agencies, in contrast to the few and paltry projects before the war, the ACE began to receive substantial special funds, becoming a channel for State Department aid to U.S. schools in Latin America and a designer of Navy personnel programs in science. In the late 1940s the ACE's annual financial statements were peppered with the federal identification numbers of contracts, task orders, and grants.[52]

Although reduced, foundation influence in ACE affairs had by no means disappeared. Plans for the ACE to launch a major review of accreditation practices collapsed for lack of any grant. In Zook's final years, the Carnegie and Rockefeller philanthropies minimized their aid to the ACE and then gave $150,000 each for general support when Arthur S. Adams became its president. At the same time the ACE received its first funds from the newly active Ford Foundation.[53]

In the most positive interpretation, this array of activities represented a vigorous response to the postwar boom in education, and well-chaired committees could achieve their ends without draining central-office energies. Not all chairs were effective, however. Zook and his staff lent a degree of order, but the ACE seemed all too ready to mount projects for whoever could pay. The Problems and Policies Committee was supposed to engage in broad thinking and general oversight, and it did occasionally redirect or block ill-considered projects. But it lost its old verve. It met only once during a twelve-month span in 1948–49, and when Barnard's Millicent Carey McIntosh declined to serve after her election to the committee, the place stayed unfilled for a year. The format of Zook's annual report symbolized the state of the council. Excerpts read at annual meetings included stirring assertions of the crucial role of education in advancing human understanding and world peace. But the report as a whole, dominating one number of the *Educational Record* each year, became an unreadable compendium, clogged by accounts of committee doings.[54]

Like Moses looking into the promised land, Zook watched the ACE move into spacious new headquarters on December 29, 1950, two days before his retirement took effect. Beginning in 1946, the ACE had annually set aside money in a building fund, with the hope that bringing various associations under one roof would "enhance the standing of the Council and of education generally in Washington." For roughly a half-million dollars, the ACE was able to buy and renovate a handsome Renaissance apartment house, once the residence of Andrew

Mellon, at 1785 Massachusetts Avenue, NW. A little further from the White House than its former location on Lafayette Park, the new address kept the ACE close to the headquarters of many other third-sector organizations.[55]

More ACE projects could now be housed together, and there was room for expansion. Fifteen other educational organizations located their offices in the building, including the land-grant association, the American Association of Junior Colleges, the National Catholic Educational Association, and the American Association of University Professors. Central duplicating and mailing facilities served them all. Other member organizations and institutions were encouraged to make the ACE building a "home in Washington," and a few small offices were reserved for use by visiting educators. The building soon assumed the unofficial name of "National Higher Education Center." Although dwarfed by its successor—One Dupont Circle, erected in the late 1960s with a grant from the W. K. Kellogg Foundation—the Massachusetts Avenue building marked the ACE as mature and prosperous, firmly entrenched in the Washington establishment of voluntary organizations. The shelter provided for other organizations made manifest the ACE's coordinating mission.[56]

ACCREDITATION RECONSIDERED

The agonizing over accreditation, damped down by the war, re-emerged in the midforties. Issues of accrediting gained urgency in part because more and more government agencies were accepting judgments of accrediting bodies. Some legislation, such as the GI Bill, linked accredited lists to eligibility for federal aid. Civil service positions and state licensing often required graduation from an "accredited" institution.[57]

Nowhere did the matter prove more explosive than in the AAU. Before the war, accreditation had developed as the most conspicuous and most expensive of the AAU's activities, justified as a way to identify college programs that prepared students effectively for graduate work. Inclusion on the AAU's "List of Approved Institutions," based on examinations that included campus visitation, counted importantly in intercollegiate competition for prestige. By comparison, the lists of the regional associations seemed too generously inclusive. Government agencies and foreign institutions relied on the AAU list, and the American Association of University Women admitted alumnae only of included institutions. Among the graduate deans were several, such as Fernandus Payne of Indiana University, longtime chair of the AAU Committee on Classification, whose involvement in the program was closely intertwined with their professional identity. Payne had disparaged the wave of criticism of accreditation just before World War II.

The AAU did not overtly accredit graduate education. Still, the judgments passed by the Committee on Membership involved something similar. Results of the investigation that followed an application for membership were shared with the individual candidate institution, though not published, and the roster of AAU members itself could be read as a list of approved graduate programs. As the war drew to a close, the AAU's position on accreditation once again became a point of contention. In 1944 Iowa State University protested that holders of its doctorates applying for positions in Public Health Service laboratories found themselves stigmatized because their degrees came from an institution not belonging to the AAU. A forceful, angry letter from the graduate dean of Iowa State told the association that it should either disavow any accrediting role in graduate education or undertake to survey the work at nonmember institutions. At Iowa State's behest, the land-grant association formally asked the AAU to address the matter. In response, the AAU set up a special committee to consider appraising graduate study. This committee, dominated by deans, reported back in favor of extension of the accreditation program and in so doing helped precipitate the radical AAU self-analysis of 1947–48.[58]

Clearly, these advocates of accreditation had overreached. They brought to the 1945 meeting a plan for the AAU to assume the task of accrediting graduate work, to do so department by department, and to begin the process with member institutions. Proponents argued that if the AAU did not take on this responsibility the regional associations or the ACE would do so, presumably less effectively. A greater threat came from the associations specialized by discipline, notably the American Chemical Society, which was already accrediting chemistry departments. The committee's report envisioned questionnaires, visitations, and follow-up appraisals. The impression of gearing up for a major operation was heightened by a complicated flow chart and the suggestion of a $2,000 contribution from each AAU member. With a degree of acrimony, skeptical delegates attacked the cumbersome apparatus proposed and expressed their fears of rigidification of Ph.D. degree requirements. Chicago's Dean Richard McKeon opposed the extension to graduate education of procedures developed to assess undergraduate programs, contending that the "more impressionistic methods" of the AAU's membership committee fit graduate work better. After a year's delay that saved face for the special committee, the AAU voted overwhelmingly not to go into graduate accrediting.[59]

Surprisingly, given recent encomiums for Dean Payne's long-standing Committee on Classification and the careful differentiation of its work appraising undergraduate programs, that undertaking also came under attack. With his harsh 1947 address, Stanford's Tresidder emerged as the most vocal opponent of the AAU's Approved List. Warning of continuous pressure to make accreditation more elaborate, he doubted if the program was worth the effort. A recent Carnegie Foundation study, he reminded his colleagues, had found no distinction between the success in graduate study by alumni of colleges on the list and others, a particularly telling result inasmuch as the foundation had been the principal source of funds to start the program. The AAU should welcome variety among colleges and universities and "lay the ghost of accreditation once and for all."[60]

As part of its report a year later, the AAU's Problems and Policies Committee recommended an end to the accreditation program, citing the many other organizations in the field, the rising cost in time and money, and the wide range of institutions asking admission to the list. The AAU's contribution was of "diminishing necessity and effectiveness." Dean Payne and a few others struggled to save the appraisal system, contending that the criteria were not mechanically applied, institutional individuality was encouraged, and AAU standards gave leverage to move stodgy trustees. Polls of colleges found that a majority—even of those rejected—favored continuation of AAU accreditation, as did representatives of the USOE, the North Central Association, and the ACE. All to no avail. As part of the revolution of 1948, the association voted by more than two-to-one to end the "annual plague of accreditation."[61]

Although they might choose not to be accreditors, the members of the AAU still found themselves subjected to accreditation. Among reasons for strengthening the AAU, Hutchins cited the need to meet "the danger that control of our institutions will be taken away from us" by professional accrediting agencies, which he unhesitatingly labeled "pressure groups." As Hancher saw it, the AAU needed to find allies in opposing "the invasion of our campuses by organizations oftentimes composed of representatives of our own institutions who meet outside and come back with proposals which they have framed." Having cooperated to bring about system, the universities now feared they had created a monster. The AAU declared itself ready to join other institutional associations in taking countermeasures.[62]

The most readily available vehicle was the Joint Committee on Accrediting, which since its founding in 1938 had limped along under the chairmanship of John J. Tigert, president of the University of Florida, mildly urging professional associations to be reasonable. The

American Chemical Society, importuned by the JCA to postpone its projected departmental accreditation, went ahead to examine and certify departments in institutions not represented in the JCA, giving them an invidious aura of quality. Examples of professional groups' overbearingness surfaced at meetings of virtually every institutional association. On what seemed arbitrarily structural grounds, for instance, a College of Veterinary Medicine might be denied accreditation because its head reported to the dean of the College of Agriculture rather than the university's president.[63]

Five institutional associations revitalized the JCA in 1949 and, with Nebraska's Reuben G. Gustavson in the lead, transformed it into the National Commission on Accrediting (NCA). Before various conventions, Gustavson traced the troubled history of accreditation and promised ways to reduce the number of fields reviewed, simplify reporting, and allow for appeals to the new NCA. Adopting the mixed membership pattern of the ACE, the commission included not only associations but also colleges and universities, of which over six hundred joined during its first year.[64]

By 1950 Wriston happily declared that some of the accrediting agencies were "displaying a healthy condition of terror." A few accrediting initiatives were indeed squelched and certain procedures simplified, but as the system-making founders of the institutional associations might have foreseen, there was no turning back from the world of standards and lists and national coordination. The NCA never fulfilled early hopes. It had a small budget, its policies were nonbinding, and, in the words of Harold Orlans, "the initial purposes of suppressing or controlling specialized accrediting were grandiloquent, unclear, or unrealistic." It was hard to hold the ranks together. Presidents who at association meetings applauded attacks on some accreditor's intrusiveness sometimes surrendered to pressure from representatives of the same field back on campus. Was it so unreasonable to give the dental school its own dean if that would attain an imprimatur valued by dental professors, alumni, and prospective students?[65]

Meanwhile the ACE had slacked off in the field of accreditation, the relevant committee being among its weakest. Gustavson's animadversions on professional-school accreditation struck Zook as excessive. If that activity had somewhat overproliferated, it was still true, he believed, that clients of professionals ultimately benefited from attention to educational standards. He doubtless felt an obligation to be even-handed, since professional as well as institutional associations were constituent members of the ACE.[66]

Not until November 1949 did the ACE sponsor a general conference on accreditation like those it had held before the war. With thirty organizations represented, accreditors of education in nursing, social work, pharmacy, and other fields explained themselves, as did the heads of two new umbrella groups, the NCA and the National Committee of Regional Accrediting Agencies (which the ACE, upset over the disappearance of the AAU's approved list of undergraduate programs, had helped bring into existence). As was the wont of ACE-sponsored conferences, this one requested that the ACE undertake further studies. The ACE set its vice-president, A. J. Brumbaugh, to work on the problem, restoring him to a post he had held earlier, chair of the Committee on Accrediting Procedures. The committee floundered, however, partly because a grant application to the Carnegie Foundation failed. Perhaps disappointed at not being chosen Zook's successor, Brumbaugh left in 1950 to become president of Shimer College. The ACE was not to continue its earlier activism in accreditation policy.[67]

Retrospect and Prospect, 1950

•

DESPITE their overlapping memberships, contrasts between the AAU and the land-grant association suggested how divergent institutional associations could be. In 1950 the AAU scrapped plans for a fiftieth-anniversary celebration, just as the ALGCU began to consider sponsoring a history of the land-grant movement. The presidents of AAU member institutions showed new determination to make the AAU their organization, restricting the graduate deans to a subsidiary; meanwhile, the ALGCU had developed a way to share governance between member institutions' chief executive officers and other administrators. The AAU had rejected suggestions for a paid executive secretaryship, an office currently proving a boon for the ALGCU and on the verge of expansion.

Three other associations had changed less strikingly in the aftermath of World War II. Although hoping to revive the distinctiveness of state universities, the NASU had launched a process of negotiation that would in time bring merger with the land-grant association, a recognition of the great similarity among complex state-supported universities. Of the major associations, the AAC remained the least happy with government activism and, in spite of its inclusiveness, stressed the values of private education. Its incumbent executive director managed to cooperate with government ventures while warning AAC members against government interference. With the largest staff among the associations, the ACE had also been established the longest in Washington. In 1950 there was promise of mounting influence in its new headquarters building, the election of a new executive head, and renewed wartime calls on its liaison capabilities.

The Korean conflict revived a familiar scenario. Once again the ACE called a special conference that pledged sacrifice and national service. Once again worries about loss of students to the armed forces dominated associational meetings. Postwar euphoria had been fading for some time, however, and Cold War

rhetoric had already begun to mark associational pronouncements. The AAC board of directors called a special session to
redesign the convention scheduled for January 1951, changing
its theme to "The Colleges and This Crisis," promising to treat
ideological, military, and financial aspects, and inviting government officials to participate. The new head of the ACE, Arthur
S. Adams, declared that the conflict had cleared the air, rendering
undeniable the "present danger." Trained at the U.S. Naval
Academy and a veteran of World War II, Adams had, while
president of the University of New Hampshire, led federal legislation committees of both the land-grant association and the
NASU. His first annual report at the ACE stressed "manpower"
problems.[1]

By 1950 those involved in higher education talked far less of
system than they had during the Age of Standards, their earlier
efforts having helped achieve the triumph of mutual certification. The national associations had enabled participants to advance an American ideal of system, derived in large part from
observing what was already practiced but made more explicit
and given national application. The more reflective or articulate
could through the associations explore and legitimize the voluntaristic, pluralistic, federative nature of American higher education.

Degree mills had not been the main cause of worry, but rather
inflated claims, difficulty in authenticating valid claims, and uncertainty about standards. Unless moderated, competition for
money, students, and prestige threatened to corrupt the academic enterprise. To meet these problems, associationalists believed, the American way of higher education should be nationally systematized—but not by the central government. Embracing
the classic liberal conviction that government must be limited,
they willingly took on quasi-governmental functions. The philanthropic foundations also had a national perspective and a leadership bent on developing system in the United States. Since
foundations provided alternative sources of power to balance
and restrain government, it was easy for the associations to accept
their gifts and guidance. Their power over the associations had
peaked in the 1920s and 1930s. Once the ACE could support
itself from dues, it was unlikely ever again to have its very constitutional declaration of mission reshaped by foundation influence.

As befit their guiding philosophy, the power of the associations
remained distinctly limited. Ultimately, it was realized, the single
institution had to choose which variety of learning it would promote and the clientele it would serve. Since gathered representatives could explain idiosyncrasies of their home institutions and
gain tolerance from each other, the associations sometimes

helped preserve differences. The delicate task of the associations was to recognize variety while still seeking the benefits of systematization. The same institutions that valued their distinctiveness and wanted freedom to please their constituents by different means desired also to be linked through mutual recognition with other institutions. Such linkage required a degree of conformity.

Associations could constrain single institutions by refusing their requests for membership or leaving them off "accepted lists." Some institutions accredited by the regionals found themselves judged inadequate by standards of certain national associations. States could issue charters and donors give money as they wished. But beneficiary institutions could not, if they valued national recognition, avoid the judgments of national bodies of academic administrators. These judgments were sometimes brought home by local academic leaders, sometimes revealed through invited surveys that relied on national standards, and sometimes (a tendency beginning in the 1940s and destined to flourish) made the basis for barring an institution from federal programs. No Morrill institution was kept out of the land-grant association for reasons of "standards." (The nonadmission of the black land-grant institutions traced to more atavistic sources.) Exclusion from the NASU was extremely rare for a clearly identified "state university." Once inside either of these associations, however, an institution was obliged to compare itself with others of its declared type, and emulation increased accordingly. In the case of the AAU, hopes for inclusion shaped important decisions within both public and private universities. The leaders of the associations favored local autonomy and institutional variation, but they expected such independence to be practiced within a framework of shared standards. Like the regionals, institutional associations after 1930 shifted away from quantitative criteria and increasingly respected an institution's own sense of purpose. Difference and healthy competition, it was demonstrated, need not bar common ventures for mutual benefit.

Faith remained strong that the associations could do much that in other nations was left to government. Still, though sometimes grudgingly and always with the proviso that voluntary organizations must balance federal action, it was agreed that the federal government played an important role in higher education. The educational associations had sought to avoid the reputation of lobbyists. They acted decorously, but they still tried to exert influence. Originally, appeals to federal officials came from elites within the associations (notably the executive committee of the land-grant group), but later, and increasingly, such appeals came also from salaried associational officers. Hoping that geographical range would make the requests look like a groundswell, presidents of member institutions encouraged each other to communicate their shared desires to congressmen. When presidents of the United States sent greetings to those attending conventions or welcomed them at the White House, the exchanges were highly ceremonial. Matters were more pointed when select delegations pressed Woodrow Wilson to back a Department of Education or asked Franklin D. Roosevelt to soften military intransigence toward academic concerns.

All in all, Washington officials did not pay much attention to education before 1950, as the persistent failure to obtain cabinet status showed. The influence of the New Deal on education would have differed little if the associations had not existed. Despite the publicity accompanying the reports of the PCHE in 1946–47, almost no federal action ensued. Some political victories, however, did come to the higher education associations. The land-grant group, which had a base in ever state, claimed among its successes the 1890 Morrill Act, the 1914 Smith-Lever Act, and the congressional reversal of VA rulings in 1950. The AAC, during an activist period in the early 1930s, helped exempt colleges from NRA provisions. The ACE in World War II forced some compromises in the military's campus training programs and made them academically less damaging than those of World War I, more attentive — to use a term of the times — to institutional "conservation." The associations took a hand in shaping the GI Bill and proved effective in its later revision. Although the reconfigurations of the late 1940s signaled no abandonment of associationalism, they confirmed acceptance, in some cases reluctant, of a greater governmental role in education. Each association took steps to provide members more opportunity to observe and influence the federal government.

The government by 1950 had ratified the assocations' view of their function by consulting with them about legislation, requesting advisory committees for administrative agencies, and letting contracts for educational services. The more influential colleges and universities sometimes chose to act directly in federal relations, and the various associations did not always favor the same policies. The ACE survived as a federation of federations by skirting the more divisive issues. Efforts by the associations to provide one voice for higher education encountered other obstacles as well: fears of seeming to coerce members, delays to await questionnaire responses, and suppositions of zero-sum games (as when the NASU and the land-grant association blocked each other's attempts to get federal support for engineering research stations). Probably the deepest tensions ran between public and private sectors, indicated by conflicting reactions to the PCHE recommendation for capital aid to public institutions. The associations repeatedly tried to moderate all of these difficulties, maintaining that disagreements were small compared to broad common interests.

Despite many limitations, the associations had by 1950 become acknowledged participants in the national governing process. The next quarter-century saw the development of a smoothly working practice of steady mutual consultation by association chief executive officers in Washington. Together they grew highly skilled at setting priorities, dividing responsibilities, and resolving disagreements. These academic chieftains also learned how to catch public attention through the media.

Like the rising professional organizations, the institutional associations offered mutual prestige enhancement and mutual counsel. In fact, they were the closest thing university presidents and deans had to professional societies. By adding this personal element to their institutional basis, the associations managed to share the élan that accompanied the professionalizing of American occupations. The resemblance to trade associations was also apparent, as in efforts to limit competitiveness by sharing information. Understandably, however, educational associations sought to differentiate themselves from profit-oriented interests. Only rarely did a disgruntled federal administrator or congressman note that educational associations sought the interests of clients and not just the common good. The rubric "nonprofit" with its connotations of altruism was gaining favor among both public and private educational institutions.

The world of learning often tried to have it both ways, presenting itself as critically useful to society yet dedicated to free inquiry independent of instrumental demands. Undeniably, the institutional associations shared in the worldly aspects of higher education. They promised to benefit business and agriculture and the military. They took pains to improve member institutions' (and their own) salary scales, balance sheets, and publicity. Still, the fact that they cared about education often led them, beyond considerations of profit and power and career success, to look for ways to enlarge humane possibilities through teaching and learning.

Harvard University might sometimes go it alone, and Black Mountain College might want no part of national affiliation, but the associations had developed widely accepted new means for institutions to work together and learn from each other. The associations themselves, coming to respect one another's special qualities, had found ways to cooperate for shared ends. To take their measure at midcentury meant recognition that, under gradualist and meliorist leadership, these organizations had promoted centralization without denying the necessary multifariousness of the human struggle against ignorance.

Note on Primary Sources

I CANNOT CLAIM that my long read through the proceedings of the institutional associations yielded unalloyed delight. I did, however, find enough evidence of little-known but important phases of the academic past to let me encourage other scholars to explore this neglected source. These variously named proceedings (see "Abbreviations") are widely available in academic libraries.

Proceedings of the land-grant association are very full, including addresses, reports, records of section meetings, and some debate. Those of the NASU include even fuller transcripts of debate for the early years. The very existence of this source has been missed by researchers who overlook the long period of NASU independence before its 1963 merger.

The AAU published lengthy participant-approved extracts from the debates that followed formal conference papers but much less from its business meetings. Its journal ends abruptly in 1948, but in the next two years the AAU's president reported on its activities to the new subsidiary Association of Graduate Schools, which continued the journal under a new name. The AAC published most of the addresses and many committee reports from annual meetings but only brief minutes.

Similarly, the ACE kept published minutes to a minimum, since it sought to make the *Educational Record* a general-interest education periodical. In fact, however, many addresses from the annual meeting appeared therein. Shorter-lived periodical publications such as the *History and Activities* series and various brochures sometimes give details of ACE undertakings unavailable through the *Educational Record*.

All these associational proceedings include committee reports—some trivial, others marking important new ways of pursuing an association's mission. Executive committee reports are often revealing; they are surpassed in importance, however, in the cases of the AAC and the ACE by the annual reports of the variously named chief salaried officer at national headquarters.

Manuscript sources proved plentiful in approximately reverse order of the founding dates of the associations. The archives of the ACE are highly inclusive and well arranged. They contain correspondence, committee minutes, draft and final committee reports, office memoranda, and—especially useful for this study—documents sent in by constituent members (other associations). The archives also include stenographic transcripts of several annual meetings.

The AAC archives are spotty but include minutes of the executive committee (later the board of directors) that are often fuller than those published, as well as full transcripts of early annual meetings. Besides a small "Historical File," there are two summational documents drawn up by Robert L. Kelly at the end of his administration, "Policies and Precedents in the History of the Association of American Colleges: Source Material Drawn from Official Records, 1914–1935" and "An Audit of Experience: A Review of the Program, Policies and Precedents Developed during the History of the Association of American Colleges, 1915–1937." The surviving correspondence falls mostly after 1950.

The AAU archives are sparse, with very little before 1950. Some stray documents have been kept, however, such as those bearing on the 1902 challenge to the association's legitimacy.

Part of the NASU records, mostly correspondence of the secretary-treasurer from the 1930s and 1940s, survives in the archives of the NASULGC at the University of Illinois, Urbana-Champaign. For the period before 1947, the same archives have less on the land-grant association. Beginning with Russell I. Thackrey's assumption of office as its executive secretary-treasurer, the collection is full of interesting correspondence, including preparation for congressional testimony and encounters with federal agencies.

To fill gaps in associational archives, papers of college and university presidents proved invaluable. Even when a president was not an active participant in an association to which his institution belonged, a meticulous filing system sometimes preserved a good run of the association's form letters, memoranda, and minutes of various committees. When a president was active, files are likely to contain frank exchanges on the workings of the association and indicate its links to current hopes and frustrations at particular institutions. Rather different are the blunt appraisals of the national bodies that crop up in correspondence between institutional presidents and in intrainstitutional memoranda. (For manuscript collections consulted and locations, see "Abbreviations.")

Circulars and bulletins of the USBE (USOE), despite their unappealing format and inadequate indexing, proved a dependable source for year-by-year educational affairs, and their statistics are the best available. The early reports and bulletins of the Carnegie Foundation for the Advancement of Teaching include survey information of value, besides being in themselves a strong influence on the institutional associations.

Memoirs helped humanize the official record. In *My Several Lives: Memoirs of a Social Inventor* (New York, 1970), James B. Conant made use of documentary sources as well as recollection. Herman B Wells's *Being Lucky: Reminiscences and Reflections* (Bloomington, Ind., 1980) is more spontaneous, reflecting the ebullient personality of its author. Guy E. Snavely's *A Search for Excellence: Memoirs of a College Administrator* (New York, 1964), though undependable in detail, tells a good deal about the ethos of the AAC, even before he became its executive director in 1937.

Abbreviations

Manuscript Collections Cited

AAC Ar. Association of American Colleges Archives, AAC national headquarters, Washington, D.C.

AAU Ar. Association of American Universities Archives, consulted at AAU national headquarters, now in the Milton S. Eisenhower Library, Johns Hopkins University

ACE Ar. American Council on Education Archives, consulted at ACE national headquarters, now in the Hoover Institution Archives, Stanford University

ACIA President's Office Records: Institutional Associations, 1934–76, Amherst College Archives

AGR Alexander G. Ruthven Papers, Bentley Library, University of Michigan

AHR Aurelia Henry Reinhardt Papers, Mills College Archives

AM Alexander Meiklejohn Papers, Amherst College Archives

AOL Armin O. Leuschner Papers, Bancroft Library, University of California, Berkeley

ASD Andrew S. Draper Papers, University of Illinois Archives, Urbana-Champaign

CCL Clarence C. Little Papers, Bentley Library, University of Michigan

CWE Charles W. Eliot Papers, Harvard University Archives

DBT Donald B. Tresidder Papers, Stanford University Archives

DK David Kinley Papers, University of Illinois Archives

EJJ	Edmund J. James Papers, University of Illinois Archives
HPJ	Harry Pratt Judson Papers, University of Chicago Archives
HS	Henry Suzzallo Papers, University of Washington Archives, Seattle
JBA	James Burrill Angell Papers, Bentley Library, University of Michigan
KLB	Kenyon L. Butterfield Papers, University of Massachusetts Archives, Amherst
MLB	Myron L. Burton Papers, Bentley Library, University of Michigan
NASULGC Ar.	National Association of State Universities and Land-Grant Colleges Archives (includes both NASU and land-grant association documents), University of Illinois Archives
RLW	Ray Lyman Wilbur Papers, Stanford University Archives
SBLP	Stephen B. L. Penrose Papers, Whittier College Archives
SPC	Samuel P. Capen Papers, State University of New York, Buffalo, Archives
UBPP	Presidents' Papers, University of Buffalo, State University of New York, Buffalo, Archives
UCPP	Presidents' Papers, University of California, Bancroft Library, University of California, Berkeley
UWPP	Presidents' Papers, University of Washington, University of Washington Archives

OTHER ABBREVIATIONS

AAA	Agricultural Adjustment Administration
AAACES Proc.	*Proceedings of the Association of American Agricultural Colleges and Experiment Stations* (1887–1919)
AAC Bul.	*Bulletin of the Association of American Colleges* (1915–58)
AAJC	American Association of Junior Colleges
AALGCSU Proc.	*Proceedings of the American Association of Land-Grant Colleges and State Universities* (1955–63)
AASA	American Association of School Administrators
AASCU	American Association of State Colleges and Universities

AAUP	American Association of University Professors
AAUP Bul.	*AAUP Bulletin*
AAU Proc.	*Association of American Universities Journal of Proceedings and Addresses* (1900–48)
ACLS	American Council of Learned Societies
ACPRA	American College Public Relations Association
AGS	Association of Graduate Schools
AGS Proc.	*Association of Graduate Schools in the Association of American Universities Journal of Proceedings and Addresses* (1948–77)
ALGC Proc.	*Proceedings of the Association of Land-Grant Colleges* (1920–25)
ALGCU Proc.	*Proceedings of the Association of Land-Grant Colleges and Universities* (1926–54)
Ar.	Archives
AR	Annual Report (of the highest salaried executive officer)
ASTP	Army Specialized Training Program
AUU	Association of Urban Universities
AVA	American Vocational Association
BDR	Board of Directors Report
Bul.	Bulletin
CCBE	Council of Church Boards of Education
CCC	Civilian Conservation Corps
CEST	Committee on Education and Special Training
CFAT	Carnegie Foundation for the Advancement of Teaching
CFAT AR	Carnegie Foundation for the Advancement of Teaching, Annual Report of the President
CFAT, Bul.	Carnegie Foundation for the Advancement of Teaching, Bulletin
CND	Council of National Defense
COFHE	Commission on Financing Higher Education
CPI	Consumer Price Index
CSHE	Center for Studies in Higher Education
CTS	Cooperative Test Service
DAB	*Dictionary of American Biography*
ECE	Emergency Council on Education
ECR	Executive Committee Report
Ed. Rec.	*Educational Record* (1920–)
EPC	Educational Policies Commission
ETS	Educational Testing Service

exec. cmte.	executive committee
GEB	General Education Board
HEQ	*History of Education Quarterly*
HUAC	House Un-American Activities Committee
IAU	International Association of Universities
IIE	Institute of International Education
IWM	Interchurch World Movement
JCA	Joint Committee on Accrediting
LACM	Liberal Arts College Movement
Lib. Ed.	*Liberal Education* (1959–)
mimeo.	mimeographed document
min.	minutes
MIT	Massachusetts Institute of Technology
NACE	National Advisory Committee on Education
NAICU	National Association of Independent Colleges and Universities
NASULGC	National Association of State Universities and Land-Grant Colleges
NASULGC Proc.	*Proceedings of the National Association of State Universities and Land-Grant Colleges* (1964–)
NASU Proc.	*National Association of State Universities Transactions and Proceedings* (1903–63)
NCAA	National Collegiate Athletic Association
NCA	National Commission on Accrediting
NEA	National Education Association
NEA Proc.	*National Education Association of the United States Addresses and Proceedings*
NRA	National Recovery Administration
NRC	National Research Council
NSF	National Science Foundation
NYA	National Youth Administration
NYU	New York University
PCHE	President's Commission on Higher Education
P&P cmte.	Problems and Plans Committee, ACE (beginning 1944, Problems and Policies)
ROTC	Reserve Officer Training Corp
S&S	*School and Society*
SATC	Students' Army Training Corps
SSRC	Social Science Research Council
SPEE	Society for the Promotion of Engineering Education
SUA	State Universities Association
TCR	*Teachers College Record*

UMT	Universal Military Training
USAFI	United States Armed Forces Institute
USBE	United States Bureau of Education
USDA	United States Department of Agriculture
USOE	United States Office of Education
VA	Veterans Administration

Notes

WHEN a person's name directly precedes the name of an association periodical, the reference is to untitled remarks. To identify the exact sources of quotations, I have included in parentheses after the relevant page number, catch words or phrases within quotation marks. A few obvious typographical errors in quotations have been silently corrected.

CHAPTER 1: GOING NATIONAL

1. Kenneth Boulding, *The Organizational Revolution: A Study in the Ethics of Economic Organization* (New York, 1953); Louis Galambos, "The Emerging Organizational Synthesis in Modern American History," *Business History Review* 44 (1970): 279–90; idem, "Technology, Political Economy, and Professionalization: Central Themes of the Organizational Synthesis," ibid. 57 (1983): 471–93; Laurence R. Veysey, "The Plural Organized Worlds of the Humanities," in Alexandra Oleson and John Voss (eds.), *The Organization of Knowledge in Modern America, 1860–1920* (Baltimore, 1979), 68–69; Charles W. Eliot, *Educational Reform: Essays and Addresses* (New York, 1898), 11.

2. David H. Everson, *Public Opinion and Interest Groups in American Politics* (New York, 1982), 81–85; Richard L. McCormick, *From Realignment to Reform: Political Change in New York State, 1893–1910* (Ithaca, N.Y., 1981), esp. 152–53. For two particularly valuable interpretive historiographical essays, see Daniel T. Rodgers, "In Search of Progressivism," *Reviews in American History* 10 (1982): 113–32; Alan Brinkley, "Richard Hofstadter's *The Age of Reform*: A Reconsideration," ibid. 13 (1985): 462–80.

3. Thomas L. Haskell, *The Emergence of Professional Social Science: The American Social Science Association and the Nineteenth-Century Crisis of Authority* (Urbana, Ill., 1977); Joseph C. Kiger, *American Learned Societies* (Washington, D.C., 1963), ch. 3.

4. *Historical Statistics of the United States* (Washington, D.C., 1975), 383 (more exact figures for number of institutions are 811 and 1,041); Robert S. Lynd and Helen Merrell Lynd, *Middletown: A Study in American Culture* (New York, 1929), 183–87, 187 ("taken"). Even Colin B. Burke's *American Collegiate Populations: A Test of the Traditional View* (New York, 1982), with its healthy warning against overstating post–Civil War changes, finds the increase in student en-

rollments significant. Much, though far from all, of Burke's case is undercut when 1920 rather than 1900 is taken as the vantage point. The more precise percentages for enrollment are 2.72 and 8.09 (*Historical Statistics of the United States* [1960 ed.], 211). For enrollments by institution, see *Biennial Survey of Education, 1918–20: Statistics* (USBE Bul. 29, Washington, D.C., 1923), table 23, pp. 309–83.

5. Kendall Birr, *Pioneering in Industrial Research* (Washington, D.C., 1956); John W. Servos, "The Industrial Relations of Science: Chemical Engineering at MIT, 1900–1939," *Isis* 71 (1980): 531–49; George Wise, *Willis R. Whitney, General Electric, and the Origins of U.S. Industrial Research* (New York, 1985); Merle Curti and Vernon Carstensen, *The University of Wisconsin: A History, 1848–1925* (Madison, Wis., 1949), 2:3, 109–10; Frederick Rudolph, *The American College and University: A History* (New York, 1962), 363–66.

6. Laurence R. Veysey, *The Emergence of the American University* (Chicago, 1965); Paula S. Fass, *The Damned and the Beautiful: American Youth in the 1920s* (New York, 1977); David O. Levine, *The American College and the Culture of Aspiration, 1915–1940* (Ithaca, N.Y., 1986), ch. 6.

7. Robert H. Wiebe, *The Search for Order, 1877–1920* (New York, 1967). For a comparative study of the national integration of higher education, see Burton R. Clark, *The Higher Education System: Academic Organization in Cross-National Perspective* (Berkeley, Calif., 1983), ch. 5, esp. 160–61.

8. Earle D. Ross, *Democracy's College: The Land-Grant Movement in the Formative Stage* (Ames, Iowa, 1942), 46–47; Rudolph, *American College and University*, 247–51; "The Morrill Act, 1862," in Richard Hofstadter and Wilson Smith (eds.), *American Higher Education: A Documentary History* (Chicago, 1961), 2:568 ("at least"); Hugh Hawkins, *Pioneer: A History of the Johns Hopkins University, 1874–1889* (Ithaca, N.Y., 1960), 17; Daniel Coit Gilman, "Our National Schools of Science," *North American Review* 105 (1867): 495–520.

9. *An Early View of the Land-Grant Colleges: Convention of Friends of Agricultural Education in 1871* (Urbana, Ill., 1967), esp. 88–107, 135–36; Alan I. Marcus, *Agricultural Science and the Quest for Legitimacy: Farmers, Agricultural Colleges, and Experiment Stations, 1870–1890* (Ames, Iowa, 1985), 130–31; Winton U. Solberg, *The University of Illinois, 1867–1894: An Intellectual and Cultural History* (Urbana, Ill., 1968), 135–37.

10. Marcus, *Agricultural Science*, 132–36, 166–81; Alfred C. True, *A History of Agricultural Education in the United States, 1785–1925* (USDA Misc. Pub. 36, Washington, D.C., 1929), 194–95, 201–2; Ross, *Democracy's College*, 168–70.

11. *Preliminary Convention: Proceedings of a Convention of Delegates from Agricultural Colleges and Experiment Stations Held at the Department of Agriculture, July 8 and 9, 1885* (Office of Experiment Stations, Special Report 9, Washington, D.C., 1885) [usually bound with *AAACES Proc.*]; True, *History of Agricultural Education*, 208–10; idem, *A History of Agricultural Experimentation and Research in the United States, 1607–1925, Including a History of the United States Department of Agriculture* (USDA Misc. Pub. 251, Washington, D.C., 1937), 125–30; Ross, *Democracy's College*, 140; Marcus, *Agricultural Science*, 192–96; Charles E. Rosenberg, *No Other Gods: On Science and American Social Thought* (Baltimore, 1976), 135–52; Roger Lea Williams, "George W. Atherton and the Beginnings of Federal Support for Higher Education" (Ed.D. diss., Pennsylvania State University, 1988) (published as *The Origins of Federal Support for Higher Education: George W. Atherton and the Land-Grant College Movement* [University Park, Pa., 1991]), ch. 4. One earlier such group, the American Medical

College Association, founded in 1876, had disbanded in 1882. See Dean F. Smiley, "History of the Association of American Medical Colleges, 1876–1956," *Journal of Medical Education* 32 (1957): 514–15; Kenneth M. Ludmerer, *Learning to Heal: The Development of American Medical Education* (New York, 1985), 62.

12. *AAACES Proc.* 1 (1887): [4] ("looking after"); Henry E. Alvord, "Annual Address of the President," ibid. 9 (1895): 22; True, *History of Agricultural Experimentation*, 129. On government grants as spawners of associations, see V. O. Key, Jr., *The Administration of Federal Grants to the States* (Chicago, 1937), ch. 7; David B. Truman, *The Governmental Process: Political Interests and Public Opinion* (New York, 1951), 92–93.

13. Edward Danforth Eddy, Jr., *Colleges for Our Land and Time: The Land-Grant Idea in American Education* (New York, 1957), 199, 255; Ross, *Democracy's College*, 178–79; True, *History of Agricultural Education*, 199–200, 212; Liberty Hyde Bailey, *AAACES Proc.* 21 (1907): 54 ("great"). The seventeen Morrill colleges for African Americans were not admitted to the association until 1954.

14. Howard Cromwell Taylor, *The Educational Significance of the Early Federal Land Ordinances* (New York, 1922), esp. chs. 5, 9, and pp. 104–5; Allen Cabaniss, *The University of Mississippi: Its First Hundred Years*, 2nd ed. (Hattiesburg, Miss., 1971), 4, 108–9.

15. "Fulton, Robert Burwell," *National Cyclopaedia of American Biography*, 13:547; Franklin L. Riley and Dumas Malone, "Fulton, Robert Burwell," *DAB*, 7:72; Cabaniss, *University of Mississippi*, 98, 109–10.

16. Robert B. Fulton, "The Organization of the National Association of State Universities," *NASU Proc.* 2 (1904): 9–11; NASU min., July 11–12, 1895 (mimeo.), ASD, box 4, where another set of NASU minutes, also never printed, those of 1896, is also found.

17. Edgar B. Wesley, *NEA: The First Hundred Years: The Building of the Teaching Profession* (New York, 1957), 44, 21–23; "Constitution," *NASU Proc.* 1 (1903): [5–6]. The NEA's Department of Higher Education traced back to the absorption of the Central College Association, organized shortly before in Illinois "as a sort of federation of state and regional associations of college men"; the department was abolished in 1924 and reinstated in 1942 (Wesley, *NEA*, 44, 104). For an earlier gathering of state university representatives, which declared itself a conference, not an association-forming convention, see *Proceedings of the Conference of Presidents and Other Delegates of State Universities and State Colleges, Held at Columbus, Ohio, December 27 and 28, 1877* (USBE Circular 2, Washington, D.C., 1879), app. B. Around the turn of the century, midwestern state university presidents met in conferences independent of the NASU. See George E. MacLean to Andrew S. Draper, Apr. 27, 1897, ASD, box 9, and William O. Thompson to Draper, Apr. 15, 1901, ASD, box 15.

18. John K. Bettersworth, *People's College: A History of Mississippi State* (University, Ala., 1953), 9–28.

19. Ross, *Democracy's College*, 178; Fulton, "Organization of the NASU," 9–16, 10 ("urgent"). The drive is recorded in various letters from Fulton to Andrew S. Draper. See esp. those of Feb. 12, Nov. 19, 1895; Jan. 29, Feb. 24, Apr. 24, Dec. 25, 1896; and Jan. 3, 1897, plus NASU exec. cmte. min., Dec. 21, 1895, all in ASD, box 4.

20. Burke A. Hinsdale, "Is It Possible and Desirable to Form a Federation

of Colleges and Universities in the United States Similar to the Association of American Medical Colleges?" *NEA Proc.* 37 (1898): 720–26, plus discussion, p. 727, and committee formation, p. 702.

21. Robert B. Fulton and Joseph Swain to "Dear Sir," June 22, 1901, ASD, box 4; George E. MacLean to Andrew S. Draper, July 16, 1901 ("older") and Apr. 20, 1901 ("even up"), both in ASD, box 9; min. of Nov. 12–13, 1901, printed in *NASU Proc.* 1 (1903): 11 ("merely"), 12; Fulton, "Organization of the NASU," ibid. 2: 15–16; ibid. 1 (1903): 20; *AAACES Proc.* 15 (1901): 40; MacLean to James B. Angell, Nov. 30, 1901, JBA, box 6 ("new"). For the perspective of the land-grant college advocates of the mining school bills, see Williams, "George W. Atherton," 367–71. In compromise form the bill was reintroduced, unsuccessfully, in 1904.

22. Robert M. Hutchins, quoted in Charles Wegener, *Liberal Education in the Modern University* (Chicago, 1978), 2n ("those which"); *AAU Proc.* 1 (1900): 13–14. Another original member, Cornell, was an unusual blend of private and public university.

23. "A Conference of American Universities on Problems Connected with Graduate Work: The Call," *AAU Proc.* 1 (1900): 11 ("our own," "raise the opinion"); Armin O. Leuschner, ibid., 2 (1901): 36; *Report of the U.S. Commissioner of Education for the Year 1898–99* (Washington, D.C., 1900), 2:1564–65 ("to pursue"); Calvin Olin Davis, *A History of the North Central Association of Colleges and Secondary Schools, 1895–1945* (Ann Arbor, Mich., 1945), 11–13. On the easy winning of German doctorates, see Jurgen Herbst, *The German Historical School in American Scholarship: A Study in the Transfer of Culture* (Ithaca, N.Y., 1965), 9. For concern over degree mills and a reference to the North Central Association as a counterforce, see John H. Finley to Andrew S. Draper, Mar. 9, 1898, ASD, box 4.

24. Armin O. Leuschner to Ida Louise Leuschner, Feb. 28, [1900], AOL, box 1; *AAU Proc.* 1 (1900): 12–15.

25. Benjamin I. Wheeler to C. W. Eliot, Dec. 1, 1899, Jan. 9, 25, 29, 1900, CWE, box 123; Nicholas M. Butler to Eliot, Feb. 1, 1900, CWE, box 103; William R. Harper to Eliot, Mar. 10, 1900, CWE, box 111. On Wheeler's ambitions for Berkeley and its need to gain prestige, see John W. Servos, *Physical Chemistry from Ostwald to Pauling: The Making of a Science in America* (Princeton, N.J., 1990), 240–49.

26. Hugh Hawkins, *Between Harvard and America: The Educational Leadership of Charles W. Eliot* (New York, 1972), 178 n. 27; idem, "Butler, Nicholas Murray," *DAB*, suppl. 4, pp. 133–38; Veysey, *Emergence of the American University*, 306–7, 362–65, 370–72; Richard J. Storr, *Harper's University: The Beginnings: A History of the University of Chicago* (Chicago, 1966), 211–22, esp. 217–19; Robert Herrick, "The University of Chicago," *Scribner's Magazine* 18 (1895): 405–6. Four liberal arts colleges were affiliated with the University of Chicago in 1902.

27. *AAU Proc.* 1 (1900): 13, 2 (1901): 23–24, 3 (Feb. 1902): 37–46, 4 (Dec. 1902): 9. On the Federation of Graduate Clubs and its efforts for interinstitutional coordination, see John Higham, "The Matrix of Specialization," in Oleson and Voss, *Knowledge in Modern America* (see n. 1), 11–12.

28. LeBaron R. Briggs to Charles W. Eliot, Mar. 5, 1901, CWE, box 102.

29. James W. Hulse, *The University of Nevada: A Centennial History* (Reno, 1974), 27–39; George Lynn Cross, *Professors, Presidents, and Politicians: Civil Rights and the University of Oklahoma, 1890–1968* (Norman, Okla., 1981), ch.

2; William T. Doherty, Jr., and Festus P. Summers, *West Virginia University: Symbol of Unity in a Sectionalized State* (Morgantown, W.Va., 1982), ch. 1.

30. Thomas Nicholson, "A Proposed Campaign for Christian Education," *AAC Bul.* 2 (1916), no. 2, p. 34; *A Forward Movement for Christian Education: A Nation-Wide Campaign for Our American Colleges and College Students* (Chicago, [1916]), CCBE brochure, copy in UCPP, box 97; CFAT AR 2 (1907): 40–57; Robert L. Kelly, "An Audit of Experience: A Review of the Program, Policies and Precedents Developed during the History of the Association of American Colleges, 1915–1937" (typescript, AAC Ar.), 5, 22; AAC min., Jan. 14–15, 1915, *AAC Bul.* 1 (1915): 6–9; Robert L. Kelly, *The American Colleges and the Social Order* (New York, 1940), 90–92. For the development of centralized denominational attention to colleges, see David B. Potts, "American Colleges in the Nineteenth Century: From Localism to Denominationalism," *HEQ* 11 (1971): 363–80.

31. *The Financial Status of the Professor in America and in Germany* (CFAT, Bul. 2, New York, [1908]), 8 ("dissipation"); Howard J. Savage, *Fruit of an Impulse: Forty-Five Years of the Carnegie Foundation, 1905–1950* (New York, 1953), 77–78; *The General Education Board: An Account of Its Activities, 1902–1914* (New York, 1915), 109–11. On the sense of threat among denominational colleges, see Gary Scott Smith, *The Seeds of Secularization: Calvinism, Culture, and Pluralism in America, 1870–1915* (Grand Rapids, Mich., 1985).

32. George E. Fellows, *AAC Bul.* 1 (1915): 49, 50 ("money providing"); Robert L. Kelly, "The Sphere and Possibilities of the Association," ibid., 2 (1916), no. 3, p. 23. For the influence of Harper's book (Chicago, 1900), see Kelly, "Audit of Experience," 33; Kelly to Kenneth I. Brown, Nov. 16, 1948, Historical File, AAC Ar. See also Veysey, *Emergence of the American University*, 237–41.

33. Edward A. Krug, *The Shaping of the American High School* (New York, 1964), 167; Edward D. Eaton, "Study of Student Mortality," *AAC Bul.* 3 (1917), no. 3, p. 75.

34. R. Watson Cooper, *AAC Bul.* 1 (1915): 46 ("playing"); Stephen B. L. Penrose, "The Relation of the College Association to Existing Associations," ibid., 54 ("not too late"); Thomas McClelland, "Discussion," ibid. 2 (1916), no. 3, p. 33 ("not of our order").

35. The foregoing account of Kelly's early career is based principally on Opal Thornburg, *Earlham: The Story of the College, 1847–1962* (Richmond, Ind., 1963), ch. 9 (p. 286, "common possession"). See also "Pres. Kelly Resigns as Head of College," *Earlham Press*, Mar. 24, 1917 ("pronounced increase"); Kelly, "Inaugural Address," *Earlhamite*, n.s. 9 (1903): 238–45; *AAC Bul.* 4 (1918), no. 1, p. 9; "Robert L. Kelly: A Memorial," *AAC Bul.* 41 (1955): 179–80; *Elbert Russell, Quaker: An Autobiography* (Jackson, Tenn., 1956), esp. 143–51.

36. Robert L. Kelly, "Sphere and Possibilities," *AAC Bul.* 2 (1916), no. 3, p. 29 ("abounding"); idem, "The Place and Function of the Proposed Association," ibid. 1 (1915): 43, 40 ("wipe off"); "Members of the Association," ibid., 15–20.

37. Kelly, "Sphere and Possibilities," *AAC Bul.* 2 (1916), no. 3, p. 29 ("to bear").

38. Parke Rexford Kolbe, *The Colleges in War Time and After: A Contemporary Account of the Effect of the War upon Higher Education in America* (New York, 1919), 21; Carol S. Gruber, *Mars and Minerva: World War I and the Uses of the*

Higher Learning in America (Baton Rouge, La., 1975), 96–97, 100 ("in no perplexity," quoting Lowell to William L. Bryan, Jan. 7, 1918); Samuel P. Capen, quoted in Richard Wayne Lykes, *Higher Education and the United States Office of Education (1867–1953)* (Washington, D.C., 1975), 70.

39. *AAU Proc.* 19 (1917): 99–100, 104–6; Herman V. Ames to Ray Lyman Wilbur, Dec. 19, 1917; Wilbur to Ames, Jan. 2, 1917 [1918], both in RLW.

40. Only the AAC, the AAU, the NASU, and the Catholic Educational Association (formed in 1904 and not limited to higher education) were formally represented at this meeting, although there was unofficial participation from the AAACES and the Association of Urban Universities, a group formed in 1914. See *The University and the Municipality: Summary of Proceedings of the First Session of the National Association of Municipal Universities* (USBE Bul. 38, Washington, D.C., 1915), 5–6. The Catholic Educational Association added the initial word "National" in 1927. See Frederick G. Hochwalt, "Highlights of the National Catholic Educational Association," ACE Ar., 13–93–13; Donald C. Horrigan, *The Shaping of NCEA* (Washington, D.C., [1979]).

41. *The Emergency Council on Education: Report of Committee on Organization (Adopted by Conference of Education Associations, Washington, January 30, 1918)*, broadside, copy in UCPP, box 112. Other relevant documents, including minutes of the meeting of Mar. 26–27, 1918, are in ACE Ar., 4–1–13. See also *AAC. Bul.* 4 (1918), pp. 10–11; "Report of Dean [Herman V.] Ames as the Representative of the Association of American Universities on the American Council on Education," *AAU Proc.* 20 (1918): 22–24; D. J. Cowling, *NASU Proc.* 16 (1918): 90–96. For a particularly detailed account of the founding of the ECE, given in July 1918, see Donald J. Cowling, "The Emergency Council on Education," *NEA Proc.* 56 (1918): 200–205. On wartime boosterism, see Sally Foreman Griffith, *Home Town News: William Allen White and the Emporia Gazette* (New York, 1989); 204; Stephen L. Vaughn, *Holding Fast the Inner Lines: Democracy, Nationalism, and the Committee on Public Information* (Chapel Hill, 1980).

42. *NASU Proc.* 16 (1918): 90–96 (including a list of the participating associations); Herman V. Ames to "Dear Sir," Feb. 12, 1918, copy in UCPP, box 111; David F. Noble, *America by Design: Science, Technology, and the Rise of Corporate Capitalism* (New York, 1977), esp. 217–19, 245–6 (however, the list of founding organizations, 219n, includes the land-grant association twice, under variant names). The accurate list in Charles G. Dobbins (ed.), *American Council on Education: Leadership and Chronology, 1918–1968* (Washington, D.C., 1968), 3–4, includes fourteen names, two groups within the NEA being given separate listings. For an account of the new council's relations with the military, see this volume, ch. 7.

43. Robert D. Cuff, "The Cooperative Impulse and War: The Origins of the Council on National Defense and Advisory Commission," in Jerry Israel (ed.), *Building the Organizational Society: Essays on Associational Activities in Modern America* (New York, 1972), 234 ("peculiar").

44. Julian Park, *Samuel P. Capen, 1878–1956* (Buffalo, N.Y., 1957), 5–13; Joseph M. McCarthy, "Capen, Samuel Paul," *DAB*, suppl. 6, pp. 98–99. Capen's detailed letters, 1914–20, to his wife, Grace Wright Capen, in SPC, provide insight into not only personal ambitions but also the social and bureaucratic elites of Washington.

45. Noble, *American by Design*, 44–45, 170, 211–12, 212 ("efficiency," quoting Capen). Although Noble's description of the SPEE as "the vanguard of

reform in higher education as a whole" (p. 170) ignores the many other sources of educational ferment in the early twentieth century, his tracing of SPEE influence constitutes a major contribution to academic history. On SPEE origins, see also Lawrence Owens, "Straight-Thinking: Vannevar Bush and the Culture of American Engineering" (Ph.D. diss., Princeton University, 1987), ch. 1.

46. Noble, *America by Design*, 211–12; Lykes, *Higher Education and the USOE*, 57–59; Samuel P. Capen, "College 'Lists' and Surveys Published by the Bureau of Education," *S&S* 6 (1917): 41.

47. A regular constitution was adopted in May 1919. See Donald J. Cowling, *NASU Proc.* 16 (1918): 96; Dobbins, *ACE Leadership*, 4–5. For similar efforts to coordinate engineering associations, see Monte A. Calvert, "The Search for Engineering Unity: The Professionalization of Special Interest," in Israel, *Building the Organizational Society*, 51. See also Samuel Haber, *Efficiency and Uplift: Scientific Management in the Progressive Era, 1890–1920* (Chicago, 1964); Robert D. Cuff, *The War Industries Board: Business-Government Relations during World War I* (Baltimore, 1973).

48. AR, *Ed. Rec.* 1 (1920): 143. For Capen's agonies during the delay, see his letters to Grace Capen, July 15 to Sept. 13, 1919, SPC, box 13. For a typical money-raising exchange of letters, see Cowling to Aurelia H. Reinhardt, June 19, 1919, and her positive answer, Aug. 6, 1919, both in AHR. For Capen's salary during his first thirteen months ($8,125), see "Report of the Auditor," *Ed. Rec.* 2 (1921): 72.

49. *NASU Proc.* 17 (1919): 63.

CHAPTER 2: SHARED IDEOLOGY, DIVERGING MISSIONS

1. For sweeping claims of altruism, see Henry E. Alvord, "Annual Address by the President," *AAACES Proc.* 9 (1895): 21; John H. MacCracken, "These Twenty Years," *Ed. Rec.* 18 (1937): 343.

2. For the defense see Truman, *Governmental Process* (see ch. 1, n. 12); Daniel Bell (ed.), *The Radical Right* (Garden City, N.Y., 1963); for a critical reformulation, see Michael T. Hayes, *Lobbyists and Legislators: A Theory of Political Markets* (New Brunswick, N.J., 1981). A fair-minded treatment by a journalist is James Deakin, *The Lobbyists* (Washington, D.C., 1966). Lewis Anthony Dexter, *How Organizations Are Represented in Washington* (Indianapolis, 1969) stresses "government relations" rather than lobbying. For a treatment of the rise of lobbying that is both more analytical and more sympathetic than most, see Margaret Susan Thompson, *The 'Spider Web': Congress and Lobbying in the Age of Grant* (Ithaca, N.Y., 1985). For quotation, see William Greider, "The Education of David Stockman," *Atlantic Monthly* 248 (Dec. 1981): 28–29.

3. For examples of such critical reinterpretation, see Corinne Lathrop Gilb, *Hidden Hierarchies: The Professions and Government* (New York, 1966); Ellen Condliffe Lagemann, *Private Power for the Public Good: A History of the Carnegie Foundation for the Advancement of Teaching* (Middletown, Conn., 1983); Roy Lubove, *The Professional Altruist: The Emergence of Social Work as a Career, 1880–1930* (Cambridge, Mass., 1965); Norman J. Ornstein and Shirley Elder, *Interest Groups, Lobbying and Policymaking* (Washington, D.C., 1978).

4. For valuable summary treatments of the cluster of ideas treated here, see Lagemann, *Private Power for Public Good*, 173–78; Peter Dobkin Hall, "A

Historical Overview of the Private Nonprofit Sector," in Walter W. Powell (ed.), *The Nonprofit Sector: A Research Handbook* (New Haven, Conn., 1987), 3–26; Paul J. Miranti, Jr., *Accountancy Comes of Age: The Development of an American Profession, 1886–1940* (Chapel Hill, N.C., 1990), ch. 1.

5. Alvord, "Annual Address," *AAACES Proc.* 9:26. Cf. V. O. Key, Jr., *Politics, Parties and Pressure Groups* (New York, 1964), 68–69; David L. Sills, "Voluntary Associations: Sociological Aspects," *International Encyclopedia of the Social Sciences* (n.p., 1968), 16:374–76.

6. Robert H. Wiebe, *Businessmen and Reform: A Study of the Progressive Movement* (Cambridge, Mass., 1962), ch. 2; David L. Carlton, *Mill and Town in South Carolina, 1880–1920* (Baton Rouge, 1982), 141–42 ("every calling"); Alvord, "Annual Address," 21 ("this is not").

7. Ellis W. Hawley, *The Great War and the Search for a Modern Order: A History of the American People and Their Institutions, 1917–1933* (New York, 1979), 52–55; Joan Hoff Wilson, *Herbert Hoover: Forgotten Progressive* (Boston, 1975), ch. 4.

8. George F. Zook and Melvin E. Haggerty, *Principles of Accrediting Higher Institutions* (Chicago, 1936), 8 ("nowhere"), 15 ("one hand").

9. Clarence A. Dykstra, "Institutional Memberships in Professional and Technical Organizations," *AAU Proc.* 40 (1938): 64; L. Nichols to R. G. Sproul, June 8, 1932; Sproul to C. B. Lipman, June 13, 1932; Violet B. Marshall to L. Nichols, Oct. 8, 1932; all in UCPP, box 311; "The University of Michigan as a Prominent Clubman," clipping, *Michigan Alumnus*, ca. 1932, ibid., Alfred Horatio Upham, "About Ourselves," *NASU Proc.* 34 (1936): 25.

10. Cf. the treatment of motives for membership in Harland G. Bloland, *Associations in Action: The Washington, D.C., Higher Education Community* (ASHE-ERIC Higher Education Report, 2, Washington, D.C., 1985), 7–12.

11. Williams, "George W. Atherton," (see ch. 1, n. 11), 329–31; J. L. Hills, "The Builders of the Association," *ALGCU Proc.* 42 (1928): 26; *AAACES Proc.* 16 (1902): 44–45; ibid. 17 (1903): 60–61.

12. *AAACES Proc.* 8 (1894): 35–38. In 1897 thirteen land-grant institutions included the terms "mechanic arts," "mechanical," "polytechnic," or "technology" in their titles. MIT, a member of the AAACES, was not an agricultural college (Ross, *Democracy's College*, 229 n. 60). For an exploration of possible motives behind the association's misnomer, see Williams, "George W. Atherton," 225–26.

13. Eddy, *Colleges for Our Land* (see ch. 1, n. 13), 146–47, 197; *AAACES Proc.* 33 (1919): 67, 40 (1926): 415–16; T. O. Walton, ibid. 55 (1941): 80.

14. Williams, "George W. Atherton," 346–54; A. Ross Hill, "The Contribution of the Land-Grant Colleges to Liberal Culture," *ALGC Proc.* 37(1923): 50–54; Dexter S. Kimball, "The Content of a Liberal Education," ibid., 75; M. E. Deutsch (UC provost) to R. G. Sproul, Nov. 9, 1937, UCPP, box 422 (see also C. B. Hutchinson to Deutsch, Feb. 13, 1934, UCPP, box 364); Herman B Wells, "President's Address," *NASU Proc.* 41 (1943): 13 ("cannot speak"). In 1936 graduate deans of arts and sciences began to meet under the ALGCU aegis, leading to the establishment of a section on graduate work three years later. See *ALGCU Proc.* 50 (1936): 144–47, 53 (1939): 211–39.

15. Association of the Separated State Universities, min., Nov. 15, 1925, CCL, box 1; *ASSU Bulletin* (mimeo.), no. 26 (Dec. 3, 1930), copy in ACE Ar., 7-2-9. For more on this organization, later known as the State Universities

Association, see this volume, ch. 6 under "The Associations and the Lawmakers" and ch. 9 under "The NASU as a Merger Prospect."

16. *NASU Proc.* 2 (1904): 6 ("men of distinction"), 5 (1907): 9.

17. Thomas F. Kane to Benjamin Ide Wheeler, Dec. 11, 1913; Guy Potter Benton to NASU exec. cmte., Feb. 6, 1914; both in UCPP, box 61; *NASU Proc.* 12 (1914): 51, 78; ibid. 29 (1931): 193–94. In 1940 Kent State University was refused membership (NASU exec. cmte. min., Dec. 29, 1940, copy in NASULGC Ar., box 10).

18. Jacob Gould Schurman, *NASU Proc.* 7 (1909): 202–3; Brown Ayres, ibid., 203 ("most important"); Benjamin Ide Wheeler to James K. Patterson, Sept. 7, 1915, and to Harry B. Hutchins, Aug. 24, 1915, both in UCPP, box 81. An even more elaborate NASU jaunt was planned for 1928: attending the twenty-fifth anniversary of the University of Puerto Rico and returning via Havana and Key West. See A. H. Upham to "Gentlemen," Dec. 30, 1927, UCPP, box 204.

19. Printed program for the 1932 NASU meeting, copy in MLB, box 15; George E. MacLean, "How Far Is the State University Justified in Undertaking Graduate Work," *NASU Proc.* 3 (1905): 52; Raymond M. Hughes to M. L. Burton, Nov. 17, 1920, Jan. 26, 1921, MLB, box 2; discussion of the Rhodes Trust, *NASU Proc.* 10 (1912): 152–77; A. H. Upham, *NASU Proc.* 29 (1931): 86–91; Herman B Wells, *Being Lucky: Reminiscences and Reflections* (Bloomington, Ind., 1980), 140 ("freely").

20. David Madsen, *The National University: Enduring Dream of the USA* (Detroit, 1966), 114–20; Irwin Shepard to James B. Angell, Sept. 14, 1907, JBA, box 7 (on national university). To strengthen the case with the CFAT, the University of Michigan, after years of avoidance, joined the NASU (Charles R. Van Hise to James B. Angell, Jan. 11, 18, 1908, JBA, box 7). On foreign relations plans, see G. E. MacLean to "Dear Mr. President," July 16, 1901, ASD, box 9; G. E. MacLean, "The Relations of State Universities Separated from State Colleges of Agriculture and Mechanic Arts to State Universities Embracing Such Colleges," *NASU Proc.* 6 (1908): 67.

21. NASU min., July 11–12, 1895, ASD, box 4; George E. Fellows to "Dear Sir," Mar. 18, 1904, ibid.; NASU exec. cmte. min., Feb. 2–3, 1939, Jan. 25–26, 1940 (re 1936 meeting), NASULGC Ar.

22. Myron L. Burton, *NASU Proc.* 18 (1920): 113–14 ("getting"); A. H. Upham, "About Ourselves," ibid. 34:26 ("assembling"); Herman G. James to Franklin V. Thomas, May 24, 1938, ACE Ar., 9-3-15 ("conformity"). On later efforts to rationalize procedures, see letters from NASU secretary-treasurer, 1946–49, Virgil M. Hancher, in NASULGC Ar.

23. Presidential dismissals aroused NASU concern in at least the following cases: Alfred Hume at the University of Mississippi ("To the National Association of State Universities: In Session at Washington, D.C., Nov. 19–20, 1930: Statement by W. O. Thompson, Chairman of the Committee on University Control," mimeo.); Arthur Griswold Crane at the University of Wyoming (Crane to Alexander Ruthven, Sept. 15, 1941, and accompanying documents); Homer P. Rainey at the University of Texas (NASU exec. cmte. min., Oct. 21, 1945); all documents in AGR, box 56; resolution on Rainey case, *NASU Proc.* 43 (1945): 121–22; on Rainey see also the interlude in this volume, "The NASU Assembles in Wartime, 1945." In contrast, when Robert B. Fulton, the NASU's first president, was forced to resign as chancellor of

the University of Mississippi, he sent a self-exculpatory but acquiescent letter to fellow presidents. See Fulton to "My dear Sir," June 20, 1906, JBA, box 7. For an interpretation of administrative professionalism that includes the presidential associations, see Mark Beach, "Professional versus Professorial Control of Higher Education," *Ed. Rec.* 49 (1968): 263–73.

24. *AAU Proc.* 4 (Dec. 1902); 12.

25. LeBaron R. Briggs to Charles W. Eliot, Mar. 5, 1901, CWE, box 102; Clarence D. Ashley et al. to the AAU, Dec. 9, 1902 (printed), CWE, box 133 ("academic expediency"); Henry M. MacCracken to William Rainey Harper, Mar. 4, 1904, AAU Ar. ("unwilling"); Theodore Francis Jones (ed.), *New York University, 1832–1932* (New York, 1933), 139–43; Ronald A. Smith, *Sports and Freedom: The Rise of Big-Time College Athletics* (New York, 1988), 198–202.

26. *AAU Proc.* 3 (Feb. 1902); 37, 4 (Dec. 1902): 12, 5 (1904): 12. Uncertainties about the AAU are described in Albion Small to Edmund J. James, Mar. 23, 1907, EJJ, Personal Correspondence, box 8: "No one is quite sure what its vocation and consequently its membership ought properly to be."

27. C. R. Van Hise to Angell, Oct. 31, 1905, JBA, box 7; *NASU Proc.* 3 (1905): 8; "Report of the Committee on Standards of American Universities" and discussion, ibid. 6 (1908): 147–57; *AAU Proc.* 8 (Nov. 1906): 10, 9 (1908): 10–11, 75; J. G. Schurman, *NASU Proc.* 5 (1907): 53–55; William K. Selden, "The Association of American Universities: An Enigma in Higher Education," *Graduate Journal* 8 (1968): 205; *NASU Proc.* 10 (1912): 79–82.

28. *AAU Proc.* 24 (1922): 24. Aware that not all Ph.D.'s were equal, one dean had suggested to the AAU in 1916 that it be considered "proper etiquette" for any listing of a Ph.D. after a person's name to specify the conferring institution (George C. Comstock, *AAU Proc.* 18 [1916]: 98.). On the "approved list," see this volume, ch. 4 under "Against Confusion: The AAU."

29. *AAU Proc.* 31 (1929): 47–72, 33 (1931): 9, 40.

30. Ibid. 34 (1932): 34, 40, 44, 38 (1936); 21–22, 143–44 (quotation on p. 144). Location of meetings was, of course, a factor. That of 1936 took place at the University of Texas. The next year at Brown University, well centered among the eastern universities, fourteen presidents attended. The AAU returned to the ACE in 1938.

31. *AAU Proc.* 13 (1911): 61; Alfred H. Lloyd to AAU exec. cmte., Feb. 12, 1924, MLB, box 13; Lloyd to Ray Lyman Wilbur, Apr. 9, 1926, DBT, 21–7; Charles B. Lipman to W. W. Campbell, Sept. 3, 1928, UCPP, box 217; *AAU Proc.* 40 (1938): 52, 20 (1918): 26, 29.

32. R. L. Wilbur to Karl Compton, Jan. 8, 1937 (and similarly to others); James R. Angell to Wilbur, Jan. 25, 1937; James B. Conant to Wilbur, Jan. 25, 1937 ("small informal"); all in DBT, 22–1; *AAU Proc.* 41 (1939): 23; "Informal Conferences of Presidents and Graduate Deans," ibid., pp. 49–50, 49 ("stronger endowed").

33. *AAU Proc.* 41 (1939): 80–105, 42 (1940): 22 ("to insure"); F. K. Richtmyer to Robert A. Millikan, Mar. 7, 1939, DBT, 22–2.

34. John H. T. Main, "The Present-Day College," *AAC Bul.* 1 (1915): 120 ("present day"), 111 ("living together," "not confused").

35. Stephen B. L. Penrose, "The Relation of the College Association to Existing Associations," *AAC Bul.* 1 (1915): 57 ("life"), 58.

36. Ibid., 12; Kelly, "Audit of Experience" (see ch. 1, n. 30), vi. Since 1920, the junior colleges had had their own American Association of Junior Colleges (Harland G. Bloland, *Higher Education Associations in a Decentralized Education*

System [Berkeley, Calif., 1969], 146; Lykes, *Higher Education and the USOE,* 83).

37. Kelly, "Audit of Experience", vi–viii; exec. cmte. min., Mar. 7, 1925, AAC Ar. ("organization"); *AAC Bul.* 15 (1929): 187.

38. *AAC Bul.* 7 (1921), no. 4, p. 28 ("existing"); exec. cmte. min., May 2, 1935, AAC Ar.; Robert L. Kelly, "Policies and Precedents in the History of the Association of American Colleges: Source Material Drawn from Official Records, 1914–1935," typescript, p. 29, AAC Ar.

39. *AAC Bul.* 4 (1918), no. 1, p. 11. See also Kelly, "Audit of Experience," 20.

40. Robert L. Kelly to Stephen B. L. Penrose, Feb. 27, 1929, SBLP ("business"); ECR, *AAC Bul.* 13 (1927): 13–14; "Book and Publicity Exhibits," ibid., 16 (1930): 183–84; Archie M. Palmer, "A College President's Professional Library," ibid., p. 307 ("professional").

41. Kelly, "Audit of Experience," 13; ECR, *AAC Bul.* 13 (1927): 13; ibid. 14 (1928): 39; exec. cmte. min., Feb. 4, 1928, AAC Ar.

42. Kelly, "Audit of Experience," 6, viii–ix; idem, "Policies and Precedents," 11; exec. cmte. min., Nov. 19, 1924, AAC Ar.; *AAC Bul.* 10 (1924): 8. There were limits to the AAC's inclusiveness, however. Besides the effectual barring of two-year colleges in 1926, normal schools and teachers colleges were refused admission when they applied (exec. cmte. min., Nov. 9, 1929, Mar. 22, 1932, AAC Ar.).

43. Solomon Katz to Hugh Hawkins, Nov. 5, 1982.

44. Donald J. Cowling, *AAU Proc.* 20 (1918); 72–73.

45. Samuel Capen, "The Colleges in a Nationalized Education Scheme," *S&S* 9 (1919): 616 ("ruthlessly"); Noble, *America by Design,* esp. 246–48; Capen, "The Cooperation of the Colleges with Industry," address of Mar. 26, 1920, typescript, SPC, box 19; ACE exec. cmte. min., Sept. 22, 1923, copy in MLB, box 13; Donald J. Cowling, "The ACE," *NASU Proc.* 16 (1918): 92 ("unifying"); Charles Riborg Mann to William Wallace Campbell, Dec. 10, 1923, UCPP, box 161; Raymond A. Kent (chairman of the ACE), "The Program of the American Council on Education," *Ed. Rec.* 17 (1936), suppl. 10, p. 61. To preserve its "peak" status, the ACE declined to become a member of any other organization (exec. cmte. min., May 2, 1921, copy in MLB, box 1).

46. AR, *Ed. Rec.* 1 (1920): 152–53.

47. John H. MacCracken, "Report of the Committee on Federal Legislation," *Ed. Rec.* 1 (1920): 95 ("bureau"); Charles Riborg Mann to D. J. Cowling, May 8, 1926, ACE Ar., 7-14-8 ("seminar"); *The American Council on Education: Its History and Activities* [1935–36] (Washington, D.C., 1935), 32.

48. Samuel Capen, *NASU Proc.* 17 (1919): 62.

49. *ACE: Its History and Activities* (1935–36), 15; *The History and Activities of the American Council on Education: Twenty-Fourth Year, 1941–42* (Washington, D.C., [1941]), 52; Paul Starr, *The Social Transformation of American Medicine* (New York, 1982), 92, citing Mancur Olson. For a blunt reference to free-riders, see Alvord, "Annual Address," 26.

50. Harry W. Tyler to Charles Riborg Mann, Jan. 30, 1923, ACE AR., 7–30–10 ("foreign friends"); *Ed. Rec.* 3 (1922): 64–65, 5 (1924): 179–80. Tyler, a professor at MIT, wanted the ACE to assert itself to become the American liaison to the League of Nation's new Committee on Intellectual Cooperation. In 1925 an independent liaison committee was set up under the leadership of Robert A. Millikan. Mann was a member, presumably as representative of

the ACE. See Vernon Kellogg, "American National Committee on International Intellectual Cooperation," ibid. 8 (1927): 17.

51. Donald J. Cowling to C. R. Mann, May 27, 1919, ACE Ar., 4-2-11; Herman V. Ames to Samuel Capen, Feb. 4, 1919, ACE Ar., 5-3-1; John H. MacCracken, "These Twenty Years," *Ed. Rec.* 18: 336; Dobbins, *ACE Leadership*, 6; David Allan Robertson, "International Relations," *Ed. Rec* 4 (1925): 13–19.

52. ECR, *Ed. Rec.* 5 (1924): 130–32; J. W. Cunliffe, "Report of the Committee on the American University Union," ibid., pp. 179–80; C. R. Mann to D. J. Cowling, Mar. 1, 27, 1924, ACE Ar., 7-14-7; D. A. Robertson, "Foreign Study for Undergraduates," *Ed. Rec.* 6 (1925): 84–90.

53. ECR, *Ed. Rec.* 8 (1927): 215–16.

54. *Ed. Rec.* 3 (1922): 181, 9 (1928): 176; *AAU Proc.* 24 (1922): 21.

55. Stanley King to Frederick J. E. Woodbridge, Nov. 7, 1934, ACIA ("pure trade"); *Ed. Rec.* 8 (1927): 201. Cf. *History and Activities of ACE (1941–42)*, 11–12.

56. *History and Activities of ACE (1941–42)*, 11–12; exec. cmte. min., Sept. 25, 1926, Mar. 12, 1927, copies in CCL, box 4.

57. *AAACES Proc.* 16 (1902): 23–26; Eddy, *Colleges for Our Land*, 157; *NASU Proc.* 19 (1921): 122–23; *AAU Proc.* 42 (1940): 53; Kelly, "Audit of Experience," 28–29; Dobbins, *ACE Leadership*, 12. For references to other projects, see this volume's interludes on annual meetings.

CHAPTER 3: FROM VOLUNTARISM TO BUREAUCRACY

1. For the quite similar structure of professional associations with individuals as members, see Gilb, *Hidden Hierarchies* (see ch. 2, n. 3), ch. 4.

2. *NASU Proc.* 10 (1912): 38–45; Kelly, "Audit of Experience," 19–21; Jeffrey M. Berry, *The Interest Group Society* (Boston, 1984), 92–95.

3. For examples of executive committee influence, see "Report of the Executive Committee," *AAACES Proc.* 15 (1901): 19–21; W. O. Thompson to "Gentlemen," Mar. 13, 1916, UCPP, box 92; R. A. Pearson to C. R. Mann, Aug. 2, 1928, ACE Ar., 7-2-8. See also *ALGCU Proc.* 49 (1935): 282–83, 332. The ACE's decision to bar members of its Problems and Plans Committee from succeeding themselves revealed some desire for the circulation of elites (AR, *Ed. Rec.* 18 [1937]: 318).

4. *AAC Bul.* 6 (1920), no. 1, pp. 6–7; C. L. Clarke, "A Study of the American Liberal College" with discussions by S. P. Capen, ibid., 10 (1924): 144–51; ibid., 12; ECR, ibid. 11 (1925): 12; "Proposed Constitution," ibid., 27, 29; ibid. 12 (1926): 39–40, 15 (1929): 186–89; Kelly, "Policies and Precedents," 17.

5. *AAU Proc.* 14 (1912): 18. Before it began inspecting colleges in the 1920s, the absence of AAU activity was suggested by its low expenditures: for example, $411 in 1905, mostly for printing the *Proceedings*, and $778 in 1915, when the largest item was the expenses of the Committee on Academic and Professional Degrees (ibid. 7 (1906): 10, 18 (1916): 18).

6. For a comparison of concern over oligarchic control within institutional associations and within learned societies, see Bloland, *Associations in Action* (see ch. 2, n. 10), 3–5. For an example of such control within a professional association, see Bruce Sinclair, *A Centennial History of the American Society of Mechanical Engineers, 1880–1980* (Toronto, 1980), 78.

7. Thomas D. Boyd, *NASU Proc.* 18 (1920): 96 ("bossed"); Thomas F. Kane, "Address of the President of the Association," *NASU Proc.* 12 (1914): 41 ("delightful"). For evidence of the secretary-treasurer's control of information being turned into influence over the incumbent NASU president, see Herman G. James to Alexander Ruthven, Mar. 26, 1942, and other correspondence, AGR, box 56.

8. Committee on Education for Citizenship min., Feb. 28, 1922 (mimeo.); Samuel P. Capen to Marion L. Burton, Mar. 15 and 16, 1922, all in MLB, box 5; *ALGCU Proc.* 40 (1926): 402–3, 48 (1935): 244; Frank L. McVey, *NASU Proc.* 18 (1920): 110; A. H. Upham, "About Ourselves," *NASU Proc.* 34: 26 ("most"). Although printing their reports in its *Proceedings,* the AAU did not bother to list committees there until 1920. By that time seven were discernible. See *AAU Proc.* 22 (1920): 15–16.

9. C. B. Hutchinson, dean of the College of Agriculture, to Monroe E. Deutsch, provost, Feb. 13, 1934, UCPP, box 364 ("very weak"); AR, *Ed. Rec.* 18 (1937): 294; James H. Baker to Benjamin I. Wheeler, May 1, 1918; Wheeler to Baker, May 16, 1918; Armin O. Leuschner to N. B. Drury, Nov. 5, 1917, all in UCPP, box 90; *AAU Proc.* 18 (1916): 16, 19 (1917): 20, 21 (1919): 19.

10. Noble, *America by Design,* 79; David M. Kennedy, *Over Here: The First World War and American Society* (New York, 1980), 113–14; Cuff, *War Industries Board* (see ch. 1, n. 47), 27, 42; John B. Rae, *The American Automobile: A Brief History* (Chicago, 1965), 39–41.

11. CFAT AR 2 (1907): 42–52, 3 (1908): 167–80; "College Boards in Education, Denominational," in Paul Monroe (ed.), *A Cyclopedia of Education* (New York, 1915), 2:84–87. William H. Crawford, "The Place and Function of the Denominational College in Education," *AAC Bul.* 1 (1915): 133–34; *Forward Movement for Christian Education,* UCPP, box 97 ("permanent"); Kelly, "Audit of Experience," 23, 7 ("thought of"). Comparison with the Catholic Educational Association is suggestive. It included higher education as a division within a more inclusive grouping. See also Kelly to S. B. L. Penrose, Feb. 27, 1929, SBLP. Kelly was preceded as exclusive secretary of the CCBE by R. Watson Cooper, who took the office when it originated in 1916. He had been president of Upper Iowa University and the first elected secretary of the AAC.

12. AR, *AAC Bul.* 5 (1919): no. 2, pp. 26–27; Kelly, "Audit of Experience," 50–51. There were complaints that Kelly had made exorbitant use of ACE funds (S. P. Capen to Grace Capen, Aug. 18, 1919, SPC, box 13).

13. In *World Survey by the Interchurch World Movement of North America: Revised Preliminary Statement and Budget* (New York, 1920), the section on American education, vol. 1, pp. 149–200, resembles contemporary writing and statistical analysis by Kelly. See also Robert L. Kelly, "The Inter-Church World Movement," *AAC Bul.* 6 (1920): no. 1, pp. 13–22; Robert T. Handy, *A Christian America: Protestant Hopes and Historical Realities* (New York, 1971), 186–90, 193–96; Alexander Meiklejohn to W. H. P. Faunce, Nov. 28, 1922, AM, box 2.

14. *AAC Bul.* 15 (1929): 175, 16 (1930); 151; AR, ibid. 16 (1930): 31–33, 17 (1931): 9–11; exec. cmte. min., Dec. 6, 1928, Mar. 29, May 6, 1929, Feb. 20, 1934, May 2, 1935, AAC Ar.; Robert L. Kelly and Bernard I. Bell, treasurer, to AAC members, Feb. 7, 1929, copy in RLW, box 4; D. J. Cowling to S. B. L. Penrose, Mar. 19, 1929, SBLP; Kelly, "Policies and Precedents," 20. The associate secretary was Archie M. Palmer, who had been assistant director of

the Institute of International Education (*AAC Bul.* 15 [1929]: 8). The Treasurer's Report for 1934 gives headquarters office expenses as $15,568, of which $12,906 was for salaries (*AAC Bul.* 21 [1935]: 165).

15. Exec. cmte. min., Jan. 25, Dec. 8, 1930, Jan. 22, 30, 1931, AAC Ar.; Kelly, "Policies and Precedents," 24; idem, "Audit of Experience," 61; "The Conference of Liberal Arts Colleges," *S&S* 31 (1930): 426–27; George L. Omwake, "The Liberal Arts College Movement," *S&S* 33 (1931): 333–34. The times were inauspicious, and the fund drive failed. The LACM led, however, to the National Conference of Church-related Colleges, which surrendered its independent existence in 1944 to become the AAC's National Commission on Christian Higher Education. Documents on the LACM are preserved in the "Historical File," AAC Ar.

16. Exec. cmte. min., Jan. 29, 1931, AAC Ar.; Robert L. Kelly, "Audit of Experience," 23, 63 ("Headquarters"); Kelly to C. R. Mann, Nov. 5, 1924, ACE 7-1-5 ("actual").

17. James R. McCain, "The Resignation of the Executive Secretary," *AAC Bul.* 23 (1937): 104–7; Kelly, "Policies and Precedents"; idem, "Audit of Experience."

18. Board of directors min., Nov. 19, 1936, Jan. 14, 1937, AAC Ar.; Guy E. Snavely, *A Search for Excellence: Memoirs of a College Administrator* (New York, 1964), ch. 10; *AAC Bul.* 24 (1938): 103, 37 (1951): 118. For Snavely's interpretation of his duties, recorded as he was leaving office, see "The Activities of the Executive Director," mimeo., Mar. 30, 1954, AAC Ar. I have used the Consumer Price Index (CPI) from *Historical Statistics of the United States* (Washington, D.C., 1975), 164, with the CPI for 1914 as 100.

19. Snavely, *Search for Excellence*, esp. 52, 157–59, and ch. 10; Snavely, AR, *AAC Bul.* 33 (1947): 214; ibid. 36 (1950): 131, 132 ("blanket"); William P. Tolley, "In Memoriam: Guy Everett Snavely, 1881–1974," *Lib. Ed.* 60 (1974): 153–55.

20. S. P. Capen to D. J. Cowling, Feb. 3, 11, Sept. 20, 1920, ACE Ar., 5-4-1; exec. cmte. min., Dec. 6, 1919, copy in AHR; AR, *Ed. Rec.* 2 (1921): 131; ibid. 3 (1922): 188.

21. S. P. Capen to Grace Capen, Aug. 20, 1914, SPC, box 9 ("clanging"), Mar. 23, 1920, SPC, box 13 ("rushed"); S. P. Capen to Helen C. Hurley, Mar. 13, 1950, UBPP, box 3 ("intelligence"); Capen, "The Registrar's Office a Barometer of Educational Tendencies," typescript, Apr. 13, 1920, SPC, box 19.

22. Park, *Samuel P. Capen* (see ch. 1, n. 44), 17; S. P. Capen to Grace Capen, Feb. 24, 1922, SPC, box 13; S. P. Capen, "Program for Progress in Education," *Ed. Rec.* 4 (1923): 16 (his inaugural); Harry W. Tyler to Henry Suzzallo, Sept. 18, 1922, telegram, Nov. 2, 1922 ("surprised"), both in HS, box 1. For an example of his continuing influence, see Capen to George F. Zook, Nov. 17, 1936, ACE Ar., 10-4-15.

23. Dobbins, *ACE Leadership*, 140–42; C. R. Mann, *Ed. Rec.* 16 (1935): 346–56; J. McKeen Cattell (ed.), *American Men of Science: A Biographical Dictionary* (New York, 1906), vi–vii, 208; Mann to Harry Pratt Judson, May 28, 1906, HPJ. For Mann's early statements on education, see his "Science in Civilization and Science in Education," *School Review* 14 (1906): 664–70; "Industrial and Technical Training in the Secondary Schools and Its Bearing on College-Entrance Requirements," ibid. 16 (1908); 425–38. For Dewey, see Mann, *The*

Teaching of Physics for Purposes of General Education (New York, 1912), xxii–xxiii.

24. C. R. Mann, *A Study of Engineering Prepared for the Joint Committee on Engineering Education of the National Engineering Societies* (CFAT, Bul. 11, New York, [1918]), esp. ix–xi, 107–8; Monte Calvert, "Search for Engineering Unity," in Israel, *Building the Organizational Society*, 42–54; Noble, *America by Design*, 203–6; Lagemann, *Private Power for Public Good*, 84–85. For a treatment of the ideals of engineering educators that includes references to Mann's thought, see Owens, "Straight-Thinking: Vannevar Bush and the Culture of American Engineering," ch. 3 (see ch. 1, n. 45).

25. Mann, *Study of Engineering Education*, 32, 63–65, 64 ("aim"), 92–94.

26. Samuel P. Capen to Grace Capen, June 27, July 10, 1918, SPC, box 12; C. R. Mann, "Education and Universal Training," *Ed. Rec.* 1 (1920): 50–53; Dobbins, *ACE Leadership*, 140–41; Noble, *America by Design*, 214–19; Mann to H. P. Judson, Mar. 26, 1917, HPJ; "A Faculty Committee on Introspection," *Technology Review* 19 (1917): 214–15; P&P cmte. min., Oct. 14, 1937, ACE Ar., 10-9-12; Mann, remarks, "Dinner in Honor of Director-Emeritus Charles Riborg Mann," *Ed. Rec.* 16 (1935): 346–56; AR, ibid. 4 (1923): 100–101; Dobbins, *ACE Leadership*, 141. The ACE published Mann's study *Education in the Army, 1919–1925* as *Ed. Rec.* 7 (1926), supp. 1. For a fuller account of Mann's wartime activities, see below, ch. 7.

27. C. R. Mann to Henry Goddard Leach, Sept. 27, 1928, ACE Ar., 8-4-8 ("cooperation"); AR, *Ed. Rec.* 7 (1926): 163 ("major"); Mann to R. L. Kelly, Oct. 10, 1927, ACE Ar., 7-2-4; *Ed. Rec.* 8 (1927): 201.

28. AR, *Ed. Rec.* 4 (1923): 100–101, 5 (1924): 129; Dobbins, *ACE Leadership*, 19, 141; C. R. Mann to Dorothy R. Dalton, Dec. 17, 1930, ACE Ar., 7-14-1; David Allan Robertson, "Educational Foreign Exchange," *S&S* 22 (1925): 409–15.

29. C. R. Mann to R. L. Kelly, Dec. 9, 1927, ACE Ar., 7-2-4 ("highly"); D. J. Cowling to Mann, Apr. 5, 1924, ACE Ar., 7-14-7; *Ed. Rec.* 5 (1924): 145, 10 (1929): 241, 14 (1933): 275; Frank F. Stephens, *A History of the University of Missouri* (Columbia, Mo., 1962), 492.

30. W. W. Campbell to C. R. Mann, Dec. 3, 1923, UCPP, box 161; A. L. Lowell to Mann, Nov. 24, Dec. 3, 1926; Donald J. Cowling to Mann, Dec. 18, 1926 (concerning Coffman); all in ACE Ar., 7-14-8; ECR, *Ed. Rec.* 11 (1930): 224.

31. C. R. Mann, "A United Attack on Personnel Problems," *Ed. Rec.* 5 (1924): 276–77; AR, *Ed. Rec.* 8 (1927): 226, 231 ("novel"), 232. Mann persuaded the head of another institutional association to vote for Hoover in 1928 (R. L. Kelly to Mann, Oct. 26, 1928, Mann to Kelly, Oct. 27, 1928, both in ACE Ar., 7-2-4). For interpretations of the long-forgotten NACE, see Gilbert E. Smith *The Limits of Reform: Politics and Federal Aid to Education, 1937–1950* (New York, 1982), 22–24; Paula S. Fass, *Outside In: Minorities and the Transformation of American Education* (New York, 1989), 117–20.

32. C. R. Mann to Brooks Fletcher, Feb. 26, 28, 1934, ACE Ar., 7-17-7; "Report of the Committee on Problems and Plans in Education," *Ed. Rec.* 14 (1933): 381–85, esp. 383; ibid. 15 (1934): 340–43.

33. *Ed. Rec.* 14 (1933): 262–64; ibid. 15 (1934): 154–59; Henry Suzzallo to S. P. Capen, May 11, 1933, HS, box 15; exec. cmte. min., May 18, 1934, mimeo., ACE Ar., 10-15-5; *ACE: Its History and Activities* (1935–36), 24. For

the two sets of constitutional changes, see *Ed. Rec.* 14 (1933): 434–36, 15 (1934): 381–83, 381 ("to advance"). For Mann's philosophical summing-up, see his *Living and Learning* (Washington, D.C., 1938).

34. Lykes, *Higher Education and the USOE*, 94, 107–9; Jack J. Cardoso, "Zook, George F.," *DAB*, suppl. 5, pp. 761–63; Vaughn, *Holding Fast the Inner Lines* (see ch. 1, n. 41), 212; S. P. Capen to Henry Suzzallo, May 6, 1933, HS, box 1; Suzzallo to Arnold Bennett Hall, Apr. 26, 1933, Suzzallo to Zook, Apr. 29, 1933, both HS, box 15; B. P. Brodinsky, "Valedictory: President of American Council Looks Back over Forty-five Years and Speaks His Mind," *Nation's Schools* 45 (1950): 27.

35. John M. MacCracken, "These Twenty Years, *Ed. Rec.* 18 (1937): 340 ("organizer"); Cardoso, "Zook," *DAB*, suppl. 5, p. 762 ("hard"); Russell I. Thackrey to Hugh Hawkins, June 1, 1986 ("underbelly"); Wells, *Being Lucky* (see ch. 2, n. 19), 374; James B. Conant, *My Several Lives: Memoirs of a Social Inventor* (New York, 1970), 425 ("tackled"), 431; AR, *Ed. Rec.* 20 (1939): 359 ("implementation"). Zook's increasing power throws light on the case of Ralph E. Himstead, executive secretary of the AAUP from 1936 to 1955, a bureaucrat neurotically attached to individual control, whose behavior during the McCarthy era froze AAUP efforts to respond. See Walter P. Metzger, "Ralph F. Fuchs and Ralph E. Himstead: A Note on the AAUP in the McCarthy Period," in *Academe: Bulletin of the AAUP* 72 (1986), no. 6, pp. 30–33; Ellen W. Schrecker, *No Ivory Tower: McCarthyism and the Universities* (New York, 1986), 318–32.

36. Samuel P. Capen, "The Committee on Problems and Plans in Education: A Summary, 1930–1936," *Ed. Rec.* 17 (1936): 484–86; George F. Zook, "Report on the Activities of the Committee on Problems and Plans in Education," ibid., 487–97; "Financial Statements of the ACE," ibid., esp. 499, 504–5; AR, ibid., 338; ibid. 22 (1941): 241–43; min. of joint meetings, P&P cmte. and exec. cmte., Dec. 19, 1941, June 16, 1942, ACE Ar., 10-20-2; AR, *Ed. Rec.* 24 (1943): 221; ibid. 25 (1944): 189, 191. The name change of 1944 came by constitutional amendment. In 1961 the P&P committee was merged with the executive committee to form the ACE "Board of Directors." See P&P cmte. min., Mar. 9, 1944, ACE Ar., 10-26-9; Dobbins, *ACE Leadership*, 50, 99.

37. *Ed. Rec.* 17 (1936): 498; AR, ibid., 334–35. A sliding scale of dues, with a $500 top, was given up in 1933 (Donald J. Shank, "Who Belongs to the Council?" *Ed. Rec.* 21 [1940]: 546). Total receipts, apart from special project funds, rose from $90,958 (1935–36) to $101,482 (1940–41) to $585,505 (1949–50). See *Ed. Rec.* 17 (1936): 501, 22 (1941): 608, 31 (1950): 477.

38. *Ed. Rec.* 17 (1939): 499; AR, ibid. 21 (1940): 308, 299, 178; Dobbins, *ACE Leadership*, 41. See *Activities of the American Youth Commission* (Washington, D.C., 1937) for its early program and staff.

39. AR, *Ed. Rec.* 26 (1945): 134; R. K. Hetzel to S. D. Shankland, Nov. 25, 1927, C. R. Mann to Hetzel, Nov. 28, 1927, both in ACE Ar., 7-2-8; "Meetings of Constituent Delegates," *Ed. Rec.* 17 (1936): 321–22; *Ed. Rec.* 24 (1943): 171, 288, 25 (1944): 306–7, 28 (1947): 87–88, 220–21; P&P cmte. min., Mar. 9, 1944, ACE Ar., 10-26-9; George F. Zook to "Dear Colleague," Mar. 3, 1947, DBT, box 1. Associate members increased from 19 in 1935 to 46 in 1941. Institutional members, under the new definitions adopted in 1936 and later, included many organizations other than colleges and universities.

40. AR, *Ed. Rec.* 26 (1945): 179–80.

41. Edward C. Elliott, "Counsel for the Council," *Ed. Rec.* 19 (1938): 304 ("gadget"); AR, *Ed. Rec.* 20 (1939): 320–21; ibid. 22 (1941): 244–47. These

central office budget figures omit all publications expenses, including those for the *Educational Record*. See *Ed. Rec.* 16 (1935): 272, 22 (1941): 609, 31 (1950): 481.

42. *ACE: Its History and Activities* (1935–36), 38 ("executive"); AR, *Ed. Rec.* 16 (1935): 252; "The American Youth Commission," ibid., 482–85; ibid. 18 (1937): 137.

43. AR, *Ed. Rec.* 31 (1950): 274 ("large"); min. of joint meeting, exec. cmte. and P&P cmte., Feb. 12, 1939, ACE Ar., 10-11-9; *Ed. Rec.* 24 (1943): 221–22.

44. The budget gave three officers' salaries: the president's, which remained unchanged at $18,000 throughout Zook's tenure; the vice-president's (earlier associate director), which rose from $9,558 in 1935–36 to $11,283 in 1949–50. Although listed by salary ($7,500 in 1935–36) and present in the office, the president emeritus mostly followed his individual inclinations. See *Ed. Rec.* 16 (1935): 268, 17 (1936): 498, 31 (1950): 475.

45. AR, *Ed. Rec.* 19 (1938): 255. There were five "executive officers" in 1937. The list rose to six, was briefly at seven in 1939, was down to three in 1944, and rose again to six in Zook's last year. It immediately rose to a new high of eight under Zook's successor. The list appeared regularly on the verso of the title page of the *Educational Record*.

46. Haber, *Efficiency and Uplift* (see ch. 1, n. 47), 146; *ALGCU Proc.* 53 (1939): 242–43, 54 (1940): 255; *NASU Proc.* 53 (1955): 189–93. My findings differ somewhat from those in Lauriston R. King, *The Washington Lobbyists for Higher Education* (Lexington, Mass., 1975), 112, where opening years of Washington offices (not central offices) are listed.

47. See Wiebe, *Search for Order* (see ch. 1, n. 7), ch. 5; Alfred D. Chandler, Jr., *Strategy and Structure: Chapters in the History of the Industrial Enterprise* (Cambridge, Mass., 1962), 8–9. For other subtle sources of staff power, see Bloland, *Higher Education Associations* (see ch. 2, n. 36), 118. For the later bureaucratic style of association staff members, see King, *Washington Lobbyists for Higher Education*, esp. ch. 3.

Interlude: The AAU Comes to the Fair, 1915

1. Samuel P. Capen to Grace Capen, Aug. 27 ("young gods"), Aug. 29 ("not so large"), 1915, SPC, box 10.

2. In the upshot, this venture was frustrated by wartime inflation. Before being discharged in 1921, the relevant committee announced that the Library of Congress, *Publishers Weekly* and the *Cumulative Book Index* had achieved the contemplated ends. Academic publishing had found its way into the mainstream.

3. S. P. Capen to Grace Capen, Aug. 27, 1915, SPC, box 10.

4. S. P. Capen to Grace Capen, Aug. 29, 1915, SPC, box 10.

Chapter 4: Toward System

1. Charles Maxwell McConn's identification of "The Age of Standards" as the period 1890–1915 seems to me to begin and end too early. See McConn, quoted in William K. Selden, *Accreditation: A Struggle over Standards in Higher Education* (New York, 1960), 28.

2. Selden, *Accreditation*, ch. 1; Harold Orlans, *Private Accreditation and Public Eligibility* (Lexington, Mass., 1975), 1–3.

3. For the AAU and the AAJC foundings, see *The University and the Municipality: Summary of Proceedings of the First Session of the National Association of Municipal Universities* (USBE Bul. 38, Washington, D.C., 1915), 5–6; George F. Zook, *Higher Education, 1918–1920* (USBE Bul. 21, Washington, D.C., 1921), 16–18; Steven Brint and Jerome Karabel, *The Diverted Dream: Community Colleges and the Promise of Educational Opportunity in America, 1900–1985* (New York, 1989), 32–33. For the rise of yet another institutional grouping, see Paul J. Edelson, "Codification and Exclusion: An Analysis of the Early Years of the National University Extension Association, 1915–1923," paper presented at the Kellogg Project Visiting Scholar Research Conference on the History of Adult Education, Syracuse University, Mar. 22, 1990, publication by Syracuse University pending.

4. The immense variety of early patterns for use of Morrill funds is a major theme of Earle D. Ross's *Democracy's College*. See also Eddy, *Colleges for Our Land*, ch. 3.

5. Eddy, *Colleges for Our Land*, 66–67; Rudolph, *American College and University*, 260; "Report of the Committee on Entrance Requirements, Courses of Study, and Degrees," *AAACES Proc.* 10 (1896): 52–54; debate, ibid., 59–62; Williams, "George W. Atherton," 349–54.

6. William Oxley Thompson, *NASU Proc.* 2 (1904): 19, A. B. Storms, "The Distinctive Work of the Land-Grant Colleges: Their Function, Scope, and Organization," *AAACES Proc.* 23 (1909): 51; J. C. Hardy, ibid. 25 (1911): 135; Bettersworth, *People's College* (see ch. 1, n. 18), ch. 2.

7. Henry Suzzallo to "Mr. Perkins," June 8, 1915 ("one great"), HS, box 11; Enoch Albert Bryan, *Historical Sketch of the State College of Washington, 1890–1925* (Spokane, Wash., 1928), 379–88.

8. James K. Patterson, "A Retrospect," *AAACES Proc.* 24 (1910): 34–35.

9. ECR, *AAACES Proc.* 14 (1900): 11 ("mission"); Winthrop Ellsworth Stone, "The Selection and Retention of an Efficient Teaching Force," ibid. 21 (1907): 72 ("stand before").

10. ECR, *AAACES Proc.* 20 (1908): 16; H. S. Pritchett, ibid., 49–51; ibid. 23 (1909): 65–71, 24 (1910): 125–36; A. B. Storms, "Distinctive Work," *AAACES Proc.* 23:57 ("decent"); Enoch Albert Bryan, ibid. 23 (1909): 58 ("national").

11. W. E. Stone, *AAACES Proc.* 23 (1909): 68, 69 ("whole"); ibid. 14 (1900): 73, 15 (1901): 22–25. For another example of emphasis on state particularism, see W. E. Drake, "The Relation of the Agricultural and Mechanical College to the State," ibid. 14 (1900): 183.

12. J. G. Schurman, "Some Problems of Our Universities—State and Endowed," *NASU Proc.* 7 (1909): 36 ("caprice"); G. E. MacLean, "The State University the Servant of the Whole State," ibid. 2 (1904): 34; G. P. Benton, "State Universities and the Educational Challenge of To-morrow," ibid. 16 (1918): 28–41; B. I. Wheeler, "The State Universities as a Factor in American Life," ibid. 173; R. E. Vinson, "Legislative Problems," ibid. 17 (1919): 136; J. K. Patterson, ibid. 6 (1908): 227–28.

13. G. E. MacLean, *NASU Proc.* 6 (1908): 204; similarly, ibid. 5 (1907): 111–12; Edmund J. James, ibid., 113 ("so-called"). For James's related resentment of foundations' advancement of new definitions and standards, see ibid. 6 (1908): 247.

14. "Report of the Committee on Standards of American Universities," *NASU Proc.* 6 (1908): 147–53, 147–48 ("typical"), discussion, pp. 177–220;

A. H. Upham, "About Ourselves," ibid. 34:22–23; Fred J. Kelly et al., *Collegiate Accreditation by Agencies within States* (USOE Bul. 3, Washington, D.C., 1940), 13; Edwin E. Slosson, *Great American Universities* (New York, 1910), 522.

15. *NASU Proc.* 4 (1906): 12–16, 5 (1907): 241; Edward A. Krug, *The Shaping of the American High School* (New York, 1964), 157; Zook and Haggerty, *Principles of Accrediting Higher Institutions* (see ch. 2, n. 8), 38–40; Selden, *Accreditation*, 34–35, 35 ("years"); Howard J. Savage, *Fruit of an Impulse: Forty-Five Years of the Carnegie Foundation, 1905–1950* (New York, 1953), 102–3.

16. *NASU Proc.* 13 (1915): 44–45; Lykes, *Higher Education and the USOE*, 51–52.

17. G. E. MacLean, *NASU Proc.* 7 (1909): 75–76; George E. Fellows to "Dear Sir," Oct. 3, 1906, mimeo., UCPP, box 33; Thomas Kane, "Standardizing the Cost of Departments," *NASU Proc.* 10 (1912): 102; George E. Vincent, "Report of the Committee on Standards of the American Universities and the A.B. Degree," ibid. 13 (1915): 45; Lykes, *Higher Education and the USOE*, 51–52; James H. Baker, "What Influence Should the Carnegie Foundation Have on Entrance Requirements?" *NASU Proc.* 7 (1909): 54–58, 57 ("large"). On the case for diversity as made by Josiah Royce in 1915, see Lagemann, *Private Power for Public Good*, 90–92, 180–83.

18. *AAU Proc.* 9 (1908): 9–11, 74–75, 10 (1909): 66; Selden, *Accreditation*, 69.

19. Samuel P. Capen to Grace Capen, Sept. 19, 1914, SPC, box 12 ("cold-blooded"); Lykes, *Higher Education and the USOE*, 45–52, 48 (quoting Day), 213–15 (for suppressed report and list); *AAU Proc.* 14 (1912): 17; D. J. Cowling, "Report of Committee on Higher Educational Statistics," *AAC Bul.* 2 (1916), no. 3, pp. 97–98; S. P. Capen, "College 'Lists' and Surveys Published by the Bureau of Education," *S&S* 6 (1917): 38–40. For a letter from the AAU to Woodrow Wilson, see *AAU Proc.* 15 (1913): 19. See also David S. Webster, "The Bureau of Education's Suppressed Rating of Colleges, 1911–1912," *HEQ* 24 (1984): 499–511. The USBE had without objection listed women's colleges in a two-level classification between 1888 and 1911. See idem, *Academic Quality Rankings of American Colleges and Universities* (Springfield, Ill., 1986), 31–33.

20. *AAU Proc.* 15 (1913): 55–62, 19 (1917): 20–21, 101–103; Kelly et al., *Collegiate Accreditation*, 13–15, 25; Zook and Haggerty, *Principles of Accrediting Higher Institutions*, 38; Davis, *North Central Association* (see ch. 1, n. 23), 57–64; Louis G. Geiger, *Voluntary Accreditation: A History of the North Central Association, 1945–1970* (Menasha, Wis., 1970), 187; Selden, *Accreditation*, 69–70; *AAU Proc.* 9 (1908): 77 ("approximately"), 78. For the relationship of the AAU list to establishment of Phi Beta Kappa chapters, see Richard Nelson Current, *Phi Beta Kappa in American Life: The First Two Hundred Years* (New York, 1990), 141–45.

21. Kendric C. Babcock, "The Present Standards of Voluntary Associations," *Ed. Rec.* 2 (1921): 93, 94 ("purely"); *AAU Proc.* 25 (1923): 20, 24–27, 26 (1924): 23, 31–35, 40 (1938): 64–65, 42 (1940): 86–97. Expenditures rose from $1,067 in 1923 to $5,518 in 1924, of which $3,794 went toward inspections. For the Fordham case, see Paul A. FitzGerald, *The Governance of Jesuit Colleges in the United States, 1920–1970* (Notre Dame, Ind., 1984), 42–44. For the (successful) efforts of the University of Buffalo to win approval, see Samuel P. Capen to Adam Leroy Jones, May 21, 1924, Nov. 24, 1926, and the printed "Memorandum of Procedure Advised for Institutions Seeking Approval of the Association for Inclusion on Its Accepted List," with re-

sponses, all in UBPP, box 13. Examples of inspection reports from 1937 are in DBT, box 22. For a general description of the AAU accrediting philosophy and procedures, see Adam Leroy Jones, "The Search for Values—Through Accrediting Agencies: The Association of American Universities," *AAC Bul.* 20 (1934): 111–17.

22. William K. Selden, "AAU: An Enigma," *Graduate Journal* 8:202. See also Webster, *Academic Quality Rankings*, ch. 11. For more on the late 1930s debates, see this volume, this chapter, under "The ACE and the Reshaping of Standardization, 1920–1940."

23. *AAU Proc.* 17 (1915): 22; ibid. 1 (1900): 15 ("separate," "federal"), 17; ibid. 18 (1916): 67–72, 69 ("academic Master's"). For recollections at the time of the committee's dissolution, see ibid. 45 (1944): 84–86.

24. Ibid., 22 (1990): 22 ("research degree"). For the committee's collaboration with professional associations, see ibid., 21–26.

25. Charles W. Eliot, *AAU Proc.* 10 (1909): 62.

26. *AAU Proc.* (Dec. 1902): 50–63, 62 ("cannot"); 5 (1904): 14–21 (discussion of Keppel's paper). See also F. P. Keppel to Benjamin Ide Wheeler, Oct. 28, 1902, UCPP, box 10.

27. *AAU Proc.* 9 (1908): 13, 10 (1909): 67–68 (first report), 68 ("institutions"), 11 (Jan. 1910): 90–91 (supplementary report setting definitions for *group, curriculum,* and *division*); "Nomenclature," *NASU Proc.* 7 (1909): 204; ibid. 8 (1910): 39–41. For a later pursuit of the same matter, see David A. Robertson, "Standard Terminology in Education," *Ed. Rec.* 8 (1927), suppl. 4.

28. *AAU Proc.* 20 (1918): 25–26, 21 (1919): 19, 22 (1920): 28.

29. William H. Crawford, "The Place and Function of the Denominational College in Education," *AAC Bul.* 1 (1915): 126–27; ibid., 7, 12.

30. Samuel Capen, "College Efficiency and Standardization; Certain Fundamental Principles," *AAC Bul.* 1 (1915): 143 ("after all"), 146–49; Donald J. Cowling, "Report of Committee on Higher Educational Statistics," ibid. 2 (1916), no. 3, pp. 96–102; Capen, *Resources and Standards of Colleges of Arts and Sciences: Report of a Committee Representing the Associations of Higher Educational Institutions* (USBE Bul. 30, Washington, D.C., 1918), 14 ("to the eye"), 15–17; Kelly, "Audit of Experience," 99.

31. Kelly, "Audit of Experience," 60, 56; Calvin H. French, "The Efficient College," *AAC Bul.* 2 (1916), no. 3, pp. 60–85; Robert L. Kelly, "The Sphere and Possibilities of the Association," ibid., 22–23; Charles Nelson Cole, ibid., 95 ("retard"); similarly, R. Watson Cooper, "The Place and Function of the Proposed Association," ibid. 1 (1915): 45. For comparable worries about too many small hospitals, see Starr, *Social Transformation of American Medicine* (see ch. 2, n. 49), 176.

32. Kelly, *American Colleges and the Social Order* (see ch. 1, n. 30), 85; idem, "Present Standards of Protestant Church Boards of Education," *Ed. Rec.* 2 (1921): 107–13; Thomas Nicholson, "A Proposed Campaign of Christian Education," *AAC Bul.* 2 (1916), no. 2, pp. 2–22; *Forward Movement for Christian Education,* p. [2] ("to assist"), UCPP, box 97; "Denominational Boards in Education," *CFAT AR* 3 (1908): 172–73. On the assumption that *efficient* had taken on offensive connotations, a later series of papers edited by Kelly for the AAC was entitled *The Effective College* (New York, 1928).

33. Raymond Walters, "Report of the Committee on Classification of Institutions of Higher Education," *AAC Bul.* 20 (1934): 93–94; Edward Everett

Rall, "The Report of the National Committee on Standard Reports for Institutions of Higher Education," ibid., 95–97; Kelly, "Sphere and Possibilities," ibid. 2 (1916), no. 3, p. 26 ("significant," "science").

34. Selden, *Accreditation*, 36–38, 98 n. 11; Kelly, "Audit of Experience," 74; *AAC Bul.* 11 (1925): 20.

35. Samuel Capen, *NASU Proc.* 17 (1919): 62; AR, *Ed. Rec.* 1 (1920): 149 ("perhaps"); "Accredited Higher Institutions," ibid., 71–80. For the last list before discontinuation, see ibid. 16 (1935): 363–71.

36. ACE exec. cmte. min., Apr. 4, 1922, Sept. 22, 1923, mimeo., MLB, boxes 5, 13; ACE Committee on Standards min., Jan. 9, 1924, MLB, box 13; AR, *Ed. Rec.* 3 (1922): 186–87; "Preliminary Recommodations [*sic*] to National, Regional and State Agencies Engaged in Defining and Accrediting Colleges," ibid., 61–63; "Report of the Committee on College Standards," ibid., 210–14; AR, ibid. 4 (1923): 95; George D. Olds, "Conference on Methods of College Standardization," ibid. 2 (1921): 81; D. A. Robertson, "Degrees for Dollars," ibid. 7 (1926): 11–24, esp. 20. The ACE committee soon broadened its purview to include junior colleges and teachers colleges. See "Report of the Committee on Standards," ibid. 5 (1924): 202–8, and *Standards for Accrediting Colleges, Junior Colleges and Teacher Training Institutions* (Washington, D.C., 1924), copy in MLB, box 13. See also Zook and Haggerty, *Principles of Accrediting Higher Institutions*, 29, 41–43.

37. "Report of the Committee on Graduate Instruction," *Ed. Rec.* 15 (1934): 192–226; FitzGerald, *Governance of Jesuit Colleges*, 36–37; Orlans, *Private Accreditation*, 17; Starr, *Social Transformation of American Medicine*, 115–16, 121.

38. "Report of the Committee on College Standards," *Ed. Rec.* 4 (1923): 138; Clark, *Higher Education System* (see ch. 1, n. 7), p. 62, ch. 5; Fritz K. Ringer, *Education and Society in Modern Europe* (Bloomington, Ind., 1979), 247–59.

39. C. R. Mann to D. J. Cowling, Mar. 19, 1925, ACE Ar., 7-14-8; *Financial Reports for Colleges and Universities* (Chicago, 1935); Kelly, "Audit of Experience," 84, 101–3; Lykes, *Higher Education and the USOE*, 97; Cowling to Mann, June 25, 1931, Mann to Cowling, June 29, 1931, both in ACE Ar., 7-14-9.

40. Orlans, *Private Accreditation*, 17 ("presidents"); Zook and Haggerty, *Principles of Accrediting Higher Institutions*, 60–61 ("stifling"); Harry Pratt Judson, "Dangers of the Standardization Movement," *Ed. Rec.* 2 (1921): 114–15.

41. Lotus D. Coffman, "Standardization of State Universities by Outside Agencies," *NASU Proc.* 21 (1923): 66–81; resolution, ibid. 22 (1924): 107 ("seriously"); H. W. Chase to "Gentlemen," Jan. 26, 1924 ("attempt"), copy in UCPP, box 170; Orlans, *Private Accreditation*, 17–18; Henry Suzzallo to "Mr. Henry," Jan. 12, 1925, HS, box 14 ("groups"); similarly, David Kinley to Frank E. Robbins, Dec. 9, 1924, MLB, box 18; "A Study of Recent Standardizing Activities of Certain Associations Affecting University Organizations and Curricula," *NASU Proc.* 24 (1926), part 2 (separately paginated). For a summary of the report presented before another association, see Fred J. Kelly, *The Influence of Standardizing Agencies in Education* (Minneapolis, 1928). See also Selden, *Accreditation*, 70; Zook and Haggerty, *Principles of Accrediting Higher Institutions*, 63–64.

42. Samuel Capen, "Discussion," in Kelly, *Influence of Standardizing Agencies*, 16–23, 17 ("persons"). Other examples of Capen's new position are "Tendencies in Professional Education," *Ed. Rec.* 5 (1924): 15–16; "A Series of Prejudices," *AAC Bul.* 13 (1927): 365–66; "The Principles Which Should

Govern Standards and Accrediting Practices," *Ed. Rec.* 12 (1931): 93–103. At the University of Buffalo, Capen's hopes for both an undergraduate tutorial program and a school of library science were undercut by accrediting agencies. See Park, *Samuel P. Capen,* 37, 45n. See also Zook and Haggerty, *Principles of Accrediting Higher Institutions,* 65.

43. Zook and Haggerty, *Principles of Accrediting Higher Institutions,* esp. v–vii; Davis, *North Central Association,* 70–72; Selden, *Accreditation,* 40–41; *Ed. Rec.* 16 (1935): 248; George F. Zook to Raymond B. Fosdick, July 16, 1937, ACE Ar., 9-3-6; Zook, "Who Should Control Our Higher Institutions?" *ALGCU Proc.* 52 (1938): 90–99.

44. [Monroe Deutsch] to Charles B. Lipman, Oct. 28, 1936, UCPP, box 416 ("standpoint"); Deutsch to R. G. Sproul, Sept. 26, 1936, UCPP, box 418; Charles B. Lipman, "Professional Associations and Associations of Professional Schools and Some Problems Which They Pose for American Universities," *AAU Proc.* 38 (1936): 131–39, esp. 134–35, and discussion, 140–143; "Memorandum for Guidance of Institutions Seeking Approval of the Association for Inclusion in Its Accepted List," ibid. 40 (1938): 25–28. For more on pharmacists, see L. P. Sieg to John J. Tigert, May 24, 1938, UWPP, 71–34, box 110.

45. Kelly et al., *Collegiate Accreditation,* esp. 212–23; George A. Works, "Voluntary Accrediting Associations," *AAU Proc.* 42 (1940): 86–92; Fernandus Payne, "Discussion," ibid., 96–97.

46. *NASU Proc.* 24 (1926), part 2, p. 1; *NASU Proc.* 36 (1938): 21–48, 79–108. The other JCA participants were the AAU, the ALGCU, and the AUU. See Selden, *Accreditation,* 71–73; Bloland, *Higher Education Associations,* 106–7.

47. Selden, *Accreditation,* 72–73; P&P cmte. min., Oct. 18–19, 1938, ACE Ar., 10-11-8; AR, *Ed. Rec.* 20 (1939): 356–59; Fernandus Payne, "Discussion," *AAU Proc.* 42 (1940): 95 ("implied"); "Report of the Joint Committee on Accrediting," Nov. 14, 1941, AGR, box 56. For a request that accrediting agencies suspend specific requirements that interfered with student acceleration during the war, see min. of joint meeting, P&P cmte. and exec. cmte., Dec. 19, 1941, ACE Ar., 10-20-2.

Chapter 5: The Philanthropic Aegis

1. J. G. Schurman, "Some Problems of Our Universities—State and Endowed," *NASU Proc.* 7 (1909): 30–31; H. S. Pritchett, "Remarks on the Carnegie Foundation," ibid., 60–62; Schurman, ibid. 8 (1910): 275, 286; William J. Kerr, "Some Land Grant College Problems," *AAACES Proc.* 24 (1910): 37–51; P. D. Hall, "Historical Overview," in Powell, *Nonprofit Sector* (see ch. 2, n. 4), 8–17. See also James Douglas, *Why Charity? The Case for a Third Sector* (Beverly Hills, Calif., 1983); Michael O'Neill, *The Third America: The Emergence of the Nonprofit Sector in the United States* (San Francisco, 1989).

2. Roger L. Geiger, *To Advance Knowledge: The Growth of American Research Universities, 1900–1940* (New York, 1986), 45. For an elaborate comparative analysis of Carnegie and Rockefeller's philanthropies, see Steven C. Wheatley, *The Politics of Philanthropy: Abraham Flexner and Medical Education* (Madison, Wis., 1988), ch. 1. For evidence that the public saw the two philanthropists in competition, see Joseph Wall, *Andrew Carnegie* (New York, 1970), 884. For

Canegie's role as advisor to other philanthropists, see ibid., 881. For an analysis of the Commission on Industrial Relations hearings in 1915, where both Rockefeller and Carnegie appeared, see Barbara Howe, "The Emergence of Scientific Philanthropy, 1900–1920: Origins, Issues, and Outcomes," in Robert F. Arnove (ed.), *Philanthropy and Cultural Imperialism: The Foundations at Home and Abroad* (Boston, 1980), 25–54.

3. Wheatley, *Politics of Philanthropy*, 36–37; Allan Nevins, *John D. Rockefeller: The Heroic Age of American Enterprise* (New York, 1940), 1:120, 226, 2:210–11; Raymond B. Fosdick, *The Story of the Rockefeller Foundation* (New York, 1952), 7 ("principles"); Storr, *Harper's University* (see ch. 1, n. 26), 9–11; Lagemann, *Private Power for Public Good*, ch. 2. The term *philanthropoid* was coined by the second generation of foundation managers (Wheatley, *Politics of Philanthrophy*, 141).

4. Raymond B. Fosdick, *Adventure in Giving: The Story of the General Education Board, a Foundation Established by John D. Rockefeller* (New York, 1962), 127 ("promote"), 131 ("no less," "formed"), 327; Nevins, *John D. Rockefeller*, 2:496; *The General Education Board: An Account of Its Activities, 1902–1914* (New York, 1915), ch. 5; Burke, *American Collegiate Populations* (see ch. 1, n. 4), 82–89; D. B. Potts, "American Colleges in the Nineteenth Century," *HEQ* 11:363–80. See also Merle Curti and Roderick Nash, *Philanthropy in the Shaping of American Higher Education* (New Brunswick, N.J., 1965).

5. Fosdick, *Adventure in Giving*, 148, 137–39; *NASU Proc.* 2 (1904): 20; *AAU Proc.* 24 (1922): 77 ("industrial"); Trevor Arnett, "Teachers' Salaries," *AAC Bul.* 15 (1929): 9–19. For the GEB's medical school program, see Fosdick, *Adventure in Giving*, ch. 12; Wheatley, *Politics of Philanthropy*, esp. ch. 3.

6. AR, *Ed. Rec.* 3 (1922): 183–84; "Report of the Commission in Charge of the Educational Finance Inquiry," ibid., 202–5; Dobbins, *ACE Leadership*, 11.

7. "The Carnegie Foundation Not a Charity But an Educational Agency," CFAT AR 2 (1907): 63–65; Lagemann, *Private Power for Public Good*, 23–29; Abraham Flexner, *Henry S. Pritchett: A Biography* (New York, 1943), 24–66; Andrew Carnegie to Charles W. Eliot, June 16, 1910, quoted in Lagemann, *Private Power for Public Good*, 52 ("good work"). Part I of this book revealingly contrasts the ideas and personalities of Carnegie and Pritchett.

8. Wall, *Andrew Carnegie*, 873; CFAT AR 1 (1906): 38–39, 21–22; Savage, *Fruit of an Impulse*, 100–103.

9. CFAT AR 2 (1907): 89–92; *AAU Proc.* 9 (1908): 11, 73 ("to assist"); Savage, *Fruit of an Impulse*, 134.

10. Andrew Carnegie to CFAT trustees, Apr. 16, 1905, printed in CFAT AR 1 (1906): 7–8; *Papers Relating to the Admission of State Institutions to the System of Retiring Allowances of the Carnegie Foundation* (CFAT, Bul. 1, New York, 1907): *AAU Proc.* 8 (1906): 65–73. In Theron F. Schlabach, *Pensions for Professors* (Madison, Wis., 1963), a meticulous work focused on this controversy, see esp. pp. 40–42.

11. Charles R. Van Hise to James B. Angell, Dec. 13, 1907, Jan. 31, 1908, JBA, box 7.

12. *NASU Proc.* 5 (1907): 214–40, 6 (1908): 49–59; Schlabach, *Pensions for Professors*, 63–66, 77–79, 83, 87; Savage, *Fruit of an Impulse*, 74–77. Although the ground for the NASU's existence was members' shared identity as public universities, in this case the association had been eager to show the ambiguities

of the public-private distinction and had in large measure succeeded. By contrast, the AAACES did include at least two institutions—Cornell and MIT—which, though receiving Morrill grants, were largely private.

13. H. S. Pritchett, *AAACES Proc.* 22 (1908): 51 ("you"); ibid., 52 ("sympathetic").

14. D. W. Working, *AAACES Proc.* 23 (1909): 70 ("pitiful"); William J. Kerr, "Some Land Grant College Problems," ibid. 24 (1910): 37–52, 38 ("unwarranted"); ECR, ibid., 112; "Indiana University and Purdue University," CFAT AR 5 (1910): 23–26. See also the discussion of agricultural education in ibid. 4 (1909): 97–107.

15. Andrew Carnegie to trustees, Apr. 16, 1905, in CFAT AR 1:8 ("control"); Savage, *Fruit of an Impulse*, 77–78, 90.

16. CFAT AR 12 (1917): 5; Schlabach, *Pensions for Professors*, 91; Savage, *Fruit of an Impulse*, 116–18, 138–40; William Graebner, *A History of Retirement: The Meaning and Function of an American Institution, 1885–1978* (New Haven, 1980), 117. The NASU held a rare executive session to discuss the suggested shift to a contributory plan (*NASU Proc.* 14 [1916]: 131).

17. Ellen Condliffe Lagemann, *The Politics of Knowledge: The Carnegie Corporation, Philanthropy, and Public Policy* (Middletown, Conn., 1989), 27–31, 29 ("accessible").

18. "The University of Wisconsin and Subsidies from Foundations," *S&S* 22 (1925): 459–61; Frederick P. Keppel, "Opportunities and Dangers of Educational Foundations," *AAU Proc.* 27 (1925): 65, 67; Lagemann, *Politics of Knowledge*, 100–103.

19. Exec. cmte. min., 1924–26, passim, AAC Ar.; Savage, *Fruit of an Impulse*, 135; R. L. Kelly, "The Teaching of the Fine Arts," *AAC Bul.* 13 (1927): 209; Lura Beam, "The Place of Art in the Liberal College," ibid., 265–88; Snavely, *Search for Excellence*, 126; Lagemann, *Politics of Knowledge*, 108–9.

20. AR, *Ed. Rec.* 3 (1922): 191–92 ("absolutely"); D. J. Cowling to C. R. Mann, May 26, 1926, ACE Ar., 7-14-8; ECR, *Ed. Rec.* 6 (1925): 173–74; Waldemar A. Nielsen, *The Big Foundations* (New York, 1972), 254. See table 3.

21. Raymond A. Kent, chairman of the ACE, "The Program of the ACE," *Ed. Rec.* 17 (1936), suppl. 10, p. 62 ("middleman"); Ray Fyfe to G. F. Zook, Mar. 2, 19, 1937; Zook to Fyfe, Mar. 9, 1937, ACE Ar., 9-3-3. For the Committee on Personnel Methods, supported by John D. Rockefeller, Jr.'s Benevolent Fund, see *Ed. Rec.* 8 (1927): 186; "The Committee on Personnel Methods," ibid. 9 (1928), suppl. 8, pp. 4.5. For Carnegie and Rockefeller connections with the testing movement, including the role of the ACE, see Lagemann, *Private Power for Public Good*, ch. 5. On central office reimbursement for administering grants, see exec. cmte. min., Feb. 27, 1924, copy in MLB, box 13 ("cost"); "Treasurer's Report," *Ed. Rec.* 9 (1928): 170.

22. Lagemann, *Private Power for Public Good*, 85–89; Fosdick, *Adventure in Giving*, 196–205; Donald T. Critchlow, *The Brookings Institution, 1916–1952: Expertise and the Public Interest in a Democratic Society* (DeKalb, Ill., 1985), 56; David W. Eakins, "The Origins of Corporate Liberal Policy Research, 1916–1922: The Political-Economic Expert and the Decline of Public Debate," in Israel, *Building the Organizational Society* (ch. 1, n. 43), 174; Lagemann, *Politics of Knowledge*, 65, 105–6; Barry D. Karl and Stanley N. Katz, "The American Private Philanthropic Foundation and the Public Sphere, 1890–1930," *Minerva* 19 (1981): 267; Geiger, *To Advance Knowledge*, ch. 4; AR, *Ed. Rec.* 3 (1922): 183 ("distinctly"); Hans Zinsser, "The Perils of Magnanimity: A Problem in

American Education," *Atlantic Monthly* 139 (1927): 248–49; Eduard C. Linde-man, *Wealth and Culture* (New York, 1936), esp. 52–54. On the legitimacy question, see Lagemann, *Private Power for Public Good*, esp. preface and ch. 8; Curti and Nash, *Philanthropy in American Higher Education*, 221–22, 227. See also J. McKeen Cattell, "Life Insurance and Annuities for Academic Teachers," *S&S* 8 (1918): 541–49, and the moderately approving R. E. Vinson, "What Foundations Are Doing," *NASU Proc.* 21 (1923): 91–97.

23. AR, *Ed. Rec.* 3 (1922): 183; Lindeman, *Wealth and Culture*, 20; Edmund E. Day to G. F. Zook, Dec. 28, 1936, ACE Ar., 9-3-5 ("probably").

24. ECR, *Ed. Rec.* 6 (1925): 174; Nielsen; *Big Foundations*, 57, 60 ("often"); Fosdick, *Story of the Rockefeller Foundation*, 207–9; J. H. MacCracken to Donald J. Cowling, Apr. 6, 1933, ACE Ar., 7-17-12.

25. On the restructuring, see above, ch. 3 under "The ACE Central Office under Capen and Mann."

26. *Activities of the American Youth Commission* (Washington, D.C., 1937); AR, *Ed. Rec.* 20 (1939): 336–39; ibid. 21 (1940): 279–86; Fosdick, *Adventure in Giving*, 240–44, 253–55; Dobbins, *ACE Leadership*, 25–26, 28, 142.

27. AR, *Ed. Rec.* 20 (1939): 362–66; ibid. 21 (1940): 262–65.

28. Ibid. 22 (1941): 241–43; "Report of the Committee on the Place of a National Organization in American Education [Works Committee]," type-script, ACE Ar., 10-17-4.

29. Min. of joint meeting, ACE exec. cmte. and P&P cmte., Sept. 6, 1941, ACE Ar., 10-19-7; ibid., Dec. 19, 1941, Apr. 30, 1942, ACE Ar., 10-20-2; AR, *Ed. Rec.* 22 (1941): 292; ibid. 23 (1942): 325, 330–31; George F. Zook to A. M. Schwitalla, Jan. 22, 1941, ACE Ar., 10-19-7; *NEA Proc.* 79 (1941): 749. As president of the ACE, Zook was already an advisory member of the EPC. Apparently, the GEB concluded that higher education's role in the EPC could be increased without formal restructuring. In 1941 James B. Conant became a member of the EPC; thenceforth, university administrators were increasingly included. In 1951 the *executive* committee of the ACE and the EPC jointly published *Education and National Security* (Washington, D.C.).

30. AR, *Ed. Rec.* 23 (1942): 330–34; P&P cmte. min., Nov. 7–8, 1950, ACE Ar., 10-65-2; Logan Wilson to Everett N. Case, Sept. 19, 1962, ACE Ar., 16-12-26; AR, *Ed. Rec.* 32 (1951): 247; Dobbins, *ACE Leadership*, 101.

31. The Ford Foundation gave the ACE a $2 million general support grant in 1962 and $3.7 million for programs over the next five years (Dobbins, *ACE Leadership*, 121). See also Dennis C. Buss, "The Ford Foundation in Public Education: Emergent Patterns," in Arnove, *Philanthropy and Cultural Imperialism*, 331–62.

INTERLUDE: THE ACE CHANGES HELMSMEN, 1935

1. This interlude draws on not only the *Educational Record* but also the stenographic transcript in ACE Ar., 9-1-7 through 9-1-9.

CHAPTER 6: WHEN IS A LOBBY NOT A LOBBY?

1. King, *Washington Lobbyists for Higher Education* (see ch. 3, n. 46), 65–67; *Congress and the Nation, 1945–64: A Review of Government and Politics in the Postwar Years* (Washington, D.C., 1965), 1549, 1562.

2. Louis Galambos, *America at Middle Age: A New History of the United States in the Twentieth Century* (New York, n.d.), 53–58; Everson, *Public Opinion and Interest Groups* (see ch. 1, n. 2), 200–201, 212 n. 35; Douglas Cater, *Power in Washington: A Critical Look at Today's Struggle to Govern in the Nation's Capital* (New York, 1964); Hugh Heclo, *A Government of Strangers: Executive Politics in Washington* (Washington, D.C., 1977); idem, "Issue Networks and the Executive Establishment," in Anthony King (ed.), *The New American Political System* (Washington, D.C., 1978), 87–124.

3. Williams, "George W. Atherton," 282; for a detailed account and astute interpretation of the association's lobbying efforts through 1906, ibid., chs. 5–6; *AAACES Proc.* 14 (1900): 12, 15 (1901): 63.

4. *AAACES Proc.* 19 (1905): 17–18; "Instructions to the Executive Committee Regarding Congressional Legislation," ibid., 45–46; ECR, ibid., 20 (1906): 18; "Memorial to Henry Cullen Adams," ibid., 37; ibid. 21 (1907): 15–16; Rosenberg, *No Other Gods* (see ch. 1, n. 11), 106, 179–80, and ch. 10; James E. Hansen II, *Democracy's College in the Centennial State: A History of Colorado State University* (Fort Collins, Colo., 1977), 163–64.

5. On mining: *AAACES Proc.* 14 (1900): 12, 19 (1905): 43; *NASU Proc.* 1 (1903): 22, 2 (1904): 15–16; Henry H. Goodell to Andrew S. Draper, various letters, esp. Jan. 30, 1902, ASD, box 4. On engineering: *AAACES Proc.* 22 (1908): 15; *ALGCU Proc.* 55 (1941): 80; NASU, "Bulletin," mimeo., Dec. 1, 1916, copy in UCPP, box 100; Daniel J. Kevles, *The Physicists: The History of a Scientific Community in America* (New York, 1978), 150–52; S. P. Capen, "Educational Bills before Congress," *Ed. Rec.* 1 (1920): 28–29; A. A. Potter, secretary, AAACES, to "Gentlemen," June 25, 1917, UCPP, box 97; Eddy, *Colleges for Our Land* (see ch. 1, n. 13), 233–34. For evidence of rising opposition to the engineering bill in one of the richer land-grant institutions, see W. W. Campbell to Anson Marston, Mar. 5, 1929, UCPP, box 227; Charles Derleth, Jr., to Robert G. Sproul, Dec. 31, 1930, ibid., box 255.

6. *AAACES Proc.* 24 (1910): 94–105, 25 (1911): 76–85, 119, 123; Howard H. Gross to Kenyon L. Butterfield, Dec. 6, 1911, and adjacent correspondence, KLB, box 20; Hansen, *Colorado State*, 253; Eddy, *Colleges for Our Land*, 140, 277; Rosenberg, *No Other Gods*, 179 ("routine").

7. G. F. Zook, "The Recommendations of the National Advisory Committee on Education," *ALGCU Proc.* 44 (1930): 48.

8. ECR, *ALGCU Proc.* 47 (1933): 113; R. A. Pearson, memoranda, Feb. 7, Mar. 6, Apr. 18, 1933, copies in UCPP, box 337; *Statistics of Higher Education, 1933–34* (USOE Bul. 2 [for 1935], Washington, D.C., [published 1937]), 428–29.

9. *ALGCU Proc.* 49 (1935): 36–37; Eddy, *Colleges for Our Land*, 198; Richard S. Kirkendall, *Social Scientists and Farm Politics in the Age of Roosevelt* (Columbia, Mo., 1966), 152–57; Gladys L. Baker et al., *Century of Service: The First 100 Years of the United States Department of Agriculture* (Washington, D.C., 1963), 254–55.

10. Robert B. Fulton, "Organization of the NASU," *NASU Proc.* 2:11–15.

11. *ASSU Bulletin*, mimeo., nos. 2, 7 ("efficiency"), 14 (all 1929), 25, 26 (both Dec. 3, 1930), copies in ACE Ar., 7-8-9; Richard C. Foster to Alexander G. Ruthven, Oct. 29, 1941, and SUA min., Nov. 7, 1941, both AGR, box 56; ALGCU exec. cmte. to "Dear Mr. President," Mar. 30, 1937, mimeo., copy in UCPP, box 442. The original membership of the Association of Separated State Universities included nineteen non-land-grant state universities, George

Washington University, and, apparently as a case of "personal membership," C. R. Mann.

12. In 1940 the NASU did start a drive to prevent cuts in NYA funding. See Guy Stanton Ford to Herman G. James, Feb. 2, 1940, NASULGC Ar., box 12.

13. J. B. Conant to R. L. Wilbur, Feb. 15, 1937, DBT, 22–1; Conant, *My Several Lives*, 179 (on his later change of opinion); Harold W. Dodds, paper for "Symposium on the Relation of the Federal Government to Higher Education," *AAU Proc.* 41 (1939): 88; Robert A. Millikan, paper for "Symposium on Centralizing Tendencies in American Education," ibid. 42 (1940): 70 ("ever increasing"). Stanford administrators opposed suspension of AAU functions during World War II for fear they might be taken over by a government agency (Ralph H. Lutz to E. B. Stouffer, Mar. 17, 1943, DBT, 22–5). Lutz wrote after conferring with Chancellor Ray Lyman Wilbur.

14. G. S. Ford, *AAU Proc.* 41 (1939): 105 ("match"); Frank Graham, ibid. 42 (1940): 77; Karl Compton, "Discussion," ibid. 41 (1939): 103–105, 105 ("just about").

15. Kelly, "Policies and Precedents," 5. Early in 1932 the executive committee empowered Kelly as executive secretary and William Preston Few, president of Duke University, "to protect the interests of the members of the Association in the new revenue bill" (exec. cmte. min., Mar. 22, 1932, AAC Ar.). For a similar case, see ibid., Jan. 18, 1938.

16. R. L. Kelly to "Dear Colleague," July 12, 1933 ("extravagant"); idem to "Members of the Association," June 3, 1933 ("building," "so-called"), both in ACIA.

17. AR, *AAC Bul.* 21 (1935): 161–63; Daniel L. Marsh, "Federal Government Aid to Colleges," ibid., 170–75, 171 ("strategically"), 175 ("self-seeking"); Kelly, "Audit of Experience," 47–49; Kelly to "Dear Colleague," Mar. 7, 1934, RLW, box 4; exec. cmte. [after Jan. 1, 1938, called "Board of Directors"] min., May 2, 1935, Jan. 18, Mar. 4, June 28, 1938, AAC Ar.; Guy E. Snavely to "Dear Colleague," Mar. 18, 1938, copy in ACE Ar., 10-8-7. In 1938 a special committee of the AAC was studying the issue of Social Security and private colleges under a Carnegie Corporation grant.

18. Exec. cmte. min., Apr. 29, 1936, AAC Ar.; Kelly, "Policies and Precedents," 29; AR, *AAC Bul.* 22 (1936): 187–88; ibid. 222; Kelly, "Audit of Experience," 49 ("colleges").

19. E. Pendleton Herring, *Group Representation before Congress* (Baltimore, 1929), 178–80, 180 ("respected"); J. H. MacCracken, "Report of the Committee on Federal Legislation," *Ed. Rec.* 1 (1920): 91–95; ibid. 3 (1922): 209 ("voluntary"); idem, "Federal Legislation," ibid. 9 (1928): 219–24; S. P. Capen to "My dear Sir," Dec. 27, 1920, Jan. 19, 1921, both in AHR; ACE Committee on Federal Legislation min., Apr. 20–22, 1919; Capen to M. L. Burton, Oct. 17, 1921, both in MLB, box 5. On the NACE, see above, ch. 3 under "The ACE Central Office under Capen and Mann." A version of the NACE's proposed federal aid for vocational education, which seemed to fit a situation of rising unemployment, became law in 1932.

20. G. F. Zook, AR, *Ed. Rec.* 20 (1939): 329 ("recent"), Lykes, *Higher Education and the USOE*, 106, 102–103; David Tyack, Robert Lowe, and Elisabeth Hansot, *Public Schools in Hard Times: The Great Depression and Recent Years* (Cambridge, Mass., 1984), 108, 102–103; *History and Activities of ACE (1941–42)*, 27–32; AR, *Ed. Rec.* 19 (1938): 282–84.

21. *Ed. Rec.* 16 (1935): 488; AR, ibid. 17 (1936): 342–47; *ACE: Its History and Activities* (1935–36), 27–28; ACE exec. cmte. min., Oct. 21, 1935 (mimeo., copy in Boston College Library); Cloyd H. Marvin to members of the ACE, July 31, 1935, mimeo., ACE Ar., 9-1-21; Dixon Ryan Fox to Robert F. Wagner, Mar. 18, 1935, copy in ACIA; G. F. Zook to Henry James, Mar. 27, 1937, ACE Ar., 10-4-11. A provision of the 1938 bill would have ended donor's opportunities to calculate assets given to charity at current rather than original value (AR, *Ed. Rec.* 18[1937]: 303; ibid. 19[1938]: 262–63).

22. John K. Norton, "Report of the Committee on Education and Government," *Ed. Rec.* 15 (1934): 350–52; AR, ibid. 18 (1937): 304–6.

23. P&P cmte. min., Oct. 18–19, 1938, ACE Ar., 10-11-18; *ACE: Its History and Activities* (1935–36), 31; *History and Activities of ACE (1941–42)*, 47–48, 57; AR, *Ed. Rec.* 18 (1937): 306–8; Barry D. Karl, *Charles E. Merriam and the Study of Politics* (Chicago, 1974), 227–30; Fosdick, *Story of the Rockefeller Foundation*, 206.

24. P&P cmte. min., Oct. 18–19, 1938, and Zook's marginal note, ACE Ar., 10-11-8; min. of joint meeting, P&P cmte. and exec. cmte., Feb. 12, 1939, p. 3, ACE Ar., 10-11-9; resolution, *Ed. Rec.* 20 (1939): 459 ("fundamental"). In his 1939 annual report, Zook raised the possibility of a "Legislative Advisory Service" to provide information to associations, institutions, and congressional committees (ibid., 364).

25. Lykes, *Higher Education and the USOE*, 33–36, 44; K. L. Babcock, "Statement," *AAACES Proc.* 24 (1910): 59–61. The Commissioner of Education was an ex officio member of the ACE's executive committee till 1956, though rarely attending after 1934. On the USBE's accredited list, see this volume, ch. 4 under "Against Confusion: The AAU." For a highly critical account of the USBE's surveys, see Clyde W. Barrow, *Universities and the Capitalist State: Corporate Liberalism and the Reconstruction of American Higher Education, 1894–1928* (Madison, Wis., 1990), 110–23.

26. Noble, *America by Design*, 212; *Survey of Land-Grant Colleges and Universities* (USOE Bul. 9, Washington, D.C., 1930), esp. vol. 1, p. vii; Arthur J. Klein, "Results of the Survey of Land-Grant Institutions," *ALGCU Proc.* 44 (1930): 72–79; Fred J. Kelly, paper for "Symposium on the Relation of the Federal Government to Higher Education," *AAU Proc.* 41 (1939): 97; Lykes, *Higher Education and the USOE*, 20–21, 43–44, 89.

27. Fred J. Kelly, paper for "Symposium," *AAU Proc.* 41:96–100; Lykes, *Higher Education and the USOE*, 165–66; "Financial Statements of the ACE," *Ed. Rec.* 17 (1936): 503, 505 (total disbursements for general fund and special funds). Kelly's list comprised the following: assessing credentials of foreign students, making surveys of state educational systems or types of institutions or individual institutions, responding to requests for information, promoting the use of standard forms, undertaking research projects, issuing bibliographies, and sponsoring conferences of educational leaders.

28. Donald R. Warren, "Tigert, John James, IV," *DAB*, suppl. 7, pp. 744–45; Samuel Capen, draft of nightletter, May 18, 1921, ACE Ar., 5-4-2 ("person"). Tigert's predecessor, Philander C. Claxton, may have been forced out because of opposition to Harding's proposal for a combined Department of Education and Welfare (Lykes, *Higher Education and the USOE*, 85). See also Charles Lee Lewis, *Philander Priestley Claxton: Crusader for Public Education* (Knoxville, Tenn., 1948), 229–31. On the "Educational Trust," see David

Tyack and Elisabeth Hansot, *Managers of Virtue: Public School Leadership in America, 1820–1980* (New York, 1982), ch. 11.

29. Leonard D. White, *The Republican Era, 1869–1901: A Study in Administrative History* (New York, 1958), 234–35.

30. Harry Pratt Judson, John H. MacCracken, and Prince L. Campbell (committee of the ECE), "Creation of a National Department of Education," in *The Emergency Council on Education: Report of Committee of Organization* ([Washington], [1918]), copy in UCPP, box 112 ("unify"); "The Moblization of Higher Education in America," *AAC Bul.* 4 (1918), no. 2, pp. 3–11; P. L. Campbell, "The Proposed Federal Department of Education," *NASU Proc.* 16 (1918): 162–68; H. V. Ames to B. I. Wheeler, May 31, 1918, UCPP, box 111; John H. MacCracken, "A National Department of Education," *Nation*, 106 (1918): 256–57; *AAC Bul.* 4 (1918), no. 1, p. 12; Kelly, "Policies and Precedents," 4–5; David B. Skillman, *The Biography of a College: Being the History of the First Century of the Life of Lafayette College* (Easton, Pa., 1932), vol. 2, pp. 210, 214, and passim.

31. Wesley, *NEA* (see ch. 1, n. 17), 246–48; Allan M. West, *The National Education Association: The Power Base for Education* (New York, 1980), 9–10; Marion L. Burton to Hugh S. Magill, Nov. 3, 1921, MLB, box 7; Tyack and Hansot, *Managers of Virtue*, 134–45 (on Strayer's educational entrepreneurship); J. H. MacCracken, "The Bill for a National Department of Education," *NEA Proc.* 56 (1918): 193–94; MacCracken, "Report of the Committee on Federal Legislation," *Ed. Rec.* 1 (1920): 91–95. The omnibus bill included appropriations for programs for combatting illiteracy, equalizing educational opportunities, Americanization of immigrants, physical education, and teacher training. See Mary C. C. Bradford, "The Work of the Commission on the Emergency in Education," *NEA Proc.* 57 (1919): 80; George D. Strayer, "A National Program for Education," ibid. 58 (1920): 42–45. On Smith, see MacCracken, "A Department of Education," *AAC Bul.* 11 (1925): 135; Charles H. Judd, "*Negative*," ibid., 153–54, 161; Dewey W. Grantham, Jr., *Hoke Smith and the Politics of the New South* (Baton Rouge, La., 1958), 333–36. See also D. J. Cowling to C. R. Mann, Dec. 6, 1923, Sept. 7, 1931, ACE Ar., 7-14-7, 7-14-9. For a valuable analysis of this movement that emphasizes opponents, see Lynn Dumenil, "'The Insatiable Maw of Bureaucracy': Antistatism and Education Reform in the 1920s," *Journal of American History* 77 (1990): 499–524.

32. S. P. Capen, "The Colleges in a Nationalized Educational Scheme," *S&S* 9 (1919): 614 ("exercise"), 618 ("coordinating"); similarly, idem, "Review of Recent Federal Legislation on Education," *Ed. Rec.* 3 (1922): 25–26.

33. Charles H. Judd, "National Problems in Education," *Ed. Rec.* 1 (1920): 118–31, 126 ("strong"); "Report of the Committee on Federal Legislation," ibid., 161–62; Lykes, *Higher Education and the USOE*, 80–81. For an interpretation of this movement that emphasizes its links to business corporations while underestimating the cross purposes among associations, see Noble, *America by Design*, 248–49. On Judd's drive for professionalization, see Ellen Condliffe Lagemann, "The Plural Worlds of Educational Research," *HEQ* 29 (1989): 204–10. On Judd and the Cleveland Conference, see Tyack and Hansot, *Managers of Virtue*, 131–33.

34. "American Council on Education: The Referendum on Federal Legislation," *Ed. Rec.* 2 (1921): 35; "The Referendum on a Federal Department

of Education," ibid., 43–51; S. P. Capen, AR, ibid., 133 ("views"). Perhaps because of Capen's own disapproval of matching grants, he understated the majority response in their favor and called opinion "nearly evenly divided" (ibid., 50). In fact, the votes on this question by individual faculty members were 553 for, 429 against; conflated faculty votes, 11 for, 5 against. In the case of associations (where executive committees voted), the vote was 22 individuals for, 6 against; and in the conflated votes, 2 for, and 1 against (ibid., 44).

35. "The Referendum on a Federal Department of Education," *Ed. Rec.* 2 (1921): 45–46 (the land-grant association response came from a committee appointed especially to consider the Smith-Towner bill); *AAU Proc.* 20 (1918): 23, 22 (1920): 33. The earlier AAU vote was in response to a request from the ECE.

36. "New Bills Affecting Education," *Ed. Rec.* 2 (1921): 73–75, 75 ("any measure," "indeed").

37. "A Petition for a Department of Education," *Ed. Rec.* 3 (1922): 37–38; J. H. MacCracken, "Report of the Committee on Federal Legislation," ibid. 4 (1923): 118–19; ibid. 5 (1924): 159 ("spokesmen"). See also Marion L. Burton to C. R. Mann, Mar. 11, 1924, MLB, box 13.

38. *AAC Bul.* 11 (1925): 22; "Debate," ibid., 141–72; John H. MacCracken, "A Department of Education," ibid., 132–40 (an insightful reminiscence of the movement during the previous seven years); C. R. Mann to Aurelia Reinhardt, Apr. 13, 1926 (a letter on the new bill sent generally to ACE members), AHR; Kelly, "Policies and Precedents," 12; MacCracken, "Report of the Committee on Federal Legislation," *Ed. Rec.* 6 (1925): 194–95; G. D. Strayer, "A Federal Department of Education," ibid., 227–33; ACE exec. cmte. min., Jan. 8, 1927, CCL, box 4.

39. C. R. Mann, "National Organization of Education," *Ed. Rec.* 6 (1925): 54 ("intelligent," "discretion"), 55 ("properly"), 56 ("various"); J. H. Mac-Cracken, "Federal Legislation," *Ed. Rec.* 9 (1928): 220–21.

40. *Ed. Rec.* 10 (1929): 244; Dobbins, *ACE Leadership,* 17; *The Memoirs of Ray Lyman Wilbur, 1875–1949* (Stanford, Calif., 1960), 469–71; *Federal Relations to Education: Report of a National Advisory Committee on Education* (Washington, D.C., 1931), part 1, pp. 93–99; West, *National Education Association,* 15.

CHAPTER 7: MINERVA AND MARS

1. Since 1866 the War Department had detailed regular officers to act as instructors at colleges—a program not limited to land-grant institutions (Ross, *Democracy's College,* 122–28, 144; Alvord, "Annual Address," *AAACES Proc.* 9: 23). J. K. Patterson, "General Drift of Education at the Land-Grant Colleges," *AAACES Proc.* 14 (1900): 99–100, 100 ("quite"). By 1914 the land-grant institutions had provided the Army three times more officers than had West Point (John S. Brubacher and Willis Rudy, *Higher Education in Transition: A History of American Colleges and Universities, 1636–1968* [New York, 1968], 231).

2. ECR, *AAACES Proc.* 16 (1902): 13; ibid., 44; J. W. Heston, "Military Instruction in Land-Grant Colleges," ibid., 73–75; G. W. Atherton, "Military Instruction in Land-Grant Colleges" and discussion, ibid. 17 (1903): 55–60; ibid., 86–87; G. W. Atherton, "Military Instruction," ibid. 18 (1904): 31; ibid., 63 ("unwise"); David Kinley, "Military Training in Universities and Colleges,"

AAU Proc. 18 (1916): 57; Williams, "George W. Atherton," 359–67, 372. For a case study of a land-grant college's troubled military relations, see Donald M. McKale (ed.), *Tradition: A History of the Presidency of Clemson University* (Macon, Ga., 1988), esp. 88–92. See also Gene M. Lyons and John W. Masland, *Education and Military Leadership: A Study of the R.O.T.C.* (Princeton, N.J., 1959), 38.

3. John Garry Clifford, *The Citizen Soldiers: The Plattsburg Training Camp Movement, 1913–1920* (Lexington, Ky., 1972), 13–22; Gruber, *Mars and Minerva* (see ch. 1, n. 38), 220.

4. J. G. Schurman, "President Schurman of Cornell Believes Every College Should Introduce Military Training," *Everybody's Magazine* 32 (1915): 179–83; Frank Strong to Guy Potter Benton, Nov. 17, 1915, copy in UCPP, box 81 ("forfeit"). For Strong's links to the Kansas peace movement, see Robert Smith Bader, *Hayseeds, Moralizers, and Methodists: The Twentieth-Century Image of Kansas* (Lawrence, Kans., 1988), 38–39. G. P. Benton to B. I. Wheeler, Feb. 8, 1916, UCPP, box 90; W. O. Thompson to "Presidents and Deans of Agricultural Colleges, and Presidents of State Universities," Mar. 13, 1916, UCPP, box 92; Lyons and Masland, *Education and Military Leadership*, 33–40; Clifford, *Citizens Soldiers*, 147–48. For the relevant sections of the National Defense Act, see Kolbe, *Colleges in War Time* (see ch. 1, n. 38), 230–35. On academic executives' interest, see Gruber, *Mars and Minerva*, 220–23.

5. Arthur Twining Hadley and David Kinley, "Military Training in Universities and Colleges," *AAU Proc.* 18 (1916): 55–60, 59 ("federal"); Gruber, *Mars and Minerva*, 222–25.

6. Gruber, *Mars and Minerva*, ch. 3, p. 100 (quoting Nicholas Murray Butler, "great army"); *AAC Bul.* 4 (1918), no. 1, pp. 14–17; *NASU Proc.* 15 (1917): 13; Noble, *America by Design*, 209 ("somewhat"). On May 4, 1917, President Benton of Vermont, head of the NASU, described Godfrey as "chairman of the Committee on Science and Research, including engineering and education, of the Council of National Defense." In fact, as Godfrey admitted, research was "cared for by the National Research Council" and medicine was under another member of the Advisory Commission. See "Proceedings of a Joint Conference between the NASU, the AAACES, the AAU and the AAC: Held at Continental Hall, Washington, D.C., May 5th, 1917," *NASU Proc.* 15 (1917): 15, 64–65, 98. See also Kevles, *The Physicists*, 115–16; Helen Wright, *Explorer of the Universe: A Biography of George Ellery Hale* (New York, 1966), 291–92. On the founding of the CND, see Cuff, *War Industries Board*, ch. 1; Samuel P. Capen and Walton C. John, *A Survey of Higher Education, 1916–1918* (USBE Bul. 22, Washington, D.C., 1919), 39.

7. Richard Watson Cooper to "My dear Mr. President," May 26, 1917, UCPP, box 105; Capen and John, *Survey of Higher Education, 1916–1918*, 39–42. A transcript of the "Joint Conference" is printed in *NASU Proc.* 15 (1917): 63–126 and of the emergency meeting of the NASU, in ibid., 13–62. Godfrey's letter calling the meeting appears on pp. 14–15. The call as conveyed by the president of NASU appears in G. P. Benton to "My dear Colleague," Apr. 17, 1917, UCPP, box 100. Lowell of Harvard soon resigned from the new committee on grounds that its meetings were ineffective (Gruber, *Mars and Minerva*, 98 n. 40). Noble has characterized the Joint Conference as "the first stage of the wartime coup d'état in American education" (*America by Design*, 209). But Godfrey came close to losing control of the meeting when Ray Lyman Wilbur, president of Stanford, denounced the proceedings as inef-

fectual and introduced a resolution urging that the government be put on a war council basis. Godfrey then became extremely modest about his powers and those of the CND ("Joint Conference," pp. 114–26). For another interpretation of higher education in World War I, see Barrow, *Universities and the Capitalist State*, ch. 5.

8. "Joint Conference," *NASU Proc.* 15:110–11 ("supreme crisis"); J. S. Nollen, AAC president, to "President, Stanford University," Apr. 26, 1917 (telegram of invitation to the May 5 meeting, "to secure"), RLW, 2–11.

9. Gruber, *Mars and Minerva*, 213–19; "Joint Conference," *NASU Proc.* 15: 111–13, 105 ("our boys").

10. AAC special meeting min., May 5, 1917, *AAC Bul.* 4 (1918), no. 1, p. 16; John S. Nollen to AAC members, Aug. 31, 1917, ibid., 21. On financial distress in 1917–18, see Kolbe, *Colleges in War Time*, 172–79.

11. W. O. Thompson to "Presidents of Land Grant Colleges," Oct. 17, 1917, UCPP, box 97 ("this would not"); Capen and John, *Survey of Higher Education, 1916–1918*, 46–47, 42 ("opening").

12. Sensitive to charges of privilege, Baker rejected the plan, citing "its effect upon the attitude of all classes in the community affected by the law." See Marion L. Burton, *AAU Proc.* 19 (1917): 98 ("rather strong"); ibid., 22 ("unswerving"); Armin O. Leuschner, Ray L. Wilbur, and Arthur E. Kennelly to Newton D. Baker, Nov. 17, 1917, ibid., 105 ("prompted").

13. "Address of President John Scholte Nollen," *NASU Proc.* 15 (1917): 82 ("unreasoning"); W. O. Thompson, ibid., 27–28; ibid., 29–34; *AAC Bul.* 4 (1918), no. 1, pp. 17, 11 ("making").

14. See this volume, ch. 1 under "Associating the Associations: The ACE."

15. Advisory Board, *Committee on Education and Special Training: A Review of Its Work during* 1918 (Washington, D.C. 1919) (hereafter cited as *CEST: Review of Its Work*), 11–13.

16. Capen and John, *Survey of Higher Education, 1916–1918*, 58; Capen, quoted in Noble, *America by Design*, 219.

17. Capen and John, *Survey of Higher Education, 1916–1918*, 58; *CEST: Review of Its Work*, 24–26; S. P. Capen to Grace Capen, Sept. 5, Aug. 12, 1918, SPC, box 11. Since the lowered draft age guaranteed a full complement for SATC programs, much of the ECE's publicity drive was rendered superfluous (Donald J. Cowling, "The American Council on Education," *NASU Proc.* 16 [1918]: 98).

18. George W. Atherton, "Military Instruction," *AAACES Proc.* 17:54 ("impression"); Clifford, *Citizen Soldiers*, 258 n. 122; Howard H. Peckham, *The Making of the University of Michigan, 1817–1967* (Ann Arbor, 1967), 134; Capen and John, *Survey of Higher Education, 1916–1918*, 59 ("unfortunate"); Gruber, *Mars and Minerva*, 233–37; *CEST: Review of Its Work*, 32.

19. Robert I. Rees, "The Plans of the Committee on Education and Special Training" and discussion, *NASU Proc.* 16 (1918): 55–74; C. R. Mann, "Difficulties of the Committee," ibid., 74–78; *CEST: Review of Its Work*, 33 ("educational experiment").

20. *CEST: Review of Its Work*, 50 ("universally"), 33; S. P. Capen, "The Colleges in a Nationalized Educational Scheme," *S&S* 9:613; Capen and John, *Survey of Higher Education, 1916–1918*, 59; F. J. Morrow, "Military Instruction in State Universities" and discussion, *NASU Proc.* 17 (1919): 88–111; F. J. Morrow, "The Reserve Officers' Training Corps" and discussion, *AAACES*

Proc. 33 (1919): 30–37; Gruber, *Mars and Minerva,* 248–50; Kolbe, *Colleges in War Time,* 81; Clifford, *Citizen Soldiers,* 259–60; Lyons and Masland, *Education and Military Leadership,* 42–43; Barrow, *Universities and the Capitalist State,* 148–49; Alexander Meiklejohn to W. H. P. Faunce, Mar. 25, 1919, AM, box 2. For the links of the CEST program to the Plattsburg idea, see Clifford, *Citizen Soldiers,* esp. ch. 7.

21. Kevles, *The Physicists,* chs. 19–21; Alice M. Rivlin, *The Role of the Federal Government in Financing Higher Education* (Washington, D.C., 1961), 31–34; Daniel S. Greenberg, *The Politics of Pure Science* (New York, 1967), chs. 4–5. For an insightful interpretation of the rise of contractualism between government and universities, see Larry Owens, "MIT and the Federal 'Angel': Academic R&D and Federal-Private Cooperation before World War II," *Isis* 81 (1990): 189–213.

22. Dobbins, *ACE Leadership,* 36, 38; committee manifesto, June 1940, quoted in William M. Tuttle, Jr., "Higher Education and the Federal Government: The Lean Years, 1940–42," *TCR* 71 (1969–70): 299 ("conservation"). In more elevated language, Zook called for "a suitable balance between the imperative immediate and the validated ultimate" (*ACE: History and Activities* [1941–42], 7). See also ibid., 42.

23. For a detailed account of the associations and the establishment of the draft, see Tuttle, "Higher Education . . . Lean Years," 298–305. See also AR, *Ed. Rec.* 22 (1941): 293–95, 293 ("necessary"); "Report of the Committee on Military Organization and Policy," *ALGCU Proc.* 55 (1941): 290; J. Garry Clifford and Samuel R. Spencer, Jr., *The First Peacetime Draft* (Lawrence, Kans., 1986), 142–43; Clifford, *Citizen Soldiers,* 299; Peckham, *University of Michigan,* 201.

24. *AAU Proc.* 43 (1941), esp. "Symposium on University Procedures and Problems Growing Out of Defense Activities," pp. 102–12; *ALGCU Proc.* 55 (1941): 313–14, 292–93; Frederick M. Hunter, "Can America Develop an Antidote for the Doctrines of Hitlerism?" ibid., 59–68; *AAC Bul.* 27 (1941): 150 ("would put").

25. *Higher Education and the War: The Report of a National Conference of College and University Presidents, Held in Baltimore, Md., January 3–4, 1942, Sponsored by the Committee on Military Affairs of the National Committee on Education and Defense and the United States Office of Education* (Washington, D.C., 1942), 16–23, 154–58.

26. Tuttle, "Higher Education . . . Lean Years," 307–12; Conant, *My Several Lives* (see ch. 3, n. 35), 340 ("jungle"), 343–44; Guy E. Snavely to William P. Tolley, June 19, 1942, copy in DBT, 64B, box 4.

27. Conference resolutions, quoted in AR, *Ed. Rec.* 24 (1943): 189–91, 190 ("continuous"), 191 ("economic").

28. AR, *Ed. Rec.* 24 (1943): 183, 188–93, 192 ("responsibility"); "The Council at Work," ibid., 438–39; G. F. Zook, "How the Colleges Went to War," *Annals of the American Academy of Political and Social Science* 231 (1944): 4–5; J. Hillis Miller and Dorothy V. N. Brooks, *The Role of Higher Education in War and After* (New York, 1944), 37–39; William M. Tuttle, Jr., "Higher Education and the Federal Government: The Triumph, 1942–1945," *TCR* 71 (1969–70): 487–88.

29. Henry M. Wriston to A. G. Ruthven, Sept. 22, 1942; NASU exec. cmte. min., Dec. 2, 1942 (mimeo.); both AGR, box 56; Goldthwaite Dorr, quoted

in Tuttle, "Higher Education . . . Triumph," 488–89 ("responsibility"); F. D. Roosevelt to Secretaries of War and Navy, Oct. 15, 1942, quoted in ibid., 490 ("highest").

30. AR, *Ed. Rec.* 24 (1943): 192–95; Miller and Brooks, *Higher Education in War*, 38–39.

31. Henry C. Herge et al., *Wartime College Training Programs of the Armed Services* (Washington, D.C., 1948), 26–34; Miller and Brooks, *Higher Education in War*, 112; Tuttle, "Higher Education . . . Triumph," 489–90; AR, *Ed. Rec.* 24 (1943): 192–200; Alonzo G. Grace et al., *Educational Lessons from Wartime Training: The General Report of the Commission on Implications of Armed Services Educational Programs* (Washington, D.C., 1948), 213–15. The ASTP and V-12 were the largest military training programs at colleges and universities and the closest to normal academic patterns, being taught by regular faculty. There were also vocational and "purely military" programs conducted under contract at academic institutions (ibid., 211).

32. George F. Zook, "How the Colleges Went to War," *Annals of the AAPSS*, 231:6 ("teachers"). By the end of the war about one-half of all institutions granting degrees for four-year programs had been used by armed service training programs, about 4 percent of junior colleges, and about 20 percent of institutions for the higher education of Negroes (Herge et al., *Wartime College Training*, 13–14). These complaints were repeated, with elaborate statistics, in hearings before the House Education Committee, whose staff was headed by the ACE's Francis J. Brown (U.S. House of Representatives, *Effect of Certain War Activities upon Colleges and Universities*, House Report No. 214, 79th Cong., 1st Sess. [Washington, D.C., 1945], 25–30).

33. "Student War Loans Program," *Annual Report of the Federal Security Agency* (Washington, D.C., 1946), 132–33; AR, *Ed. Rec.* 24 (1943): 200; Grace et al., *Educational Lessons from Wartime*, 218–19.

34. Francis J. Brown, summary of remarks, "A Conference of Constituent Members," *Ed. Rec.* 25 (1944): 304; Herge et al., *Wartime College Training*, 36–39, 38 ("curtailment"); Paul K. Conkin, *Gone with the Ivy: A Biography of Vanderbilt University* (Knoxville, Tenn., 1985), 419–20.

35. Richard G. Axt, *The Federal Government and Financing Higher Education* (New York, 1952), 264; Conant, *My Several Lives*, 340; Robert R. Palmer, Bell I. Wiley, and William R. Keast, *The Procurement and Training of Ground Combat Troops* (Washington, D.C., 1948), 37–39; Andrew J. Green, ".014 Again," *AAUP Bul.* 36 (1950): 679–88; Tuttle, "Higher Education . . . Triumph," 496–97; Henry L. Stimson and McGeorge Bundy, *On Active Service in Peace and War* (New York, 1948), 457–61; *Effect of Certain War Activities* (see n. 32 above), 45; AR, *AAC Bul.* 31 (1945): 130; J. C. West, *NASU Proc.* 42 (1944): 107–8.

36. Robert P. Patterson, quoted in Tuttle, "Higher Education . . . Triumph," 495–96. See also Palmer, Wiley, and Keast, *Procurement and Training*, 29–31.

37. AR, *Ed. Rec.* 24 (1943), esp. 186, 220. For a useful history of the ACE's then recent past, see William E. Wickenden, "Higher Education and Government in Wartime," *Ed. Rec.* 27 (1946): 389–400.

38. Clifford, *Citizen Soldiers*, 299; Axt, *Federal Government and Financing Higher Education*, 263 ("had an air"). The associations were not the only channels available to heads of colleges and universities seeking to influence government policy. Harvard's Conant, for instance, vice president of the AAC in 1942 and a member of the Problems and Plans Committee of the ACE, joined with various associational committees in calling on government leaders.

But he also advanced his ideas for military training in colleges through his annual reports and direct correspondence with high government officials (Conant, *My Several Lives*, 341–44).

39. AR, *Ed. Rec.* 24 (1943): 218–19; Dobbins, *ACE Leadership*, 46–47, 54–55; *Higher Education and the War* (see n. 25 above), 157.

40. BDR, *AAC Bul.* 28 (1942): 66–67; Francis J. Brown, "Higher Education Serves Total Defense," *AAU Proc.* 43 (1941): 101; AR, *Ed. Rec.* 24 (1943): 217–18: "The Council at Work," ibid., 438–49; David D. Henry, *Challenges Past, Challenges Present: An Analysis of American Higher Education since 1930* (San Francisco, 1975), 56. Information on ACE testimony on the pending bills is in ACE Ar., 10-27-1ff. In 1943 an AAC commission, while advocating educational aid to veterans, cautioned against direct federal grants to institutions (Miller and Brooks, *Higher Education in War*, 182).

41. Keith W. Olson, *The G.I. Bill, the Veterans, and the Colleges* (Lexington, Ky., 1974), 13–14, 22–23; Davis R. B. Ross, *Preparing for Ulysses: Politics and Veterans During World War II* (New York, 1969), 94, 96–97; "A Conference of Constituent Members," *Ed. Rec.* 25 (1944): 300–303.

42. Ross, *Preparing for Ulysses*, 95–96, 101, 108, 112–13; Olson, *G.I. Bill*, 17–18; "Conference of Constituent Members," *Ed. Rec.* 25:302–3.

43. Rivlin, *Role of the Federal Government*, 64–70; Henry, *Challenges Past*, 65–68; Olson, *G.I. Bill*, ch. 1; ECR, *ALGCU Proc.* 60 (1946): 106; *NASU Proc.* 43 (1945): 74–86.

44. AR, *Ed. Rec.* 25 (1944): 187–89; Conant, *My Several Lives*, 351–52; P&P cmte. min., Mar. 9, 1944, ACE Ar., 10-26-9. A verbatim transcript of the joint meeting, Mar. 11, 1944, is in ACE Ar., 11-23-16. The three visitors to the White House were Conant, W. H. Cowley, president of Colgate, and Francis J. Brown. The quotation from Roosevelt, as recollected by Conant, is in the transcript, p. 92. Roosevelt did, however, reply to a similar argument for delay on UMT submitted to him later by the ACE's Youth Problems Committee; he indicated that pending congressional hearings obviated any need for the requested presidential study commission (P&P cmte. min., Mar. 10–11, 1945, ACE Ar., 10-31-17; F. D. Roosevelt to G. F. Zook, Dec. 14, 1944, ACE Ar., 10-32-15). For the efforts within Congress to establish postwar UMT during World War II, see Martin L. Fausold, *James W. Wadsworth, Jr.: The Gentleman from New York* (Syracuse, N.Y., 1975), 349–54.

45. Conant, *My Several Lives*, 354. A meeting of the constituent associations in May 1944 confirmed the position against UMT seventy to five (*Ed. Rec.* 25 [1944]: 291–92).

46. Henry, *Challenges Past*, 42; James P. Baxter, 3rd, "Commission on Liberal Education Report," *AAC Bul.* 29 (1943): 273; Miller and Brooks, *Higher Education in War*, 182. In 1945–46 higher education income from the federal government was down to 21 percent. See *Biennial Survey of Education in the United States, 1944–46* (USOE, Washington, D.C., 1950), ch. 4, p. 24.

47. For the origins of the January 1945 report, which was made jointly with the Educational Policies Commission of the NEA, see P&P cmte. min., Feb. 21 and May 6, 1943, ACE Ar., 10-23-3. Both Dodds and Day urged modifications to make the report more strongly adverse to federal controls. H. W. Dodds to G. F. Zook, Nov. 3, 1944 ("overwhelming"); E. E. Day to Zook, Nov. 8, 1944; both in ACE Ar., 10-31-16; *Effect of Certain War Activities* (see n. 32 above), 14 ("maintained"), 25 ("privately"), 44.

48. Levine, *American College and the Culture of Aspiration* (see ch. 1, n. 6),

esp. chs. 4 and 9; Abbott L. Ferriss, *Indicators of Trends in American Education* (New York, 1969), 387.

49. Grace et al., *Educational Lessons from Wartime*, 37, 221–31, 242 ("technique"), 243–44 ("need"). See also Edward C. Elliott, "The Effects of Wartime Research upon Institutions of Higher Learning," in Herge et al., *Wartime College Training*, 204. For a summary and appraisal of the Grace Report, see Henry, *Challenges Past*, 49–54.

CHAPTER 8: INTO THE POSTWAR WORLD

1. Stephen E. Ambrose and Richard H. Immerman, *Milton S. Eisenhower: Educational Statesman* (Baltimore, 1983), 87–88.

2. The GI Bill of Rights was the Servicemen's Readjustment Act of 1944, Public Law 346, 78th Cong. Many of its effects on educational institutions were reenforced by the more generous provisions in Public Law 16, 78th Cong., passed in 1943 for the vocational rehabilitation of disabled veterans. Public Law 16 accounted for under 10 percent of World War II veterans enrolled in college. Unlike 346, it had a World War I forerunner (Axt, *Federal Government and Financing Higher Education*, 123).

3. Olson, *G.I. Bill*, 64–65, 78; AR, *Ed. Rec.* 28 (1947): 322–23; Russell I. Thackrey to Hugh Hawkins, Aug. 8, 1981. For suspicion of student veterans' motives, see testimony gathered during debate over the Korean War GI Bill, cited in Olson, *G.I. Bill*, 106–7.

4. ECR, *ALGCU Proc.* 61 (1947): 72; Olson, *G.I. Bill*, 62–63.

5. ECR, *ALGCU Proc.* 63 (1949): 109–10; ibid., 267 ("opportune"), 273–75; "Report of the Joint Committee on Veterans Affairs," ibid. 64 (1950): 278–79; "Report of Joint Committee of Business Officers," ibid., 284; Axt, *Federal Government and Financing Higher Education*, 125–34; R. I. Thackrey, "Like It Is," ibid. 83 (1969): 118 ("Yankees"); AR, *Ed. Rec.* 27 (1946): 276–77; "Public Law 571," *Laws Relating to Veterans* (Washington, D.C., 1951), 2: 1449.

6. A. J. Brumbaugh, "Freedom to Teach and Freedom to Learn," *Ed. Rec.* 31 (1950): 423–27; Karl F. Pfitzer to Francis J. Brown, July 18, 1950 ("vague"); Brown to Pfitzer, July 25, 1950; both in ACE Ar., 9-26-7; Axt, *Federal Government and Higher Education*, 135.

7. AR, *Ed. Rec.* 27 (1946): 252–53. A telegram to Truman urging this course grew out of an AAU meeting but was sent on behalf of institutional presidents, not in the name of the association. See Harold W. Dodds to A. G. Ruthven, Oct. 23, 29, 1946, AGR, box 45.

8. AR, *Ed. Rec.* 28 (1947): 314–21; ibid. 29 (1948): 207–12, 207 ("strong"); Conant, *My Several Lives*, 357–58.

9. *ALGCU Proc.* 60 (1946): 223–24; Daniel A. Poling, "Universal Military Training," ibid. 61 (1947): 45–56; ibid., 168, 177–78; ibid. 62 (1948): 259.

10. *AAC Bul.* 34 (1948): 162; AR, ibid. 31 (1945): 131–32.

11. AR, *Ed. Rec.* 29 (1948): 206–9, 213–16; James M. Weisbard, "Universal Military Training, Selective Service, and American Society, 1944–1964" (B.A. thesis, Amherst College, 1987); Arthur A. Hauck, "Legislation before the Congress Affecting Higher Education," *NASU Proc.* 50 (1952): 29–30. In October 1950, the AAU was hoping to defeat UMT by supporting Conant's plan for two years of national service by all men at age eighteen (Henry M.

Wriston, "Informal Report from the President of the AAU," *AGS Proc.* 2 [1950]: 107–8).

12. AR, *Ed. Rec.* 30 (1949): 235; ibid., 333; *NASU Proc.* 46 (1948): 145–46; George Q. Flynn, *Lewis B. Hershey, Mr. Selective Service* (Chapel Hill, N.C., 1985), ch. 8.

13. "Letter of Appointment of Commission Members," *Higher Education for American Democracy: A Report of the President's Commission on Higher Education* (hereafter cited as *PCHE Report*) (6 vols. in one; New York, [1948]), unpaginated front matter ("our system"); Axt, *Federal Government and Financing Higher Education*, 189; James Earl Russell, *Federal Activities in Higher Education after the Second World War . . .* (New York, 1951), 92; *Higher Education and National Affairs*, no. 102 (July 18, 1946), p. 7. For Zook's thinking shortly before the PCHE was appointed, see his Inglis Lecture of 1945, *The Role of the Federal Government in Education* (Cambridge, Mass., 1945).

14. *PCHE Report* 1:101 ("American colleges," punctuation slightly modified), 41, 27–35; 2:5–6; 1:39–43, 49 ("not sharply"). For earlier, similar calculations of "able students lost to higher education," see Vannevar Bush, *Science, the Endless Frontier* (Washington, D.C., 1945), 166–76.

15. *PCHE Report* 2:45–57; 5:59–61; 2:22; 3:5–14; 2:22–23, 27–28. On the new name, see Brint and Karabel, *Diverted Dream* (see ch. 4, n. 3), 70–71.

16. AR, *Ed. Rec.* 28 (1947): 250–53; ibid. 30 (1949): 225–30. For two recent sources that recognize the significance of the PCHE, see Diane Ravitch, *The Troubled Crusade: American Education, 1945–1980* (New York, 1983), 15–19, and the forthcoming volume by Richard Freeland, working title "Academia's Golden Age: Universities in Massachusetts, 1945–1970" (New York, 1992).

17. AR, *Ed. Rec.* 29 (1948): 217–22; P&P cmte. min., June 23–24, 1948, copy in ACIA.

18. Robert M. Hutchins, "The Report of the President's Commission on Higher Education," *Ed. Rec.* 29 (1948): 107; William P. Tolley, "Some Observations on the Report of the President's Commission on Higher Education," ibid., 371–80. For a balanced anthology of responses, see Gail Kennedy (ed.), *Education for Democracy: The Debate over the Report of the President's Commission on Higher Education* (Boston, 1952).

19. Lyman E. Jackson, "Findings of the Seminar on the Report of the PCHE," *ALGCU Proc.* 62 (1948): 77–79; J. L. Morrill, "The Challenge of Change," ibid., 37–39.

20. Lewis W. Jones, "The Challenge of the President's Commission," *ALGCU Proc.* 62 (1948): 44 ("peanut butter"), 45 ("dangerous"), 46. James B. Conant, who considered the PCHE's national scholarship plan much too ambitious, dwelt on the German example in his *Education in a Divided World: The Function of the Public Schools in Our Unique Society* (Cambridge, Mass., 1948), 195–99.

21. John A. Hannah, " 'Nor Lose the Common Touch,' " *ALGCU Proc.* 63 (1949): 42–43 ("every year"); Earl J. McGrath, "On the Outside—Looking In," ibid., 98–106, 105 ("civilian"); "Report of the Special Committee on Federal Legislation," ibid., 271–72. On the USOE proposal, see also Arthur S. Adams, "New Federal Legislation," *NASU Proc.* 47 (1949): 31–32.

22. Gordon Keith Chalmers, "A Critique of the Harvard Report," *AAC Bul.* 31 (1945): 594–96; idem, "The Place of Letters in Liberal Education," ibid. 33 (1947): 693 ("study"), 698. The claim for Greek brought dissents

from President Harry D. Gideonse of Brooklyn College and Minnesota's Dean T. R. McConnell.

23. G. K. Chalmers, "Report of Commission on Liberal Education," *AAC Bul.* 34 (1948): 144–45, 145n; Mordecai W. Johnson, ibid., 164–65.

24. G. K. Chalmers, "Report of Commission on Liberal Education," *AAC Bul.* 35 (1949): 161 ("intellectual"), 161–62 ("educational"); ibid., 182–83.

25. AR, *AAC Bul.* 36 (1950): 131 ("notion"); Carter Davidson, ibid. 35 (1949): 215. Cf. *PCHE Report* 1:43. There turned out to be 3.6 million students enrolled for degree credit in 1960, up from 2.4 million in 1948 (*Historical Statistics of the United States* [Washington, D.C., 1975], 383).

26. *Historical Statistics*, 382; Ferriss, *Indicators of Trends*, 175, 387; Axt, *Federal Government and Financing Higher Education*, 199–200, 209, 211; Rivlin, *Role of the Federal Government*, 101. On the failure in the House between 1948 and 1950 of bills for federal school aid which had passed the Senate, see Smith, *Limits of Reform* (see ch. 3, n. 31), chs. 6–8; Ravitch, *Troubled Crusade*, 27–41.

27. Axt, *Federal Government and Financing Higher Education*, 212.

28. AR, *Ed. Rec.* 27 (1946): 250 ("alternately"); Francis J. Brown (ed.), *Emergency Problems in Higher Education: The Report of a Conference of Government Officials, Military Officers, and Representatives of American Colleges and Universities, July 11–13, 1946* (Washington, D.C., 1946).

29. Hollis P. Allen, *The Federal Government and Education: The Original and Complete Study of Education for the Hoover Commission Task Force on Public Welfare* (New York, 1950), 280 ("institutions," punctuation slightly modified), 249–50; Axt, *Federal Government and Financing Higher Education*, 127; Olson, *G.I. Bill*, 59, 66–68. Various attitudes toward NSF legislation are informally presented in Ora L. Wildermuth (secretary of the Association of Governing Boards of State Universities and Allied Institutions), "Report on Meeting of American Council on Education, May 2 & 3, 1947," mimeo., AGR, box 42.

30. Lewis Webster Jones, "The Challenge of the President's Commission," *ALGCU Proc.* 62:45; Hannah, " 'Nor Lose the Common Touch,' " ibid. 63:45; J. L. Morrill, "Challenge of Change," ibid. 62:33–34; ECR, ibid. 64 (1950): 104; "Report of the Joint Committee of Business Officers," ibid., 284–90.

31. Edmund E. Day, "Comments on the National Science Foundation," *ALGCU Proc.* 60 (1946): 83–87, 86 ("vision").

32. Conant, *My Several Lives*, 244–45; Lee A. DuBridge, *AAU Proc.* 46 (1945): 23; *AAC Bul.* 32 (1946): 125–27; ibid. 33 (1947): 260–61; *ALGCU Proc.* 60 (1946): 221; ibid. 64 (1950): 302; *NASU Proc.* 46 (1948): 147–50; NASU exec. cmte. min., Oct. 21, 1945, AGR, box 56.

33. Dorothy Schaffter, *The National Science Foundation* (New York, 1969), 7–10, 95–100, 239–40; Kevles, *The Physicists* (see ch. 6, n. 5), 356–66; Allen, *Federal Government and Education*, 264, 271, 274; Don K. Price, *The Scientific Estate* (Cambridge, Mass., 1965), 238–40.

34. Robert A. Taft, "Education in the Congress" and discussion, *Ed. Rec.* 30 (1949): 337–56; Ravitch, *Troubled Crusade*, 28–29, 33. On the shift in 1944 by the National Catholic Welfare Council toward favoring federal aid to education if it included nonpublic schools, see Horrigan, *Shaping of NCEA*, 17.

35. *AAC Bul.* 32 (1946): 125 ("far more"), 33 (1947): 261 ("studies"); H. M. Wriston, "Report of the President of the AAU," *AGS Proc.* 1 (1949): 25–26; Commission on Financing Higher Education, *The Impact of Inflation upon Higher Education: An Interim Statement* (n.p., n.d.); John D. Millett, "Foreword," in Axt, *Federal Government and Financing Higher Education*, ix–xiv. On

the COFHE as a reaction to the PCHE, see the forthcoming volume by Richard Freeland referred to above, n. 16.

36. BDR, *AAC Bul.* 34 (1948): 130–34, 132 ("devoted"); ibid., 161; *Ed. Rec.* 30 (1949): 377–78.

37. ECR, *ALGCU Proc.* 62 (1948): 99–100; AR, *Ed. Rec.* 29 (1948): 222–24; ibid. 32 (1951): 261–62. See also H. M. Wriston, "Report of the President of the AAU," *AGS Proc.* 1:24; ACE P&P cmte. min., June 23–24, 1948, copy in ACIA.

38. AR, *Ed. Rec.* 32 (1951): 260–61; Mark H. Ingraham, "Report of Commission on Insurance and Annuities," *AAC Bul.* 33 (1947): 237–38; ibid., 254; R. McAllister Lloyd, "The College President and Social Security," ibid. 36 (1950): 529–33; *NASU Proc.* 49 (1951): 67.

39. AR, *Ed. Rec.* 32 (1951): 263–64; H. M. Wriston, "Report of the President of the AAU," *AGS Proc.* 1:24–25; "Recommendations on Federal Aid for Medical Education," draft AAU cmte. report, enclosed in Robert M. Hutchins to A. G. Ruthven, Mar. 1, 1949, AGR, box 46; Stephen P. Strickland, *Politics, Science and Dread Disease: A Short History of United States Medical Research Policy* (Cambridge, Mass., 1972), 55–66.

40. AR, *Ed. Rec.* 31 (1950): 214–15, 219–20; A. J. Brumbaugh, "A Statement on Freedom to Teach and Freedom to Learn" (mimeo.), Nov. 6, 1949, copy in ACIA. Brumbaugh presented a moderated version of this paper before a meeting of the ACE constituent members in January 1950. See Brumbaugh, "Freedom to Teach and Freedom to Learn," *Ed. Rec.* 31 (1950): 418–28.

41. AR, *Ed. Rec.* 29 (1948): 205; *ALGCU Proc.* 61 (1947): 177–78; ECR, ibid. 62 (1948): 99–100; "Report of the Special Committee on Federal Legislation," ibid., 259–62; A. S. Adams, ibid. 63 (1949): 112; "Report of the Special Committee on Federal Legislation," ibid., 268–75; R. I. Thackrey to Hugh Hawkins, Aug. 8, 1981 ("genius"). See also Paul L. Dressel, *College to University: The Hannah Years at Michigan State, 1935–1969* (East Lansing, Mich., 1987).

42. AR, *Ed. Rec.* 30 (1949): 225, 229–30; ibid. 31 (1950): 215. To follow some of the themes of this section through the 1950s, see Homer D. Babbidge, Jr., and Robert M. Rosenzweig, *The Federal Interest in Higher Education* (New York, 1962).

43. Richard Polenberg, *War and Society: The United States, 1941–1945* (Philadelphia, 1972), ch. 4, pp. 137–38, 243; Olson, *G.I. Bill*, 69–71; Marcia Graham Synnott, *The Half-Opened Door: Discrimination and Admissions at Harvard, Yale, and Princeton, 1900–1970* (Westport, Conn., 1979), 201–202; Current, *Phi Beta Kappa in American Life* (see ch. 4, n. 20), 220; AR, *Ed. Rec.* 29 (1948): 280 ("fully").

44. BDR, *AAC Bul.* 34 (1948): 129; ibid. 35 (1949): 132; Snavely, *Search for Excellence*, 131; Kenneth I. Brown, "American Education and a Mirror," *AAC Bul.* 35 (1949): 17–21; Vincent J. Flynn, "Can Americans Continue Living Together?" ibid. 36 (1950): 7–15; Sydney E. Ahlstrom, *A Religious History of the American People* (New Haven, Conn., 1972), ch. 56.

45. BDR, *AAC Bul.* 34 (1948): 130–34; ibid., 161 ("on account").

46. Mildred McAfee Horton, "Presidential Address," ibid., 5–14; William P. Tolley, "Report of the Committee on Minority Groups in Higher Education," ibid. 34 (1948): 150–55, 150 ("deep concern").

47. *AAC Bul.* 34 (1948): 166–69, 167 ("solved," "repeal").

48. Ibid. 35 (1949): 163–69, 168 ("harm"); ibid. 36 (1950): 159–61.

49. Martin D. Jenkins, "Significant Programs in Institutions of Higher Education of Negroes," *Ed. Rec.* 26 (1945): 301–11, 311 ("typically"), 302 ("almost").

50. AR, *Ed. Rec.* 27 (1946): 315–28, 323 ("current"); ibid. 28 (1947): 274–78, 278 ("it is not"); Lloyd Allen Cook (ed.), *College Programs in Intergroup Relations: A Report by Twenty-Four Colleges Participating in the College Study in Intergroup Relations, 1945–1949* (Washington, D.C., 1950), esp. 7; AR, *Ed. Rec.* 29 (1948): 279–82, 281 ("whatever").

51. AR, *Ed. Rec.* 29 (1948): 287–88; ibid. 39 (1949): 289–90; *Factors Affecting the Admission of High School Seniors to College* (Washington, D.C., 1949), iii ("purely," "number"). The report indicated class inequities with its finding that 83 percent of students said they would go to college if assured of admission and given half of their living costs, yet only 35 percent applied.

52. Francis J. Brown (ed.), *Discriminations in College Admissions: A Report of a Conference Held under the Auspices of the American Council on Education in Cooperation with the Anti-Defamation League of B'nai B'rith, Chicago, Illinois, November 4–5, 1949* (Washington, D.C., 1950), 3–12, 9 ("American"); Francis J. Brown and Richard B. Anliot (eds.), *Human Relations in Higher Education: A Report of a National Student Conference Held at Earlham College, March 29–31, 1951* (Washington, D.C., 1951), esp. 4–10; AR, *Ed. Rec.* 31 (1950): 252–54; ibid. 32 (1951): 286–88. For the report of a dean who left the Chicago conference reassured that graduate schools were "most fair in their admissions policies," see *AGS Proc.* 2 (1950): 92. Full proceedings of the Chicago conference are in Committee on Discriminations in College Admissions min., May 4, 1950, ACE Ar., 10-60-7.

53. Russell I. Thackrey, "How the Land-Grant Association, the Conference of Presidents of Negro Land-Grant Colleges, the National Association of State Universities, and the State Universities Association, Were Brought Together in One Organization," typescript (1982), copy in my possession; Eddy, *Colleges for Our Land* (see ch. 1, n. 13), 265; *ALGCU Proc.* 68 (1954): 86. See also Clyde L. Orr, "An Analytical Study of the Conference of Presidents of Negro Land-Grant Colleges" (Ed.D. diss., University of Kentucky, 1959). Besides Day, Thackrey listed Hannah, Morrill, Gustavson, and President Carl Borgmann of the University of Vermont as among those pressing for inclusion of the black presidents.

54. AR, *Ed. Rec.* 19 (1938): 284–86, 285 ("mad"); *ACE: History and Activities (1941–42)*, 23; G. F. Zook to George D. Stoddard, Oct. 6, 1947, copy in AGR, box 45.

55. AR, *Ed. Rec.* 25 (1944): 189–90; ibid. 27 (1946): 305–7; Wells, *Being Lucky* (see ch. 2, n. 19), 375; "Gourmet & President," *Time,* Apr. 4, 1938, reprinted in ibid., 458 ("jolly"); Dobbins, *ACE Leadership,* 54; Tuttle, "Higher Education . . . Triumph," *TCR* 71: 498.

56. James F. Tent, *Mission on the Rhine: Reeducation and Denazification in American-occupied Germany* (Chicago, 1982), 112–18, 251–53, 300–303, 115 ("high pressure"); AR, *Ed. Rec.* 30 (1949): 254–56. See also Herman L. Donovan, "Report on Survey of Higher Educational Institutions in Germany," *NASU Proc.* 46 (1948): 115–18; Wells, *Being Lucky,* ch. 20.

57. ACE exec. cmte. min., May 2, 1946, ACE Ar., 13-39-1; *Ed. Rec.* 27 (1946): 507; AR, ibid. 29 (1948): 229–31. For a comparative treatment of the four councils, see Homer P. Rainey, "Educational Councils and Similar Associations," *AAU Proc.* 42 (1940): 77–85.

58. *AAU Proc.* 47 (1946): 123, 48 (1947): 44, 75; G. F. Zook, "International University Association," *AAC Bul.* 35 (1949): 90; resolution, ibid. 34 (1948): 163–64; Ben M. Cherrington, "Pending Legislation," *AAC Bul.* 34 (1948): 78–81; idem, "Ten Years After," ibid. 511–15; idem, "Report of the Commission on International Cultural Relations," ibid. 36 (1950): 156–58; ACE P&P cmte. min., Mar. 23–24, 1948, copy in ACIA.

59. Surviving for a year after the end of the Carnegie grant, the commission dissolved in 1949. See AR, *Ed. Rec.* 29 (1948): 265–68, 267 ("misunderstanding"); ibid. 30 (1949): 246, 251–53.

60. AR, *Ed. Rec.* 27 (1946): 302–3; "The Council at Work," ibid., 120 ("acquaint"), 224; Milton S. Eisenhower, "United Nations Educational, Scientific and Cultural Organizations [*sic*]," *ALGCU Proc.* 60 (1946): 100–105.

61. Milton S. Eisenhower, "UNESCO—Three Years of Accomplishment," *ALGCU Proc.* 63 (1949): 67–83; G. F. Zook, AR, *Ed. Rec.* 28 (1947): 328–32, 329 ("I cannot"), 330 ("age-old"). For a positive response to the first meeting of the U.S. Commission for UNESCO, see William S. Carlson, "Report on the National Conference on UNESCO," *NASU Proc.* 45 (1947): 86–95.

62. AR, *Ed. Rec.* 29 (1948): 272; George F. Zook, "The International University Conference in Utrecht," *Ed. Rec.* 29 (1948): 341–52, 344 ("debates"); Francis J. Brown, "Universities in World Cooperation," *ALGCU Proc.* 62 (1948): 70–77. The International Association of Universities held its first regular general assembly in 1955, thereafter meeting quinquennially (Wells, *Being Lucky*, 378).

63. AR, *Ed. Rec.* 30 (1949): 247–48; ibid. 31 (1950): 234–35. For a survey of ACE international projects, see ibid. 30 (1949): 251–66. For the related movement to establish a "World University Alliance," see G. F. Zook to A. G. Ruthven, Jan. 4, 1946, and enclosures, AGR, box 40.

64. C. B. Hutchinson, "A Mission to China," *ALGCU Proc.* 60 (1946): 68–75; R. E. Buchanan, "The Stake of the Land-Grant College in the Arab World," ibid., 75–83; ECR, ibid. 63 (1949): 110; ECR, ibid. 64 (1950): 103–4; Eddy, *Colleges for Our Land*, 249–54.

65. J. B. Conant to Raymond B. Allen, Jan. 26, 1951, UWPP, 70–28, box 6; *AGS Proc.* 2 (1950): 84–85, 107; William K. Selden, "The AAU: An Enigma," *Graduate Journal* 8:206.

CHAPTER 9: RECONFIGURATIONS

1. Lyman E. Jackson, "Functioning under the New Constitution," *ALGCU Proc.* 60 (1946): 50–59, 51 ("form"); John A. Hannah, *ALGCU Proc.* 63 (1949): 106; Russell I. Thackrey to Hugh Hawkins, Aug. 8, 1981. The new constitution, with simultaneously adopted bylaws, including slight changes from the original proposal, appears in *ALGCU Proc.* 61 (1947): 23–28. After approval by two successive conventions, the constitution formally took effect at the conclusion of the 1946 meeting. For the previous constitution, see *ALGCU Proc.* 58 (1944): 17–19, and for a useful tracing of past efforts at constitutional revision, Thomas P. Cooper, "Remodeling," *ALGCU Proc.* 60 (1946): 32–34.

2. James Gray, *Open Wide the Door: The Story of the University of Minnesota* (New York, 1958), 200–204; "Morrill, J(ames) L(ewis)," *Current Biography* (New York, 1951), 438–41; Morrill, "Challenge of Change," *ALGCU Proc.* 62:34.

3. ECR, *ALGCU Proc.* 63 (1949): 107.

4. *AAACES Proc.* 33 (1919): 73–75; *ALGCU Proc.* 64 (1950): 1–12.

5. Council on Graduate Work min., *ALGCU Proc.* 62 (1948): 245–46; ibid. 63 (1949): 268; Eddy, *Colleges for Our Land,* 254–55.

6. ECR, *ALGCU Proc.* 63 (1949): 107 ("nerve-center"). The institutional presidents on the executive committee were elected by the senate. The presidents had a slight numerical edge, since the association's immediate past president served as chairman, with its current president as vice-chairman.

7. Ibid. 53 (1939): 83–84; "Report of Assistant Secretary," ibid. 55 (1941): 317–20; ibid. 59 (1945): 45 ("conduct").

8. Ambrose and Immerman, *Milton S. Eisenhower,* chs. 4–6; James C. Carey, *Kansas State University: The Quest for Identity* (Lawrence, Kans., 1977), 161–64, 178–79; T. P. Cooper, "Remodeling," *ALGCU Proc.* 60:30.

9. *ALGCU Proc.* 60 (1946): 192, 61 (1947): 75; J. L. Morrill, "Challenge of Change," ibid. 62 (1948): 38; ibid. 63 (1949): 107; "Russ Thackrey, Man of Quality," *Manhattan* [Kans.] *Mercury,* Mar. 13, 1990. Thackrey's educational ideas appear in his *The Future of the State University* (Urbana, Ill., 1971).

10. *ALGCU Proc.* 61 (1947): 150, 63 (1949): 157, 64 (1950): 278–79; John A. Hannah, ECR, ibid. 64 (1950): 100 ("total program"); R. I. Thackrey, AR, ibid., 269. For salary, see ibid. 61 (1947): 150, 63 (1949): 157, 64 (1950): 271.

11. *ALGCU Proc.* 61 (1947): 169 ("reasonable"), 177–78; ECR, ibid. 61 (1947): 74–75 ("duly designated"). The new committee recommended against taking any position on the proposed federal department (ibid. 62 [1948]: 259–60). For Thackrey's reminiscences at the time of his retirement, see his "Like It Is," *NASULGC Proc.* 83 (1969): 117–25. For the 1962 judgment, see Babbidge and Rosenzweig, *Federal Interest,* 114.

12. "President's Address," *NASU Proc.* 41 (1943): 14 ("individual"); ibid. 42 (1944): 44 ("essentially"), 43 (1945): 34.

13. Deane W. Malott, "Membership Committee Report," ibid. 47 (1949): 70–71. See also ibid. 46 (1948): 124.

14. *NASU Proc.* 48 (1950): 10–11; Arthur S. Adams, "New Federal Legislation," ibid. 47 (1949): 31–33; ibid., 82–83.

15. *NASU Proc.* 46 (1948): 149, 48 (1950): 67, 50 (1952): 102–4.

16. Ibid. 47 (1949): 83 ("possibility"); *ALGCU Proc.* 64 (1950): 273–75. For arguments pro and con, see "Proposed Merger of the NASU with the ALGCU," *NASU Proc.* 48 (1950): 63–77 (report on pp. 64–67); "Recommendations of the Joint Committee on the Proposed Merger of the NASU and the ALGCU," ibid. 50 (1952): 101–10 (includes report of successor committee).

17. "Notes on NASU and ALGCU," enclosure in Harold W. Stoke to members of the NASU, Sept. 1, 1949; Frederick A. Middlebush to A. G. Ruthven, Oct. 18, 1950; both in AGR, box 57; *ALGCU Proc.* 63 (1949): 268; John A. Hannah, ibid. 64 (1950): 277 ("shotgun"); *NASU Proc.* 48 (1950): 77.

18. J. L. Morrill, ECR, *ALGCU Proc.* 63 (1949): 108 ("public-supported"); ibid. 64 (1950): 277; H. K. Newburn, *NASU Proc.* 48 (1950): 73; Hannah, "'Nor Lose the Common Touch,'" *ALGCU Proc.* 63:42–45.

19. Virgil M. Hancher to A. G. Ruthven, Mar. 9, 1949; Ruthven to Hancher, Mar. 18, 1949; both in AGR, box 57; Jane Sanders, *Cold War on the Campus: Academic Freedom at the University of Washington, 1946–64* (Seattle, 1979), chs. 1–3; *NASU Proc.* 48 (1950): 68.

20. J. C. West to John D. Williams, Aug. 5, 1949; Virgil M. Hancher to A. G. Ruthven, Aug. 19, 1949; J. C. West to Harold W. Stoke, Sept. 12, 1949 ("might well"); George H. Denny to J. C. West, Apr. 18, 1950 ("cruel invasion"); all in AGR, box 57; Stow Persons, *The University of Iowa in the Twentieth Century:*

An Institutional History (Iowa City, 1990), 72, 166–67; Bryan, *State College of Washington*, 382 ("cow college").

21. *NASU Proc.* 48 (1950): 25, 34–48 (1951): 57.

22. *NASU Proc.* 49 (1951): 71 ("crabbing"); ECR, *ALGCU Proc.* 63 (1949): 107–8.

23. *ALGCU Proc.* 64 (1950): 102–3, 277, 317–18; Eddy, *Colleges for Our Land*, 255.

24. *NASU Proc.* 50 (1952): 102–10.

25. *ALGCU Proc.* 64 (1950): 43; SUA annual meeting min., May 4, 1948, AGR, box 57; ibid., Apr. 30, 1950, AGR, box 50; W. C. Toepelman to R. B. Allen, Oct. 23, 1950; SUA min., July 21, 1952; both in UWPP, 70–28, box 7.

26. John D. Williams to Gregg M. Sinclair, Aug. 4, 1954, NASULGC Ar., box 10; AR, *AALGCSU Proc.* 72 (1958): 83; O. Meredith Wilson, "Work of the Joint Office of Institutional Research," ibid., 95–98; [Charles P. McCurdy, Jr.], "AAU: Report of the Executive Secretary," May 1–2, 1963, ACE Ar., 16-14-1; Russell I. Thackrey to Hugh Hawkins, Aug. 8, 1981; Thackrey, "How the Land-Grant Association . . ." (see ch. 8, n. 53).

27. *AAU Proc.* 47 (1946): 107–8, 111.

28. G. F. Zook, "The Veteran in Graduate and Professional Schools," *AAU Proc.* 46 (1945): 29–38 (a rather unfocused address that inspired no discussion); Zook, ibid. 47 (1946): 125; Donald B. Tresidder, "The Aim and Scope of the AAU," ibid. 48 (1947): 25–26; ibid. 49 (1948): 45, 47 (1946): 123, 48 (1947): 44.

29. Alan Valentine, *AAU Proc.* 47 (1946): 121–22; Donald B. Tresidder, ibid. 46 (1945): 67, 139; idem, "Aim and Scope," ibid. 48:21.

30. *AAU Proc.* 46 (1945): 10; Lagemann, *Private Power for Public Good*, 115–20.

31. Donald B. Tresidder, "Aim and Scope," *AAU Proc.* 48:18–27, 24 ("dull-witted").

32. Frederick A. Middlebush, "The Scope and Purposes of the AAU," *AAU Proc.* 48 (1947): 27–32 and discussion, pp. 32–46; ibid., 140.

33. *AAU Proc.* 49 (1948): 28.

34. Ibid., 8–16, 11 ("university," "nationally), 14 ("unified"); "Report of Committee on Problems and Policies of the AAU: Suggested Reorganization of the AAU," mimeo. (1948), AGR, box 46. Only excerpts from the report were printed.

35. *AAU Proc.* 49 (1948): 16–42, 22 ("encroachment"), 23 ("as it stands").

36. Ferdandus Payne, ibid., 24–25; "Concluding Discussion of Report on Problems and Policies," ibid., 43–66.

37. The far more inclusive Council of Graduate Schools, created in 1960, assumed some functions of the AGS but did not bring its termination.

38. "Concluding Discussion," *AAU Proc.* 49:43–58; ibid., 106 ("surgical"), 143–44 (constitution as amended).

39. Henry M. Wriston, "Report of the President of the AAU," *AGS Proc.* 1 (1949): 22–33, 28 ("typical"), 29 ("scrupulously"), 16. See also Deane W. Malott to A. G. Ruthven, Nov. 10, 1948, AGR, box 46. For the AAU's later intensification of its federal relations role, see King, *Washington Lobbyists for Higher Education*, 86–89; Bloland, *Associations in Action*, 63.

40. *AAC Bul.* 36 (1950): 177; "Academic Retirement and Related Subjects: Report of a Study Conducted by a Joint Committee of the AAUP and the AAC," ibid., 308–28.

41. J. P. Baxter III, "Contribution of the Academic World to the War Effort," *AAC Bul.* 32 (1946): 5–7. Baxter expanded this interpretation, with concrete examples, in his *Scientists against Time* (Boston, 1946).

42. *AAC Bul.* 35 (1949): 132–33; Frank W. Abrams, "How Can American Business Help American Education?" ibid., 33–40; Laird Bell, "Touching Corporations," ibid., 41–49; Snavely, *Search for Excellence*, 127–28. Although the AAU was its nominal sponsor, the new foundation-supported Commission on Financing Higher Education was welcomed by the AAC. See John D. Millett, "Commission on Financing Higher Education," *AAC Bul.* 36 (1950): 72–75.

43. *AAC Bul.* 32 (1946): 109, 33 (1947): 241, 35 (1949): 170 ("friendliness"), 36 (1950): 136; Eleanor Rust Collier, "American College Public Relations Association," ibid., 569–72; Snavely, *Search for Excellence*, 131; R. I. Thackrey to J. L. Morrill, Apr. 11, 1949; Morrill to Thackrey, Apr. 14, 1949; both in NASULGC Ar., box 10.

44. Snavely, *Search for Excellence*, 129–31.

45. For this and other post-1950 developments in the AAC, see Bloland, *Higher Education Associations*, 142–44; idem, *Associations in Action*, 15, 64–65; King, *Washington Lobbyists for Higher Education*, 86–89. See also Edgar M. Carlson, "The National Representation Project—A Report and an Accounting," *Lib. Ed.*, 62 (1976): 274–83; BDR, ibid., 288–89; "Report of the Treasurer," ibid., 304; Frederick W. Ness to "Dear Colleague," Feb. 20, 1976, mimeo.; Theodore D. Lockwood to "Dear Colleague," May 12, 1976, mimeo.; both in AAC Ar.

46. AR, *Ed. Rec.* 32 (1951): 307–8; summary of section discussions, annual meeting min., ibid., 319.

47. AR, *Ed. Rec.* 30 (1949): 269–70; B. P. Brodinsky, "Valedictory," *Nation's Schools* 45:27; *Ed. Rec.* 32 (1951): 314; C. G. Dobbins to Bill Hamm, Apr. 25, 1957, ACE Ar., 13-90-1 ("primarily interested"). The NEA's revived interest went back to 1942, when it voted to reestablish its Department of Higher Education, dropped in 1924. The department became the Association for Higher Education in 1952 (the American Association for Higher Education after 1967). See Wesley, *NEA,* 104–5; Bloland, *Higher Education Associations,* 148; Wells, *Being Lucky,* 385. Several letters responding to the NEA "incursion," notably Cloyd H. Marvin to Arthur S. Adams, June 15, 1951, are in ACE Ar., 13-9-14.

48. AR, *Ed. Rec.* 27 (1946): 244–51, 337–40; ibid. 30 (1949): 212, 266 ("not easy"). For the effectiveness of the Commission on Cooperation in Teacher Education in interassociational liaison, see Karl W. Bigelow to Guy Snavely, July 26, 1947, ACE Ar., 9-17-3.

49. Bloland, *Higher Education Associations,* 153–60; idem, *Associations in Action,* 26, 40, 60–62, 84–87; King, *Washington Lobbyists for Higher Education,* 51–53; Joseph P. Cosand et al., "Summary Report: Presidential Views of Higher Education's National Institutional Membership Associations" (Ann Arbor, Center for the Study of Higher Education, University of Michigan, [1980]), esp. 9. In the Cosand study, 64 percent of 1,284 responding presidents ranked the "current, pluralistic system" first or second out of five possibilities offered regarding interassociational relationships; 52 percent ranked a "stronger coordinated model" first or second. A useful insider's view is Stephen K. Bailey, *Education Interest Groups in the Nation's Capital* (Washington, D.C., 1975). See also Thomas A. Bartlett et al., *A Report to the Coordinating Committee from the*

Subcommittee on Association Relations (Washington, D.C., 1980) ["the Fretwell Report," after the subcommittee chairman, E. K. Fretwell, Jr.].

50. Grants and contracts provided $831,150 of the 1948–49 budget of approximately $1,190,150 (AR, *Ed. Rec.* 30 [1949]: 216). For a history of the Pharmaceutical Survey, see ibid. 31 (1950): 270–71.

51. Ibid. 27 (1946): 283–91, 30 (1949): 284–86, 31 (1950): 254–55; A. J. Brumbaugh, "George F. Zook: 1885–1951," ibid. 32 (1951): 331–32; Lagemann, *Private Power for Public Good*, 108–21; Conant, *My Several Lives*, 425, 429–32; Harold S. Wechsler, *The Qualified Student: A History of Selective College Admission in America* (New York, 1977), 245–49. For the ACE's concern over financial loss through the merger, see P&P cmte. min., Oct. 27–28, 1947, ACE Ar., 10-50-4.

52. For example, *Ed. Rec.* 30 (1949): 496–98. The ACE's total receipts from the federal government, 1941–60, were approximately ten million dollars, constituting toward the end of the period over 50 percent of ACE income (Kiger, *American Learned Societies* [see ch. 1, n. 3], 181).

53. AR, *Ed. Rec.* 31 (1950): 249, 32 (1951): 247–50.

54. Ibid. 30 (1949): 223, 32 (1951): 317.

55. Ibid. 28 (1947): 239 ("enhance"), 31 (1950): 202–3; Wells, *Being Lucky*, 376. For a picture of the new building, see Dobbins, *ACE Leadership*, 70.

56. AR, *Ed. Rec.* 32 (1951): 250–52, 31 (1950): 203; Ralph E. Himstead, "The Association's New and Permanent Home," *AAUP Bul.* 37 (1951): 229–37.

57. Selden, *Accreditation*, 5, 100–101; Orlans, *Private Accreditation*, chs. 1–3; Gilb, *Hidden Hierarchies* (see ch. 2, n. 3), 59.

58. *AAU Proc.* 45 (1944): 101–15. On the AAU's self-reformation, see this volume, this chapter, under "Revolution from Above at the AAU."

59. *AAU Proc.* 46 (1945): 39–70, 64 ("impressionistic"); ibid. 47 (1946): 11–27; Special Committee on Accreditation, "Memorandum on the History of the Discussion of Accreditation by the AAU," mimeo., AGR, box 42.

60. Donald B. Tresidder, "Aim and Scope," *AAU Proc.* 48:22–23, 25 ("ghost").

61. *AAU Proc.* 49 (1948): 13 ("diminishing"), 13–14, 29–42. For the final vote—twenty-three for abolition, ten against, and one not voting—see ibid., p. 3. During the next year, the AAU's president received "oceans of correspondence" from complaining groups that had relied on the Approved Lists for various purposes (*AGS Proc.* 1[1949]: 24). See also Selden, *Accreditation*, 74–75.

62. *AAU Proc.* 49 (1948): 42. For similar remarks by two other presidents, Frank Graham and Frederick Middlebush, see ibid., 30–32.

63. Reuben G. Gustavson, "Joint Committee on Accreditment [*sic*]," *AAC Bul.* 35 (1949): 53.

64. The five participating associations were the AAC, the AAU, the ALGCU, the AUU, and the NASU. The AAC was invited to join on the ground that professional accreditation was encroaching on liberal education, as with the American Chemical Society's appraisals of undergraduate departments. See R. G. Gustavson, "Joint Committee," *AAC Bul.* 35:50–55; idem, "National Commission on Accrediting Procedures," *Ed. Rec.* 31 (1950): 74–76; idem, "Report of National Commission on Accrediting," *NASU Proc.* 48 (1950): 48–51; *ALGCU Proc.* 62 (1948): 286–87.

65. Henry M. Wriston, "Informal Report from the President of the AAU,"

AGS Proc. 2 (1950): 107. Matters for the NCA were also complicated by the simultaneous emergence of a national committee of the regional associations. The two bodies, which have been likened to "two bears in a cage," united in 1975 as the Council on Postsecondary Accreditation. For accounts of the two groups with developments beyond 1950, see Orlans, *Private Accreditation,* 18–27, 19 ("initial"), 26 ("bears"); Selden, *Accreditation,* 76–79. See also "Report of the Joint Committee on Accrediting," *AGS Proc.* 1 (1949): 77–80. The Council on Dental Education refused to approve Columbia University's Dental School because it was under the Medical School dean (ibid., 77).

66. AR, *Ed. Rec.* 30 (1949): 275–81.

67. A. J. Brumbaugh, "The Accrediting Agencies Face Their Common Problems," *Ed. Rec.* 31 (1950): 59–92 (a report of the November 1949 conference); AR, ibid., 247–50; ibid. 32 (1951): 288; Selden, *Accreditation,* 75–76, 105 n. 34; P&P cmte. min., Mar. 2–3, 1950, E. E. Day to G. F. Zook, Apr. 4, 1950; both in ACE Ar., 10-62-4; Dobbins, *ACE Leadership,* 68–69. On the NCA and the National Committee of Regional Accrediting Agencies, see above, n. 65.

Postlude: Retrospect and Prospect, 1950

1. *AAC Bul.* 36 (1950): 453; AR, *Ed. Rec.* 32 (1951): 237 ("present"); Arthur S. Adams, "In Retrospect . . . 1951–61," in Dobbins, *ACE Leadership,* 147–48. See also Adams's presidential address to the land-grant association, "The Lasting Strength," *ALGCU Proc.* 64 (1950): 44–50.

Acknowledgments

IT IS A TRUTH universally acknowledged that a lone scholar in possession of a good idea, must be in want of a friend. I have been fortunate in finding many friends, both old and new, to help me do better at thinking, searching, and writing.

Historians kind enough to read and comment on drafts of this book include Tilden Edelstein, Richard Freeland, Roger Geiger, Allen Guttmann (who read the entire manuscript twice), and John Servos. Ellen Condliffe Lagemann gave chapter 5 the benefit of her special knowledge. Perhaps I should have accepted more of these scholars' suggestions, but I am grateful for the decided improvements made by the many recommendations I followed. Robert A. Gross, though not serving as a reader, bettered the outcome through his probing questions about what I was up to. Roger L. Williams generously shared his dissertation on the early land-grant association. Carol Gruber cheerfully agreed to my use of her book's title (with order reversed) in naming my chapter 7. Although Laurence Veysey chose not to read much of the manuscript for this book, I am in his debt for discussions over many years as well as the example of his scholarship.

Having been twice a visiting associate at the Center for Studies in Higher Education (CSHE) at the University of California, Berkeley, I can testify to its invigorating spirit. I recall with gratitude the chance to exchange ideas there with Gert Brieger, Geraldine Clifford, Paula Fass, Oliver Fulton, Marion Gade, Sheldon Rothblatt, Janet Ruyle, Barbara Shapiro, and Martin Trow. During my second visit two then-graduate students, Patrick Miller and Maresi Nerad, organized within the CSHE a seminar on the history of American higher education. Happily for me, its penetrating meetings included as participants Samuel Haber and Frederick Rudolph. Conversations with Clark Kerr and T. R. McConnell brought to my project the thinking of longtime associational insiders.

Two correspondents whom I never met were kind enough to share their memories. In the initial planning stages of this work, the late Laura Horowitz, a former staff member at the NASULGC, sent me a ten-page letter with her impressions of the Washington representatives of higher education. Russell I. Thackrey, who retired as executive director of the NASULGC in 1970 and died in 1990, answered continuing requests for inaccessible information. Our correspondence widened into a delightful epistolary friendship.

In the mechanics of manuscript preparation at Amherst College, I am grateful for the good will and talents of Rhea Cabin, Diane Beck, Margaret Ferro, and especially Friederike Dewitz, who answered repeated calls for help. Betty Steele, director of the Amherst College Academic Computer Center, went far beyond normal collegial assistance in addressing a series of complex problems. The following students took on research chores for me: Marc Lieber at Berkeley and Ann Marie Marciarille and Daniel Shelton at Amherst.

In Berkeley I relied on the excellent services of the various University of California libraries. In western Massachusetts I am one of many beneficiaries of the widely admired interlibrary cooperation among Five Colleges, Inc. (Amherst, Hampshire, Mt. Holyoke, and Smith Colleges and the University of Massachusetts). These libraries supplemented each other's holdings splendidly for my purposes. My deepest obligation among them is to Robert Frost Library, Amherst College, which provided, besides other benefits, a physical home for most of the composition of this book. Willis E. Bridegam, Jr., librarian of the college, directs with rare sensitivity a dedicated group of specialists. Those whom I called on most unrelentingly include Leeta Bailey, Daria D'Arienzo, Margaret Groesbeck, Michael Kasper, John Lancaster, and Floyd Merritt.

Happily for me, the archives of the ACE and the AAU were still housed in their national headquarters when I did my research, and I was able to gather some impressions of the organizations that have emerged from the earlier stages I trace in this volume. The AAC still retains its archives in its Washington headquarters, which—appropriate to its special nature—is not found at One Dupont Circle. For their arranging of the ACE archives as well as their welcome, I thank Judith A. Pfeiffer and Linda J. Ebben. Thanks also to Jill Bogard for follow-up assistance. At the AAC, Diane Haddick took pains to provide comfortable access to all records, and William O'Connell discussed recent AAC developments with me. At the AAU, I learned from conversations with Robert Rosenzweig and John Vaughan. I saw least of the NASULGC, since its archives are located elsewhere, but appreciated the chance to discuss its current functions with Nevin Brown.

The list of collections preceding the notes names the archives on which I have drawn. I thank their staffs for many courtesies. As representatives of the archival profession, I name the following, on whom, if memory serves, I made particularly extensive demands: Richard C. Berner, Gary Lundell, and Uli Haller at the University of Washington; Shonnie Finnegan and Chris Densmore at SUNY Buffalo; Maynard Brichford at the University of Illinois; Thomas D. Hamm at Earlham College; Harley P. Holden at Harvard University; and Matthew T. Schaefer at the University of Michigan.

At the Johns Hopkins University Press I have benefited in many ways from the editorial guidance of Robert Brugger, Barbara Lamb, and Penny Moudrianakis. I would also like to thank Linda Forlifer, my copy editor.

A National Endowment for the Humanities fellowship provided me financial assistance, as did a research travel grant from Amherst College, thoughtfully arranged by Deans Ralph Beals and Ronald Rosbottom.

For their expressions of love and confidence over the years, I thank members of my traditional and nontraditional families—Helene Tidd, Ruth Hardwick, Rena Allen, and Walter Richard.

I appreciate the support the persons named have given me, even when they found my explanations of the project somewhat obscure. Part of the trouble may have been my reluctance to pronounce "higher education institutional associations." For this group of organizations, unhappily, no convenient acronym has emerged.

Index

Designed by Jim Billingsley

Composed by Capitol Communication Systems, Inc.,
in Baskerville text and display

Printed by Thomson-Shore, Inc.,
on 50-lb. Glatfelter B-16, and bound in Holliston Roxite